Research on Library Computerisation

Research on Library Computerisation

Editors:
M. Bavakutty
Muhammed Salih T.K.
Mohamed Haneefa K.

Ess Ess Publications

4837/24, Ansari Road, Darya Ganj,
New Delhi-110002
✆ : 23260807, 51563444
Fax : 011-51563334
E-mail: info@essessreference.com
url:http://www.essessreference.com

First Published **2006**

ISBN: 81-7000-478-0

Rs.1225/-

Published by:
Ess Ess Publications
4837/24, Ansari Road, Darya Ganj, New Delhi-110 002
Tel: 011-23260807, 51563444 Fax: 011-51563334
E-mail: info@essessreference.com
url: www.essessreference.com

Printed in India at:
Printline, New Delhi

CONTENTS

Preface

Using computers and other information technology gadgets to perform the library activities and to provide library and information services are generally known as library computerization. Library is to provide better library and information services with added benefits and is involved in acquiring, processing, retrieving and providing information services from machine-readable databases. Reasons that necessitate dependence of modern libraries on computers are many.

There has been a tremendous increase in the generation of information in all fields of knowledge due to intensive researches taking place in almost all fields of knowledge. This further widens the horizon of knowledge and causes multiplication of knowledge often termed by information scientists as 'information explosion'. In addition to the enormous quantity of print documents, the volume of information available electronically is also increasing tremendously. Therefore it has become difficult to track, retrieve and disseminate up-to-date information needed for research and development. As such modern libraries in recent years have experienced new challenges of adapting to the new environment of information technology.

The cost of documents and other information sources are increasing regularly. But, the fund allocation to libraries is never incresed in proportion to this raise. There has also been a continuous devaluation of currency. Hence no library is presently able to procure all the resources needed by its users. So this situation also adds to the reasons for libraries turning to computerisation, as it facilitates effective resource sharing through networking.

The shift in the medium of publication from print to electronic is another important reason that necessitated computer applications in libraries. It has been estimated that the world produces between 1 and 2 exabytes of unique information per year, which is roughly 250 megabytes for every man, woman, and child on earth (An exabyte is a billion gigabytes, or 10^{18} bytes). On the other hand printed documents of all kinds contain only 0.003% of the total. Magnetic storage is by far is the most rapidly growing and the largest medium for storing information. As such it is becoming the universal medium for information storage. So the shift in the volume of sources of information and its format in recently have made the traditional libraries not capable of meeting the current library and information requirements of the academics and researchers.

The library collection is increasing regularly, reducing the available space in libraries. No library can provide additional space every year, although collection will grow continuously. Computer application can solve this problem, as computer is capable of storing huge volume of information on tiny storage mediums.

Information Technology is an amalgam of wonderful inventions of the 20th century in Electronics and Communication. During a very short span of time it has acquired an important place in almost all walks of human life and particularly in the field of education with a greater impact on the universities and its libraries. Over the last couple of decades, there has been a significant change in higher education occasioned by Information Technology.

The recent developments in Information Communication Technology have effected innovative changes in the way in which information is collected, stored, retrieved and disseminated and literally the rapid developments in the field of computers and communication have virtually shrunk the size of the earth. The availability of a number of specialized databases, online and offline information services over Internet and in CDs and DVDs, resources sharing networks, availability of e-contents etc. further necessitates computerisation of libraries.

Is is well known that computer is capable of storing large amount of data, processing it accurately and speedily and retrieving the same within the shortest possible time. Speed, storage, accuracy, versatility, compactness, reliability, repetitiveness, diligence etc. are considered to be the common features of computers. With rapid developments in technological revolution, computer hardware cost has declined considerably and at the same time the speed and capabilitis of computers have increased significantly. Hence if we match the requirements of a modern library and the capabilities of information and communication technology, we will find that computer application is unavoidable for modern libraries to achieve its objectives.

The availability of information at right time and in the right form is of utmost importance in all the developmental activities. It has become very difficult to manage the information manually due to the explosive growth of knowledge. Almost all fields of knowledge is increasing tremendously in a multidimensional way. Hence there is a need for proper organisation and management of knowledge. The advent of digital computers, advances in telecommunication technology, widespread use of networking, explosive growth of Internet, world wide packet networks, optical discs and other mass storage media, interactive video technology, image technology, computer graphic technology, virtual reality and the growth of public and private databases have opened up new possibilities in dealing with the collection, organisation, retrieval and dissemination of information. Now information can not only be stored, retrieved, communicated and broadcasted electronically in enormous quantities at phenomenal speed, but can also be rearranged, selected and transformed.

Modern libraries have become more and more aware

of the revolutionary impact of developments in Information and Communication Technology (ICT) on their major activities. Access to collections of other libraries is no longer a mere convenience; it is a matter of urgent necessity in view of the huge amount of information being produced every year and the costs to acquire and organise it. This necessitates co-operation and resource sharing among libraries and information centres. Resource sharing is successful only through computer and telecommunication networking and to participate in such network, the application of ICT is very essential. The information seeking behaviour of users is also changing owing to the interdisciplinary nature of learning. The application of ICT facilitates to provide pinpointed, expeditious and exhaustive information at the right time to the right user. It provides opportunities for libraries and information centres to widen the scope of their resources and services and to increase their significance within the organization they serve. The increasing availability of information in machine readable form allows many information needs to be satisfied with decreased involvement of libraries and librarians.

Though ICT has potential for modernising the library activities, there is a wide gap between what is told and what has been achieved. However, the application of Information and Communication Technologies in different types of libraries in India has gained much momentum. New and emerging technologies such as Wireless Networking, Radio Frequency Identification technology, multimedia technology, graphical user interfaces, etc have immense possibilities for libraries. Although the use of ICT in libraries in the country at present is quite low, it is expected to go up in the coming years with continued reduction in the prices of the hardware and software. The extent of use of ICT in the libraries, which are already using it, will increase substantially. Libraries will use expert systems and artificial intelligence systems. Remote browsing of databases and tele-delivery of documents will increase. Packet-switched networks will be common. Use of CD-ROM and DVD-ROM will increase further. The World Wide Web is going to be more interactive and multidimensional, incorporating multimedia presentations.

It is in this context two research studies on library computerisation have been conducted under my supervision and guidance. This book, which contains the core of the reports of these research studies, has two parts, Part I 'Computerisation of University Libraries' conducted by **Dr. Mohammed Salih T K** and Part II 'Application of Information Communication Technology in Special Libraries' carried out by **Dr. Muhamed Haneefa K.**

Part I, **'Computerisation of University Libraries'** has four chapters. Chapter 1 is the 'Introduction' to the subject of study, covering the need and importance of the University Library computerisation, areas of library computerisation, computer based services to users, system librarianship, new dimensions in library automation, the role of INFLIBNET in computerisation of University Libraries. Chapter 2 gives the Methodology of the study covering the need and significance of the study, objectives, hypotheses formulated, limitations of the study, various data sources, selection of sample, data collection and the methods of analysis adopted. Chapter 3 confined to the Analysis of the data and Interpretations, contains analysis of data on library collections, financial assistances, manpower, infra structure available, various services and INFLIBNET support and participation in computerisation. It also includes the analysis of the websites of the University Libraries. Chapter 4 entitled 'Summary of the Findings and Suggestions' gives the major findings of the study and makes conclusions on the basis of the analysis. It also puts forward certain suggestions for the improvement of the computerisation process of the University libraries studied. A selected bibliography and three questionnairs used for the study are given at the end.

Part II, **'Application of ICT in Special Libraries'** has five chapters. Chapter 1 'Introduction' describes the reasons and problems of application of ICT in libraries, features of Special Libraries, Special libraries in Kerala, need, significance and limitation of the research study. Chapter 2, Application of ICT in Libraries, contains descriptions of Online Public Access Catalogues, Storage Technologies, Database and Database Management Systems, Library Networking, Library Consortia, Internet, Intranet and Extranet, Wireless Technologies, Digital Library, Virtual Library, Multimedia, Electronic Journals, Emerging Technologies, Skill and Expertise of Library Professionals in the Electronic Environment. Chapter 3, Methodology of the study includes Objectives, Hypotheses and Research Design. Chapter 4 confines to Analysis and Interpretation of the data on Collections of Special Libraries, Library Professionals, Information and Communication Technology Infrastructure in Special Libraries, Computer Applications, Telecommunication and Networking, ICT Based Library Services, Training in ICT Based Services and Operations, Objectives of Information and Communication Technology Application, Factors Influencing the Provision of ICT Based Library Resources and Services, Barriers of ICT Application in Special Libraries, Librarians' Attitude Towards ICT Application in Libraries, Future Plans, Librarians' Comments and Suggestions about the State-of-the-Art application of ICT in their Libraries, Use of ICT Based Resources and Services and views of the users. And Chapter 5 includes the Summary of Findings and Suggestions for Improving ICT Application in Special Libraries. A select Bibliography and five appendices, namely Questionnaire to the Librarians, Questionnaire to the Users, Interview Schedule, Observation and the List of Special

Libraries studied are given at the end.

I am sure that this volume containing reports of case studies on a current subject will be of immence use to the practicing professional librarians for planning and executing similar studies and comparison of the findings. This will also be extreamely helpful to the students, the researchers and the faculty in Library and Information Science who would like to carry out research studies on library computerization and allied subjects.

Dr. Mohammed Salih and Dr. Muhamed Haneefa deserve special credits and congradulations for conducting these two outstanding research studies systematically and sincerely. I express my earnest gratitude to Mr. Sumit Sethi, the Managing Director of Ess Ess Publications, New Delhi for the timely publication of this book.

Calicut University Campus **Prof. M. Bavakutty**

1st Novermber 2005

Part I

Muhammed Salih T K

Computerisation of University Libraries

1.1
Introduction

This chapter throws light on the subject under study, 'Computerisation of University Libraries' that encompasses various facets. All related aspects including the necessity for computerisation of University Libraries, areas of computer applications in libraries, various services provided under a computerised environment, the potential of open sources in libraries, System Librarianship, latest trends in computerisation etc. are covered. It is with the establishment of the Information and Library Network (INFLIBNET) Ahmedabad; the momentum of computerisation of University Libraries in the country started and its role in this endeavor is undisputable. So the contribution of INFLIBNET is also dealt with in detail.

Indian Universities constitute one of the largest higher education systems in the world, with 294 university level institutions which includes 52 Deemed Universities, 40 Agricultural Universities, 33 Technical, 18 Medical, 3 Information Technology, 1 Journalism, 6 Law and 10 Open Universities, 13150 affiliated colleges, 88.21 Lakh students and 4.27 Lakh teachers[1]. The government of independent India realized the need for studying in detail the national education set up and appointed several committees and commissions. All these committees while evaluating the status of higher education in the country and making solid recommendations for their restructuring have also examined the role of libraries in the academic institutions and made several recommendations for the proper development of the University Library System.

ROLE OF UNIVERSITY LIBRARY IN HIGHER EDUCATION

Universities have certain objectives and the role of its libraries in attaining the set objectives is undisputable. The important role that the University Library could play in a university setup began to be duly recognized in India during the second quarter of the 20th century only. However, the real boost and momentum in the growth and development of university libraries took place only after the country attaining independence in 1947. University Library is the hub of all academic activities in a university and is supposed to meet all the information requirements of its academic community by providing every possible information sources to the clientele. Radhakrishnan Commission (1948- 49) has rightly pointed out the importance of the University Library in a University setup, as "Teaching is a co-operative enterprise. Teachers must have the necessary tools for teaching purposes in the shape of libraries and laboratories and also the right type of students. The library is the heart of all the university's work, directly so as regards its research work, and indirectly as regards its educational work. Scientific research needs a library as well as its laboratories while for humanistic research, the library is both the library and laboratory in one"[2]. It has been rightly reported "Education, especially at higher levels, has been described more as a process of learning than of teaching, signifying the self-efforts to be put in by the students. According to this concept, students in higher education are to be provided with the facilities necessary for mastering the subject matter, techniques, skills, and habits of thought and methods of work in their chosen field. Classroom instruction alone will not provide all the opportunities needed for attaining all these complex educational objectives. It is here the libraries come to help the students"[3]

NEED AND IMPORTANCE OF UNIVERSITY LIBRARY COMPUTERISATION

All human activities are controlled by knowledge

derived from information, which is the essential input for study and research activities and it becomes valuable only when it reaches its target users. Till recently, the University Libraries have been manually providing traditional library and information services mainly contained in print media such as books, journals etc. Information has become catalyst in the socio-economic, scientific, technological and cultural development of the society. Hence easy availability of required information to the academic community is imperative. Any study and research activity need quick access to right information and its efficient and rapid processing. So the need for quick information retrieval forces libraries to depend on some means that makes information processing and retrieval efficient and rapid. One of the basic jobs done by computer is information processing and retrieval in a very rapid manner; hence it has become an aid in information management. Library computerisation is to provide a better service with added benefits and is involved in acquiring, processing and providing information services from machine-readable databases.

The objectives of library computerisation has been described as[4]:

* To improve access to collection;
* To improve the quality of existing services;
* To reduce the routine and time consuming clerical works;
* To improve the speed of cataloguing, technical processing and putting items on shelves faster;
* To offer improved range of services;
* To improve co-operation and resource sharing among libraries;
* To easily participate and utilize national and international computer networks; and

* To provide more current and comprehensive reporting of library information to managers.

The objectives of the use of computers in libraries have been viewed from a slightly different perspective as[5]:

* To maintain bibliographic records for all materials;
* To provide bibliographical details through a single enumerative access point of all type of materials;
* To reduce repetition (drudgery) in the technical process of library work;
* To provide accurate information at a fast rate;
* To share the resources in the networking project;
* To improve precision and scope of research activity;
* To innovate new IT processes to provide high quality information

The major reasons that necessitate dependence on computers in University Libraries can be summed up to the following headings.

INFORMATION EXPLOSION

"Information overload is not a new phenomenon: the potential for overload has existed ever since information became an important input to any human activity. For example, once the scientific disciplines began to clearly emerge in the 17th to 19th centuries, it gradually became impossible for anyone to keep abreast of all the work in what had been called 'natural philosophy'. In some fields, the degree of specialisation is so high that, even within the same discipline, people are unable to keep abreast of all sub-areas and, in fact, may be completely unable to understand some of them. Throughout the 20th century, the explosion of information outputs in the form of journal papers, patents, books, 'grey' literature, and so forth continued and that explosion gained even more force in the period immediately following the Second World War."[6]. According to Kamath[7] in the field of

Science and Technology alone about three million documents are published each year which include articles, conference papers, books, technical reports and theses. He maintains that the rate doubles every eight to 10 years. The Faxton Company USA, statistics reveals that the number of fulfilable journal titles rose from 38079 in 1974 to 1,04,714 in 1989 – an increase of 66,635 or 175 per cent.

In addition to the large quantity of print materials, the volume of information available electronically is also increasing exponentially. Today Internet has become the biggest source of information and the findings at the University of California that printed documents of all kinds comprise only 0.003% of the total information generation is an indicator of the dominance of digital information in our knowledge sources. The number of Internet hosts has increased many folds in recent years. With interdisciplinary and multidisciplinary initiatives and with the emergence of new disciplines, it is likely that the volume of information will continue to increase. The latest ISC (Internet Systems Consortium, Inc.) Internet Domain Survey released its report in January 2004. The survey attempted to discover every host on the Internet by doing a complete search of the Domain Name System and discovered a fast growth in the number of domains during the last 10 years and the growth is well evident in the Figure[8] 1.1

It has become difficult to track and disseminate up-to-date information needed for Research and Development. Hence modern libraries in recent decades have experienced new challenges of adapting to the new environment of information technology.

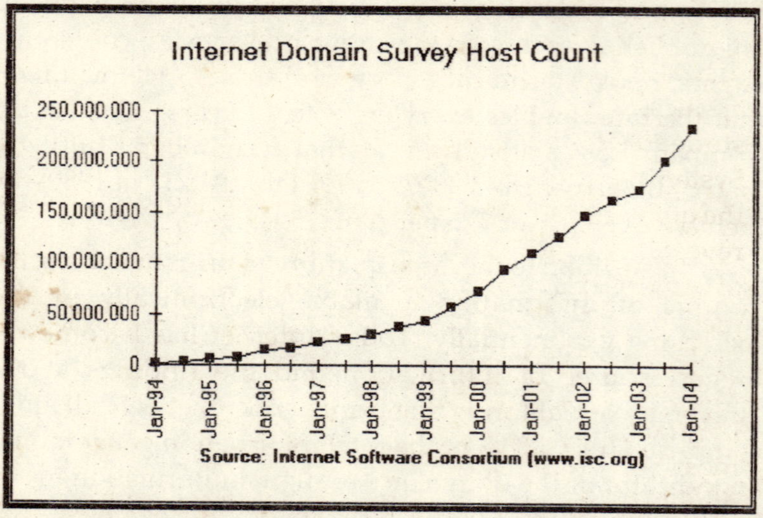

Figure 1.1 Growth of Internet Domain Hosts during the last decade

SHRINKING BUDGET AND PRICE HIKE OF DOCUMENTS

The cost of books and other information sources are escalating year by year. But the fund allocation to University Libraries in our country is not increasing in proportion with this increase. There has been a continuous devaluation of currency also. Hence no library is able to procure all the resources needed by its users. The Faxton Companys' (USA) statistics revealed that the average price per serial title paid by college and university libraries in 1979 was $ 50.11; by 1989 it had risen to $125.87, Scientific and Technological libraries pay an average of $234 per serial title a year. "The average price of foreign titles has risen from $41.34 per title in 1976 to $143.09 in 1989"[9]. So this situation also adds to the reasons for libraries turning to computerisation as a computerised library can co-operate with other libraries for effective resource sharing through networks, overcoming the barriers of limited resources in terms of finance and library collections.

SHIFT IN THE MEDIUM OF PUBLICATIONS

The shift in the medium of publication from print to digital is another important factor that necessitated computer applications in libraries. A study conducted by faculty and students at the School of Information Management and Systems at the University of California at Berkeley to measure the quantity of information produced in the world each year revealed that the world produces between 1 and 2 exabytes of unique information per year, which is roughly 250 megabytes for every man, woman, and child on earth. An exabyte is a billion gigabytes, or 10^{18} bytes. Printed documents of all kinds comprise only 0.003% of the total. Magnetic storage is by far the largest medium for storing information and is the most rapidly growing, with shipped hard drive capacity doubling every year. Magnetic storage is rapidly becoming the universal medium for information storage[10]. So the shift in the volume of sources of information and its format in recent years have made the traditional libraries not capable of meeting the present day library and information requirements of the academic community.

LACK OF ADEQUATE SPACE

Every year the size of the library collection increases reducing the area of available free space in libraries. "The size of the recorded information is ever growing whereas space available at the disposal of each library is limited. No library can think of getting additional space every year, although collection will grow continuously. Weeding of books is a small solution but books cannot be weeded out as speedily as these are acquired. Computer application can solve this problem, as computer is capable of storing huge bulk of information on tiny storage mediums"[11]. Lack of required space in libraries is one of the reasons that coerce libraries to turn to tiny storage mediums for storing information.

IMPACT OF INFORMATION TECHNOLOGY

Information Technology is an amalgam of wonderful inventions of the 20th century in Electronics and Communication. During a very short span of time it has acquired an important place in almost all walks of human life and particularly in the field of education with a greater impact on the universities and its libraries. Over the last couple of decades, there has been a significant change in higher education occasioned by Information Technology.

The recent developments in ICT, which comprises computer and communication technology, have effected revolutionary changes in the way in which information is collected, stored and disseminated and literally the rapid developments in the field of computers and communication have virtually shrunk the size of the earth. The availability of a number of specialized databases, online and offline information services (over Internet and in CDs and DVDs), resources sharing networks, availability of e-contents etc. further necessitates computerisation of libraries.

In order to achieve progress in any field whether it is academic or non-academic, authentic data is an indispensable requirement. The age-old methods of organizing data are no more applicable in a dynamic and ever growing society. Due to a high need for quick retrieval and dissemination of information and better services for its users, use of computers in library housekeeping operations has become indispensable. In a nutshell following are the main factors, which necessitates computerisation of libraries[12].

* Explosion of knowledge resulting in numerous specialization and flow of almost non-stop information;
* In-ability of users to explore unlimited literature and information of interest;
* Wastage of lot of precious time in handling routine and repetitive library operations; and

* Impossibility of a single library to acquire and make available the entire published materials.

It has been reported that "the world's total production of information amounts to about 250 megabytes for each man, woman, and child on earth. It is clear that we are all drowning in a sea of information. The challenge is to learn to swim in that sea, rather than drown in it. Better understanding and better tools are desperately needed if we are to take full advantage of the ever-increasing supply of information"[13].

Thus University Libraries are found now-a-days struggling in many ways in their routine affairs like inability to manage the ever growing huge collection of books and other reading materials, price hike of information sources coupled with shrinking fund allocations, shift in the medium of publications in the form of availability of some of the sources of knowledge only in digital form like CDROM, DVD and websites, reduction in the size of available space in libraries, the overall impact of IT on society and consequent ever increasing demand from users, lack of adequate staff to perform different tasks that are mainly repetitive in nature etc. Similarly no library can be self sufficient in this era and there is a need for obtaining resources from other libraries, publishers and information providers located in far away places through computer networks. Computer is an electronic device capable of storing large amount of data, processing it accurately and speedily and retrieving the same within the shortest possible time. Speed, storage, accuracy, versatility, compactness, reliability, repetitiveness, diligence etc. are the common features of computers. With rapid strides in technological revolution, computer hardware cost has declined considerably from year to year and at the same time the number of circuits per millimeter on a computer chip doubles every year increasing the speed and capacity of computers. More over computer and communication technology has made acquiring of information from far away places very easy. Hence if we match the requirements of a modern University Library and the capabilities of computers, we will find that computer application is unavoidable for University Libraries to achieve its objectives. In brief, computers are needed in libraries to manage the huge collections which has become almost humanly unmanageable, to avoid jobs of a repetitive nature, to provide better access to collection including access from and to remote sources and to exploit the increasing potential of the technology for better services and operations.

AREAS OF LIBRARY COMPUTERISATION

The impact of computers has permeated all sectors of librarianship. Housekeeping applications of computers in libraries include Acquisition control, Serials control, Circulation control, Technical processing comprising Cataloguing and Classification, and Stock verification. Computerisation helps achieving greater standardization, efficiency, cooperation and improved services in libraries.

Computerised information retrieval systems offer more convenient, more flexible and more comprehensive retrieval than manual systems and there are large numbers of internationally accessible Information Retrieval Systems (IRS). It is possible to provide various services using the data collected and processed in housekeeping operations. Such information retrieval activities include OPACs, generation of various types of bibliographies, Current Awareness Services, SDI services, Abstracting work, compilation of union catalogues/lists, indexing services etc. OPAC is the most prominent IRS used in libraries by all types and categories of members. Computerised system is also needed for providing management statistics etc. for an effective

Library housekeeping operations are particularly suited for computerisation because of its' repetitive nature. Many of the sections in the library use the same data for their operations and services. It is because of this nature of the library, computers were made use of in libraries first rather than in many other organizations. Computers are capable of handling many of the mundane repetitive tasks that are necessary but are time consuming. Effective computerisation will drastically reduce the amount of work needed to organise, maintain and retrieve information. There needs a provision for Nodes from different sections to access the data made available from a central Server.

Computers are widely made use of in library housekeeping operations by keeping the record of the stock of the library as to its whereabouts and status. Computer permits the reduction of the number of repetitive jobs performed in the library by keying in the data once and manipulating it several times as and when required. All library housekeeping routines are directed towards controlling the stock of the library and such routines may include selection, ordering, procurement, invoice processing, accessioning etc. of the documents that come under the Acquisition procedures; labeling cataloguing, assigning keywords, subject descriptors and class numbers etc. that come under the Technical Processing or Cataloguing procedures; Circulation procedures such as issue/return, recall, fine collection, addition / modification / deletion of membership details etc; Serials control module including procurement procedures related with serial publications and many other routine as well as occasional tasks performed in the library.

ACQUISITION PROCEDURES

The routine acquisition procedure in libraries is very much suited for computerisation as it involves repetitive clerical tasks. The procurement of items made in this section is mostly monographs of once-and-for-all purchases. The following basic functions of the Acquisition module have been identified[14]:

* To receive records of items to be acquired;
* To establish whether items requested are already in stock or on order;
* To print orders or otherwise order items;
* To check when orders are overdue and follow up overdue orders;
* To maintain a file of records of items on order;
* To note the arrival of ordered items and prepare for payment;
* To maintain book-fund statistics and accounts.

Apart from these functions, report generation at various stages of procurement for managerial purposes as well as for staff and users of the library is also needed in this module. The module should be capable of accepting standard data from different sources like other online and offline databases also. It should manage databases like vendors, financial sources, currencies and its corresponding local rates etc.

TECHNICAL PROCESSING OF DOCUMENTS

The jobs involved in technical processing of documents have been minimized due to the use of computers. Catalogue has always been regarded as an important tool and the primary record of the stock of the library for the users. Several physical forms exist with regard to the catalogue and different cataloguing rules are in prevalence. Computers permit to produce catalogues according to desired rules using the predefined instructions and the data acquired from acquisition. Further data can be accepted from external and remote sites according to various standards. More over the use of computer helps to retrieve data through all the entry elements that have been fed in to the computer.

Use of subject descriptors to provide subject approach to the resources has become very easy in a computerised environment. By using an authority list the system itself is able to display the possible subject descriptors and the technical staff need to make an appropriate selection only. Similarly assigning class numbers for shelf arrangement as well as information retrieval has also become a relatively light job now days. Internet can also be used as an aid in the technical processing by obtaining class numbers and catalogue formats from other sources.

The functions of the computerised cataloguing system are[15]:

* Inputting complete details of new documents that is bibliographic and indexing elements;
* Maintaining the database of master file of bibliographic records and index files. Carry out functions like add, delete and modify;
* Generating various lists like author, subjects and other bibliographies, list of additions and indexes etc.
* Providing for search of the database by various access points;
* Generating selected records in book form or card form;
* Generating out put in various catalogue formats like ISSD (M), AACR etc.
* Integrate with other subsystems like circulation, acquisition and reference systems.

CIRCULATION PROCEDURES

Circulation control in libraries impinge upon one of the primary functions of the library i.e. document delivery to its clientele for use outside the library. It is more concerned with controlling stock within one library or library system. While stating the principles of circulation control Rowley[16] noted that in order to achieve maximum availability of material, all libraries must control circulation, by keeping, at the very least, record to specify:

* What material is in the library stock or readily accessible through other channels;
* Which material is on loan, and from whom or where it can be retrieved;
* When material on loan next be available in the library for other customers.

In addition to controlling the movement of documents such as check-in/check-out, follow-up, overdue collection etc. the circulation module need to generate various information and report to support the general queries from the users as well as to provide management information for the library management.

Though relatively an old technology bar coding is a very important one used in libraries. Barcodes are self-contained messages with information encoded in a series of black bars of varying breadths and white spaces between every two of them. Libraries use this technology for charging and discharging of documents and also for stock verification for the reasons – operational efficiency, speed and accuracy. The main objectives[17] of using bar code in libraries are to improve operational efficiency; to achieve accuracy; to make stock verification an easy process and to reduce overall cost. In a bar-coded system, the accession number and member identity code, which are scanned at the time of charging/ discharging, will ensure the accuracy. On the other hand in a manual or semi automated system, the typographical error may result in charging/discharging a wrong document to a wrong member. In future the RFID technology may take up the functions of barcodes, yet this is the most economical and feasible technology available and used at present.

STOCK VERIFICATION

The library resources that are being issued to its members are prone to loss. An inventory control system is needed to collect information on such losses. A computerised system reduces the labour involved in such a task. Usage of barcodes for feeding data of available book is highly recognized. After taking stock of all the collections, it is to be compared with the library database and a list of missing items generated.

ONLINE CATALOGUES AND WEB OPACS

OPAC entertains queries with regard to the availability and status of the library resources through different access points. It has become the primary key for the clientele to the collection of the libraries replacing the traditional card catalogues in our universities. It can be made available over the LAN, Intranet as wells as Internet providing access without any geographical barriers. Thus web OPACs are very common these days. It serves the clientele in a much more convenient manner than the traditional catalogues by providing the current status of the item and several other features like options to request for new titles of all kinds of resources, facility for document reservation etc.

SERIALS CONTROL AND ARTICLES DATABASE MANAGEMENT

Serials module in an automated library system is supposed to look after the procurement and other activities related to serial publications. From the programmers point of view this module poses much problems due to the changing nature of serial publications like frequently occurring changes in title, frequency, publisher etc. Serials control is one of the most complex procedures in libraries. The complexities of the procedure of procurement, claiming and entering of issues, follow-ups to be taken in case of missing issues - it occurs very frequently in case of journals, Article indexing, Routing, Selective Dissemination of Information etc. makes it a much complex activity compared to other routine works in the library.

The functions of the Serials control system are[18]:

* Inputting serials data;
* Ordering new serials;
* Renewing presently subscribed serials;
* Accessioning of individual issues as and when the issues are received;
* Sending reminders;
* Selective follow up of missing issues;
* Preparation of various lists like: periodicals received, journals subscribed, journals exchanged, journal received as gift and list of holdings with their status on shelf, binding, circulation etc. by subject, title etc.
* Keeping track of the amount spent on subscriptions, bindings etc.
* Estimation of the budget for the next academic/financial year, and
* Binding control.

Article indexing facilities provides more convenient and exhaustive search facilities to the users and helps the library to provide effective and innovative services in the libraries like Selective Dissemination of Information and Current Awareness Services.

MANAGEMENT INFORMATION SYSTEMS

Apart from making provisions for various automated operations and services in libraries, the library management system has to generate necessary information required for the top-level management to make plans and take decisions. This could be about the need for procurement of a particular title or type of document or about extending or reducing the working hours of the library or increasing or reducing the number of staff. Bailey[19] observed "the need for statistical and analytical information to be able to justify their decisions and provide accountability. Intelligence can take the form of:

* Report showing how much is spent with particular supplier
* Reports showing percentage increases in prices
* Ability to accurately predict annual budgets
* Savings made from cancellations
* Breakdown of expenditure by budget codes
* Breakdown of expenditure by budget different formats
* Copyright licensing audit figures
* Statistics on the use of resources
* Statistics on time and costs for research activities

Compiling such information can be a time-consuming and costly exercise in itself, and thus managers are demanding the ability to produce reports and statistics from their systems with ease and speed". Provision of required information will enable the management to take suitable decision at the right time.

COMPUTERISED SERVICES TO USERS

User service refers to what a library does to facilitate retrieval of information and access to information for patrons. There are a wide variety of services that can be rendered to its users by a computerised library system. These may include Current Awareness Service, Selective Dissemination of Information, Reference Service, Circulation of Accession List, Content page Service, Online database services, Online bibliographic services, Online Full Text E – Journals, CD ROM and DVD based services including multimedia, Internet services, computer aided User Education programmes etc.

CURRENT AWARENESS SERVICE (CAS)

CAS helps the user keep him/herself up to date about the developments within a wider subject field. An automated CAS system reviews the information source immediately upon its receipt. The information or the description about the source is then routed to the person with whose interest the information is related. Title announcements, contents list etc. forms parts of CAS. A computerised system can easily provide such a service with the matching of the content of the document and the user's subject area. This can be routed through the email id of the patrons for quick service.

SELECTIVE DISSEMINATION OF INFORMATION (SDI)

SDI service helps to route all the information in a particular area of interest to a user by matching the subject profile of the person with the subject of the information. This enables the user to get all the information arriving at the library that falls within his area of study. An effective SDI service can be developed by storing a user profile and marking the subject area of the document. The efficiency of the system depends on the profile construction of the user as well as the information source. Under this service the users' subject profile is collected and stored in the system and periodically matched with the profiles of new entries in the database and matching references are routed to the user either through email or through a printed copy.

REFERENCE SERVICE

Computerised reference service is requested and provided over a network or the Internet, usually via e-mail, instant messaging ("chat"), or Web-based submission forms, and are usually answered by librarians in the reference department of the library. Sometimes the participants in a collaborative reference system serving more than one institution may answer it like "Ask a librarian..." <http://www.loc.gov/rr/askalib/> from the Library of Congress. Synonymous terms used for this service includes chat reference, e-reference, online reference, and virtual reference.

CIRCULATION OF ACCESSION LIST

An automated library system can very easily generate the new additions list on a periodic basis and make it available to the users through different channels so as to make them aware about the latest additions to the library. This service is intended to increase the use of the newly added documents. Here the user is kept up to date regarding the holdings of the library and can select the document according to his/her interest.

CONTENT PAGE SERVICE

Content page service is provided to the users to make them aware about the contents of the latest journals so that they needn't go thorough the whole journal to make a selection of the required article. Mostly the content pages are scanned and stored to some format like 'pdf' and then routed to the users either through email or through print copies. If the reader is interested in any of the article he/she can request the source journal and get the article. If the copy is a digital one, it can be served through the network even.

ONLINE DATABASE SERVICES

At present several online databases are available such as STN, BIOSIS, SciFinder, INSPEC, COMPENDEX PLUS etc. Access to those databases is mostly limited to subscribed users only. Individuals cannot afford to subscribe such highly charged databases and libraries can only come to their rescue. Many databases are now available in CDs and DVDs and fast access to such databases can be provided within the library through the library LAN.

ONLINE BIBLIOGRAPHIC SERVICES

A bibliographic service does not provide always the required information rather it makes available the information about the source of information. An online bibliographic service system is a computer file consisting of electronic entries, each containing a uniform description of a specific document or bibliographic item, usually retrievable by author, title, subject heading or keywords. An increasing number of such databases now provide the full-text of at least a portion of the sources indexed. Most electronic bibliographic databases are proprietary, available by licensing agreement from vendors, or directly from the abstracting and indexing services that create them. Libraries as part of their user services do providing access to such databases.

ONLINE FULL TEXT SERVICES

Online Full Text is an electronic resource that provides the entire text of a single work or of articles published in one or more journals, magazines, and/or newspapers. Such a bibliographic database provides the complete text of a significant proportion of the works indexed, in addition to the bibliographic citation and (in many cases) an abstract of the content. Many journal publishers have made their publications available in the digital format. Science Direct, Emerald, JSTOR, Cambridge University Press etc are examples for this service. These are made accessible over Internet and in some cases are also available on CDROM and DVD. In some cases full text of articles is available free of cost and in most of the cases it is priced. Subscribers of the journal get the privilege of accessing the electronic version of the same article through Internet. Full text of article is now made available mainly through library consortia and is either IP number based access or by verification of user id and password. This service enables the user to access the article immediately on its publication and effective search of articles is very much possible. More over in case of electronic copy of articles, there is no question of tear because of constant use of the article. Libraries make available the article either on the basis of individual subscription or through participating in consortia.

CD ROM AND DVD BASED SERVICES

Many valuable databases are available in the form of CDs and DVDs. Biological Abstracts, Chemical Abstracts etc. are best examples for this. A good number of books, journals, reference sources, theses, dissertations etc. are available in these formats and making it available over a network through a CD/DVD server provides users with much easiness of accessing these valuable sources. These sources may include multimedia resources also and serving it over a network makes multiple accesses to the resources. It provides users with speed of access, capability to search using various search strategies etc. and there is no fear of the source getting mutilated because of constant use.

INTERNET SERVICES

The number of information resources that are available on the Internet is enormous and growing rapidly, and because of their number and their variability in subject, treatment, complexity, language, etc., they provide something of potential value to all members of the higher education community.

"By the mid 1990s, most academic librarians recognized that the Internet could be used to satisfy a wide variety of information needs and that members of the higher education community needed assistance in using it as an information source. Over the last decade, academic libraries have facilitated the use of the Internet by their clients in several ways"[20]. There is a critical need to provide University Library clients more efficient and effective access to Internet information resources that have value for higher education.

USER EDUCATION PROGRAMMES

A good user education programme helps the user to understand the facilities and services of a library for its better exploitation. Applications of computers, incorporating text, graphics, animation, sound and video, in imparting user education progrmmes have made it more effective and meaningful. Availability of different presentation packages like Microsoft Power Point, Harvard Graphics etc. have reduced the task of libraries in preparing the user education programmes. Users can make use of the programme even without the direct intervention of the library staff and such provision will really help the users in making best use of the library. The computer as a multimedia workstation has created a major shift from traditional modes of teaching and learning to a multitude of new and exciting options for instructors and users. The increased potential of multimedia capabilities for computing with new devices such as DVD-ROMs and increased network bandwidth provide exciting opportunities for the delivery of audio, video, and graphics. Utilizing multimedia for teaching is really just another tool that provides a new type of learning environment. Libraries are now able to host their multimedia supported user education programmes in their websites.

DIGITIZATION

Digitization is a process by which a character or text, chart, picture, sound, video etc. is converted to digital format. The ultimate goal of a digital library is to provide ways of organizing and efficiently managing large data collections. Digitization changes the material in to digital form that is easier to store and retrieve. Digital information can be created using OCR technology, digital cameras or directly keying the information. Digitized information has many advantages like universal availability, minimum cost, easy use, does not get mutilated by use or time and doesn't perish after a long time. It can easily be put on a network to make multiple accesses. Digitization provides access to multi media documents including full text, sound and motion films. Digitization of some documents has become very important to protect such valuable information sources that are prone to total loss or disappearance due to its oldness.

Setting up a digital collection or library has become a relatively easy task using the current database technology as most of the components and tools for doing it are open sources and easily available. Libraries have always striven to collect process and disseminate information and information exists in many forms. Digital libraries break the barrier of physical boundaries and strive to give access to varied domains and communities.

ELECTRONIC THESES AND DISSERTATIONS (ETD)

An ETD is an electronic document that contains the research work of a scholar. The ETD is similar to its paper predecessor. It has all the features of an ordinary thesis or dissertation with the additional benefits of being electronic in physical form. There has been a move from paper theses and dissertations to electronic format with much acceptance among universities in the international community. It provides a technologically advanced medium for expressing ideas. The benefits of providing electronic resources has been listed by the Virginia Polytechnic Institute and State University website[21] as:

* More access to research
* research is available on campus
* research is accessible worldwide
* Less expense to authors and libraries
* no paper costs
* no physical shelf space
* lower cataloging costs
* Better presentation of research (not available in paper format)
* addition of multimedia files
* more dynamic presentation of data
* hyperlinks
* programs and code

Universities play a major role in generation and dissemination of knowledge by conducting research works and producing theses and dissertations as a unique genre of information sources. These theses are unique sources that contain very valuable findings. Many of such works are not published and not available elsewhere. There is no clear-cut policy in our universities for making available the theses and dissertations to other researchers and academics. Usually a copy is sent to the University Library. Even if it is not made available to the library, the same is not being traced and acquired by the libraries. Digital libraries of Electronic Theses and Dissertations offer an alternative to this waste of valuable scholarship.

The practice of submission of theses in electronic format only has not begun in our country, yet initiatives have begun to convert the existing theses to digital format by projects like Vidyanidhi at Mysore University. Further the huge collection of theses and dissertations in our universities are getting deteriorated and loosing readability day by day due to several reasons like typewritten text and poor quality papers etc. Hence these need to be digitized for better preservation and accessibility and concrete initiatives need to be taken in this direction. The copyright of such resources lies with the concerned universities and what is needed is an attitude to share the unique source of information. Each individual library has to take measures to digitize the existing collection and insist the researchers to submit a copy of their work in a standard digital format. Since all theses are produced in electronic format the researchers can easily do this. INFLIBNET can take a central initiative and insist all the universities to make available the theses to a central database.

NETWORKING AND RESOURCE SHARING

Resource sharing has been in existence in our libraries in different forms like inter library loan, sharing of cataloguing data, sharing manual expertise and skills etc. for many decades. But with the advent of computer networks its potential increased many folds. The most obvious benefit of computer network is that it can retrieve virtually any kind of data including textual, audio and even video. It enables to combine the skills of different people and the power of different equipment, regardless of the physical locations of the people or equipment.

There are several factors that compel one Library to depend on other Libraries and Information Centres like reduction in budgetary provision, increasing prices of documents, lack of infra structure and expertise etc. Rao[22] has traced the expenditure analysis on procuring library resources. India is spending more than Rs 5,000 million a year on procuring new library resources, and of that around Rs 2,000 million is spent on the acquisition of overseas journals. The annual increase in price of these resources means that even financially sound organizations experience difficulties in meeting their cost. Also, the increase in information generation at an estimated rate of 13 per cent per annum has made the task of collection, organization and retrieval of information very difficult. These two main factors have influenced libraries and information centres to automate their services and share resources through networking. The Faxon company, USA, which maintains statistics from 1974 on, reveals that the number of journal titles rose from 38,079 in 1974 to 104,714 in 1989, and that the average price per serial title paid by university libraries in 1979 was US$50.11; by 1989 it had risen to US $125.87. Also, the science and technology libraries pay an average of US $ 234 per serial title a year.

The growth of Indian library networks may be traced to the efforts made during the last four decades. The 1958 Scientific Policy resolution enabled the appointment of different committees and commissions that looked into specific issues and produced recommendations in the form of Sinha Committee's Report (1959), the Ranganathan Report to the University Grants Commission (1965), the Peter Lazar Report and the Kamath Report (1972). In 1984 the Working Group of the Planning Commission recommended to the

Government the need for modernization of library services and informatics during the Seventh Five Year Plan (1985-1990). The Ninth Five Year Plan (1997-2002) Working Group on libraries and informatics highlighted the challenges to be faced by the Indian libraries of the twenty-first century due to unprecedented developments in IT, networking and the Internet.

Telecommunication networks form an integral part of accessing, communicating and transmitting information. In India, the Department of Telecommunications (DOT), Bharat Sanchar Nigam Limited (BSNL), and the Government of India are responsible for providing and maintaining national and international telecommunication facilities. Now private investments in this field have been made by companies like Reliance, Indicom, Asianet etc. and are making provisions for effective data transmission across the country. Several library and information networks have been developed in different parts of the country since 1988 prominent include INFLIBNET and DELNET. In 1950s and 60s United States and Europe felt pressures for increased cooperation and effective dissemination of information, for which the following factors[23] were responsible:

1. Enormous growth of published records;
2. Need for effective control of library resources for retrieval purposes;
3. Inability of library staff to handle enormous data;
4. Complexity of user demands;
5. Limitation of library space and finance;
6. Spurt in research activity due to sufficient grants available for research institutions and research scholars;
7. Interaction between major disciplines which resulted in the creation of new disciplines like geophysics, biophysics, physical chemistry etc.;

8. Advances in computer science in terms of hardware and software capabilities to effectively handle bibliographic storage and retrieval;
9. Advances in library networking; and
10. Availability of funds for automation, networking and retrospective conversion".

Networking of Library and Information Centres for achieving their stated objectives should involve the increased application of IT, the most dynamic technology in so far as breakthroughs are concerned. According to Moore's Law, the number crunching capacity of the computer doubles and the price halves every 18 months. Hence, the future of library networking is in this dynamic technology. Just as electronic books are replacing physical books, the conventional LICs are undergoing transformation in size, location, operations and in shape as they become digital LICs.

Rao[24] has further observed "developing countries like India being late entrants into the field of IT have an advantage over developed countries in that they skip intermediate technological stages. This means India can build its national LIN better and cheaper than those in developed countries. Several initiatives have taken place at different levels since 1988, such as INFLIBNET, DELNET, BTIS, CALIBNET, MALIBNET, BONET, and in the next few years all these networks in India will have to be linked to the NII, and access extended to all educational institutions". This is applicable to the networking scenario in Kerala where it is nonexistent. A network that brings the resources in the university libraries of Kerala under one umbrella is the need of the hour. Interlinking of the four major university libraries in Kerala through Asianet leased line for UGC Infonet connectivity has widened the scope for resource sharing among these universities. It can now operate a Virtual Private Network (VPN) for an effective communication and networking. The modalities and financial resources need to be explored for such a venture.

There are certain security issues related with the networks. Protection of networks is a vital issue to be considered against external attacks to the databases. A common method of protection is the use of firewalls. These are systems comprising hardware and / or software. They are usually placed in between an institution's network and the Internet, though they can also be used internally. A firewall could be placed between a university's administrative system and the student side of its network. Firewalls employ one or more of four techniques: packet filter, application gateway, circuit-level gateway, and proxy server. "In a perfect world, network security wouldn't exist. It's a barrier and, generally speaking, has an inverse relationship with functionality. Librarians and other users of information systems usually find network security to be a nuisance. But just as we understand we should lock our cars when we leave them in parking lots, so we know that we must secure our networks"[25]. Libraries are now making available their databases over networks including Internet and adequate steps need to be taken to protect their valuable resources from any possible damage.

CONSORTIA INITIATIVES

Although resource sharing and cooperation among libraries have been an international tradition for many decades, the phenomenal growth of consortia over the past decade clearly has been fueled by the rapid transformation made possible through technology. Today, many libraries, especially academic and research libraries are already a part of one or more consortia, and those that are not are rapidly taking steps to develop these strategic partnerships with other libraries. In developed countries, although the consortium movement initially was most pronounced in academic libraries, today public, school and even corporate libraries are exploring new ways to provide shared services and to reduce their costs through consortia purchase of resources.

Consortia approach has got certain advantages from the point of view of publishers as well as library and information centers. Hurtt[26] discussed the advantages of consortia from the publishers' point of view. The first advantage for publishers working with consortia is that they can help to simplify the sales process in some of the same ways that working with wholesalers can. In developing a multi-consortium or national consortia approach, a publisher usually needs to have one contact for marketing, selling, negotiating a price and licensing. This works most efficiently when a publisher can work with consortia that have strong centralized administration. Those consortia that can sign license agreements on behalf of their members, and those that accept and pay from one invoice certainly cut down on the time and paperwork needed when dealing with each library.

The second advantage, according to him is that consortia can help publishers increase their market penetration and communication with more libraries, and to do so more quickly than the publisher can do on its own. Consortia, with their Web sites, newsletters (distributed via both mail and e-mail), regular meetings, and listservs are often able to communicate publisher information quickly to their membership about new products, trials and price offers quickly and efficiently.

These first two advantages contribute to the third advantage to the publisher: faster sales. Working through consortia can help publishers achieve a faster rate of adoption or sales, especially when the offer requires that the libraries subscribe to the product by a set deadline date. It is possible to sell an online product to an entire state or to a substantial percentage of the membership of consortia within three months when conditions are right and everything in the process runs smoothly. By contrast, traditional mechanisms

- such as direct mail, telemarketing or visits from field sales representatives - could require one-to-three years to achieve similar results.

The biggest advantage libraries can take from consortia is that they will get more resources for less amount than what they get if they purchase as a single client. Vijaya Kumar and Sreekumar[27] listed the benefits that libraries can reap from consortia as:

* Sharing of information with improved resource sharing;
* Joint pricing negotiations, which gives ability to control expenses and reduce overall costs including information costs;
* Contracts covering multiple countries and strategic alliance with institutions that have common interests for building a larger political coalition and critical mass.

They further listed the benefits of purchasing e-journals through consortia as:

* A single interface and access point;
* A wider range of electronic journals available;
* E-journals organized by subject;
* Links to and from indexing and abstracting services;
* Enhanced search facilities; and
* Customizable institution interface.

The UGC Infonet has provided University Libraries in the country an opportunity to reap the benefits of consortia and there needs to be more initiatives in this direction according to the typical information needs of universities. There are problems with regard to funding management etc, nevertheless such an approach will enable each individual library participating in the consortia to have resources that were not attainable earlier. "To succeed as a collective activity, almost every group has had to overcome political hurdles, funding challenges and the egos of individuals and institutions. Library consortia are having an important impact around the world"[28].

INTERNET AND ITS' IMPACT ON LIBRARY INFORMATION SERVICES

Advent of Internet to the provision of information has a tremendous impact on libraries. "Libraries have always been concerned with public service and access to collections. Traditionally, service and access have been provided on an as-needed basis to those people who actually enter the library building - it has been that presence in the library that has been the characteristic for distinguishing library patrons. This approach allowed librarians to help those who had a specific and defined need for information and defined the library as the place to go for help"[29]. With the advent of automated library systems, library collections became more accessible within the library. Libraries made the transition from the card catalog to the online catalog, allowing electronic access to the information and making keyword searching a real possibility, a real boon to novice library users. Telnet and gopher access to libraries were the first popular manifestations of information-sharing and communication technologies, allowing remote access to collections and predicting the global information networks available today. Now the access provided to information by the libraries are not confined within the walls of the library rather it is extended universally through Internet to reach the users far away. More over libraries provides Internet services to its clientele enabling them to trace the information available elsewhere as well as to provide them communication facilities. Here the libraries have to play the dual role of providing information to remote clientele and enabling its local members to get information from remote sites.

One of the main objectives of the university libraries is to support research and university libraries worldwide started to recognize that research habits significantly changed with the availability of research information on the Internet. Individuals, publishers and other research organizations provide more and more research publications online. This makes the often time-consuming process of obtaining a printed copy through the local library faster and more convenient. It necessitates provision of Internet services in university libraries to retain its role as the main provider of information in higher education.

OPEN SOURCE SOFTWARE FOR LIBRARIES

Libraries looking for alternatives to restrictive software licenses and expensive software can go for open source software. In recent years, there have been a number of developments in library-related open source software about which many of the library professionals are not aware. Libraries in India have made use of CDS/ISIS and Winisis packages for database creation. It is freely available form Unesco site and further developments are possible in ISIS using Pascal programming interface.

Bretthauer[30] throws light on the availability of open source software for library related operations. Open source software is supplied with the source code, the underlying programming that is used to create any software package. In the case of proprietary software, the end user cannot legally view or change the source code rather he gets an executable form of the program. Contrary to this, open source software users are encouraged to look at the source code and offer improvements wherever possible, using a process which is similar to peer review. Over the past decade, open source software proponents have created some stunning successes: Linux, FreeBSD, OpenBSD, Apache, MySQL, PostgreSQL, PHP, PERL, and Python are all open source products Opensource.org also has a certification process for licenses intended to protect the use of the term "open source".

One notable example in open source is the Open Book

integrated library system, for which source code was not available until after the product's first public demonstration. Other examples are Infomine and the Internet Scout Portal Toolkit. They use open source packages such as Apache and MySQL to create sophisticated software. MyLibrary (*http://hegel.lib.ncsu.edu/development/mylibrary/*) has been used in production user portals by several libraries beyond NCSU, where it was initially developed and is still maintained, both in the USA and elsewhere.

Libproxy is a rewriting pass-through proxy system, which is intended to permit authenticated users to access library resources from outside a library's IP range. Patrons of libraries which use this software to provide access to IP-authenticated electronic resources from outside the library's IP range are not required to modify their Web browsers. The current version has been implemented in production use.

Citation Manager (*http://stalefish.lib.sfu.ca/Citation Manager/*) is an open source online citation database for end users. It provides an easy way for institutions to give all patrons equal access to simple bibliographic organization tools both on-site and at home. It's author, Todd Holbrook (2001) of Simon Fraser University Library, describes the package as "still at an alpha stage as I add features, but it's stable so far and usable, if limited". This package may be of interest to libraries, which support commercial citation management packages. Work also continues on several open source integrated library systems. Generally open source ILSs are probably best considered as up-and-coming but not quite ready for production use. Koha (*http://www.koha.org/*) has been in production use in its home library, the Horowhenua Library Trust, Levin, New Zealand since the beginning of 2000, and development continues. OpenBook suffered a slight setback when its sponsoring organization, the Technology Resource Foundation, lost its funding. OpenBook is MARC21-compliant, has a Web interface, support for multiple languages, includes a Z39.50 server and client, and is geared toward collections of up to 25,000 items. Avanti (*http://www.avantilibrarysystems.com/*) also continues development, and is being tested.

A most significant development in open source software for libraries was a meeting sponsored by the Digital Library Federation in October 2001. Organized by Aaron Trehub, Eric Lease Morgan, and Martin Halbert, and facilitated by Dan Greenstein of the DLF, the meeting's focus was on mainstreaming open source software in libraries. Many of the attendees of the meeting represent ARL libraries. There were two major outcomes of the meeting. First is an effort to develop a portal approach to exhibiting library-related open source software, including the ability to sort or find products used by type of library and by type of project. The goal of such a project would be to help libraries determine what packages would be suitable for use. The intent was to build on the strengths and accomplishments of Dan Chudnov's *www.oss4lib.org*, rather than compete with this successful site, which has functioned for several years with minimal support. That idea has been prototyped by Eric Lease Morgan and Notre Dame Libraries' Digital Access and Information Architecture Department, with the intent of pursuing grant funding opportunities and building awareness of open source within some library circles. The second outcome was to sponsor, or help sponsor, a research project which would test a number of hypotheses about open source software. The report of this meeting can be found at *http://www.diglib.org/architectures/ossrep.htm* Koha (*http://www.koha.org/*) is an effective open source suited for libraries. Greenstone has excellent provisions for managing a digital library collection.

The popularity of Linux, the open source operating system has grown visibly over recent years. It attracts attention of many because of different reasons such as free availability, reputation for stability, reliability, user-friendliness etc. Many libraries are opting for this powerful operating system and there are many reasons for its popularity. It provides a range of choices that few other Operating Systems can match. These choices include a healthy selection of Linux distributions, an extensive array of supported hardware, a growing number of application programs and an assortment of organizations that are willing to provide technical support for Linux systems. Now Linux has become a viable alternative to any other Operating Systems including DOS, Windows, Unix, NetWare and so on.

Open source software specific to meeting different library needs are evolving and is beginning to fulfill its potential for replacing increasingly restrictive software licenses and software subscriptions with a useful, viable alternative. Libraries in under developed and developing countries that find it difficult to raise source for obtaining highly charged commercial software should think of opting for open sources.

SYSTEM LIBRARIANSHIP

Due to the impact of technology on libraries, the roles of librarians have undergone considerable change. The use of the technology as the basis of information service has highlighted the need for library personnel with special skills to help information seekers. The skills needed in the latest information technology has caused professionals from other fields especially from computer field enter the area of information provision. Ramakrishnan[31] has rightly pointed out "As is evident from the use of Internet and other IT devices by information seekers, a large number of non-library professionals are in the field. In fact, the term 'Information Professional' can be used as a broader term to include the term 'Library professional' as well. It is for the traditional library professionals to equip themselves with IT skills so as to function effectively in this IT age i.e. the twenty first century". Availability of the right kind of manpower in terms of necessary quality and quantity at various levels in the hierarchy of library is a pre requisite for the success of automated systems.

Now a new 'breed' of professionals with skills in library science as well as in computer applications known as 'system librarians' have come up in developed countries. System librarianship in India is a profession of recent origin. System librarians are computer professionals and librarians simultaneously. Jordan[32] has defined systems-librarian as "a librarian who is responsible for managing the information technology used in a library". Among librarians, those dealing with systems represent a subspecies whose place within the hierarchy has been shifting. Systems librarians handle all things dealing with computers in libraries. It is an ecological niche that requires skills that are not taught in most library and information science schools today, and certainly were not taught at the time when most senior practicing librarians studied library science. Qualified librarians, in both library and computer science, to take on the challenge of making a library's automated system and electronic resources work are also so few that demand remains high. Seadle[33] has identified the role of systems librarians as "Systems librarians represent a service profession for a service profession. They are the plumbers who get called in an emergency, the carpenters who make additions to the house, the roofers whose work is supposed to last for a decade but sometimes leaks. They are absolutely necessary to accomplish what we do in libraries today".

Wilson[34] articulates in detail what systems librarians commonly do on the job. He identifies the following to be the typical responsibilities of systems librarians:

* Integrated library system management;
* Network design and management;
* Server and host administration;

* Desktop computing;
* Training, documentation, and support;
* Application development;
* Planning and budget;
* Specification and purchasing;
* Technology exploration and evaluation;
* Miscellaneous technology support;
* Technical risk management; and
* Communication and coordination.

Above listed of responsibilities and skills illustrates how comprehensive the job description of a systems librarian can be and how important his role in the organization. Yet, the exact combination of these items will depend on the size and functions and services of library or organization, the skills and responsibilities of others working with the systems librarian, and several other factors. White[35] has given the following as the primary responsibilities of a system librarian:

* Developing original applications;
* Troubleshooting;
* Software evaluation;
* Hardware/software monitoring, maintenance, and upgrading,
* Data protection;
* Staff training;
* System documentation; and
* Negotiation and communication.

While library schools have taken interest in recent years in instilling knowledge about the latest digital technologies, few if any schools currently offer courses in introductory systems librarianship. If we go through the syllabi of library schools we can find that the focus tends to be mostly on human-computer interaction, application packages like word processors or minor database applications rather than the basics of operating system administration, network administration, database design, or languages like Java, Perl, or C++. This fits with a trend in library schools to provide a broader and more intellectual education, rather than train students to step immediately into a specific library job like cataloging or reference.

Seadle[36] has further emphasized, "a good systems librarian is in fact more like an expert bibliographer than like a technician. Both should bring scholarly expertise, plus substantial language or methodological training, to the job. Their status is not equal. But in the end, what makes libraries work is the balance of skills. The real professional's professional in the library world can be anyone who provides a set of skills that others need. Systems librarians are certainly among them". Information technology applications are changing always and the systems librarian's mission is to keep him/herself up to date and to work with constantly changing technology. Both library staff and library users have rapidly changing information needs and technology skills; systems librarians need to seek and help design systems to serve such a diverse population.

System administration is a very important task to be performed by the system people like system librarians or computer professionals. It involves maintaining the databases, providing access to the system according to privileges; creating/deleting users, protecting databases and taking back up to avoid data loss etc.

In order to protect the database backup of the data is to be taken regularly and system administrators generally adopt automatic methods of backup like mirroring of disk drives, RAID facility, using certain software like cloning software etc. Cloning software is now becoming quite popular in all types of libraries. Pricing is such that even many libraries can afford it. It takes an image of an entire hard drive and stores it on some kind of media such as zip disks, compact disks, or a server's hard drive. It can be used to roll out a group of new computers or as a backup system. It can be especially helpful to libraries that have limited staffing resources to devote to troubleshooting computer software problems. If a software problem occurs on a computer, it can basically be restored in a matter of minutes to the state it was in at the time the image was created. It is well worth the cost when purchasing computers in bulk for a new building or replacing a batch of old computers.

NEW DIMENSIONS IN LIBRARY AUTOMATION

Computer technology always found to be fast growing is bringing out new applications. Due to intensive research taking place in computer applications many new technologies are coming up. Automated library systems are now moving to a totally automated one where the user of the library need not interact with any staff member for obtaining assistance and is able to get the services with the help of computers. This provides users with greater easiness. Facilities like Radio frequency controlled document security systems, automated check-in/check-out systems, use of smart cards for user identification and microchips for document identification etc. are implemented in India also and it is expected that these highly sophisticated technologies will be affordable for our university libraries also when the present high cost comes down. It is a fact that in a country like India where a big number of graduates and post-graduates in librarianship are in want of jobs, introduction of these sorts of facilities in libraries may cause resistance from the library staff in fear of loosing the job.

RFID TECHNOLOGY

Radio Frequency Identification (RFID) technology has changed the concept of security all over the world by giving Smart Cards for individuals' identification. The use of RFID has now been extended to libraries so as to keep them efficient and competitive in an ever-changing environment. The technology is applied to a variety of activities in libraries now a days like totally automated check in/check out (without the intervention of the library staff), theft detection, stock verification etc. and comprises many components including RFID Tags/Labels, Library Staff Station, Security Gate, Self Service Units, Shelf Management etc. and it can be extended to many more areas in future. Being a new technology its potential is to be elaborated a little.

RFID tags are flexible paper-thin with an electronic chip. When placed in to books or other media, theses tags/labels can be read and written to using radio frequency, that operate without contact and line of sight. It has an in-built EAS function to detect thefts and is designed to last for lifetime of the item they identify. The Library Staff Station facilitates handling of materials having RFID tags. Through a modern graphical user interface, many functions can be run on this station.

Once the label is placed in the document, its identification such as Accession Number/shelf location is registered in the chip of the label. This information is either to be taken from the library database or it is directly taken from the book by scanning the barcode on the book. Thus this ID tags are used for check in/check out purposes.

After establishing the validity of the member through the Smart Card, the documents to be checked out are placed on the deck of the station. Library database is updated automatically by putting the book in the borrower's account and theft detection system of the label is deactivated. When the document is to be returned, the borrower has to place it on the deck and it gets checked in and the theft detection mechanism is activated. Fine, if any, would be calculated and a slip may be printed at this time. If the document is to be renewed, it is to be placed on the deck and can be renewed after checking the validity of renewal and new due date is to be confirmed.

Sorting the document for re shelving can also be done by this technology. When it is placed on the deck, it is capable of displaying the collection and shelf number of the document. Security Gates are two or more Theft Detection Pedestals that are independent of each other and may have overlapping protection zones providing additional security. Any item that has not been checked-out by staff station or self-checkout station, will be detected as it passes through these pedestal zones.

Self Service Units are stations where the books are checked out of the library independently by the borrower without any intervention of library staff. It is an interactive station with touch screen that prompts the member to enter his/her identity card. The system checks the validity of the member card, and if found satisfactory further prompts to place the books on the deck of the borrowing station one by one. The status of each item is changed as checked out and the theft detection mechanism is deactivated so as to make a smooth passage through the security gate. Another system facilitates the self-check-in process. Here the documents to be returned are to be placed in the equipment for this purpose. System updates the database by changing the status of the document and account of the borrower appropriately and deactivates the theft detection mechanism. Just like the ATM facility in banks this automatic check-in facility can be made available 24 hours even if the library is closed.

RFID technology can very well be applied in stock verification function also. Special hand held terminals will help to check the availability of the item in the shelves without the document being taken out of the shelf.

WIRELESS APPLICATIONS IN LIBRARIES

Wireless access within the library is provided in many

advanced countries to enable the clientele to access the resources with ease. There are different standards used in wireless technology such as 802.11a, 802.11b, Bluetooth, HomeRF etc. and adoption of standards may differ from library to library. Graham[37] noted the reasons for use of Wireless technology in library networks and found it divided in US along two lines relevant to the type of libraries. Public libraries use wireless technology as a cost effective way to extend networking in buildings, where the addition or expansion or traditional network cabling was costly and difficult due to structural issues. Application of wireless technology in College and University libraries addresses specific needs, in particular providing access for community members' laptops. Laptops are not common in our universities today, but the reason specified by Graham in the case of public libraries may be applicable to our university libraries as well.

ROLE OF INFLIBNET IN COMPUTERISATION OF UNIVERSITY LIBRARIES

Information and Library Network (INFLIBNET), Ahmedabad is an autonomous inter university center of the UGC, established in 1991 and located at Gujrat University campus, Ahmedabad. It is directed towards modernization of libraries and information centers for information transfer and access, to support scholarship, learning and academic pursuits by establishing a national network of libraries and information centers in universities, institutions of higher learning and R&D institutions in India. It is basically a co-operative endeavor in resource development, sharing and its utilization at national level. In May1996 it attained the status of an autonomous Inter-University Centre under UGC. INFLIBNET is set out to be a major player in promoting scholarly communication among academicians and researchers in India. It is with the coming up of INFLIBNET that the trend of computer application in university libraries in the country started and the role of INFLIBNET in this momentum is very great.

Major objectives[38] of the INFLIBNET are:

* To promote and establish communication facilities to improve capability in information transfer and access, that provide support to scholarship, learning, research and academic pursuits through cooperation and involvement of agencies concerned
* To establish Information and Library Network (INFLIBNET) – a computer communication network for linking libraries and information centers in universities, deemed to be universities, colleges, UGC information centers, institutions of national importance and R&D institutions etc. avoiding duplication of efforts in acquiring resources.

FUNCTIONS OF INFLIBNET

In order to fulfill the broad objectives, INFLIBNET has undertaken the following activities[39]:

* Promote and implement computerisation of operations and services in the libraries and information centres of the country, following a uniform standard.
* Evolve standards and uniform guidelines in techniques, methods, procedures, computer hardware and software, services and promote their adoption in actual practice by all libraries, in order to facilitate pooling, sharing and exchange of information towards optimal use of resources and facilities.
* Evolve a national network interconnecting various libraries and information centres in the country and to improve capability in information handling and service.
* Provide reliable access to document collection of libraries by creating on-line union catalogue of serials, theses/dissertations, books, monographs and non-book

materials (manuscripts, audio-visuals, computer data, multimedia, etc.) in various libraries in India.

* Provide access to bibliographic information sources with citations, abstracts etc. through indigenously created databases of the Sectoral Information Centres of NISSAT, UGC Information Centres, City Networks and such others and by establishing gateways for on-line accessing of national and international databases held by national and international information networks and centres respectively.
* Develop new methods and techniques for archival of valuable information available as manuscripts and information documents in different Indian Languages, in the form of digital images using high-density storage media.
* Optimise information resource utilization through shared cataloguing, inter-library loan service, catalogue production, collection development and thus avoiding duplication in acquisition to the extent possible.
* Enable the users dispersed all over the country, irrespective of location and distance, to have access to information regarding serials, theses/dissertations, books, monographs and non-book materials by locating the sources wherefrom available and to obtain it through the facilities of INFLIBNET and union catalogue of documents.
* Create databases of projects, institutions, specialists, etc. for providing on-line information service.
* Encourage co-operation among libraries, documentation centres and information centres in the country, so that the resources can be pooled for the benefit of helping the weaker resource centres by stronger ones.
* Train and develop human resources in the field of

computerised library operations and networking to establish, manage and sustain INFLIBNET.

* Facilitate academic communication amongst scientists, engineers, social scientists, academics, faculties, researchers and students through electronic mail, file transfer, computer/audio/video conferencing, etc.
* Undertake system design and studies in the field of communications, computer networking, information handling and data management.
* Establish appropriate control and monitoring system for the communication network and organise maintenance.
* Collaborate with institutions, libraries, information centres and other organisations in India and abroad in the field relevant to the objectives of the Centre.
* Create and promote R&D and other facilities and technical positions for realising the objectives of the Centre.
* Generate revenue by providing consultancies and information services.
* Do all other such things as may be necessary, incidental or conducive to the attainment of all or any of the above objectives

"The automation of university libraries is a pre-requisite for networking and resource sharing. INFLIBNET Centre, through UGC, has been providing the required support to universities in phases. Till 1999-2000, 123 universities have been given initial grant of Rs. 6.5 lakhs each to develop infrastructure for automation.INFLIBNET Centre also desires that each university should establish a LAN in it's campus linking all the departments including library. This LAN in turn will be connected to the WAN"[40].

ACHIEVEMENTS OF INFLIBNET

The major achievements of INFLIBNET include financial assistance for automation of university libraries, development of SOUL, a library management software, library and information science human resource development and consultancy, development of Union Database, bibliographic standards and latest being UGC Infonet.

FINANCIAL ASSISTANCE FOR AUTOMATION OF UNIVERSITY LIBRARIES

INFLIBNET, through UGC provided both initial and recurring grants to the 142 universities identified under the programme. Non-recurring grants enabled the universities to procure hardware, software (OS), modem, telephone, air-conditioners etc. Universities were also provided with recurring grant for the first five years after the installation of the systems to help them maintain the same and retro-conversion of bibliographical data. This has definitely helped to create an IT conscious environment in university libraries in India. Further, to manage the automation activities in university libraries the post of Information Scientist in the scale of pay of Lecturer was sanctioned with financial support for the first five years.

DEVELOPMENT OF SOUL SOFTWARE

INFLIBNET has developed SOUL software to facilitate automation of libraries. It works in Client/Server mode in Windows environment using MS-SQL server as back end tool. It is web compatible and supports barcode technology to generate labels and is developed in conformity with international standards like MARC21, CCF, AACR II, ISO 2709 etc. Certain utility software developed at the Centre are available to the universities on request such as software for searching the data from union databases (OPAC), Catalogue card generation, Duplicate checking of records, Customised software for Books, Theses, Serials, Data Conversion from Dbase, FoxPro and text file to ISO-2709 format.

HUMAN RESOURCE DEVELOPMENT AND CONSULTANCY

To enhance the skills of University Library staff for implementation of INFLIBNET Programme, the following training courses are conducted. 20 training courses of four-week duration for operational staff working in the university libraries were prominent. This is mainly meant for operational staff of libraries. They are given exhaustive training on application of computers to library and information services and 7 workshops of one-week duration for senior library staff such as University Librarian and Deputy Librarian, focusing on managing automation and networking. IRTPLA, a new series of training programs are conducted at different locations in collaboration with universities across the country to train college librarians at regional level. More than 800 professionals have been trained under a total of more than 35 programs. Special workshops on Network Management for Libraries have also been conducted. Ten Librarians from different universities spent a week at INFLIBNET to solve their problems in using ILMS software. SOUL was installed at 304 Libraries and onsite training of one-week duration to the library staff was provided at each site. Apart from these, an annual convention called CALIBER is conducted at various places. It helps the library as well as IT professionals to interact with each other and discuss issues for mutual benefit.

DEVELOPMENT OF UNION DATABASE

Development of Union Database is one of the most important activities of INFLIBNET Centre. Its Book database consists of 60 Lakh records received from 89 universities and has around 12 Lakh unique records. Theses database consists of more than 1.4 Lakh records of doctoral theses submitted to various Indian universities. Serial holdings database has more than 13750 unique serial titles having over 47,000 holdings of various universities in the country. Experts database provides useful data related to the names of experts in different disciplines and it consists of more than 13000 records and is growing steadily. Research projects database has more than 9000 records. Apart from these the NISSAT-Project Database has more than 20000 experts profiles in the area of Science and Technology and is provided access on the URL *http://nissat.inflibnet.ac.in*.

BIBLIOGRAPHIC STANDARDS

To maintain consistency and quality in databases created by the participating libraries, each participating library has to follow the standards adopted by INFLIBNET. The document "INFLIBNET Standards and Guidelines for Data Capturing" is made available to all university libraries. INFLIBNET also recommends the standard, Anglo American Cataloguing Rules - Rev. 2 and Library of Congress Subject Headings to assign subject headings. Libraries following INFLIBNET standards will find it easy to convert their records in to MARC 21 format. INFLIBNET also brings out several publications and provides in ormation services like Document Delivery Service (DDS).

UGC INFONET

UGC under the auspices of INFLIBNET launched an ambitious programme to bring about a qualitative change in the academic infrastructure, especially for higher education. Under this initiative UGC plans to modernize the university campuses with state-of-the-art campus wide networks and setting up its own nationwide communication network named UGC-Infonet. It uses ICT and Internet to transform learning environment from a mono-dimensional to multi-dimensional one.

Infonet provides access to highly precious databases like Chemical Abstract and Biological Abstract and E-journals covering all fields of learning of relevance to various universities including Arts, Humanities, Social Sciences, Physical and Chemical Sciences, Life Sciences, Computer Science, Mathematics and Statistics. The literature made available includes full text access to journals covering research articles, reviews and abstracting databases. Access is provided to current as well as archival literature. Its future programs include developing modules on E-Learning, Education and Tele Conferencing, collaboration with national documentation centers and other resourceful libraries.

UGC-Infonet will be a boon to the higher education systems in several ways:

* UGC-Infonet will become a vehicle for distance learning to facilitate spread of quality education all over the country.
* UGC-Infonet will be a tool to distribute education material and journals to the remotest of areas.
* UGC-Infonet will be a resource for researchers and scholars for tapping the most up-to-date information.
* UGC-Infonet will form a medium for collaboration among teachers and students, not only within the country but also all over the world.
* UGC-Infonet will be an Intranet for University Automation.
* UGC-Infonet will encompass entire University Systems for most efficient utilization of precious network resources.

UGC-Infonet is aimed at establishing a channel for Globalisation of Education and to facilitate the universities in marketing their services and developments. Infonet proposes mirror sites for content hosting in major cities of the country as shown in Figure 1.2.

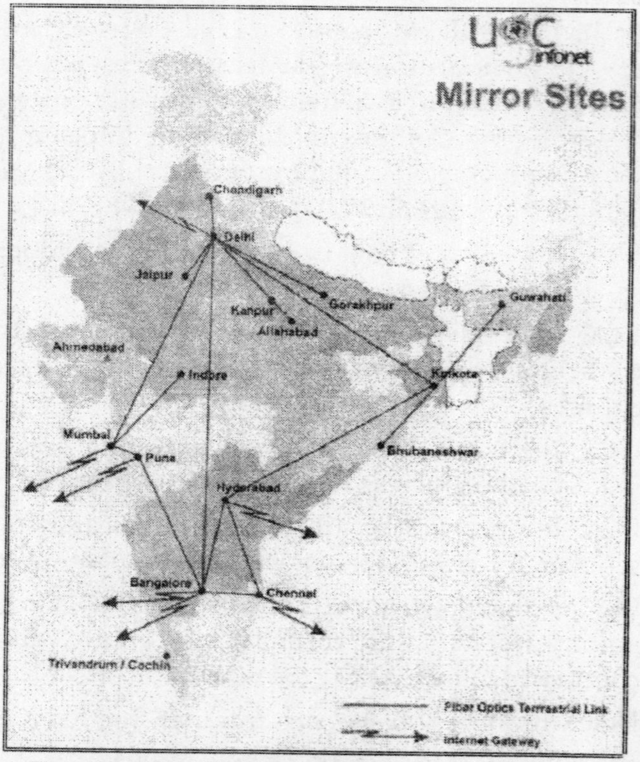

Figure 1. 2 UGC Infonet Mirror Sites in the Country
Courtesy: ***http://web.inflibnet .ac.in***

NETWORK ARCHITECTURE OF THE INFONET

UGC Infonet is based on open IP platform, employing state-of-the-art technologies like IP, enabling on-line response to queries. Open system architecture will ensure support for current and future applications. Users from educational Institutions would enjoy high data rates while accessing Intranet and Internet resources.

FEATURES OF THE UGC-INFONET

The main features of the UGC-INFONET are:

* Scaleable Architecture to grow from Universities to affiliated Colleges

* Nation-wide Terrestrial Backbone using Fiber Optic links
* Integrated Satellite WAN supporting broadband and SCPC VSAT technology
* Comprehensive Network Management Systems for overall monitoring of the network, down to each and every device.
* Linkage with other Academic and Research Networks all over the world.
* Data security and virus protection using firewalls and Intrusion Detection Systems
* Dedicated Data Center for Web hosting, e-Journals and Mail Boxes.
* Mirror sites spread all over the country for content hosting.
* Broadband Multimedia and Video Channels for Distance Learning

INTRANET FOR UNIVERSITIES

Availability of Reliable and Stable network infrastructure will facilitate increased usage of computers in the University Campuses. Campus Management will be more efficient and student friendly. Interlinking of the universities will expand the reach of students and faculty to other universities providing them with better avenues for wider horizontal growth. UGC-Infonet is aimed at establishing a seamless link between the UGC and the universities. This will help to provide a more accurate and up-to-date picture of the Universities, while at the same time it will enable universities to have timely information about the various schemes of the UGC. Consequently, this is expected to bring a qualitative change in the UGC-Universities interaction. The huge and multifaceted Indian Education Systems would achieve greatest efficiency through e-governance of UGC.

IMPLEMENTATION OF INFONET

The UGC-Infonet is overlaid on ERNET Infrastructure in a manner so as to provide assured quality of service and optimal utilization of bandwidth resources. The network is run and managed by ERNET India. The project is funded by UGC with 100% capital investment and up to 90% of recurring costs. A joint technical and tariff committee, consisting of leading experts in the country is setup to guide and monitor the design, implementation and operations of UGC-Infonet. INFLIBNET is the nodal agency for coordination of the UGC-Infonet and facilitate linkage between ERNET and the Universities. In the long run, each University will become a hub for the colleges affiliated to it. ERNET entrusted Asianet Satellite Communications, the responsibility of providing connectivity to the universities in Kerala. Leased line connectivity with one Mbps bandwidth has been provided to the four universities viz. Kerala, Calicut, Mahathma Gandhi and CUSAT.

CAMPUS LANS AT UNIVERSITIES

Infrastructure at the University campus is also critical to take full advantage of the UGC-Infonet. Campus LAN technology is evolving rapidly and many universities may not have the expertise to setup the most modern and cost effective LANs. ERNET India has participated with many institutions in the planning and implementation of their campus computing facilities. The expertise generated thus will be extended to the Universities so that every university can have a state of the art infrastructure.

To conclude, a decade ago library automation, at least in our country, was regarded as an addition to the facilities in a library rather than a necessity. Today the situation has changed and automation has become the dire need of libraries to discharge its duties to build up and process its collection, to facilitate operations, to provide services to its clientele and to support the management decision-making. No library, especially in higher education, can survive in the present era without the application of computers.

It is in this context, that a detailed study of the computerisation of university libraries in Kerala is conducted covering a wide spectrum of facets such as its areas of applications, different hardware available and software in use, features and use of OPACs, INFLIBNET support received, various standards in use, utilization of open source software, financial resources available, services provided and operations performed using computers, digitization initiatives, network facilities available, Internet services provided to the members as well as services provided through the library website to remote users, the human resources available for computerization activities, response of users with regard to the computerised circulation system, OPAC and Internet services, responses of the person in charge of the computerised activities regarding the duties and responsibilities, facilities available, difficulties faced in the process of computerisation of the university libraries under study and to identify the solutions to the problems etc. This study will help to understand the status of computerisation of the university libraries and to identify the lacunas in the system and will further be able to put forward suggestions for its improvement.

REFERENCES

1. *http://web.inflibnet.ac.in/info/indUniv.jsp* (Accessed on 30/05/2004).
2. Government of India (1962). **Report of the University Education Commission, 1948.** v1. New Delhi: Manager of Publications, pp 111- 22.
3. Bavakutty, M. (1988) ***Libraries in higher education***. New Delhi: Ess Ess Publications, p. 1.

4. Venkata Ramana P and Rao, V Chandrasekhar. (2003). **Use of Information Technology in Central University Libraries of India**. *DESIDOC Bulletin of Information Technology*. **23** (2): p. 31.

5. Kanakachary, M et.al. (1990). **Approach to library automation: some basic issues**. In *Computerisation & Library Network*. Thirty Sixth All India Library Conference, Jodhpur, India, 26-29 December, 1990, Organized by University of Jodhpur, edited by C P Vashisth. New Delhi: ILA p.74.

6. *www.informationr.net/tdw/publ/ppt/overload/sld005.htm* (Accessed on 22/07/2004).

7. Kamath V A (1983). **Evolution of information technology: an overview**. *IASLIC Bulletin*. **28** (4): p.178.

8. *http://www.isc.org/* (Accessed on 30/05/2004).

9. Graves, Daniel J and Wulfff, Yvonne L. (1990). **The economics behind resource sharing: implications for collection development and future of libraries**. *Advances in Resource Sharing*. pp 52-53.

10. *http://www.sims.berkeley.edu/research/projects/how-much-info/summary.html* (Accessed on 23/07/2004).

11. Sharma, Pandey S K. (1993). ***Library computerisation: theory and practice***. New Delhi: Ess Ess Publications. p 94.

12. Rama varma and Janakraj. **Practical aspects of library automation in the Indian context**. In *Information Technology Applications in academic libraries*. Fourth National Convention for Automation of Libraries in Education and Research (CALIBER 97), Patiala, India. 6-8 March 1997, Organized by Information and Library Network Centre, Ahmedabad and Thapar Institute of Engineering and Technology, Patiala, edited by A L Moorthy and P B Mangla. Ahmedabad: INFLIBNET. p10.

13. *http://www.sims.berkeley.edu/research/projects/how-much-info/summary .html* (Accessed on 23/07/2004).

14. Rowley, JE. (1988). ***Computers for libraries.*** London: Clive Bingley. p. 145.

15. Nair, R Raman. (1992). ***Computer application to library and information services.*** New Delhi: Ess Ess Publications, p. 236 – 7.

16. Rowley, JE. (1988). ***Computers for libraries.*** London: Clive Bingley. p. 163.

17. Manjunath, GK and Pujar, SM. (2002). **Barcoding of library documents: planning, techniques and tools**. *Annals of Library and Information Studies,* **49** (4): p. 119.

18. Nair, R Raman. (1992). ***Computer application to library and information services.*** New Delhi: Ess Ess Publications, p. 235.

19. Bailey, Penny. (2004). **Internet, Interaction and Intelligence: Latest development in library automation.** *Managing information.* **11** (3): April 2004. p38.

20. Waldhart, Thomas J. et. al. **Provision of local assisted access to selected internet information resources by ARL academic libraries.** *Journal of Academic Librarianship.* **26** (2): p. 101.

21. *http://etd.vt.edu/background/whatis.html* (Accessed on 24/06/2004).

22. Rao, Siriginidi Subba. (2001). **Networking of libraries and information centres: challenges in India.** *Library Hi Tech.* **19** (2): p. 167.

23. Kaul, H K. (1999). ***Library Resource Sharing and Network.*** New Delhi: Virgo Publications. p 37.

24. Rao, Siriginidi Subba. (2001). **Networking of libraries and information centres: challenges in India.** *Library Hi Tech.* **19** (2): p. 175.

25. Cain, Mark. (2003). **Cybertheft, network security, and the library without walls.** *The Journal of Academic Librarianship*, **29** (4): p. 246.
26. Hurtt, James. (2000). **Fitting the pieces together: selling to regional networks, consortia and libraries.** *Library Consortium Management: An International Journal*, 2 (1): p. 5.
27. Vijaya Kumar, J K and Sreekumar, M G. (2002). **Consortia approach among the higher education and research libraries in India: a dire need of the hour.** In *Library Co-operation in a networked world*. National Seminar on Library Co-operation in a networked world, University of Calicut, India, 25 – 26 May 2001. Organized by C H Mohammed Koya Library and Department of Library and Information Science, University of Calicut, edited by M Bavakautty, M C K Veeran and T K Muhammed Salih. New Delhi: Ess Ess Publications, p. 78.
28. Friend, Frederik J. (1999). **New wine in a new bottle: purchasing by library consortia in the United Kingdom**. *Information Technology and Libraries*. **18** (3): p146.
29. Arant, Wendi and Payne, Leila. (2001). **The common user interface in academic libraries: myth or reality?**. *Library Hi Tech*, **19** (1): p. 64.
30. Bretthauer, David. (2002). **Open Source Software in Libraries an Update**. *Library Hi Tech News incorporating Online and CD Notes*. **19** (5):
31. Ramakrishnan, M N. (2002). **Library Profession in Kerala: a SWOT analysis**. In *Organisation of Libraries and Information Centres in the 21st Century*. National Seminar on Organisation of Libraries and Information Centres in the 21st Century, University of Calicut, India, 26 – 27 May 2000. Organized by C H Mohammed Koya

Library and Department of Library and Information Science, University of Calicut, edited by M Bavakautty, M C K Veeran and T K Muhammed Salih. New Delhi: Ess Ess Publications. p. 54.

32. Jordan, Mark. (2003). **The self-education of systems librarians**. *Library Hi Tech*. **21** (3): p. 275.
33. Seadle, Michael. (2003). **The status of systems librarians**. *Library Hi Tech*. **21** (3): p. 269.
34. Wilson, T.C. (1998). ***The Systems Librarian: Designing Roles, Defining Skills***. Chicago: ALA.
35. White, H.S. (1990). **The role of the automation librarian in the medium-sized library**. *Canadian Library Journal*. **47**(4): pp. 257-62.
36. Seadle, Michael. (2003). **The status of systems librarians**. *Library Hi Tech*. **21** (3): p. 269.
37. Graham, Rebecca A. (2002). **Wireless use in libraries.** *Library Hi Tech*. **20** (2): pp 238.
38. *http://web.inflibnet.ac.in/about/objective.jsp* (Accessed on 23/06/2004).
39. *http://web.inflibnet.ac.in/about/functions.jsp* (Accessed on 23/06/2004).
40. *http://web.inflibnet.ac.in/* (Accessed on 23/07/2004).

1.2
Research Methodology

The purpose of this study was to make a survey of the computerisation scenario of the University Libraries in the state of Kerala for obtaining a clear picture of the level of application of computers in the libraries and to assess the extend of its reach to the targeted users of the library and to put forward suggestions for the improvement of the existing system. This chapter covers the Objectives of the study, Hypotheses, Sources of data, Selection of samples and methods of analysis of data and its presentation.

The importance of the University Library in the academic society as the prime agency for dissemination of information required to satisfy the information needs of the academics is well established. It is well known that the traditional methods of management of the libraries will not be able to tackle the impact of 'Information Explosion'. Use of computers proved to be an excellent solution to this. Today, computers are doing a yeomen service to libraries with its superb capabilities to do humanly unmanageable works with splendid speed that may act in nanoseconds. Its capabilities such as tremendous speed, huge capacity to store ocean of information on to tiny storage medium like CDs and DVDs, immense capabilities to perform repetitive jobs in libraries without fatigue, the radical power to sort, arrange, retrieve and disseminate information, its capacity to collect information from anywhere in the world through world wide networks overcoming all the geographical barriers etc. has made the computer indispensable in libraries. The use of

Internet facilities in the provision of information in libraries has acquired greater significance and utilization of its full potential in our libraries is to be made.

NEED AND SIGNIFICANCE OF THE STUDY

The major University Libraries in the state of Kerala started computerisation of their operations and services almost a decade ago. Here attempt is made to examine whether the libraries have applied computers in all the potential areas of application and whether the computerised services are outreaching and benefiting to the users of these libraries. It is to be ascertained whether the libraries have provision of adequate finance, hardware, software, manpower and necessary other infrastructure for the smooth furtherance of the task. It is to be further investigated whether the libraries are making proper utilization of Open Source software. Such a study will help to find out not only the lacunas in the present system, but the problems faced by the staff and the users of the automated library system also, and to suggest measures for solving the problems that persist.

OBJECTIVES OF THE STUDY

The study that is aimed at investigating various aspects of Computerisation of University Libraries in Kerala has the following specific objectives:

1. To identify and compare the application of computers in housekeeping operations in libraries with regard to:
   (a) Database Management
   (b) Acquisition procedures
   (c) Technical Processing
   (d) Serials Control
   (e) Document Circulation Operations, and
   (f) Stock Verification.
2. To identify the availability of hardware and the

proprietary as well as open source software along with the operating systems in use;

3. To identify the various sources of available finance for computerisation and to assess the sufficiency of financial resources available;
4. To study the support received from INFLIBNET for library computerisation and the contribution of the library to the union database of INFLIBNET;
5. To identify the collections available in various types of documents, the standards followed in the technical processing of documents and the satisfaction of the library over the standards followed;
6. To identify the provisions made in each university library for accessing the OPAC, options and access points provided, various access points made use by the users, and to ascertain the satisfaction of the users over the library OPAC;
7. To identify the services provided by the library and the application of computers in various services and operations of the library and the opinion of the users about the computerised circulation services;
8. To identify the network infrastructure available in the library and in the university for providing computerised services and extending the services of the library beyond its premises; and the security measures taken to protect the network;
9. To study the provisions of Internet Services in the University Libraries, to identify the purposes of Internet use of Students, Research Scholars and Teachers and to identify various services used and to assess the speed of the connection and availability of required information and the services provided by the libraries;
10. To study and compare the websites of the University

Libraries so as to ascertain its role in the provision of information by the University Libraries.

11. To identify the infrastructure available and the efforts taken by the University Libraries for digitization of documents;
12. To identify the total personnel engaged in the computerised activities and their competency for the work in terms of their qualifications;
13. To study the duties, responsibilities and qualifications of the person in charge of the computerised library system;
14. To identify difficulties faced by the person in charge of the computerised library system, the methods through which it is over come, options available for improving his/her works, the freedom enjoyed in incorporating own ideas to the works and guidance as well as support received from within the library and to study his/her opinion over the facilities available;
15. To assess the utilization of the computerized services by the users and to identify the difficulties faced by them in making benefit of computerisation;

A thorough examination of the professional literature was made to acquire ample knowledge about the subject under study. Mostly journal articles and conference proceedings volumes were consulted for this purpose. Books published on the subject and articles available over Internet as well as websites of some libraries and other organizations were also referred. The examination of the literature particularly the related studies enabled the investigator to arrive at some assumptions that are presented as hypotheses of this study for detailed verification.

HYPOTHESES

The following are the specific hypotheses formulated for the study:

1. The University Libraries in Kerala have overlooked the need for development of the E-Resources collections.
2. Computerisation of the University Libraries in Kerala is not being fairly supported in terms of finance.
3. University Libraries in Kerala are not adequately equipped with latest hardware and software to provide modern computerised services to their clientele.
4. University Libraries in Kerala do not have adequate number of qualified and skilled personnel to shoulder the computerisation processes.
5. University Libraries in Kerala are yet to make computerisation in some of the basic and potential areas including services and operations.
6. Lack of proper User Education in the University Libraries in Kerala makes the available computerised services under utilized.
7. The users of the University Libraries in Kerala are making best use of the OPAC utilizing the full provisions made in the OPAC.
8. University Libraries in Kerala lack good computer network infrastructure to extend the services beyond the library premises and the libraries have not utilized Internet to provide modern library and information services.
9. The academic community in the universities of the state considers the 'Internet' as an important source of information but the University Libraries have not reckon with this and are not supporting them properly.
10. University Libraries in Kerala have not begun digitization though there are unique and valuable collections that are prone to deterioration.

LIMITATIONS OF THE STUDY

The present study is only at the level of a particular

State, i.e. the state of Kerala and a particular type of academic libraries i.e. University Libraries. There are Seven Universities in Kerala. They are:

1. University of Kerala, Thiruvananthapuram,
2. Mahathma Gandhi University, Kottayam,
3. Cochin University of Science and Technology (CUSAT), Kochi,
4. Sri Sankaracharya University of Sanskrit, Kaladi,
5. Kerala Agricultural University, Vellanikkara, Thrissur,
6. University of Calicut, Thenhippalam and
7. Kannur University, Kannur

Out of these 7 universities, Kerala Agricultural University (KAU) is devoted to a specific discipline, i.e. Agricultural Sciences. Its funding sources, mode of governance etc. are different from the other universities in the state. Hence KAU is not covered under this study. There are two other institutions in the state with the status of deemed university, Sree Chithra Tirunal Institute of Medical Science and Technology, Thiruvananthapuram and National Institute of Technology, Calicut. These institutes are imparting education in two special disciplines, i.e. Medical Science and Engineering respectively. Hence these also do not come under the purview of this study.

Sri Sankaracharya University of Sanskrit and Kannur University are recently established universities and their university libraries are still in its infancy stage. Sri Sankara Sanskrit University has its campus at Kaladi and presently the library is functioning in the Administrative building of the University. There is no permanent staff in the library and is presently run by 3 professionals on deputation from Mahathma Gandhi University and a few fresh graduates in library science on contract basis. The University is yet to get the UGC recognition. Kannur University attained the recognition of UGC very recently and is yet to make any considerable move in the direction of computerisation of the University Library. It is too early to study and review the automation status of University Libraries of these two universities and hence these two universities are not included in this study.

As such this study covered the university libraries of four major universities in the state of Kerala Viz. University of Kerala, Mahathma Gandhi University, Cochin University of Science and Technology and University of Calicut.

DATA SOURCES

Survey method was used to ascertain information regarding the computerisation of University Libraries in Kerala through means of questionnaires and by personal observations. The investigator resorted to a combination of these two methods to ascertain the problem in its real and correct perspective.

The following are the sources of data used in this study:

1. Questionnaires administered to the persons in charge of the University Libraries in Kerala
2. Questionnaires administered to the persons who are in charge of the computerisation/ computerised activities in respective university libraries.
3. Questionnaires administered to users (Teachers, Research Scholars and Students) for whom the University library is mainly intended.
4. Websites of the university libraries.

The Questionnaires are given as appendices.

SELECTION OF SAMPLE AND DATA COLLECTION

The first questionnaire discussed above was administered to the persons in charge of the University Libraries and the second one was administered to the person in charge of the Computer Section/Computerisation of the

Table 1.2.1 Selection of the Sample of users from the Universities

Name of Library	Students				Research Scholars				Teachers			
	Science		Social Sci.		Science		Social Sci.		Science		Social Sci.	
	Served	Responded	Served	Responded	Served	Responded	Served	Responded	Served	Responded	Served	Responded
KUL	100	68	100	84	25	25	25	18	25	13	15	7
CUL	100	85	100	57	25	15	25	15	25	11	15	7
CUSATL	100	92	26	26	25	22	5	5	25	10	4	4
MGUL	100	95	100	58	25	16	15	10	25	17	10	5

university libraries under study for collecting data for the study. The third questionnaire is administered to a representative sample of the users namely Post Graduate Students, Research Scholars and Teachers from Science as well as Social Science subjects. The details of the users taken as sample from each of the university are given on Table 2.1.

In certain cases, especially in Social Science subjects, the sample available was very less in number. Hence in such cases the questionnaires were served to the whole users.

METHODS OF ANALYSIS AND PRESENTATION OF DATA

The data obtained were analysed using Microsoft Excel and STATISTICA 6.0, a special data analysis software. Quantitative study and percentage analysis is used and in appropriate cases Chi-square test was done to find out the significance of association between variables of study. The data is interpreted and presented using Tables, Charts and Figures.

STATISTICAL TOOLS USED

The Chi-square test is mainly used for testing the association between two attributes. (Example: the association between the University Libraries and the use of Internet services). Chi-square is the measure of discrepancy between actual observation and expected value under the hypothesis of no association between attributes. Lower value of Chi-square means lesser the association. In computation, we find the Chi-Square and corresponding P-value. If $P < 0.01$ the association is highly significant. If P is in between 0.01 and 0.05 the association is significant at 5% level and if $P > 0.05$ there is no significant association between the attributes.

1.3
Analysis of the Data and Interpretations

The data collected from the University Libraries, the academic community of the universities under study and the University Library websites have been analysed and interpreted here. Data were collected using questionnaires from the four University Libraries and from the selected sample of users of the University Libraries in the state. The success of any computerised library system greatly depends upon its capability to outreach the target users. Hence the responses of the library users regarding the computerised system have great significance in rating the performance of the system. Responses were collected from sample groups of users consisting Post Graduate Students, Research Scholars and Teachers of the four Universities under study, to ascertain their views about and experiences regarding the services provided by these libraries.

LIBRARY COLLECTIONS

Table 3.1 shows the number of various collections available in the University Libraries under study as on 31st March 2004.

Table 1.3.1 Collections of Documents in the University libraries under study

Type of Document	*KUL*	*MGUL*	*CUSATL*	*CUL*
Books	286155	33379	55882	89568
Bound Vol. Journals		2881	20798	2105
Theses & Dissertations		428	573	3005
Reports	-	-	-	-
Patents	-	-	1891	
Standards	-	-	-	-
Audio Cassettes	-	-	-	1
Video Cassettes	150	-	-	1
Microfiches	1500	-	-	205
CDs	3000	150	168	140
DVDs	2	-	-	-
Any Other	-	-	-	-

The Library collection is one of the main factors that determine the value of the library. A good, qualitative, properly processed and arranged collection of different types of documents on a varied range of subjects makes the platform for providing effective service to the clientele of a university library.

Kerala University Library (KUL) was not able to provide the exact figures of documents available in each category. The given figure 286155 includes their collections of Books, Bound volumes of Journals, Theses and Dissertations. All these collections are accessioned in a continuous serial order and also fed in to the computer making no distinction on categories. All the other data provided by KUL pertaining to Video Cassettes, Microfiches and Compact Discs are also approximate, as these items are not properly recorded in the library and no exact figures were available. In a computerised environment one has to be able to provide the exact data regarding its collection. But even after making complete retrospective conversion KUL finds it difficult to figure out the numbers in each category. This can be regarded as a handicap of the system the KUL has developed. Mahathma Gandhi University Library (MGUL) has a collection of 33379 books, 2881 bound volumes of journals and 428 Theses. Cochin University of Science and Technology Library (CUSATL) has a collection of 55882 books, 20798 bound volumes of journals, 573 theses and dissertations, 1891 Patents and 168 CDs.

The Calicut University Library (CUL) has a collection of 89568 books and 2105 bound volumes of journals, 3005 theses and dissertations, 140 CDs and 205 Microfiches. It was observed that most of the CDs available in libraries were not specifically procured rather they were received free along with the hardcopy of books. It seems that the size of various collections available in the libraries is in proportion with the year of establishment of each library. KUL, the oldest library established in the year 1942 has the highest collection while CUL established in the year 1969 stands second and CUSATL established in 1977 stands third and MGUL established in 1989 is in the fourth position.

JOURNALS AND ONLINE DATABASES

University libraries are intended to support the higher education that mainly consists research activities. Researchers largely depend on journal articles for obtaining latest information in any field of knowledge. So a good collection of journals with properly processed set up is a necessity in any university library. In a computerised environment, making the articles available along with the abstract to the users over the library as well as the campus LAN will enhance the use of journals. Table 3.2 provides details of subscriptions of journals by the University Libraries.

The KUL subscribes to the highest number of journals i.e. 294 followed by MGUL 269 and CUSATL 220 and CUL subscribes to the lowest number i.e. 197 titles. CUSATL gets the highest number of 118 journals as gift while CUL gets 48 and MGUL only 2. No information was available from KUL regarding the number of journals received as gift as they are not recorded in the library. Out of the 294 journals subscribed in KUL, 56 are foreign and 238 are Indian journals. In MGUL 107 are foreign journals while 162 are Indian. CUSATL subscribes to more number of foreign journals, out of the 220 journals, 122 are foreign and only 98 are Indian. In CUL out of 197 journals, 36 are foreign and 161 are published within the country. The KUL and MGUL subscribe to 2 online databases each while CUSATL and CUL do not subscribe to any online databases.

Table 1.3.2 Subscription of Journals and Online Databases

Journals	*KUL*	*MGUL*	*CUSATL*	*CUL*
Total Subscribed	294	269	220	197
Received as Gift	No details	2	118	48
Foreign Journals	56	107	122	36
Indian Journals	238	162	98	161
Online Databases	2	2	Nil	Nil

MGUL has not computerised their Serial Control while all other libraries are doing the Serial Control through their computerised system. MGUL stands second in the number of journals subscribed with a total of 269 journals. Making a proper article indexing through their Serial Control module will help MGUL to provide better services to its users. CUSATL has computerised the serial control functions, but has not started article indexing. CUSATL has the highest number of foreign journals among the libraries under study. However this library does not index the articles in the journals. Unless journals are not properly indexed, many of the valuable articles may not get the attention of the users. Since the OPAC of CUSATL is accessible over the campus LAN, providing the article index over the campus LAN will definitely enhance the use of the valuable journals in the University Library.

The analysis clearly reveals the poor share of online

resources in the University libraries under study. CUL stands last in the matter of subscription to periodical literature and the reason may be the least allocation of fund. Other libraries subscribe to fairly good number of journals.

TECHNICAL PROCESSING

Technical processing comprising classification, cataloguing and assigning of subject descriptors to the documents are done so as to provide better services to users as well as for better management of the information resources within the library. More over adhering to international standards helps the libraries in sharing the information smoothly in a resource-sharing atmosphere in the present networked world. Table 1.3.3 gives details about the standards followed by the university libraries under study in technical processing of documents.

Table 1.3.3 Standards used for Technical Processing of Documents

Category	*KUL*	*MGUL*	*CUSATL*	*CUL*
Classification Scheme	CC	DDC	UDC	DDC
Cataloguing Code	CCC	AACRII	AACRII	AACRII
Subject Descriptor	Chain Procedure	LC Subject Headings	Sears' List	LC Subject Headings

KUL is following the traditional Indian standards for their technical processing of documents. Colon Classification (CC), the classification scheme used by KUL is not much popular these days and is not considered user friendly also. More over CC schedules are not updated and revised regularly. The cataloguing code as well as method of assigning subject descriptors used in KUL are also not widely used and almost absent in the international scenario. So adherence to such standards will pause difficulty while cooperating with other libraries for resource sharing. Similarly the library may find it difficult to process the documents procured in the newly emerging subjects if the standards followed are not revised and updated frequently. Dewey Decimal Scheme of Classification is the most widely accepted classification scheme all over the world. And INFLIBNET which is the prime agency inspiring computerisation activities and hosting a union database of university libraries in the country insists on the Common Communication Format, AACR II and Library of Congress Subject Headings as the standard tools for all the participating libraries[1]. MGUL and CUL are following DDC, AACR II and Library of Congress Subject Headings. CUSATL is following AACR II for cataloguing rules but for classification the library is using UDC, because the collection is mainly confined to Science and Technology subjects for which UDC is considered more appropriate. CUSATL is following Sear's List of Subject Headings for assigning subject descriptors and not found to be satisfied with the use of the same. Regarding the satisfaction over the above standards followed, MGUL and CUL who are following the standards suggested by INFLIBNET as well as widely accepted all over the world, are found to be fully satisfied. KUL expressed their total dissatisfaction over the standards followed in Classification, Cataloguing and assigning Subject Descriptors by them and wanted to change to the standards suggested by INFLIBNET. CUSATL is only partially satisfied and wanted to change the subject descriptor from Sear's List to 'one which incorporate latest developments in subjects'. It is clearly depicted that the standards followed by MGUL and CUL in all three processes are within the suggestions of INFLIBNET and within the international practice while KUL is trailing totally and CUSATL partially in this matter.

SERVICES PROVIDED BY THE UNIVERSITY LIBRARIES

Library is essentially a service institution and all the collections developed, infrastructure built up and personnel appointed are to serve as a base for providing effective services to its clientele. Data were obtained from libraries to know what are the traditional library and information services provided by them. Table 1.3.4 lists the services provided by each of the library.

Table 1.3.4 Services Provided by the University libraries under study

Services	*KUL*	*MGUL*	*CUSATL*	*CUL*
Book Lending	Yes	Yes	Yes	Yes
Reprographic Services	Yes	Yes	Yes	Yes
Selective Dissemination of Information	No	Yes	Yes	No
Circulation of Accession List	Yes	No	No	Yes
Content Page Service	No	No	No	No
Compilation of Bibliographies	Yes	Yes	No	Yes
Local Abstracting/ Indexing Service	No	No	No	No
Inter Library Loan	Yes	Yes	Yes	No
Reference Service	Yes	Yes	Yes	Yes
Current Awareness Service	No	Yes	Yes	No
Routing of Periodicals	No	No	No	No
User Education	No	Yes	Yes	No
Translation Services	No	No	No	No
Other Services	-	-	-	-

All the University Libraries studied are found to be providing Book Lending Service, Reprographic Service and Reference Service. Regarding the provisions of other services the libraries differ. MGUL and CUSATL provide Selective Dissemination of Information while KUL and CUL does not provide this service. KUL and CUL provide Circulation of Accession Lists while other two are not offering the same. Compilation of bibliographies is done by KUL, MGUL and

CUL while CUSATL does not make provision for this service. All the University Libraries except CUL provide Inter Library Loan and except KUL and CUL others are providing User Education services. Current Awareness Service is provided by MGUL and CUSATL. None of the libraries under study provide Content Page Service, Local Abstracting/ Indexing Service, Routing of Periodicals and Translation Services. And no library pointed out any other service provided by them. This analysis is a purely quantitative one and does not go to the frequency or quality of the service provided by the libraries. On observation it was found that some of the services provided by the libraries are not regular in nature.

In terms of the number of services provided KUL and MGUL stands ahead of others. CUL stands behind other libraries in this aspect, though as shown in the Table 4.19 the major portion of the library budget is set apart to meet the salary of the staff. Even after making such huge investment on the manpower library lags behind in the matter of providing proper library and information services.

LIBRARY MEMBERSHIP

KUL was not able to provide the exact number of members in different categories in the library. The figures provided include even old memberships that are no more valid. The members have been serially numbered from the past without making any distinction among different categories. It is strange that the KUL is not able to provide the statistics of current live membership in different categories. All the other three libraries were able to provide the figures of their membership in various categories. Table 4.5 gives the details of the membership in each library.

Table 4.5 Membership Details of Different Categories

Category	*KUL*	*MGUL*	*CUSATL*	*CUL*
Under Graduates	18985	-	331	110
Post Graduates		1100	1873	1717
Researchers		280	272	29
Teachers	3192	530	223	20
Non Teaching Staff		504	564	170
Public	20127	-	80	158
Others	-	-	8 (Institutions)	2
Total	42304	2414	3351	2265

In all the cases post graduate students constitute the biggest category of members. They are the students of the Teaching Departments and Schools situated in the university campuses. It is notable that the number of registered researchers in CUL is very low. This is due to the fact that there is a decrease in the number of students registered for research in various departments in the University recently. Similarly live membership in the category of Teachers is also low. The number of Teachers in the MGUL includes teachers from the university Departments and Schools as well as from the Affiliated Colleges. The very objective of the university library is to support the higher education by providing all possible sources of information to the academics consisting of Students, Research Scholars and Faculty members. As mentioned in the previous chapter on methodology, here the user samples were taken among from these categories and attempt was made to ascertain their purpose of library visits, its frequency and the duration of the time they usually spend on a visit. It is hoped that such an analysis will help to understand the dependence of the users on libraries under study in the matter of fulfilling their information needs.

PURPOSE OF LIBRARY VISITS BY THE USERS

The purposes of library visits were obtained from the

users through a question with 4 specified options. Users were also given opportunity to mark any other purposes.

The specified purposes were Study, Research, Official and Recreational and apart from these some of the respondents mentioned the purpose of visit as to read newspapers. The users marked the responses under single option as well as under multiple options. University wise analysis of the purpose of visit is shown in Table 1.3.6. Official and Recreational purposes of library visit is recorded here very rarely only. University libraries are supposed to meet the information requirements for the higher education. It is found

Table 1.3.6 Purpose of Library Visits by the Users - University Library wise

Purpose of Visit	*KUL*	*MGUL*	*CUSATL*	*CUL*	*Total*
Study	148 (68.84%)	120 (59.70%)	109 (68.55%)	114 (60.00%)	491 (64.18%)
Research	38 (17.67%)	27 (13.43%)	14 (8.81%)	25 (13.16%)	104 (13.59%)
Recreational	0(0.00%)	1(0.50%)	1(0.63%)	6(3.16%)	8(1.05%)
Other - (News Paper Reading)	0(0.00%)	0(0.00%)	0(0.00%)	1(0.53%)	1(0.13%)
Study and Research	25 (11.63%)	23 (11.44%)	20 (12.58%)	28 (14.74%)	96 (12.55%)
Study and Recreational	1 (0.47%)	22 (10.95%)	10 (6.29%)	15 (7.89%)	48 (6.27%)
Study and Other (News Paper Reading)	0(0.00%)	3(1.49%)	0(0.00%)	0(0.00%)	3(0.39%)
Research and Official	0(0.00%)	1(0.50%)	0(0.00%)	0(0.00%)	1(0.13%)
Research and Recreational	0(0.00%)	0(0.00%)	1(0.63%)	0(0.00%)	1(0.13%)
Study, Research and Official	1(0.47%)	1(0.50%)	0(0.00%)	0(0.00%)	2(0.26%)
Study, Research and Recreational	2(0.93%)	3(1.49%)	4(2.52%)	1(0.53%)	10(1.31%)

that Study and Research are the main purposes for which the users of all the University Libraries under study depend their respective libraries.

Table 1.3.7 gives the details of the analysis based on the subject background of the users.

Table 1.3.7 Purpose of Library Visits by the Users - Subject wise

Purpose of Visits	*Social Science*	*Science*	*Total*
Study	191(64.31%)	300(64.1%)	491(64.18%)
Research	50(16.84%)	54(11.54%)	104(13.59%)
Recreational	2(0.67%)	6(1.28%)	8(1.05%)
Other – (News Paper Reading)	0(0.00%)	1(0.21%)	1(0.13%)
Study and Research	34(11.45%)	62(13.25%)	96(12.55%)
Study and Recreational	12(4.04%)	36(7.69%)	48(6.27%)
Study and Other (News Paper Reading)	2(0.67%)	1(0.21%)	3(0.39%)
Research and Official	0(0.00%)	1(0.21%)	1(0.13%)
Research and Recreational	1(0.34%)	0(0.00%)	1(0.13%)
Study, Research and Official	1(0.34%)	1(0.21%)	2(0.26%)
Study, Research and Recreational	4(1.35%)	6(1.28%)	10(1.31%)

The table shows that the users with Social Science as well as Science backgrounds make library visits for almost similar purpose.

Table 1.3.8 has the details regarding the purpose of library visit by various categories of users in the University libraries under study.

Table 1.3.8 Purpose of Library Visits by the Users - Status wise

Purpose of	*Students*	*Researchers*	*Teachers*	*Total*
Study	459 (81.24%)	20 (15.87%)	12 (16.22%)	491 (64.18%)
Research	18 (3.19%)	72 (57.14%)	14 (18.92%)	104 (13.59%)
Recreational	7(1.24%)	1(0.79%)	0(0.00%)	8(1.05%)
Other - (News Paper Reading)	1(0.18%)	0(0.00%)	0(0.00%)	1(0.13%)
Study and Research	24(4.25%)	29(23.02%)	43(58.11%)	96(12.55%)
Study and Recreational	48(8.50%)	0(0.00%)	0(0.00%)	48(6.27%)
Study and Other (News Paper Reading)	3(0.53%)	0(0.00%)	0(0.00%)	3(0.39%)
Research and Official	0(0.00%)	0(0.00%)	1(1.35%)	1(0.13%)
Research and Recreational	0(0.00%)	0(0.00%)	1(1.35%)	1(0.13%)
Study, Research and Official	0(0.00%)	0(0.00%)	2(2.70%)	2(0.26%)
Study, Research and Recreational	5(0.88%)	5(3.17%)	1(1.35%)	10(1.31%)

The Table shows that the main purposes mentioned by all the categories include either study or research purpose or both. This shows that irrespective of the status, the users make use of the University Libraries for the purposes for which it is intended.

FREQUENCY OF LIBRARY VISIT BY THE USERS

Analysis on the frequency of visits made by the users to the library gives an idea about the use of library made by the clientele as well as how important the library is to the users.

Table 1.3.9 Frequency of Library Visits by the Users - Library wise

Library	*Daily*	*Once in 2 Days*	*Once in 3 days*	*Once in a week*	*Rarely*	*Total*
KUL	102 (47.44%)	31 (14.42%)	23 (10.70%)	45 (20.93%)	14 (6.51%)	215
MGUL	98 (48.76%)	48 (23.88%)	23 (11.44%)	28 (13.93%)	4 (1.99%)	201
CUSATL	46 (28.93%)	34 (21.38%)	29 (18.24%)	41 (25.79%)	9 (5.66%)	159
CUL	60 (31.58%)	42 (22.11%)	18 (9.47%)	47 (24.74%)	23 (12.11%)	190
All Libs	306 (40.00%)	155 (20.26%)	93 (12.16%)	161 (21.05%)	50 (6.54%)	765

If the library is found very rarely used by its clientele it may be because of the triviality of the library to the user. If the library is so inevitable to the user he may visit it frequently to collect the required information. Analysis on the frequency of visit by users in the university libraries under study showed that overall 60 per cent of the users are daily or alternative days visitors to the library. The perceptions and priorities of such a user population have greater relevance in rating the performance of the libraries. Table1.3.9 gives a detailed frequency of visit statistics of the users of various libraries under study.

Overall 40 per cent of the users are daily visitors to the library while 20.26 per cent are making visit on alternative days. 21.05 per cent of the respondents make visit once in a week only while 12.16 per cent are visiting once in three days and the percentage of users who make rare visit to the library are 6.54 per cent only. The rate of daily visitors is highest in MGUL while the lowest is in the CUSATL. The highest rate of rare visitors is in CUL while MGUL has got the least number of rare visitors.

Subject wise analysis of library visits presented in Table1.3.10 shows that Social Science (53.54%) users visit the library daily and are far ahead of their Science (31.41%) counter parts in visiting the library daily. This may be because of the fact that for the users of the Social Science, virtually the library is both the library and the laboratory in one.

Table 1.3.10: Frequency of Library Visits by the Users - Subject wise

Subjects	*Daily*	*Once in 2 Days*	*Once in 3 days*	*Once in a week*	*Rarely*	*Total*
Social Science	159 (53.54%)	48 (16.16%)	25 (8.42%)	45 (15.15%)	20 (6.73%)	297
Science	147 (31.41%)	107 (22.86%)	68 (14.53%)	116 (24.79%)	30 (6.41%)	468
All Groups	306 (40.00%)	155 (20.26%)	93 (12.16%)	161 (21.05%)	50 (6.54%)	765

Status wise analysis of users in Table 1.3.11 showed that Students (42.83%) are ahead of Research Scholars (39.68%) and Teachers (18.92%) in making daily visit to the library. Among the Teachers the highest percentage (29.73%) visit the library once in a week only. The highest percentage (13.51%) of rare visitors is also from the teachers and this is more than double of the average (6.54%) of total rare visitors.

The analysis of the data proved that majority of users usually make regular visit to the library daily or on alternative days basis. As such it can be assumed that the users, particularly the students find the library crucial for satisfying their information needs.

Table 1.3.11 Frequency of Library Visits by the Users - Status wise

Status	*Daily*	*Once in 2 Days*	*Once in 3 days*	*Once in a week*	*Rarely*	*Total*
Students	242 (42.83%)	108 (19.12%)	69 (12.21%)	115 (20.35%)	31 (5.49%)	565
Research Scholars	50 (39.68%)	35 (27.78%)	8 (6.35%)	24 (19.05%)	9 (7.14%)	126
Teachers	14 (18.92%)	12 (16.22%)	16 (21.62%)	22 (29.73%)	10 (13.51%)	74
All Groups	306 (40.00%)	155 (20.26%)	93 (12.16%)	161 (21.05%)	50 (6.54%)	765

TIME SPENT BY THE USERS IN THE LIBRARY

Analysis was made to determine the average time spent by the users in the library on a visit. Table 1.3.12 provides the details.

Table 1.3.12 Time Spent in the Library by the Users - Library wise

Library	*Less than ½ Hour*	*½ to 2 Hours*	*2 to 5 Hours*	*More Than 5 Hours*	*Total*
KUL	43(20.00%)	121(56.28%)	49(22.79%)	2(0.93%)	215
MGUL	31(15.42%)	141(70.15%)	27(13.43%)	2(1.00%)	201
CUSATL	43(27.04%)	107(67.30%)	8(5.03%)	1(0.63%)	159
CUL	55(28.95%)	113(59.47%)	22(11.58%)	0(0.00%)	190
All Libs	172(22.48%)	482(63.01%)	106(13.86%)	5(0.65%)	765

Table shows that majority (63.01%) of the users use to spend in the library 'half an hour to 2 hours' on a visit. In all the libraries under study majority of users belong to this category only. Similarly in all the cases, but KUL, the second highest category belongs to those who spend 'less than 30 minutes' on a visit. In KUL second highest category (22.79%) belongs to those who spend '2 to 5 hours' on a visit. This may be because of the reason that the KUL is situated away from the main campus and users may prefer to stay for a long time once they make a visit to the library. Library wise analysis of users showed that in KUL 20 per cent spending 'less than half an hour' in the library while 56.28 per cent spending '30 minutes to 2 hours' on a visit to the library. Only one per cent or below are found to be spending 'more than 5 hours' on a visit to the library. In CUL no one has claimed to be spending 'more than 5 hours' on a visit.

The subject wise analysis showed that those who spend more time in the library belong to Social Science subjects. Table 1.3.13 gives the details.

Table 1.3.13 Time Spent in the Library by the Users-Subject wise

Subject	*Less than ½ Hour*	*½ to 2 Hours*	*2 to 5 Hours*	*More Than 5 Hours*	*Total*
Social Science	59(19.87%)	162(54.55%)	72(24.24%)	4(1.35%)	297
Science	113(24.15%)	320(68.38%)	34(7.26%)	1(0.21%)	468
All Groups	172(22.48%)	482(63.01%)	106(13.86%)	5(0.65%)	765

In the categories of users spending 'less than 2 hours' the percentage of Science users are high where as in the categories of those who spend 'more than 2 hours', the percentage of Social Science users are high.

Table 1.3.14 Time Spent in the Library by the Users - Status wise

Status	*Less than ½ Hour*	*½ to 2 Hours*	*2 to 5 Hours*	*More Than 5 Hours*	*Total*
Students	129(22.83%)	357(63.19%)	74(13.10%)	5(0.88%)	565
Research Scholars	29(23.02%)	74(58.73%)	23(18.25%)	0(0.00%)	126
Teachers	14(18.92%)	51(68.92%)	9(12.16%)	0(0.00%)	74
All Groups	172(22.48%)	482(63.01%)	106(13.86%)	5(0.65%)	765

Status wise analysis also proved that the habit of spending time in the library by different categories is not different from the general trend. In all the cases the highest percentage was recorded in the second category of 'half an hour to 2 hours' and the second highest was in the first category of spending 'less than 30 minutes'. Table 1.3.14 has the details.

It is notable that none from Teachers and Research Scholars are spending 'more than 5 hours' in the library while 0.88 per cent of students claimed that they use to spend 'more than 5 hours' on a visit to the library. The above analysis on the time spent by the users in the library has proved that respondents use to spend a reasonable time in the library on a visit.

It can be concluded from the analysis on Frequency of visit, Purpose of library visit and Time spent on a visit that the academic community under study is serious users of the university libraries and they heavily depend their respective university libraries for meeting their information requirements with regard to their higher education purposes.

FINANCIAL ASSISTANCE FOR COMPUTERISATION

Adequate funding is a pre requisite for the successful implementation of any programme. All the libraries under study started their computerisation process in the middle of the last decade or just prior to that. During this period the price of computers and its peripherals were comparatively high and the libraries needed huge amount for implementation of computerisation processes. The financial aid received from INFLIBNET was crucial in the beginning of the computerisation of these libraries. All the university libraries under study have received grants from INFLIBNET. KUL and CUL received the grant in 1995 while MGUL received it in 1998 and CUSATL in 1999. Being an old university, KUL was fortunate to receive a handsome amount of Rs. 52 Lakhs while all other universities got Rs. 6.5 Lakhs each. Table 1.3.15 depicts the details of the grants received from various sources by different university libraries for their computerisation.

Table 1.3.15: Financial Assistance Received for Library Computerisation

Name of the Agency	KUL		MGUL		CUSATL		CUL	
	Amountin Lakh	Year	Amount in Lakh	Year	Amount in Lakh	Year	Amount in Lakh	Year
INFLIBNET, UGC	52	1995	6.5	1998	6.5	1999	6.5	1995
State Govt.	8	2002	33	1992-2003	-	-	10	1995
Others	-	-	-	-	200 from MHO Project	-	-	-

The assistance received from State Government seemed to be varying in libraries. KUL received an amount of Rs. 8 Lakhs in the year 2002 while MGUL received a total amount of Rs. 33 Lakhs during the period between 1992 and 2003. CUL received Rs. 10 Lakhs from the State Government in the year 1995 while CUSATL has not received any amount so far from the Government. But CUSATL received a very huge amount of around Rs. 2 Crores as part of the aid received by the university from Netherlands. This amount is approximate and no exact figure was available as the amount was allocated and utilized for the university as a whole. The above figures disclose that there is a disparity among libraries in getting the amount for computerisation and the amount received by CUL is too less compared to other universities. Yet CUL was able to automate most of the library procedures. On the other hand it is to be noted that even after receiving a huge allotment from INFLIBNET, KUL is not yet able to extend their computerisation to all the sections of the library especially to circulation procedures.

BUDGET ALLOCATION TO UNIVERSITY LIBRARIES UNDER STUDY

The internal allocation in the university budget is the main source of regular finance for various offices in universities for it's functioning. Each university library also gets its share every financial year. Information was obtained from university libraries regarding the allocation of funds for activities related with computerisation, staff salary and procurement of books and journals. It is found that the major allotment in the university budget is devoted for meeting the staff salary in most of the cases. The other important allocation is for the purchase of books and journals. All other purposes get a very skimpy amount and many of the highly essential needs like procurement of necessary hardware and software, online subscriptions, AMC charges, recurring expenses related with computers etc. are seemed to be quite overlooked in the university budgets. University wise allocations of budget are discussed below.

BUDGET OF THE KERALA UNIVERSITY LIBRARY

Table 1.3.16 shows the budgetary allocation on Salary, Books and Journals and Computerisation related purposes in Kerala University in the last three financial years. As the table reveals allocation of the amount for computer related purposes in KUL is very less during last three years. The university budget has not made any provision for subscription to online databases, procurement of hardware and software, recurring charges related with computers and AMC for software. Yet it is notable that the budget has made provision for the AMC of computer hardware. More than half of the allocation made was for meeting the staff salary in 2002-03 and 2004-05 while in 2003-04 the allocation for procurement of books and journals were increased slightly bringing down the proportion of staff salary allotment.

It is very clear that a mammoth amount is spent on its staff salary. It is significant to note that KUL has not utilized the support provided by INFLIBENT in appointing the Information Scientist. As such there is no qualified person to look after the computerised activities. This is an indicator of the negligence of the library for properly manning the computerised activities.

Table 1.3.16 : KUL Budget during Last 3 Years

Purpose	**2002-03**		**2003-04**		**2004-05**	
	Amount	%	*Amount*	%	*Amount*	%
Staff Salary	10052438	57.74	10427890	46.85	10592500	55.50
Books and Journals	4620447	26.54	5000000	22.46	3000000	15.72
Online subscription (journals, databases etc.)	-	-	-	-	-	-
Procurement of Computer Hardware and Software	-	-	-	-	-	-
Recurring charges like Internet subscription	-	-	-	-	-	-
AMC charges for Hardware	162200	0.93	100000	0.44	150000	0.78
AMC charges for software	-	-	-	-	-	-
Total	17407760		22253400		19083300	

* '%' is the percentage of the total amount allocated as the Budget for the year that includes other allocations that are not mentioned in the Table also.

BUDGET OF THE MAHATHMA GANDHI UNIVERSITY LIBRARY

The budgetary allocation on Salary, Books and Journals and Computerisation related purposes in the MGUL during the last three financial years are shown in the following Table 1.3.17.

Table 1.3.17 : MGUL Budget during Last 3 Years

Purpose	*2002-03* *Amount*	*%*	*2003-04* *Amount*	*%*	*2004-05* *Amount*	*%*
Staff Salary	7000000	47.61	7000000	46.66	7400000	48.05
Books and Journals	5500000	37.41	6000000	40	6000000	38.96
Online subscription (journals, databases etc.)	-	-	-	-	-	-
Procurement of Computer Hardware and Software	1000000	6.80	500000	3.33	600000	3.89
Recurring charges like Internet subscription	300000	2.04	300000	2	300000	1.94
AMC charges for Hardware	170000	1.15	200000	1.33	300000	1.94
AMC charges for software	-	-	-	-	-	-
Total	14700000		15000000		15400000	

* '%' is the percentage of the total amount allocated as the Budget for the year that includes other allocations that are not mentioned in the Table also.

Though the biggest chunk is devoted to staff salary in the MGUL budget also, it is noteworthy that they have made provisions for many computer related affairs in their budget. Allocations made for procurement of hardware and software, recurring charges and AMC of hardware are notable allocations. But the budget does not make any provision for subscription to online databases.

It is seen that quiet a substantial amount has been allocated for books and journals purchase. But the importance of the procurement of online databases has not been taken seriously by the MGUL also and no amount has been set apart for this purpose.

BUDGET OF THE COCHIN UNIVERSITY OF SCIENCE AND TECHNOLOGY LIBRARY

The budgetary allocation on Salary, Books and Journals and Computerisation related purposes in CUSATL for the last three financial years is represented in the Table 4.18. In CUSAT, the library budget has not seriously considered the provision for computerised activities. In the financial year 2004-05, they have allotted Rs.15 Lakhs for the procurement of hardware and software and it is the only one allocation they made in the last three years for computer related matters in the library. It is the only library under study that spends more on purchase of books and journals than the staff salary. Yet they have also not set apart any amount for the procurement of online databases and journals.

Table 1.3.18 : CUSATL Budget during Last 3 Years

Purpose	*2002-03*		*2003-04*		*2004-05*	
	Amount	*%*	*Amount*	*%*	*Amount*	*%*
Staff Salary	5715000	50.06	5676000	48.83	5737000	40.39
Books and Journals	5500000	48.18	6700000	57.05	6700000	47.17
Online subscription (journals, databases etc.)	-	-	-	-	-	-
Procurement of Computer Hardware and Software	-	-	-	-	1500000	10.56
Recurring charges like Internet subscription	-	-	-	-	-	-
AMC charges for Hardware	-	-	-	-	-	-
AMC charges for software	-	-	-	-	-	-
Total	11415000		11744000		14202000	*

* '%' is the percentage of the total amount allocated as the Budget for the year that includes other allocations that are not mentioned in the Table also.

The total amount allocated for the library has shown an increasing trend in last three years and needs to be a separate fund allocation for computerisation related activities. CUSATL is the single instance of allocating more amounts to purchase of documents than to the library staff salary. Yet in CUSATL also no allocation was made for the subscription to E-Resources and Online journals and databases.

BUDGET OF THE CALICUT UNIVERSITY LIBRARY

The budgetary allocation on Salary, Books and Journals and Computerisation related purposes in the CUL in the last three financial years is shown in Table 1.3.19.

Table 1.3.19 : CUL Budget during Last 3 Years

Purpose	*2002-03*		*2003-04*		*2004-05*	
	Amount	%	*Amount*	%	*Amount*	%
Staff Salary	10168000	83.85	7775000	78.37	7931000	76.97
Books and Journals	885000	7.29	900000	9.07	1050000	10.19
Online subscription (journals, databases etc.)	-	-	-	-	-	-
Procurement of Computer Hardware and Software	-	-	-	-	-	-
Recurring charges like Internet subscription	380000	3.13	380000	3.83	380000	3.68
AMC charges for Hardware	225000	1.85	240000	2.41	250000	2.42
AMC charges for software	-	-	-	-	-	-
Total amount allotted to the library	12125700		9920200		10303200	

* '%' is the percentage of the total amount allocated as

the Budget for the year that includes other allocations that are not mentioned in the Table also.

In CUL major portion of the fund is set apart for meeting the staff salary and the allocation for even books and journals procurement is very low. Allocation has not been made for subscription to online databases and journals in the CUL budget. Nevertheless, it is notable that regular provisions have been made for AMC of Hardware and Recurring charges for Internet etc. An amount of Rs. 3,80,000 has been allocated every year for Internet subscription and an amount of more than Rs. 2,25,000 have been allocated for AMC of computers. But there is no allocation for the AMC of software in the CUL budget also.

It is notable that the major portion of allocation is for meeting staff salary, but the Table 1.3.22 reveals that the numbers of staff members are less in the CUL. This may be because of the reason that the CUL is the only library that gives UGC scales of pay to its professional staff. But there should be a proportionate qualitative as well as quantitative increase in the services provided by the library also.

COMPARISON OF BUDGET ALLOCATIONS OF UNIVERSITY LIBRARIES

The analysis on budget allocation in all the four universities revealed that in last three years the internal allocation of funds in the universities for computerisation was negligible. All the libraries, except CUSATL, have spent more on staff salary. KUL spent 52.89 per cent while MGUL spent 47.45 per cent and CUL was much ahead of others by making 79.98 per cent of the budget allocation for their staff salary. In CUSATL the amount spent was 45.84 per cent and they allocated 50.58 per cent on procurement of Books and Journals. In CUL 8.76 per cent, in MGUL 38.8 per cent and in KUL 21.48 per cent were set apart for the procurement of Books and Journals. The Table 1.3.20 gives the average of the

Table 1.3.20 : Comparison of the Fund Allocations of the University Libraries

Purpose	*KUL*		*MGUL*		*CUSATL*		*CUL*	
	AverageAmount	*%*	*AverageAmount*	*%*	*AverageAmount*	*%*	*AverageAmount*	*%*
Staff Salary	10357609	52.89	7133333	47.45	5709333	45.84	8624667	79.98
Books and Journals	4206816	21.48	5833333.	38.8	6300000	50.58	945000	8.76
OnlineSubscription	-	-	-	-	-	-	-	-
Procurement of ComputerHardware and Software	-	-	700000	4.65	500000	4.01	-	-
Recurring charges likeInternet subscription	-	-	300000	1.99	-	-	380000	3.52
AMC charges for Hardware	137400	0.7	223333	1.48	-	-	238333	2.21
AMC charges for software	-	-	-	-	-	-	-	-
Total	19581487		15033333		12453667		10783033	

allotment in last three financial years in the four University Libraries.

The MGUL has made provision of an average of Rs. 7 Lakh in last three years for the procurement of computer hardware and software while CUSATL made an average of Rs. 5 Lakhs. The KUL and CUL did not make any provision towards the procurement of hardware and software at all. MGUL has allotted Rs. 3,00,000 towards recurring charges while in the CUL the amount is Rs. 3,80,000. KUL and CUSATL have not made any provision for this. It is observed that KUL meets such expenses from the fee collected from users of Internet and Infonet services. All the libraries except CUSATL have provisions in their budget for AMC of computer hardware. KUL has set apart an average amount of Rs. 1,37,400 while MGUL made provision for Rs. 2,23,333 and CUL for Rs. 2,38,333 for hardware maintenance.

It is clearly revealed that the university authorities have not properly taken into consideration the expenditure towards the application of computers in the libraries shown in the right side of the figure. With regard to the procurement of E-Resources such as databases in the form of CDs and DVDs as well as subscription to online resources very serious negligence is found from the part of libraries.

Allocation of funds in the university budgets for the computerised set up is essential since a system once installed needs to be properly maintained and developed further. So regular allotment of funds has to be made for computerised activities in the library.

COMPUTER HARDWARE AVAILABLE IN THE UNIVERSITY LIBRARIES

Computers and other peripherals are the most essential part of the computerisation process. Computer technology is fast changing and advancing. Availability of required number of computers for the users and computers and other related gadgets for the staff makes the computerisation process more momentous and meaningful. Table 1.3.21 gives the details of computers and other peripherals available in the libraries under study.

There are wide ranges of computers available in the market and the processor speed, capacity of memory and hard disc etc. are the main determinants of the performance of the computers. Similarly the basic technology decides the quality of the outputs of the printers. Computers and other peripherals with latest configurations and provision of a good network infrastructure along with a dynamic library management software provides a platform for providing good computerised services to the users. Computers have passed through many generations and the older ones were much inferior compared to the latest ones available in the market. It is the technology of the microprocessor that decides the superiority of the machine over other machines. There were significant changes in the technology in the past, but the university libraries in the state started computerisation mostly around a decade ago and Pentium machines were available in those days. So almost all the machines available in the University Libraries are Pentium machines. The existence of machines prior to that is only reported from MGUL where two computers are 486 machines.

In an integrated library management system all the computers in various sections depend the Server machine for data storage and retrieval. So the availability of good Server class machines is a necessity for having a powerful computer network in the library. All the university libraries studied are found to have Server class machines to use as their Servers. MGUL has two Servers while KUL, CUSATL and CUL have 3 each.

Laptop computers are portable ones that can be easily handled just like brief cases. It can be used for various management purposes and in libraries it can be used especially for conducting user education programmes. Except CUL none of the libraries have Laptop machines.

When the libraries in Kerala started computerisation it was the Pentium I computers dominating the market. KUL has 7 P I machines, MGUL has 2 and CUL has 23 and CUSATL do not have PI machines. More number of Pentium II group computers is available in the libraries under study. In KUL only two P II machines are available while in MGUL13 and in CUSATL 35 are available. In CUL there is only a single PII machine. MGUL has got 4 P III machines while CUSATL has 3 and CUL has one. KUL has 6 Pentium IV machines, MGUL has got 5 and KUL has two machines in this category. There are 8 Celron machines in KUL and 11 in CUL. Other libraries have no machines with Celron processors.

KUL, MGUL and CUSATL have CD Server while in CUL there is no CD Server. CD ROM Towers are available in KUL, CUSATL and CUL while MGUL does not have this. Except CUSATL all others are having systems with DVD drives.

Barcode printers are the dedicated printers that are used to print barcodes. None of the libraries other than CUSATL have barcode printers. CUSATL have 2 such printers one in the Circulation Section to print the membership card and other one in the Technical Section to print the accession numbers of the documents

Printers of various qualities are essential for use in various sections of the library. The basic technology of the printer decides the quality of the output of the printer. Laser printers provide high quality printing while in Inkjet printer quality is not that much high. Dot matrix printers provide hardcopies that are more economical. KUL has got 4 Dot Matrix printers, MGUL 2, CUSATL 4 and CUL has 8 such printers. KUL and CUL have one each Ink Jet Printer, MGUL has 6 and CUSATL do not have any Inkjet printer. KUL has

Table 1.3.21 Computer Hardware available in the University libraries under study

Items	*KUL*	*MGUL*	*CUSATL*	*CUL*
Server Class machines	3	2	3	3
Laptop Computers	-	-	-	1
486 Machines	-	2	-	-
Pentium I	7	2	-	23
Pentium II	2	13	35	1
Pentium III	-	4	2	1
Pentium IV	6	5	-	
Celron Machine	8			11
Dot Matrix Printers	4	2	4	8
Inkjet Printers	1	6		1
Laser Printers	1	2	2	2
Heavy Duty Network Printers	-	1	-	-
CD Server	1	1	1	-
CD ROM Tower	1		1	1
Systems with DVD Drives	1	1		1
Barcode Printer	-	-	2	-
Flat Bed Scanners	-	2	1	1
Over Head Scanners	-	-	-	-
Barcode Scanners	-	2	3	3
Modems	2	2	-	7
Hubs	3	2	1	3
Switches	1	1	1	1
Router	-	-	1	1
LCD Projector	-	-	-	-
Web Camera	-	-	-	-
UPS	16	5	16	5

a single Laser Printer while all others have 2 each. Heavy Duty Network Printers are needed for providing hardcopies to users without time delay, especially for taking print out of materials that are downloaded bulkily from Internet from different machines in a network. These printers usually have faster printouts and additional facilities such as scanning options. Only MGUL has got a network printer while no one else is found having such a facility.

Scanners are needed to scan texts and images to make digital copies. KUL do not have any scanner while in MGUL there are 2 Flat Bed Scanners and CUSATL and CUL have one each. None of the libraries are having Over Head Scanners that are high-resolution, high-quality and high-volume scanners used for bulk digitization purposes. Barcode scanners are needed for scanning the barcodes in document transactions and in inventory control. CUSATL and CUL have 3 such scanners and MGUL has two while KUL does not have barcode scanners, as the library has not yet computerised their circulation procedures.

KUL and MGUL have 2 modems each while CUL has 7 modems. CUSATL does not have any modem as they have an Optical Fiber backbone in the campus. There are three hubs in each KUL and CUL while two in MGUL and one in CUSATL. All the libraries have single switch for connecting the network. CUSATL and CUL have Router in the library.

LCD Projector is used to project the visual out put to a wider screen. It addresses a group of viewers and helps to make presentations very effectively. It is helpful in conducting demonstrations, user education programmes and training programmes in libraries. None of the university libraries under study are having LCD Projector. Web camera is used for visual interaction especially in Internet sessions of communications. Cost wise it is much cheaper and widely available in the market. Yet no one among the university libraries under study is found possessing any web camera.

Continuous power supply is very essential for keeping the computerised system up all the time. Proper arrangements need to be made to make regular power supply in the library.

MGUL and CUL have 5 UPS systems while KUL and CUSATL have 16 systems each. UPS are available with a variety of back up options and if the back up hours are more less systems may be needed. But more number of UPS systems, even if with lesser back up time, makes provisions for alternative sources of power supply and keeps the system up even when one or two UPS systems are down. All the libraries are found to be having enough number of UPS to provide continuous power supply.

All the libraries under study found to be having adequate Server class machines. Pentium IV machines, the latest in personal computers, are available in the market for last three years and its availability to the libraries under study found to do too less with CUSATL and CUL do not possess any machine in this category. This shows that the libraries under study mostly depends old machines that may put limitations on them in using some of the applications especially in web related applications. Similarly a Laptop computer that helps in conducting effective user education programmes both inside as well as out side the library is not available in majority of the libraries. LCD projector, which is a must in conducting effective training programmes and user education programmes is not available in any of the library under study. Internet related equipments like web camera are not available in any of the library and there should be adequate equipments and tools available for conducting video conferencing especially among the university libraries in the state for creating an effective communication channel between the libraries in higher education in the state. Over-Head Scanners that are necessary for high volume digitization work are also not available in the libraries under study. With a good number of Theses and Dissertation collection in the libraries, these libraries need to have such Scanners for initiating digitization works. These equipments need to be made available in all the university libraries. Other equipments available found to be in tune with the requirements of the libraries under study.

COMPUTER SOFTWARE AVAILABLE IN THE UNIVERSITY LIBRARIES

Software used for the housekeeping operations is the most important software required in libraries. Out of the four libraries, two libraries i.e. KUL and CUL are using the Libsys software for their house keeping operations. KUL uses it on

Table 1.3.22 Computer Software Used in the University libraries under study

Purpose	*KUL*	*MGUL*	*CUSATL*	*CUL*
Housekeeping Operations	Libsys4/ WindowsNT	SOUL/ Windows	ADLIB/ Windows	Libsys4/ Sco Unix
Word Processing	MS Word/ Windows	MS Word/ Windows	MS Word/ Windows	MS Word/ Windows
Spreadsheets	MS Excel/ Windows	MS Excel/ Windows	MS Excel/ Windows	MS Excel/ Windows
Presentation Software	MS Power Point/ Windows	MS Power Point/ Windows	MS Power Point/ Windows	MS Power Point/ Windows
Web Browsing	Internet Explorer/ Windows	Internet Explorer/ Windows	Internet Explorer/ Windows	Netscape, Mozilla/ Linux IE/ Windows
DTP		Page Maker/ Windows		ISM Publisher, PageMaker / Windows
Digital Library software	TechFocus / Linux	-	ACADO/ Windows	-
OCR (Optical Character Recognition)	-	-	-	-
Any Other				Barcode: Label Works/ Windows

the Windows NT platform while CUL on Sco Unix on server side and Windows95/98 on client side. MGUL is using the SOUL software on Windows platform developed by INFLIBNET. CUSATL makes use of ADLIB software on Windows platform. It is foreign software received as part of the aid received by the library from Netherlands. It was found that CUSATL only has a web enabled library system. Table 1.3.22 gives details of the software in use in different University Libraries.

For the purposes of Word processors, spreadsheets and presentation software all the libraries are making use of Microsoft Office products MS Word, MS Excel and MS Power Point respectively. For web browsing libraries mostly depend Microsoft product Internet Explorer on Windows operating systems and CUL makes use of Mozilla and Netscape Navigator on Linux platform. For DTP works MGUL uses Page Maker that helps to design the page settings and CUL uses Page Maker and ISM Publisher that provides necessary fonts for DTP works. Both are used on Windows platforms. KUL and CUSATL have made use of digital library software. KUL uses TechFocus on Linux platform while CUSATL uses ACADO on Windows platform. CUL uses separate software for barcode generation called Label Works and its platform is Windows98. None of the libraries have seen started using Optical Character Recognition software that is needed for recognizing the scanned texts and images. Its application is mainly in the digitization works and none of the libraries have done the digitization process to any considerable extent.

It is found that all the libraries are making use of commercial software while the potential of the open sources are totally neglected by the libraries. The only instance of making use of open source is the use of Linux operating system for very limited applications in CUL and KUL. It can be ascertained that KUL and CUL have spent a large amount on software while MGUL has obtained software with reasonable price. CUSATL received the software under the CUSAT-Netherlands Government project. Open sources like digital library application software, Greenstone should be utilized by the university libraries in the state. Since some of the libraries are investing huge amount on the house keeping software that is not affordable to them also and on observation it was found that all the libraries are not satisfied with the software they are using. In such a situation the university libraries in the state must take a joint initiative to develop software that suits their requirements and that is affordable to them also. Since all the university libraries have almost the same objectives and requirements such an initiative will be most feasible.

MANPOWER IN THE UNIVERSITY LIBRARIES UNDER STUDY

Qualified and trained manpower is an asset for any library. There should be a combination of both professional as well as non-professional staff available for the smooth functioning of a university library. Qualified personnel is needed for performing various tasks that needs professional skill and expertise while non-professionals are to supplement the tasks of professionals in rendering services to the clientele. Apart from these, professionals with computer skill and qualifications are a necessity of recent origin.

PROFESSIONAL STAFF STRENGTH IN THE UNIVERSITY LIBRARIES

Professional staff is needed for performing various skilled professional jobs in libraries. The availability of professional staff varies from university to university under study. It is notable that among the libraries under study, only a single library, i.e. CUSATL has a University Librarian, the Head of the library. In all the other libraries the position of the University Librarian is vacant and the senior most professional staff member is put in charge of the University Librarian. Many of the implementation tasks related with computer applications need comparatively long term planning and for making such planning, a full time University Librarian is essential. Persons with short-term assignment may not dare to initiate tasks that need more financial investments, as the person himself/herself has to settle the amount with the university. Table 1.3.23 gives the details of the professional staff strength in each library.

Table 1.3.23 Professional Staff Strength in the University libraries under study

Category	*KUL*	*MGUL*	*CUSATL*	*CUL*
Deputy Librarian	2	1	-	1
Asst. Librarian Sel. Gr.	4		4	5
Asst. Librarian Sr. Scale	-	1	2	3
Asst. Librarian	-	-	4	2
Asst. Librarian Gr. I	7	-	-	-
Asst. Librarian Gr. II	13	10	-	-
Jr. Librarian/Reference Assistant	7	5	6	-
Profl. Asst. Gr I/ Technical Asst.	10	6	5	5
Profl Asst. Gr. II/ Library Assistant	6	-	1	-
Total	**49**	**23**	**22**	**16**

KUL has two Deputy Librarians while MGUL and CUL have one each. In CUSATL there is no Deputy Librarian, but it is the only library in the entire state with a University Librarian. There are 5 Assistant Librarians Selection Grade in CUL while KUL and MGUL have 4 each and MGUL has none in this grade. CUL has 3 Assistant Librarian Senior Grade while CUSATL has 2 and MGUL has 1. In KUL there is no Senior Grade Assistant Librarian. Junior Librarian and Reference Assistant are in the same grade and there are 7 Reference Assistants in KUL, 5 in MGUL, 6 in CUSATL and none in CUL. Professional Assistants Gr I and Technical Assistants are in the same grade and KUL has 10 Technical

Assistants, MGUL has 6 and CUATL and CUL have 5 each. Professional Assistant Gr. II and Library Assistant are in the same grade and KUL has 6 and CUSATL has one while the other two university libraries have none in this category. Altogether there are 49 professionals in KUL, 23 in MGUL, 22 in CUSATL and 16 in CUL. CUL invests more on its staff who are supposed to provide good service; the number of services provided by this library is found to be the lowest among the libraries under study.

NON-PROFESSIONAL STAFF

Non-professional staff is technically not qualified and are needed to perform routine jobs other than those performed by the professional staff. The non-professional staff who help the professionals in their duties and services include Library Attenders / Library Assistants and peons. Table 1.3.24 gives details regarding the availability of non-professional staff in the library.

Table 1.3.24 Non- Professional Staff Strength in the University libraries under study

Category	*KUL*	*MGUL*	*CUSATL*	*CUL*
Library Assistant/Attender	2	-	-	8
Peon	1	5	5	2

Only KUL and CUL have Library Attenders or Assistants. KUL has 2 Attenders while CUL has 8. KUL has One Peon while MGUL and CUSATL have 5 each and CUL has 2 peons.

Professional as well as Non-professional staff are needed for performing traditional library duties and services while specially qualified and skilled staff are needed for performing jobs related with computer applications in library routines and services.

PERSONNEL ENGAGED IN LIBRARY COMPUTERISATION

Among the librarians, those dealing with systems represent a subspecies and are called System Librarians. They exist to handle all things dealing with computers. This unique breed of librarian is a necessity, keeping the library technologically connected and serving as a conduit to the underworld of computer improvements and advancements. They are actually the vital innovators implementing services that allow the library to maintain a valuable place in the lives of the clientele. In our country this profession has not been purely recognized as System Librarianship and those who perform the computer related jobs include both library professionals and computer professionals. In many of the cases, in university libraries, help is sought from the Computer Department. Nevertheless there is a need for regular and fulltime qualified staff in the library. Table 1.3.25 gives the details of the staff members who are working in the Computer Sections of the University Libraries under study.

Staff working in this section needs qualifications and training in both librarianship and computer applications. Though UGC made provisions for appointing Information Scientists to manage the computerised services and operations only two University Libraries i.e. CUSATL and CUL have filled up these posts.

Table 1.3.25 Staff Strength of Computer Section in the University libraries under study

Designation		***Qualifications (General)***	***Qualifications in Computer Science/IT***
KUL	Assistant Librarian	MA, M.Lib.Sc.	-
	Reference Assistant	MA, M.Lib.Sc.	-
	Technical Assistant	MA, M.Lib.Sc.	DCA
	Library Assistant	MA, M.Lib.Sc.	-
MGUL	Assistant Librarian	MLISc.	-
	Assistant Librarian	MLISc.	-
	Reference Assistant	MLISc.	-
	Reference Assistant	BLISc.	PGDCA
CUSATL	Information Scientist	-	M.Tech.
CUL	Information Scientist	MA, MLib.Sc.	PGDCA, PGDLAN
	Professional Assistant	MA, BLISc.	-
	Professional Assistant	MLISc.	-

In KUL four library professionals are working in the computer section and they are postgraduates in Library and Information Science and only one among them has got a formal qualification in computer application, Diploma in Computer Applications, and he is only the third person in the professional hierarchy of the Section.

In MGUL also, there are four persons working in the section and only a single person is having a formal qualification in computer application i.e. PG Diploma in Computer Applications and the person is last in the professional hierarchy and holds only a degree in Library and Information Science while other three persons are having Post Graduation in Library and Information Science.

In CUSATL, there is no formal Computer Section and all the library professionals are involved in the computerised activities. CUSATL has recently appointed Information Scientist under the INFLIBNET scheme to manage the automated activities. This person is purely a computer professional with Post Graduate degree in Computer Technology. She lacks any experience in library computerisation.

CUL has three persons working in the computer section. One is the Information Scientist appointed under the INFLIBNET scheme and others are pure library professionals on contract basis. Information Scientist is a postgraduate in Library Science and holds Post Graduate Diploma in Computer Applications as well as in Library Automation and Networking.

The study reveals that the University Libraries in the state are not equipped with adequate qualified staff to handle computerised activities. In KUL and MGUL there is no qualified staff for managing the computerised operations and services where as in CUSATL and CUL the number of supporting staff in the computer section is quiet inadequate.

ADMINISTRATION OF THE COMPUTERISED ACTIVITIES

UGC has recognized the need for properly manning the computerised library systems and sanctioned the post of Information Scientist with stipulated qualifications. Among the libraries under study the CUSATL and CUL have utilized this provision and appointed Information Scientist while KUL and MGUL have not utilized. In KUL and MGUL Assistant Librarians without any qualification in Computer Science have been put in charge of the computerised activities. CUSATL appointed the Information Scientist with a pure Computer Science background during 2003 while in CUL the post was filled in 2001 with a person with qualifications in Library Science as well as computer applications. Table 1.3.26 gives information about the persons in charge of computerisation in various libraries. The Table reveals that the service details of the persons in charge of computerisation are not uniform in the university libraries under study.

Table 1.3.26 Details of the Personnel in charge of the Computer Sections of University Libraries

Designation	***KUL Assistant Librarian (Sel. Grade)***	***MGUL Assistant Librarian Gr II***	***CUSATL Information Scientist***	***CUL Information Scientist***
Qualifications (General)	M,A, M.Lib. Sc.	M.Sc.; M.L.I.Sc.	-	M.A, M.Lib.Sc.
Qualifications (Computer)	Nil	Nil	M.Tech (Comp & Inf Sc)	PGDCA, PGDLAN
Date of Joining	8-11-75	7-9-89	28-8-03	19-2-01
Scale of Pay	12000 - 18300	6675 - 10500	8000 - 13500	8000 - 13500

KUL and MGUL have put Assistant Librarians in charge of Computer Section who were not appointed by the library for the management of Computerised activities. They lack any formal qualifications in the Computer Application also.

In the United States and in most of the developed nations of the Europe, this profession has been recognized as 'System Librarianship' and System Librarians are required to have formal qualifications in Library and Information Science as well as in Computer Science in order to cope with the skills needed for both end of the profession. Efforts needs to be made to recognize the requirements of the profession and to develop the skills needed for both library and information services and for computer applications.

In-service training programmes help to gain skill in computer applications especially in case of persons without any formal qualifications in Computer Science / Applications. Similarly it helps pure computer professionals in attaining skills in library related applications. Today library services are moving towards web-based services. The skills required to keep abreast of library technology has exploded since the introduction of the World Wide Web and professionals need to get trained and acquainted with web related technologies and applications also.

Table 1.3.27 provides details of training obtained in library computerisation by the persons in charge of computerisation. The person in charge in CUSATL has not undergone any training programme as she has been appointed recently though she has no exposure in library computerisation. All others have been trained in different aspects of library computerisation varyingly.

DUTIES AND RESPONSIBILITIES OF THE PERSONS IN CHARGE OF COMPUTERISATION

The duties and responsibilities of the persons in charge of the computerisation found to be varying in the universities. More involvement in the activities of the section was found among the persons with Library Science background while the person with pure Computer Science background seemed to be not that much involved. Table 1.3.28 gives details of the

Table 1.3.27 Training Obtained by the Persons in charge of Computerisation

	Sl. No.	Training Programme	Agency	Duration	Course Content
KUL	1	Training on Library Automation	Dept. of Lib & Inf. Sci., Kerala University	4 Weeks	Use of CDS/ISIS
	2	Training in use of SOUL software	INFLIBNET	1 Week	SOUL Software
MGUL	1	Training on Library Automation	INFLIBNET	1 Month	Basics of Computers and CDS/ISIS
	2	Training on Digital Library	Osmania University	1 Week	Digital Library
	3	UGC Infonet Training	INFLIBNET	1 Week	Use of Infonet Resources
	4	Workshop on Web Page Designing	Dept of Lib & Inf. Sc., Kerala University	1 Week	Web Page Designing
CUL	1	Training on Library Automation	INFLIBNET	1 Month	Basics of Computers and CDS/ISIS
	2	Intensive training on use of ILMS Software	INFLIBNET	1 Week	ILMS software
	3	Training on Digital Library	DRTC Bangalore	1 Week	Digital Library Applications
	4	UGC Infonet Training	INFLIBNET	1 Week	Use of Infonet Resources

duties and responsibilities of the persons in charge of computerisation in various University Libraries.

Table 1.3.28 Duties and Responsibilities of the Persons in charge of Computerisation

Duties and Responsibilities	*KUL*	*MGUL*	*CUSATL*	*CUL*
Over all management of section	Yes	Yes	No	Yes
Database administration	Yes	Yes	No	Yes
Training the library staff	No	Yes	No	Yes
Training users	Yes	Yes	No	Yes
Software development	No	No	No	No
Providing services to users	Yes	Yes	Yes	Yes
Communicating with vendors	Yes	Yes	Yes	Yes
Planning future programmes/ services	Yes	Yes	No	Yes
File works	Yes	Yes	No	Yes
Hardware maintenance	No	Yes	Yes	Yes
Software maintenance	No	Yes	Yes	Yes
Network Management	No	Yes	Yes	Yes

Not much uniformity is found among the persons in charge of the computerised activities in terms of duties and responsibilities. None among the persons found to be doing the job of software development while all found to be providing services to users as well as corresponding with the vendors. Duties and responsibilities of the persons in MGUL and CUL found to be exactly same.

WORKING ENVIRONMENT

Adequate physical facility is a pre requisite for discharging one's duties and responsibilities smoothly. Regarding the physical facility provided, persons from all the libraries found to be satisfied. Required numbers of systems and peripherals is essential for carrying out the job in a computerised environment. Similarly adequate manuals and reference materials are essential for performing the job smoothly. Regarding a question about the provision of sufficient systems and peripherals the persons in charge of computer sections in KUL, MGUL and CUSATL responded that they are provided with sufficient computers and peripherals while the person from CUL responded as 'no'. With regard to the availability of sufficient manuals and reference materials the persons from KUL and MGUL found to be satisfied while the persons from CUSATL and CUL does not found to be satisfied.

Timely attention from vendors and service contractors will enable to keep the system up without any break. With regard to the support from vendors and service contractors, persons from KUL, MGUL and CUL found to be satisfied while the person in charge in CUSATL is dissatisfied.

Freedom in incorporating one's ideas into his work may enable to introduce new and innovative services to the users. The persons in charge of the systems may be more aware about the potential of the automated systems and may be in a better position, compared to the superiors who have not much knowledge about the library computerisation, in chalking out the new programmes. So the freedom granted to the persons in charge may result in improving the existing services as well as introducing new ones. With regard to the question on such freedom, the persons from MGUL, CUSATL and CUL responded that they enjoy such freedom while the person from KUL did not respond to the question.

Guidance from superiors and assistance from colleagues reduces the workload and provides a conducive atmosphere for working. In response to questions about the guidance from superiors and assistance from colleagues all found to be satisfied while about the encouragement from superiors the person from MGUL found to be dissatisfied.

Communication with counterparts in other institutions enables to discuss the problems as well as prospects in the profession and gain knowledge about developments in the profession. Regarding the question on communication with counterparts in other institutions persons from KUL, MGUL and CUL responded that they communicate with others and discuss their problems while the person from CUSATL responded as 'no'. Similarly the persons from KUL, MGUL and CUL responded that they use to attend Conferences/ Seminars/Workshops/User-group meet and found to be getting valuable information to improve their work.

Non-library professional as in charge of the Computer Section of the CUSATL seems to be a fish out of water. The person is not found communicating with counterparts in other universities and has not shown much interest in participating in Workshops/Seminars etc. on the specific field. It is also found the person has not much involvement in the computerisation activities.

AREAS OF APPLICATIONS OF COMPUTERS

None of the University Library formally conducted a system analysis prior to the computerisation process. Yet all of them made certain planning in an informal way. Regarding the status of computerisation MGUL, CUSATL and CUL have claimed to be fully computerised while KUL claimed to be partially computerised. Table 1.3.29 gives details about the areas of computer application in various University Libraries under study.

A close examination of the data in the Table reveals that all the libraries are yet to computerise some of the essential operations or services. Above Table reveals that all the libraries have computerised database creation, information retrieval, acquisition procedures, cataloguing works (including online catalogues), inter office communication and office file works. All the libraries except KUL have automated their circulation procedures. KUL is not yet able to provide computerised circulation services to its users even after almost a decade of use of computers in the library. All the three

Table 1.3.29 : Areas of Applications of Computers in the University Libraries

Areas of Applications	*KUL*	*MGUL*	*CUSATL*	*CUL*
Database Creation	Yes	Yes	Yes	Yes
Information Retrieval	Yes	Yes	Yes	Yes
Circulation Procedures	No	Yes	Yes	Yes
Acquisition Procedures	Yes	Yes	Yes	Yes
Serials Control	Yes	No	Yes	Yes
Cataloguing	Yes	Yes	Yes	Yes
OPAC	Yes	Yes	Yes	Yes
Digitization of Documents	No	No	Yes	No
Stock Verification	No	No	No	Yes
Reference Services	No	No	Yes	No
Inter Office Communication	Yes	Yes	Yes	Yes
Intra Library Communication	No	No	Yes	No
Financial Management	No	No	No	No
Office File Works	Yes	Yes	Yes	Yes

libraries except MGUL have made use of computers in Serial Control. CUSATL only makes use of computers for communication within the library while no one has made use of computers in the financial management of the library. CUL only has made use of computer in Stock verification. The Figure 1.3.9 represents the number of areas where computer applications are made in these libraries.

Out of the total of 14 possible areas of applications ascertained CUSATL has made applications in 12 areas where as CUL has made in 10 and KUL and MGUL have made in 8 areas each. Thus CUATL found to be the forerunner in the number of areas of computer application in the University Libraries under study.

COMPUTERISED SERVICES AND OPERATIONS

Libraries make use of computers mainly for performing its house keeping operations and for providing services to its users. Table 1.3.30 gives the details of computerised services and operations in these libraries.

Table 1.3.30 Details of Application of Computers in Services and Operations

	Areas	*KUL*	*MGUL*	*CUSATL*	*CUL*
Serv-ices	Current Awareness Services	No	Yes	Yes	No
	SDI Service	No	Yes	Yes	No
	Circulation of Accession List	Yes	Yes	Yes	Yes
	Content Page Service	No	No	No	No
	Online Services (Database and Full Text)	Yes	Yes	Yes	Yes
	Multimedia Services	Yes	Yes	Yes	No
	CD/DVD based Services	Yes	Yes	Yes	No
	Internet Services	Yes	Yes	Yes	Yes
	User Education Programs	No	Yes	Yes	No
Oper-ations	Bar code for stock verification	No	No	No	Yes
	Smart Card for member identification	No	No	No	No
	Microchips for document identification	No	No	No	No
	Totally automated check in/Check out	No	No	No	No
	Electronic theft detection systems	No	No	No	No

It is found that all the libraries are providing Internet Services, Online Services (Database and Full Text) and Circulation of Accession List to its users. None of the libraries under study is providing Content Page Service. CUL does not provide any multi media services to its users. On observation it was found that other three libraries are also not providing multimedia services to any considerable extent though they have claimed so. MGUL and CUSATL are using computers for imparting User Education programmes while KUL and CUL are not providing such services. Computerised

Current Awareness Service, Selective Dissemination of Information and CD/DVD based services are provided by only MGUL and CUSATL. It was observed that the computerised Reference Service through which a user can collect information from a database or post a query to the Reference Librarian is not being provided by any of the library under study.

Latest applications of computers in libraries are found to be absent in the libraries under study. None of the libraries are using Smart Card for member identification, Microchips for document identification, Totally Automated Check-in/Check-out Systems and Electronic Theft Detection Systems. It was observed that RFID Technology has not been introduced in the libraries under study. Only CUL have computerised stock verification system as well as using barcodes for feeding the data of documents during stock verification.

USER AWARENESS ABOUT DIFFERENT COMPUTERISED SERVICES AND AVAILABILITY OF THESE SERVICES TO THE USERS

The user awareness about different computerised services and its availability to them through their respective libraries were ascertained. Table 1.3.31 gives the details.

CURRENT AWARENESS SERVICE

The Users were asked whether they are aware about CAS and do they get the service from their library. In KUL 50.23 per cent, in MGUL 57.21 percent, in CUSATL 59.75 percent and in CUL 41.58 per cent responded that they are aware about this particular service provided using computers. Table 1.3.30 has revealed that MGUL and CUSATL are providing computerised CAS to its users. But in MGUL 45.27 per cent and in CUSATL 52.83 per cent only have responded that they are getting the service from their library. It shows that overall less than half of the population is getting the service and it is not reaching to the majority of the users. In

KUL and CUL, where the service is not provided, 8.37 and 20.53 per cent respectively have claimed that they are getting the service and it shows the ignorance of the users regarding the services provided by the libraries. An overall 51.9 per cent awareness was recorded while the libraries where the service is provided it is available to only 49.05 per cent.

The analysis showed that 51.9 per cent of the users are aware about the service and majority (50.05%) of the users are not getting Current Awareness Service where it is provided.

SELECTIVE DISSEMINATION OF INFORMATION

As in the case of CAS, MGUL and CUSATL have claimed to be providing this service. An overall 25.36 per cent awareness was found about this specialized service. In KUL 28.37 per cent, in MGUL 27.86 per cent in CUSATL 23.27 per cent and in CUL 21.05 per cent only are aware about this service. It is notable that this service is available to only 18.82 per cent of the respondents with 19.4 per cent in MGUL and 18.24 per cent in CUSATL. KUL and CUL are not providing the service, but as in the earlier case of CAS, here also contrary to the fact 7.44 per cent from KUL and 10 percent from CUL have claimed that they are getting the service.

It is revealed that this service is also not reaching to the majority (81.18%) of the users. The awareness about the service among users is also very poor with 74.64 per cent of them being ignorant about the specialized library service.

CIRCULATION OF NEW ADDITIONS LIST

Circulation of New Additions List enables the user to be aware about the latest additions of documents to the library collection. In a computerised library system this service can be provided very easily. Computer can generate such report and it can be sent on periodic basis to the users either by means of a hardcopy or the soft copy can be posted to the email box of the users on regular intervals. All the libraries under study are providing this service and an overall 34.77

per cent of users are aware about this service. In KUL 28.37 per cent, in MGUL 44.28 per cent, in CUSATL 38.36 per cent and in CUL 28.95 per cent are aware about this service. But it was found that this service is also not reaching to majority of the users. In KUL 19.07 per cent, in MGUL 33.83 per cent, in CUSATL 32.08 per cent and in CUL 24.21 per cent only have said that they are getting this service.

It is found that 65.23 per cent of the users are not aware about this service and overall availability of the service is to 26.93 per cent of users only leaving the majority of the other 73.07 per cent of users not benefiting from this service.

ONLINE DATABASE SERVICES

All the universities under study are coming under the purview of UGC Infonet and are supposed to get many of the modern computer based information services like Online Database Services and E-Journal Fulltext Services Online Bibliographic Services etc. through Infonet. Comparatively, better awareness (41.7%) was found with regard to Online Database Service among the users. In KUL 41.86 per cent, in MGUL 46.27 per cent, in CUSATL 54.72 per cent and in CUL 25.79 per cent are aware about this service. But this service is also not reaching to majority of the users. In KUL 30.7 per cent, in MGUL 38.81 per cent, in CUSATL 43.40 per cent and in CUL only 11.58 per cent have responded that they are getting online database services. In CUSATL the service is reaching to more than half of the users while in CUL it is very low with 11.58 per cent only getting the benefit of such valuable services.

It is revealed that 58.3 per cent of the users are not aware about the Online Database Service. Only 30.72 per cent of users are getting the service while rest of the 69.28 per cent are not getting benefit of the service.

ONLINE FULL TEXT SERVICES

With regard to the online full text services better

awareness is found among the users. An overall 53.07 per cent of the users are found to be aware about full text services. All the libraries are getting full text service as part of Infonet Consortia and apart from this, these libraries subscribe to some of the full text databases. In KUL 51.63 per cent, in MGUL 69.65 per cent, in CUSATL 55.97 per cent and in CUL 34.74 per cent of the users are aware about this service. But the overall availability of the service is only 40.39 per cent only with 34.88 per cent in KUL, 61.69 per cent in MGUL, 42.77 per cent in CUSATL and only 22.11 per cent in CUL. It is in MGUL the service is reaching to a wider community where as in CUL the situation is pathetic. UGC has invested huge amount on providing E-resources to the universities in the form of database access and E-Journal access. The universities under study were fortunate to receive these privileges in the first phase itself. Yet it is frustrating to note that the services are not reaching to the majority of users. Effective steps should be taken to make maximum use of these valuable services.

It is unveiled that 46.93 per cent of the users are not aware about the service and 59.61 per cent are not utilizing the Full text services.

CD ROM / DVD BASED SERVICES

Except CUL, all the other three libraries under study are providing CD ROM / DVD based services using dedicated Servers for this purpose. An overall 41.83 per cent awareness is found among the users regarding this service. In KUL 42.33 per cent, in MGUL 59.7 per cent, in CUSATL 43.4 per cent and in CUL 21.05 per cent are aware about this service. 20 per cent in KUL, 51.74 per cent in MGUL, 27.04 per cent in CUSATL have responded that they are getting this service from their respective libraries. In CUL where this service is not provided 2.11 per cent have wrongly stated that they are getting this service. It is notable that the service is reaching only to 33.04 per cent of the users in case of the libraries where it is provided.

As in the case of other computerised services, this service also needs to be brought to the users effectively.

It is found that 58.17 per cent of the users are not aware of the service and 66.96 per cent of the users are not utilizing this service where it is provided.

INTERNET SERVICES

All the libraries under study are providing Internet services and are found to be the most popular service provided by these libraries with an awareness of 93.2 per cent among the users and to 85.62 per cent the service is available. The high rate of awareness among the users may be part of the popularity of the Internet due to its advent in to the daily life of the society, but it is notable that 85.62 per cent have claimed that this service available to them. Analysis revealed that in KUL the awareness is just below 90 per cent where as among the users of other libraries it is above 90 per cent. 85.58 per cent in KUL, 94.53 per cent in MGUL, 93.08 per cent in CUSATL and 70 per cent in CUL claimed that this service is available to them.

It is revealed that only 6.8 per cent are ignorant about the service and to 14.38 per cent the service is not reaching.

USER EDUCATION SERVICES

User education programmes are conducted to educate the users regarding their privileges in the library. Yet it is notable that users are poorly aware about such facility itself. Awareness about User Education services is recorded as 26.98 per cent in KUL, 31.84 per cent in MGUL, 37.74 per cent in CUSATL and 16.84 per cent in CUL.

It is revealed that a huge majority of 72.03 per cent of the users is not aware about User Education Programmes and it is not available to 77.22 per cent of the users.

It is revealed that except the Internet services, all other services are not reaching the target users properly. This handicap is reflected in the general awareness about the services also. Libraries under study have claimed that they are providing many of the services. But it was observed that the libraries are not providing the services in a structured and regular basis. Here it is to be noted that the services they are providing is available to a narrow minority only. It means that majority of the services are not properly interpreted to users and are not reaching to them. Though MGUL and CUSATL are providing user education services, it is revealed that only 22.78 per cent are getting any orientation in the use of services provided by them. In case of the other two libraries no user education programmes are conducted and there is a pressing need for bringing the services to the notice of the users. But none of the libraries under study possess an LCD Projector, a hardware that is highly essential for interpreting computerised services to users. Without such a facility no university library in this era can properly educate the users about the use of various computerised services provided by them.

COMPUTER APPLICATIONS IN VARIOUS OPERATIONS AND SERVICES

The libraries under study are using computers for various services and operations. The sub-areas of applications within each area were ascertained which are discussed below:

DATABASE CREATION

Creation of the database is considered to be the first step in computerizing a library. Without a database in digital form, no library can make effective use of computers. All the libraries have prepared their databases in digital form and the details of its application are given in Table 1.3.32, which shows that all the libraries have completed their retrospective conversion and databases are available in the digital form. All the libraries used catalogue cards as data source for their retrospective conversion. CUL have made use of Accession

Register also but only to complete the data that were not available in the catalogue cards. All the three libraries except CUSATL developed the database in-house while CUSATL got the work done by external agency. KUL and CUL utilized the services of the Library staff as well as data entry operators while MGUL depended only on the library staff for data entry. Three persons were engaged in the data entry in MGUL and completed the work within two years.

In CUSATL the retro-conversion was done by external agency involving 4 to 10 persons and managed to complete the work within 6 months. In CUL the work took 2 years and a total of 6 persons consisting of staff members and data entry operators were involved in the work. In KUL the work took only 6 months to 1 year but the data regarding the number of persons involved in the work is not available.

STANDARDS FOLLOWED FOR LIBRARY DATABASE

Regarding the adherence to the standards for database description, it is more dependent on the software used by the libraries than the policy of the library. It is learnt that all the software used by the libraries adheres to ISO 2709 standard and are also Z39.5 compatible. In the case of Classification numbers, Cataloguing rules for description of data element and assigning keywords the libraries adhered to the standards they were following in the library traditionally.

DATA SECURITY MEASURES

It is very important to back up the database so as to secure the valuable data from any possible damage or loss. In a totally automated system, any damage to the database will bring the whole system in to a halt. Regarding the back up of the data CUSATL is found to be more conscious. CUSATL takes the back up daily and they use to have a separate weekly and monthly back up additionally. MGUL and CUL take the backup daily. KUL use to back up the data once in two days only because they have not computerised their circulation

Table 1.3.32 Computer Applications in Library Database

Database Creation	*KUL*	*MGUL*	*CUSATL*	*CUL*
Status of retrospective conversion	Completed	Completed	Completed	Completed
Document source used for conversion	Catalogue Card	Catalogue Card	Catalogue Card	Catalogue Card then Accession Register
By whom created	In house	In house	External Agency	In house
Created in house by	Staff & data	Staff members entry perators	NA	Staff and data entry operators
Number of persons engaged	Not known	3	4 to 10 persons	6
Document in languages other than English entered by means of	Transliteration	Transliteration	Transliteration	Transliteration/Using Gist Card
Duration taken for database creation	6 months to 1 year	1 to 2 years	Up to 6 months	1 to 2 Years
Standards followed	ISO 2709	ISO 2709	ISO 2709	ISO 2709
Classification notation used in the database	CC	DDC	UDC	DDC
Cataloguing Rules followed	CCC	AACR II	AACR II	AACR II
Subject descriptor standard followed	Chain Indexing	LC Subject Headings	Sears List	LC Subject Headings
Frequency of database back up taken	Once in 2 days	Daily	Daily, Weekly Monthly	Daily
Medium used for backup	CD	DAT Drive & Harddisc	Cartridge	Harddisc and CD
Automatic back up mechanism	Nil	Nil	Nil	RAID
Stand by server used	No	Yes	Yes	No

procedures and have no transaction data. KUL is using Compact Discs as the backup medium while MGUL uses DAT drives and hard discs for back up. CUSATL uses Cartridge for backup while CUL makes use of hard disc as well as re-writable CDs for making the data secure. Except CUL none of the libraries have any automatic back up mechanism to secure the data. In CUL the server has RAID feature which automatically copies the contents of the original hard disc to one or more separate hard discs. MGUL and CUSATL have stand by Servers for making use during any emergency while KUL and CUL does not have standby machines.

All the libraries have made their complete bibliographical database and found using the standards for technical processing as used by them traditionally. The standards followed by MGUL and CUL are as per the internationally widely used standards while the standards followed by KUL are not up to international standards and CUSATL is found using the internationally well accepted standard for cataloguing rules only. Proper care have been taken by all the libraries in securing their data from any damage and MGUL and CUSATL have provision for using stand by Server to bring the system back immediately during any failure of Server.

AREAS OF APPLICATIONS IN ACQUISITION PROCEDURES

The job involved in the acquisition works of documents includes procedures from accepting the request for acquisition of the document to making the document the property of the library by accessioning it. Table 1.3.33 gives the details of applications of computers in various works in the Acquisition procedures in different libraries.

Table 1.3.33 Computer Applications in the Acquisition Works

Areas	*KUL*	*MGUL*	*CUSATL*	*CUL*
Duplication Checking	Yes	Yes	Yes	Yes
Ordering	Yes	Yes	Yes	Yes
Receipt of Document	Yes	Yes	Yes	Yes
Accessioning	Yes	Yes	Yes	Yes
Invoice Processing	Yes	Yes	No	Yes
Budget Handling	No	Yes	No	Yes
Any other areas	-	-	-	-

MGUL and CUL found to be making use of all the options listed in the questionnaire. CUSATL does not make use of computers for Invoice processing and budget handling. KUL also is not using computer for the budget handling in the Acquisition works. None of the libraries mentioned any other area in the Acquisition procedure where computer is used.

All the University Libraries were found occasionally using Internet as an aid in the acquisition work such as to know the availability and price of documents and the exchange rate of currencies etc. On observation it was found that the Acquisition modules in the library under study have provision for sending the titles to be procured for the approval of a higher committee or authority. None of the library found using this option as the library do not follow such practices. Apart from the functions discussed above report generation at several stages are possible and the libraries were found not making use of the facility, as they do not require it.

APPLICATIONS IN CIRCULATION PROCEDURES

Computerisation of circulation procedures helps to save time of the library staff as well as the users of the library and provide better service to users. It is an area of computerisation that has a direct bearing on the users. Table 1.3.34 shows the areas of application within the circulation procedure in various libraries.

Table 1.3.34 Computer Applications in Circulation Procedures

Areas	*KUL*	*MGUL*	*CUSATL*	*CUL*
Membership Management	Yes	Yes	Yes	Yes
Check out/Check in/ Renewal	No	Yes	Yes	Yes
Enquiries	No	Yes	Yes	Yes
Reservation of documents	No	Yes	Yes	Yes
Fine collection	No	Yes	No	Yes
Sending reminders	No	Yes	Yes	Yes
Use of barcode inCheck out/ Check in	No	Yes	Yes	Yes

The KUL has not yet started computerised circulation procedures. They have just started the creation of the member database for initiating a computerised circulation system. All the other libraries are making use of computers for circulation of documents. Over due charges calculation is one of the most important applications of computer in the circulation of documents. It helps to save time of the members as well as the staff at the circulation desk. During rush hours manual calculation of fine may cause for overcrowding at the circulation counter. Despite all these factors CUSATL has not computerised the fine collection works in the circulation. Documents as well as members are identified on the basis of numbers allotted in the circulation counter and feeding the accurate number to the computer is crucial. So use of barcodes for identifying the members as well as the document is a necessity for avoiding keying in wrong numbers, which may lead to chaos. All the libraries under study that provides computerised circulation services are found to be using this technology. All, but KUL, are using computers for issue/ return of documents, renewal of documents, reservation of documents and sending reminders for long overdue items.

USER RESPONSE ABOUT CIRCULATION SERVICES

Computerised Circulation Services are one of the areas of library computerisation where the users get direct benefit of the facility. In a purely manual system users in large libraries may have to wait a long time for getting documents issued out and returned. Similarly the overdue charges collection procedure is a cumbersome process especially in rush hours stealing a good amount of time of the users as well as the library staff. A computerised circulation procedure makes provisions for effective document reservation facilities and is capable of entertaining different enquiries from the users that are not possible in a purely manual system. Thus a computerised circulation system provides many fold advantages over the traditional circulation procedures. As already mentioned, among the four university libraries studied the KUL does not provide computerised circulation services. Users were asked to express their awareness about the computerised circulation services. Table 1.3.35 gives university wise details of the responses of the users.

Table 1.3.35 User Awareness about Computerised Circulation Services

Library	*Yes*	*%*	*No*	*%*	*Total*
KUL	7	3.26	208	96.74	215
MGUL	170	84.58	31	15.42	201
CUSATL	122	76.73	37	23.27	159
CUL	175	92.11	15	7.89	190
All Libs.	467	84.91	83	15.09	550

Pearson Chi-square: 15.9980, df=2, p=.000336

It is fairly evident from the Table that users are almost aware about the facility and getting the services from their libraries. In KUL where the services are not provided 1.3.26 per cent have wrongly responded that they are getting the facility. It is notable that in CUSATL where the facility is provided 23.27 per cent have said that they are not getting the service. This shows their ignorance about the library services. Similarly in MGUL 15.42 per cent have responded that the facility is not available. But in CUL only 7.89 per cent are ignorant about the service. Yet it is notable that in all the libraries where the service is available a good number of users are not aware about the services and may not be making use of the service. This service needs to be brought to the notice of the users. The Chi-square test proved that the association between awareness of the users regarding computerised circulation services and the University Library is highly significant.

COMPUTERISED CIRCULATION SERVICES

Users were asked about the computerised services available to them under the circulation module so as to check the level of reach of different services to the users. Table 1.3.36 gives details of the responses marked by them.

Table 1.3.36 Computerised Circulation Services Available toUsers

Circulation Services	*MGUL*	*CUSATL*	*CUL*	*Total*
Issue/Return/Renewal	65(38.24%)	60(49.18%)	81(46.29%)	206(44.11%)
Reservation	0(0.00%)	4(3.28%)	1(0.57%)	5(1.07%)
Fine collection	1(0.59%)	0(0.00%)	2(1.14%)	3(0.64%)
Enquiry	1(0.59%)	0(0.00%)	0(0.00%)	1(0.21%)
Issue/Return/Renewal and Reservation	27(15.88%)	13(10.66%)	10(5.71%)	50(13.06%)
Issue/Return/Renewal and Fine collection	10(5.88%)	10(8.20%)	40(22.86%)	60(12.85%)
Issue/Return/Renewal and Enquiry	4(2.35%)	12(9.84%)	9(5.14%)	25(5.35%)
Issue/Return/ Renewal, Reservation and Fine Collection	18(10.59%)	2(1.64%)	4(2.29%)	24(5.14%)
Issue/Return/ Renewal, Reservation and Enquiry	6(3.53%)	9(7.38%)	2(1.14%)	17(3.64%)
Issue/Return/ Renewal, Fine collection and Enquiry	6(3.53%)	4(3.28%)	18(10.29%)	28(6.00%)
Issue/Return/Renewal Reservation, Fine collection and Enquiry	32(18.82%)	8(6.56%)	8(4.57%)	48(10.28%)

In all the university libraries most of the users responded that they are getting the document issue, return and renewal facilities only. The other features of the system like its capability to reserve documents as well as to entertain different queries from the users are not seen familiar to the users.

TIME SAVING IN THE CIRCULATION PROCEDURES

A computerised circulation procedure, apart from providing additional facilities to the users, should be time saving also. It was observed that the libraries though make use of computers for circulation of documents, are still maintaining the traditional manual system as a safety measure. Users were asked whether they find the system time saving for them. Table 1.3.37 reveals the responses of the users to the question.

Table 1.3.37 User Response Regarding Time Saving in the Circulation Procedures

Library	*Yes*	*%*	*No*	*%*	*No Response*	*%*	*Total*
MGUL	162	95.29	2	1.18	6	3.53	170
CUSATL	103	84.43	9	7.38	10	8.20	122
CUL	160	91.43	15	8.57	0	0.00	175
All Libs.	425	91.01	26	5.57	16	3.43	467

Pearson Chi-square: 24.4737, df=4, p=.007314

91.01 per cent of the users find the computerised circulation procedure time saving while 5.57 per cent have the opinion that it is not time saving. 1.3.43 per cent did not respond to this question. Libraries under study were found to be using traditional record keeping procedures for the circulation of documents as an additional precautionary measure. Yet it is significant that above 90 per cent find the system time saving. In MGUL the highest percentage rated the system as time saving while in CUSATL the lowest rated so. The Chi-square test proved the association between the time saving in circulation procedures and the university library is significant.

IMPROVEMENT OVER THE EXISTING CIRCULATION SERVICES

In order to know the perception of the users regarding improvement over the existing circulation services, question was asked whether they need any other computerised circulation services. Majority of the users found to be satisfied with the existing services and did not feel the need for any other services in this aspect. Table 1.3.38 gives details of the responses of the users.

Table 1.3.38 Computerised Circulation Services needed by the Users

Library	*Yes*	*%*	*No*	*%*	*Total*
MGUL	11	6.47	159	93.53	170
CUSATL	16	13.11	106	86.89	122
CUL	18	10.29	157	89.71	175
All Libs.	45	9.64	422	90.36	467

A very small portion of the users responded that they need other computerised circulation services. But none, but a very few, were able to specify what other services are needed by them. A Teacher from KUL suggested for Totally Automated Check in/Check out System so that the time delay as well as staff intervention can be eliminated. Similarly a Student respondent from CUSATL suggested for getting the item checked out through Internet and making the item available through home delivery.

AREAS OF APPLICATIONS IN SERIALS CONTROL

Serials Control is the module that creates a lot of problems from the point of view of the designers of the module as well as the librarians because of the ever-changing nature of different aspects of the periodicals publications. Serials are considered to be the resources in the library that have the highest potential value for research. A well-designed serials module helps to reduce the manual work done in the periodicals section of the library and to provide a wide range of services to the users of the library. Table 1.3.39 given below provides the details of applications of computers in the serials control module in various university libraries.

Table 1.3.39 Computer Applications in Serials Control

Areas	*KUL*	*MGUL*	*CUSATL*	*CUL*
Ordering	No	Yes	Yes	Yes
Receipt	No	Yes	Yes	Yes
Reminders	No	No	Yes	Yes
Budget Handling	No	No	Yes	Yes
Invoice Processing	No	No	Yes	Yes
Routing	No	No	No	No
Sending for Bindery	No	No	No	Yes
Accessioning	No	No	Yes	Yes
Article Indexing	Yes	No	No	Yes
Current Awareness Service	No	No	Yes	No
Selective Dissemination of Information	No	No	No	No
Check in/Check out	No	No	No	No

All the libraries studied found to be making use of Internet as an aid in the Serial Control work such as obtaining details of Serials, communicating with vendors etc. None of the university libraries under study found making total utilization of the computerised serial system. KUL has not started making use of the serials control module of the software they use. Yet they have started indexing of journal articles with the help of computers. KUL and CUL are using the same house keeping operation software and CUL is found to be making use of the module to a good extent. This means that KUL is not making proper use of the serials control system available with them and are still depending on manual system that have many limitations in providing advanced services. MGUL is also not making use of the serials module to any considerable extent and are using it only for ordering and receipt of the journals only. CUSATL and CUL use computers for some of the operations of serial module. But both of these libraries are not making use of the system for providing advanced services like routing of periodicals and Selective Dissemination of Information. CUL use it for article indexing while CUSATL is not using it for this purpose. Similarly CUSATL uses it for Current Awareness Service while CUL does not use the same. None of them are using it for check-in / check-out of the Serials, as they do not provide this service for serials collection. The above analysis shows that the use of computers in the serials module is more confined to the house keeping operations whereas its use in the provisions of services to the clientele is very limited.

AREAS OF APPLICATIONS AND PROVISIONS MADE IN OPACS

Online Public Access catalogues are the most commonly and heavily used computer based service by the library users. It replaces the traditional card and other forms of catalogues and provides many fold additional facilities to the users of the library. It is one of the first areas of computer applications in libraries. All the university libraries under study have developed their online catalogues and are accessible to its members. Table 1.3.40 gives the details of the OPACs of various university libraries.

Access points provided by all the OPACs include Author, Title, Words in title and Subject. Access through class number is not given by the CUSATL while all other libraries have this provision. KUL and MGUL do not provide access through Place of publication of the document while CUSATL and CUL OPACs have this provision. Access through Publisher is not given by CUSTAL while other three library OPAC have this provision. MGUL online catalogue entertains access through the series of publication of the document while no other library has this provision. CUSATL

OPAC only makes provision for access through the year of publication of the document.

Libraries may have different databases for different category of documents and all these databases can be made available over OPAC. MGUL and CUL have made books, journals and theses databases available over the OPAC while KUL has only book database and the other two are in the development stage only. CUSATL has Books, Journals and Audiovisual materials databases available over their OPAC.

There are different search strategies that can be entertained by a computerised catalogue where as in a traditional library catalogue no such provision could be made. This includes Boolean search comprising 'AND', 'OR' and 'NOT' operators, Truncation and Word Proximity searches. All the OPAC under study supports Boolean search and provides users with greater easiness while making a comprehensive search of the library catalogue. Truncation search helps to search the documents that have certain words beginning with the same characters. Providing option to search such words helps the user to retrieve information on a comprehensive subject. All the libraries under study have this provision in their OPAC. Word proximity search helps the occurrence of one term in relation with another term and helps for advanced search of the catalogue. KUL and CUL have this provision in their catalogue.

Apart from making provisions for searching the database of the library, OPACs can be used as tool for interaction between the automated system and the user. Users can use the OPAC for making suggestions or giving feedback to the library. One such application found in OPACs is the provision for suggesting new titles to be procured. By providing such option valid members of the library can post their suggestion for the required title without meeting the library staff. Only the OPAC of KUL provides such a privilege while other libraries are not giving the option to users of

Table 1.3.40 Online Public Access Catalogues in the University Libraries

		KUL	MGUL	CUSATL	CUL
Access points Provided	Author	Yes	Yes	Yes	Yes
	Title	Yes	Yes	Yes	Yes
	Words in Title	Yes	Yes	Yes	Yes
	Subject	Yes	Yes	Yes	Yes
	Class Number	Yes	Yes	No	Yes
	Place	No	No	Yes	Yes
	Publisher	Yes	Yes	No	Yes
	Series	No	Yes	No	No
	Year	No	No	Yes	No
Databases Available	Books	Yes	Yes	Yes	Yes
	Journals	No	Yes	Yes	Yes
	Thesis	No	Yes	Yes	Yes
	Other	-	-	Audio Visual Materials	-
Search facilities	Boolean Search	Yes	Yes	Yes	Yes
	Truncation	Yes	Yes	Yes	Yes
	Word Proximity	Yes	No	No	Yes
Provisions	To Reserve Document	No	No	No	No
	To Know Current Status of document	Yes	Yes	Yes	Yes
	To Suggest New Titles	Yes	No	No	No
	To Access Over Campus LAN	N	N	Yes	No
	Web OPAC	No	No	Yes	No
Numbers of Terminals Provided for Users		1	2	4	2

OPAC. Similarly the user through OPAC can reserve documents that are issued out. KUL has not computerised the circulation procedure and is not making provision for this facility. All the other libraries under study have made provision to the users for knowing the current status of the document. The OPAC of KUL, MGUL and CUL are accessible only within the library while the OPAC of CUSATL is available over the campus LAN as well as over the Internet making the services available to a very wider community round the clock. Similarly within the library also CUSATL has made provision for more members to access the catalogue at a time by providing 4 terminals to the users, while MGUL and CUL have made two nodes available and KUL has provided only a single machine to the members of the library.

AWARENESS OF USERS ABOUT OPAC

Library OPACs are the primary key to the resources of a computerised library. It has many advantages over the traditional card and other forms of catalogue and is extensively being made use in modern computerised libraries. Apart from providing several access points for search, OPAC has provisions to entertain several complex search queries. Online catalogue is one of the first areas of services provided by computerised libraries. All the libraries under study have their OPAC and it was observed that they are maintaining the traditional catalogue also as these traditional catalogues are also still found to be used by many. A question was asked to the users in order to check their awareness about the existence of OPAC in their respective university library as the traditional card catalogues are also in use. Table 1.3.41 gives the details about the awareness of users about OPAC.

Table 1.3.41 User Awareness about OPAC

Library	Yes	%	No	%	Total
KUL	155	72.09	60	27.91	215
MGUL	191	95.02	10	4.98	201
CUSATL	145	91.19	14	8.81	159
CUL	178	93.68	12	6.32	190
All Libs.	669	87.45	96	12.55	765

Pearson Chi-square: 65.4737, df=3, p=.000000

All the users of the library except KUL are well aware about the OPAC. In KUL 27.91 per cent responded that they do not have an OPAC and it shows that they are not aware about the provision of the online catalogue in the library and may be using the traditional card catalogue for searching documents. An over all 87.45 per cent are aware about the existence of OPAC and the remaining 12.55 per cent are ignorant about this. MGUL has got the highest rate regarding the awareness about OPAC with 95.02 per cent responding positively. The Chi-square test proved that the association between the awareness of users about OPAC and the university library is highly significant.

Table 1.3.42 User Awareness about Library OPAC - Subject Wise

Subject	Yes	%	No	%	Total
Social Sc.	245	82.49	52	17.51	297
Science	424	90.60	44	9.40	468
All Groups	669	87.45	96	12.55	765

Pearson Chi-square: 10.8807, df=1, p=.000973

An analysis based on the subject background of the users about their awareness on OPAC shows that respondents belong to Science subjects are more aware than those in Social Science subjects. Table 1.3.42 gives the details of the subject wise analysis of awareness among those who belongs to Science subjects is above 90 percent while among Social

Sciences group it is around 82.5 per cent only. The Chi-square test proved the association between the subject group of the respondents and awareness about OPAC is highly significant.

Status wise analysis showed that Research Scholars have the least awareness while Teachers have a high degree of awareness about OPAC. Table 1.3.43 gives the details.

Table 1.3.43 User Awareness about OPAC - Status wise

Status	*Yes*	%	*No*	%	*Total*
Students	494	87.43	71	12.57	565
Research Scholars	104	82.54	22	17.46	126
Teachers	71	95.95	3	4.05	74
All Groups	669	87.45	96	12.55	765

Pearson Chi-square: 7.63567, df=2, p=.021985

The Chi-square test proved that the association between the Status of the user and awareness about OPAC is significant. The table clearly indicates the high degree of awareness among the Faculty members while among students it is 87.43 per cent and among Research Scholars it is 82.54 per cent. Overall, much difference is not found among various categories of users regarding awareness about OPAC.

USERS OF OPAC IN THE UNIVERSITY LIBRARIES

Out of the total 765 respondents only 669 were found aware about OPAC and out of this, only 634 found to be using OPAC. Remaining 35 are though aware about the OPAC, did not mark to show their use of OPAC. The figure of 131 not using OPAC includes those who are not aware about the OPAC as well as those 35 who are aware but not using the OPAC.

Table 1.3.44 shows an overall 82.88 per cent of the users are making use of OPAC for searching the library resources. Library wise analysis of users showed that in CUL 93.68 per cent users are making use where as in KUL it is only 61.86 per cent. In MGUL and CUSATL also library users extensively make use of OPAC and the percentage of use are 91.04 and 88.05 respectively.

Table 1.3.44 Users of OPAC - Library wise

Library	*Yes*	*%*	*No*	*%*	*Total*
KUL	133	61.86	82	38.14	215
MGUL	183	91.04	18	8.96	201
CUSATL	140	88.05	19	11.95	159
CUL	178	93.68	12	6.32	190
All Libs.	634	82.88	131	17.12	765

Pearson Chi-square: 94.9986, df=3, p=.000000

The Chi-square test proved that the association between the use of OPAC made and the university library is highly significant. A much higher level of OPAC use is found in CUL while in KUL it is comparatively low.

Subject wise analysis of users of OPAC showed that people from Science subjects are making more use of OPAC compared to those from Social Sciences. In Social Sciences the usage rate is 77.78 per cent only while in Science subjects it is 86.11 per cent. Regarding the awareness about OPAC also Science people were found ahead of those from Social Sciences. Details have been given in Table 1.3.45.

Table 1.3.45 Users of OPAC - Subject wise

Subject	*Yes*	*%*	*No*	*%*	*Total*
Social Science	231	77.78	66	22.22	297
Science	403	86.11	65	13.89	468
All Groups	634	82.88	131	17.12	765

Pearson Chi-square: 8.89080, df=1, p=.002868

The Chi-square test proved that there is a significant association between the use of OPAC made and the subject background of the users.

Status wise analysis of OPAC usage showed that

Teachers are the highest users of OPAC. It is notable that Research Scholars who usually spend a period more than Post Graduate Students in universities are making less use of OPAC compared to the Students.

Table 1.3.46 Users of OPAC - Status wise

Status	*Yes*	*%*	*No*	*%*	*Total*
Students	473	83.72	92	16.28	565
Research Scholars	95	75.40	31	24.60	126
Teachers	66	89.19	8	10.81	74
All Groups	634	82.88	131	17.12	765

Pearson Chi-square: 7.32606, df=2, p=.025665

The Chi-square test did not proved any significant association in the case of status wise analysis.

Comparatively lower level of OPAC use found among Research Scholars and higher level among Teachers are visible in the above figure.

ACCESS POINTS AND LEVEL OF USAGE OF OPAC

Various access points provided in OPAC enables the user to locate document as well as to filter the query for obtaining result of an advanced search. Advanced search provides details of the documents that satisfy particular features or characteristics. Question was asked to disclose the access points generally used by the respondents. Choices were given and users were allowed to specify the access points used by them. Table 1.3.47 below gives the details of the access points used by various categories of users. It was found that the most used search key is the author and is followed by the title and the subject. Words in the title was also found to be made use by many users while the usage of other points were too limited.

Table 1.3.47 Use of Various Access Points in OPAC - Status wise

Access Point	Students		Researchers		Teachers		Average
	Yes	No	Yes	No	Yes	No	Yes
Author	415(87.74%)	58(12.26%)	77(81.05%)	18(18.95%)	54(81.82%)	12(18.18%)	86.12%
Title	348(73.57%)	125(26.43%)	68(71.58%)	27(28.42%)	47(71.21%)	19(28.79%)	73.03%
Words in Title	95(20.08%)	378(79.92%)	35(36.84%)	60(63.16%)	19(28.79%)	47(71.21%)	23.50%
Subject	279(58.99%)	194(41.01%)	58(61.05%)	37(38.95%)	36(54.55%)	30(45.45%)	58.83%
Class Number	37(7.82%)	436(92.18%)	8(8.42%)	87(91.58%)	2(3.03%)	64(96.97%)	7.41%
Place	20(4.23%)	453(95.77%)	4(4.21%)	91(95.79%)	2(3.03%)	64(96.97%)	4.10%
Publisher	38(8.03%)	435(91.97%)	14(14.74%)	81(85.26%)	3(4.55%)	63(95.45%)	8.68%
Series	14(2.96%)	459(97.04%)	5(5.26%)	90(94.74%)	3(4.55%)	63(95.45%)	3.47%
Boolean	6(1.27%)	467(98.73%)	2(2.11%)	93(97.89%)	3(4.55%)	63(95.45%)	1.74%
Truncation	2(0.42%)	471(99.58%)	0(0.00%)	95(100%)	0(0.00%)	66(100%)	0.32%
Word Proximity	2(0.42%)	471(99.58%)	0(0.00%)	95(100%)	1(1.52%)	65(98.48%)	0.47%

It was found that name of the author is preferred by the majority of (86.12%) users while title is used by 73.03 per cent and 58.83 per cent using subject of the document as the access points. Keywords in title, that were usually not available in the traditional catalogue, are used by 23.5 per cent of the users. All other access points like Place of Publication; Publisher and Series of the document are used by a very limited number of users only. The access point, year of publication was not listed and was not mentioned also by anyone as making use. The other three terms listed were Boolean search, Truncation search and word proximity search. These are the typical features of electronic catalogue and were not at all possible with the traditional catalogues. It helps the users to filter their query and find out their document of interest very easily and save their time considerably. It is unfortunate to find that the users are not exploring these potentials of the OPAC properly. This may be because of the fact that users do not know the proper use of these methods. This indicates the need for proper interpretation of the service through effective user education programme.

Here it is evident that the access points used by different categories are almost same and in the traditional catalogue also almost the same access points are found used. This leads to the conclusion that the peculiar features of electronic catalogue have not been made use by any category to any considerable extent.

SATISFACTION OF USERS OVER ACCESS POINTS PROVIDED IN OPAC

Question was asked to ascertain whether the users are satisfied over the access points provided in the OPACs in their respective libraries and the analysis showed that the users are highly satisfied with the access points provided.

Table 1.3.48 Satisfaction Over Access Points Provided in OPAC - Library wise

Library	*Yes*	*%*	*No*	*%*	*Total*
KUL	126	94.74	7	5.26	133
MGUL	177	96.72	6	3.28	183
CUSATL	128	91.43	12	8.57	140
CUL	168	94.38	10	5.62	178
All Libs.	599	94.48	35	5.52	634

Pearson Chi-square: 4.28194, df=3, p=.232607

As shown in Table 1.3.48 analysis revealed that an overall 94.48 per cent are satisfied with the provisions made in the OPACs for finding out the library resources and not much difference exists among the users of different libraries with regard to the provision of access points in OPAC. The Chi-square test did not reveal any association between the University Library and the satisfaction of the users. This shows that irrespective of the library users are highly satisfied over the access points.

Subject wise analysis also did not show any dissatisfaction over the access points available in OPACs as shown in Table 1.3.49.

Table 1.3.49 Satisfaction Over Access Points Provided in OPAC - Subject wise

Subjects	*Yes*	*%*	*No*	*%*	*Total*
Social Science	218	94.37	13	5.63	231
Science	381	94.54	22	5.46	403
All Groups	599	94.48	35	5.52	634

Pearson Chi-square: .008007, df=1, p=.928699

The Chi-square test proved any relation between the subject background and the user satisfaction highly insignificant. It was examined whether there is any difference in the level of satisfaction between various categories of users over the provisions of access points made in OPAC. It showed, as seen in Table 1.3.50, that all the status group have of almost the same level of satisfaction in the provided access points. The Chi-square test proved that the association between the level of satisfaction over the access points in OPAC and the category of users is quiet insignificant.

Table 1.3.50 Satisfaction Over Access Points Provided in OPAC- Status wise

Status	*Yes*	*%*	*No*	*%*	*Total*
Students	445	94.08	28	5.92	473
Research Scholars	91	95.79	4	4.21	95
Teachers	63	95.45	3	4.55	66
All Groups	599	94.48	35	5.52	634

Pearson Chi-square: .577354, df=2, p=.749256

The above analysis showed that the users irrespective of library, status group, sex, subject and age group found to be satisfied over the access points provided in OPAC and Chi-square test did not prove any association between the category of users and satisfaction over access points.

ORIENTATION IN THE USE OF OPAC

OPAC is a development of recent origin and not older than 6 years in these libraries. So providing proper orientation is a must for making best use of the facility. OPAC has got several advanced features that were not available or possible in the traditional catalogues. It entertains complex search queries and enables the users to get more concrete bibliographical information. Being a development of recent origin providing proper orientation will help the users to reap the maximum benefits of the OPAC.

Table 1.3.51 Orientation in the Use of OPAC – University Library wise

Library	*Yes*	*%*	*No*	*%*	*Total*
KUL	44	33.08	89	66.92	133
MGUL	83	45.36	100	54.64	183
CUSATL	49	35.00	91	65.00	140
CUL	43	24.16	135	75.84	178
All Libs.	219	34.54	415	65.46	634

Pearson Chi-square: 18.0913, df=3, p=.000422

Library wise analysis showed that users were not being adequately trained in the use of OPAC. Table 1.3.51 revealed that more than 65 per cent have not received any orientation in the use of Online Public Access Catalogue in the libraries. In MGUL just above 45 per cent have received orientation while in CUL it is below 25 per cent. In KUL 33.08 per cent responded that they have received orientation in the use of OPAC while in CUSATL 35 per cent received orientation. Chi-square test showed significant difference between the users of different libraries in the orientation received in the use of OPAC.

As Table 1.3.52 revealed there was no subject wise distinction among the users in getting orientation in the use of OPAC and around 35 per cent in both subjects only received orientation in the use of OPAC. The Chi-square test proved that any relation between the Subject background and the level of orientation received is highly insignificant.

Table 1.3.52 Orientation in the Use of OPAC - Subject wise

Subjects	*Yes*	*%*	*No*	*%*	*Total*
Social Science	80	34.63	151	65.37	231
Science	139	34.49	264	65.51	403
All Groups	219	34.54	415	65.46	634

Pearson Chi-square: .001286, df=1, p=.971394

Status wise analysis of the users showed that Research Scholars are the category that got the highest rate of orientation (38.95%) in the use of OPAC. Among teacher respondents only 31.82 per cent got orientation in the use of OPAC. Chi-square test did not show any association between the subject backgrounds of the user and level of orientation received by them.

Table 1.3.53 Orientation in the Use of OPAC - Status wise

Status	*Yes*	*%*	*No*	*%*	*Total*
Students	161	34.04	312	65.96	473
Research Scholars	37	38.95	58	61.05	95
Teachers	21	31.82	45	68.18	66
All Groups	219	34.54	415	65.46	634

Pearson Chi-square: 1.08510, df=2, p=.581270

The fact that advanced features of the OPAC like Boolean search, truncation search and word proximity searches have not been explored by the users should be viewed in the light of absence of proper orientation to the users. Once the potential of the OPAC is exposed to the users, they will definitely get real benefits of the electronic catalogue.

METHODS ADOPTED FOR LEARNING USE OF OPAC

Question was asked to those who have not received any orientation, about the method adopted by them in understanding the use of OPAC. Since 82.88 per cent of the users found to be using OPAC and only less than 35 per cent among them have received orientation in the use of OPAC, this question has greater relevance. Three possible choices were given and users were asked to indicate any other method (if any) also. Table 4.54 shows the details of the methods and combinations of methods adopted by users in making use of OPAC.

Table 1.3.54 Details of Methods adopted for learning use of OPAC

Method	*KUL*	*MGUL*	*CUSATL*	*CUL*	*All Libs*
Trial and Error	32 (35.96%)	42 (42.00%)	35(38.46%)	60 (44.44%)	169 (40.72%)
By Observing Others	13 (14.61%)	14 (14.00%)	14(15.38%)	27(20.00%)	68 (16.39%)
From friends	39 (43.82%)	34 (34.00%)	26(28.57%)	30 (22.22%)	129(31.08%)
Other methods	1(1.12%)	0(0.00%)	0(0.00%)	2(1.48%)	3(0.72%)
Trial and Error and By observing Others	1(1.12%)	5(5.00%)	6(7.69%)	7(4.44%)	19(4.58%)
Trial and Error and From friends	3(3.37%)	3(3.00%)	4(4.40%)	9(6.67%)	19(4.58%)
By Observing Others and From friends	0(0.00%)	2(2.00%)	2(2.20%)	1(0.74%)	5(1.20%)
Trial & error, observing others and From friends	0(0.00%)	0(0.00%)	3(3.30%)	0(0.00%)	3(0.72%)

The adoption of methods found to be varying among universities. The first two methods were seen made use by more users in the CUL. 'Trial and error method' of self-learning was adopted by 44.44 per cent and 'observing others use the OPAC' were adopted by 20 per cent of users in CUL. In KUL 43.82 per cent adopted 'learning from friends' and 'self-learning' was adopted by 35.96 per cent. In MGUL the main method was 'trial and error' (42%) while 34 per cent 'learned it from their friends'. In CUSATL, majority (38.46%) of the users adopted the method of 'trial & error' while the method of 'learning from friends' (28.57%) was also adopted considerably. As shown in the Table in certain cases more than one method was seen adopted by users to know the use of OPAC and these were below 8 per cent only.

Learning from other users enables only to understand the methods and techniques that are known to others and there may be limitations in such cases. 'Trial and error' method will also not enable one to explore the full potential of the OPAC. Using the help file will solve this problem up to certain extent. Providing adequate training by the library staff is the best method to make maximum use of the technology. Large libraries will find it difficult to train the users individually. Hence demonstrations with the help of LCD Projectors at the beginning of the academic session will help the students in acquiring skill in using the OPAC. Such training programmes should be conducted on regular intervals so that newly joined members can attain skill in using OPAC.

AVAILABILITY OF TERMINALS FOR USING OPAC

In order to ascertain the adequacy of terminals to the users, question was asked whether the users had to wait for their turn while some one else is using the OPAC terminal. Table 1.3.21 has revealed that in KUL a single terminal has been provided as OPAC while in MGUL and CUL there are two each and in CUSATL there are 4 terminals provided for users to browse the OPAC. Table shows the user response about this question. It is evident that there is a higher level of dissatisfaction among users over the number of terminals provided in the libraries under study. Table 1.3.55 reveals the library wise details of satisfaction over terminals provided.

Table 1.3.55 Availability of OPAC Terminals - Library wise

Library	*Yes*	*%*	*No*	*%*	*Total*
KUL	78	58.65	55	41.35	133
MGUL	122	66.67	61	33.33	183
CUSATL	64	45.71	76	54.29	140
CUL	124	69.66	54	30.34	178
All Libs.	388	61.20	246	38.80	634

Pearson Chi-square: 22.1754, df=3, p=.000060

In CUL 69.66 per cent have said that they had to wait for their turn to use the OPAC while in MGUL 66.67 per cent and in KUL 58.65 per cent have responded similarly. In CUSATL where 4 nodes a2e provided for users only 45.71 per cent have said that they keep on waiting for their turn to use the OPAC. Chi-square test proved significant association between the University Library and the availability of OPAC terminals.

Though two terminals are provided in MGUL and CUL the percentage of users who responded 'yes' to this question were higher compared to KUL. But it is notable that the percentage of users of OPAC in KUL was only 61.86 per cent while this was 91.04 per cent and 93.68 per cent in MGUL and CUL respectively. This analysis shows that the numbers of terminals provided in the libraries under study are inadequate when the demand from the users is considered. The Chi-square test analysis proved that the association between the availability of terminals and university library is highly significant.

INFLIBNET SUPPORT AND ASSISTANCE

It is with the establishment of the INFLIBNET the

momentum of computer applications in university libraries in the country started. Since the very beginning of it's coming into existence the INFLIBNET has played a key role in the process through different activities mainly through providing financial assistance to the libraries and helping the libraries to develop manpower required for computerisation. Table 4.7 has given the picture of financial assistance provided by the INFLIBNET to the libraries under study. Considering the importance of qualified personnel needed for the development and management of a computerised system, the INFLIBENT sanctioned a post of Information Scientist to each library in the scale of pay equal to that of Lecturer. As in the case of other UGC posts this post is also supported by the UGC for the initial 5 years period. After that the concerned state government has to support this post. Out of the 4 universities under study only two universities i.e. University of Calicut and CUSAT filled up the post while the other two universities did not take any initiatives in filling up the post. Table 1.3.56 gives the details of the support provided by INFLIBENT in developing manpower to look after the computerised systems in these libraries.

It is with the training programmes conducted by the INFLIBNET, majority of the university libraries in the country gained initial know how in automating library procedures. The Table reveals that all the libraries under study have received manpower training from the INFLIBNET. The one-month training in Application of computer to Library and Information Services was catalyst in the process of starting database creation in libraries. Similarly all the libraries have obtained training in the use of Infonet resources also. The other training programmes such as those conducted in the use of automation packages like ILMS and SOUL have also been obtained by the libraries varyingly. KUL and MGUL have received on site training programme conducted by the INFLIBNET.

Table 1.3.56 Training Obtained from INFLIBNET by the Library Professionals

Library	*Name of Training Programme*	*No. of persons*	*Duration*
KUL	Application of Computer to Library & Information Services	3	One month
	Use of Infonet Resources	1	One week
	On site training programme	20	One day
	SOUL software training	1	Two weeks
MGUL	Application of Computer to Library & Information Services	3	One month
	On site training programme on SOUL	20	One Week
	Use of Infonet Resources	1	One Week
	Use of Internet Resources	2	One Week
CUS ATL	Application of Computer to Library & Information Services	1	One month
	Use of Infonet Resources	1	One Week
CUL	Application of Computer to Library & Information Services	2	One month
	Use of ILMS	1	One week
	Use of Infonet Resources	1	One week

RECORDS PROVIDED TO THE UNION DATABASE

The INFLIBNET maintains a union database of documents available in the Indian universities. All the universities provide their data with CCF tags to the INFLIBNET for making it available through Internet. Table 1.3.57 gives the details of the data sent by each university along with the total number of documents available in the library.

Table 1.3.57 Records Contributed to INFLIBNET Union Database

Library	*Document*	*Sent to INFLIBNET*	*Available in Library*
KUL	Books	1,45,000	286155
	Theses	1500	
	Serials	1133 Titles	
MGUL	Books	28000	33379
	Theses	282	4282
	Serials	470 Titles	500
CUSATL	Books	Nil	55882
	Theses	552	552
	Serials	220 Titles	220
CUL	Books	68200	89568
	Theses	2800	3005
	Serials	409 Titles	409

Table 1.3.57 shows that bibliographical details of a good number of documents especially books in the universities are yet to be sent to the INFLIBNET. The KUL maintains a special collection on Kerala Studies and availability of the complete details of such unique collection in the union database is very much appreciable. Regarding the serial titles all the universities have sent the details of their available holdings summary to the INFLIBNET.

UGC INFONET AND PARTICIPATION OF THE UNIVERSITY LIBRARIES

All the universities under study come under the UGC Infonet purview and are provided with 1 Mbps bandwidth Leased Line connection through Asianet under UGC Infonet programme. All the libraries have provided the connection to the existing Internet provision in the library and KUL and CUSATL have extended the connection to the teaching departments while in MGUL and CUL the services have not been extended beyond the library premises. Since the facility is provided through the existing channel KUL and CUL are charging fee for the use of Internet provision through which Infonet resources are also accessed. But in CUL exclusive center for access to Infonet resources without charging any fee is under construction and expected to be completed shortly. MGUL and CUSATL are not charging any fee for Infonet use and in all libraries the category of members given access is not different from that of Internet use, which is given in the Table 1.3.28.

INFLIBNET REGIONAL TRAINING PROGRAMME IN LIBRARY AUTOMATION

INFLIBNET Regional Training Programme in Library Automation abbreviated as IRTPLA, is a training programme conducted by INFLIBNET at various universities providing training in the use of SOUL software. It is mainly intended at training library professionals from Colleges and Universities. In a programme 20 persons are admitted and hands on training is imparted in the use of SOUL. Among the universities under study all except CUSATL conducted the programme helping library professionals from universities and affiliated colleges to gain knowledge in the use of SOUL. MGUL has conducted the programme twice, training a total of 50 librarians.

NETWORK FACILITIES IN THE UNIVERSITY LIBRARIES

Use of integrated library systems necessitates computer network facilities in libraries. It is needed for providing facilities for all sections in the library to access the database and for effective communication between various sections. Table 1.3.58 gives the details of network infrastructure available in the libraries under study. All the libraries under study are using integrated library management systems and most of the housekeeping operations are done using computers. So all the libraries have developed a Local Area Network within the library building. Except CUSATL all the libraries have UTP cables as medium of transmission while CUSATL uses Optical Fiber Cable for its networking. Only KUL and CUSATL have LAN in the campus and CUSATL has made their library accessible over their LAN. KUL is not available over their campus LAN as the library is somewhat away from the campus. MGUL and CUL have no LANs in their campus and the library resources and services are available inside the library only. Yet the website of CUL is available over Internet providing certain information while MGUL has not yet hosted their website.

CUSATL and CUL have Router in the library that connects the LAN with the Internet. But only the Library services network of CUSATL is accessible through campus LAN and Internet. In CUL the LAN set up for library functions are not connected with the Internet and there is a separate network for accessing Internet. This is done to secure the library network. In both instances Firewall implementation is done through software restricting unauthorized access from outside. All the libraries are participating in the INFLIBNET while CUSATL and MGUL are making use of DELNET resources. MGUL is also making use of American Information Resource Center (AIRC) network. No other participation in any other network is worth mentioning in the case of the libraries under study.

Table 1.3.58 Network Infrastructure Available in University libraries under study

		KUL	MGUL	CUSATL	CUL
LAN in Library		Yes	Yes	Yes	Yes
Medium of Transmission		UTP Cable	UTP Cable	OFC	UTP Cable
LAN in Campus		Yes	No	Yes	No
Participation in Networks	INFLIBNET	Yes	Yes	Yes	Yes
	DELNET	No	Yes	Yes	No
	Others	-	AIRC	-	-
Library Services Network accessible through campus LAN/Internet		No	No	Yes	No
Availability of Router in Library		No	No	Yes	Yes
Implemented Firewall		NA	NA	Yes	Yes
Mode of Protection		NA	NA	Through Software	Through Software

INTERNET SERVICES AND FACILITIES IN THE UNIVERSITY LIBRARIES

All the libraries under study have Internet facilities and are providing Internet based services to its users. It is found that with the introduction of Infonet facilities all the libraries were able to get high-speed connection with comparatively good bandwidth. The university libraries under study have different types of Internet connectivity with different service providing agencies through different modes of transmission. Table 1.3.59 gives the details of the Internet connectivity as well as the provisions of services to the users. All the libraries have got 1 Mbps leased line connection through Asianet for accessing UGC Infonet. Considering the Internet infrastructure in the state, this is found to be a good option providing a high-speed connection for the universities. KUL, MGUL and CUL have a separate 64 Kbps ISDN dialup connection through BSNL. KUL has got another 256 Kbps leased line through BSNL while MGUL has a PSTN dial up connection using the services provided by Satyam Online and CUSATL has another leased line connection from BSNL. All these alternative sources make provision for a non-stop Internet service facility in the university libraries under study.

Numbers of computers made available to the members found to be scanty in all the University Libraries. KUL and CUSATL have made available 12 computers to the users while in MGUL and CUL it is only 10. It is notable that in the Universities of Kerala and Cochin the departments have Internet connection and Infonet resources are also available in the departments. But in MGUL and CUL these facilities are not available in the department and the number of terminals provided in the central facility is too inadequate. All the libraries are providing Internet services to the Students, the Research Scholars, the Teachers and the Non-teaching staff while KUL alone has extended the service to the public also. MGUL and CUSATL are providing the service without charging any fee while KUL charges a fee on hourly basis while CUL charges it on a yearly basis. In KUL students and

Research Scholars are charged Rs. 15 for one hour of Internet use while staff, both teaching and non-teaching, and public are charged Rs. 20 per use of the facility for one hour. In CUL the fee is charged on a yearly membership basis and the rate charged has a proportionate increase every financial year. The rate prevalent in the current financial year is Rs.350 for students, Rs. 525 for Research Scholars and Rs. 875 for Teaching and Non-teaching staff. They are permitted to use the facility unlimited subject to the availability of the machine.

Table 1.3.59 Internet connectivity and provisions of services

		KUL	MGUL	CUSATL	CUL
Type of Connectivity/ Service Provider/ Bandwidth of the connection		1. ISDN Dial up/BSNL/ 64 Kbps 2. Leased Line/Asianet/ 1Mbps 3. Leased Line/BSNL/ 256Kbps	1. ISDN Dial up/BSNL/ 64 Kbps 2. Leased Line/Asianet/ 1Mbps 3. PSTN Dialup/Satyam Online/ 9.6 Kbps	1. Leased Line/BSNL/ 512Kbps 2. Leased Line/Asianet/ 1Mbps	1. ISDN Dial up/BSNL/ 64 Kbps 2. Leased Line/Asianet/ 1Mbps
Training in the use of Internet provided to users		Yes	Yes	Yes	Yes
No. of machines provided to users		12	10	12	10
Status of Users and Fee Rates	Students	Rs.15/ Hour	Nil	Nil	Rs.350/ Year
	Research Scholars	Rs.15/ Hour	Nil	Nil	Rs.525/ Year
	Teaching Staff	Rs.20/ Hour	Nil	Nil	Rs.875/ Year
	Non Teaching Staff	Rs.20/ Hour	Nil	Nil	Rs.875/ Year
	Public	Rs.20/ Hour	NA	NA	NA

UTILIZATION OF INTERNET SERVICES

Internet is the most popular source of information today. With its dynamic features it fetches required information in many formats like text, sound, vision etc. from anywhere in the world without any geographical or time barriers. One third of the respondents were found to be using the Internet services in the University libraries under study. Table 1.3.60 provides details of the users of Internet in various university libraries. The highest use rate was recorded in the MGUL and the lowest in the Calicut University Library.

Table 1.3.60 Internet Users in the Universities in Kerala - Library wise

Library	*Yes*	*%*	*No*	*%*	*Total*
KUL	163	75.81	52	24.19	215
MGUL	179	89.05	22	10.95	201
CUSATL	135	84.91	24	15.09	159
CUL	101	53.16	89	46.84	190
All Libs	578	75.56	187	24.44	765

Pearson Chi-square: 78.9734, df=3, p=.000000

In three universities except Calicut University more than 75 per cent of the respondents are using the Internet facility while in the University of Calicut it is only 53.16 per cent. In CUSATL and MGUL where the Internet services are provided without charging any fee the usage rate is found to be very high. The Chi-square test analysis proved that association between the use of Internet and University Library is highly significant. The low rate of Internet usage in CUL may be because of the high fee charged.

A faculty-wise analysis of the respondents showed that users from Science subjects are using Internet services more than those from Social Science subjects. 83.97 per cent of the respondents from Science faculty are using the Internet services while the rate among Social Science subjects respondents are only 62.29 per cent. Table 1.3.61 reveals the data of faculty wise use of Internet by respondents. The Chi-square test analysis proved that association between the use of Internet and the subject background of the respondents is highly significant.

Table 1.3.61 Internet Users in the University Libraries in Kerala - Subject wise

Subject	*Yes*	*%*	*No*	*%*	*Total*
Social Science	185	62.29	112	37.71	297
Science	393	83.97	75	16.03	468
All Groups	578	75.56	187	24.44	765

Pearson Chi-square: 46.2599, df=1, p=.000000

The Chi-square test proved that the association between the subject background and the use of Internet services is highly significant.

Status wise analysis showed that there is not much difference among Students, Research Scholars and Faculty members in the matter of using Internet services. Table 1.3.62 has the details.

Table 1.3.62 Status wise Details of Internet Users in the University libraries under study

Status	*Yes*	*%*	*No*	*%*	*Total*
Students	419	74.16	146	25.84	565
Research Scholars	94	74.60	32	25.40	126
Teachers	65	87.84	9	12.16	74
All Groups	578	75.56	187	24.44	765

Pearson Chi-square: 6.70254, df=2, p=.035052

The Table shows that the use of Internet among teacher community under study is 87.84 per cent while among students and researchers it is around 75 per cent only. The Chi-square test analysis proved that association between the use of Internet and the category of the respondents is insignificant.

Almost similar level of usage habit among various categories of users is clearly depicted in the table.

INTERNET SERVICES USED

Internet services used were listed in the questionnaire as Web Browsing, Email, Chatting, Newsgroups, Discussion Groups, Searching Databases, Accessing E Journals, Accessing Reference Sources, Accessing the Catalogues and Databases of Other Libraries and also provided option for marking any other purposes used by the respondents. On the basis of the preferences made by the users these purposes could be grouped in to five as Browsing (browsing), Communication (Email, Chatting), Forums (News groups, Discussion Groups), E-Contents (Searching Databases, Accessing E Journals, Accessing Reference sources) and Accessing other Libraries

Table 1.3.63 Internet Services Usage in the University Libraries in Kerala - Library wise

Services & Combinations	*KUL*	*MGUL*	*CUSATL*	*CUL*	*Total*
Browsing	21(12.88%)	12(6.70%)	13(9.63%)	9(8.91%)	55(9.52%)
Communication	13(7.98%)	7(3.91%)	2(1.48%)	5(4.95%)	27(4.67%)
E-Contents	13(7.98%)	12(6.70%)	6(4.44%)	5(4.95%)	36(6.23%)
Browsing & Communication	28(17.18%)	19(10.61%)	25(18.52%)	23(22.77%)	95(16.44%)
Browsing & E Contents	7(4.29%)	12(6.70%)	7(5.19%)	6(5.94%)	32(5.54%)
Communication & E-Contents	12(7.36%)	18(10.06%)	4(2.96%)	9(8.91%)	43(7.44%)
Browsing, Communication & Forums	2(1.23%)	14(7.82%)	11(8.15%)	11(10.89%)	38(6.57%)
Browsing, Communication & E-Contents	45(27.61%)	58(32.40%)	33(24.44%)	18(17.82%)	154(26.64%)
Browsing, Communication & Accessing Other Libraries	1(0.61%)	0(0.00%)	6(4.44%)	0(0.00%)	7(1.21%)
Browsing, Forums & E-Contents	4(2.45%)	2(1.12%)	3(2.22%)	1(0.99%)	10(1.73%)
Browsing, Communication, Forums & E-Contents	8(4.91%)	16(8.94%)	13(9.63%)	10(9.90%)	47(8.13%)
Browsing, Communication, E-Contents & Accessing Other Libraries	8(4.91%)	8(4.47%)	6(4.44%)	3(2.97%)	25(4.33%)
Browsing, Communication, Forums, E-Contents & Accessing Other Libraries	1(0.61%)	1(0.56%)	6(4.44%)	1(0.99%)	9(1.56%)

(access the Catalogues and databases of other libraries). The following Table 1.3.63 provides the details of the purposes of the users library wise.

Out of the total 578 persons using the net services, the combination of Browsing, Communication and E-Contents found to be the top priority of the 26.64 per cent of users. Browsing, Communication and Accessing Other Libraries is the combination least used with a total of 1.21 per cent only. Analysis on the various Internet services and its different combinations used by respondents from Science and Social Science backgrounds are given in Table 1.3.64.

Table 1.3.64 Internet Services Usage in the University libraries under study - Subject wise

Services and Combinations of services	*Social Science*	*Science*	*Total*
Browsing	27(14.59%)	28(7.12%)	55(9.52%)
Communication	8(4.32%)	19(4.83%)	27(4.67%)
E-Contents	14(7.57%)	22(5.60%)	36(6.23%)
Browsing andCommunication	40(21.62%)	55(13.99%)	95(16.44%)
Browsing andE Contents	7(3.78%)	25(6.36%)	32(5.54%)
Communication and E-Contents	8(4.32%)	35(8.91%)	43(7.44%)
Browsing, Communication and Forums	16(8.65%)	22(5.60%)	38(6.57%)
Browsing, Communication and E-Contents	33 (17.84%)	121 (30.79%)	154 (26.64%)
Browsing, Communication and Accessing Other Libraries	1(0.54%)	6(1.53%)	7(1.21%)
Browsing, Forums andE-Contents	6(3.24%)	4(1.02%)	10(1.73%)
Browsing, Communication, Forums andE-Contents	14(7.57%)	33(8.40%)	47(8.13%)
Browsing, Communication, E-Contents and Accessing Other Libraries	7(3.78%)	18(4.58%)	25(4.33%)
Browsing, Communication, Forums, E-Contents and Accessing Other Libraries	4(2.16%)	5(1.27%)	9(1.56%)

Analysis based on the subject background of the users showed that users with Science background are ahead of Social Science users in the use of 'E-contents' such as databases, full text articles etc., which are more needed for academic purposes. In the other combinations not much significant difference was found between these two groups.

Status wise analysis of various Internet services used is given in Table 1.3.65.

Table 1.3.65 Internet Services Usage in the University libraries under study - Status wise

Services & Combinations	*Students*	*Research Scholars*	*Teachers*	*Total*
Browsing	45(10.74%)	4(4.26%)	6(9.23%)	55(9.52%)
Communication	23(5.49%)	3(3.19%)	1(1.54%)	27(4.67%)
E-Contents	23(5.49%)	8(8.51%)	5(7.69%)	36(6.23%)
Browsing & Communication	76(18.14%)	9(9.57%)	10(15.38%)	95(16.44%)
Browsing & E Contents	18(4.30%)	9(9.57%)	5(7.69%)	32(5.54%)
Communication & E-Contents	31(7.4%)	8(8.51%)	4(6.15%)	43(7.44%)
Browsing, Communication & Forums	33(7.38%)	3(3.19%)	2(3.08%)	38(6.57%)
Browsing, Communication & E-Contents	110 (26.25%)	34 (36.17%)	10 (15.38%)	154 (26.64%)
Browsing, Communication & Accessing Other Libraries	2(0.48%)	0(0.00%)	5(7.69%)	7(1.21%)
Browsing, Forums & E-Contents	9(2.15%)	0(0.00%)	1(1.54%)	10(1.73%)
Browsing, Communication, Forums & E-Contents	34(8.11%)	6(6.38%)	7(10.77%)	47(8.13%)
Browsing, Communication, E-Contents & Accessing Other Libraries	9(2.15%)	9(9.57%)	7(10.77%)	25(4.33%)
Browsing, Communication, Forums, E-Contents & Accessing Other Libraries	6(1.43%)	1(1.06%)	2(3.08%)	9(1.56%)

Here it is seen that majority of the Students (26.25%) and Research Scholars (36.17%) makes use of the Internet the services Browsing, Communication & E-Contents that are usually needed for general purpose, communication purposes and Study and Research purposes. Among the Teachers the same purpose is mentioned by majority (15.38%) of users while the same percentage is found to be using the services Browsing and Communication alone excluding the E-Contents.

The analysis showed that Research Scholars are using Internet services that are more related with academic purposes while Students comes to next to them and Teachers found to be behind others in this aspect.

PURPOSE OF INTERNET USE

Users were asked about their purpose of Internet use and they were given choices such as Study, Research, General, Recreational and Communication and were given option to indicate Any Other purposes of Internet use. Multiple choices were indicated by most of the users and the choices and their combinations as marked by the users are given in Table 1.3.66.

The main purposes indicated by the users were Study as well as Research and the combinations consisting both purposes.. Non-serious purpose of Internet use found to be very limited with only 0.52 per cent responding as their purpose of Internet use as mere Recreational. An over all 78.32 per cent found to be using Internet for their Study purposes while 43.89 per cent is using it for Research purposes. A total of 9.51 per cent found to be using Internet neither for Study nor for Research purposes and their interest was focused towards purposes other than these.

Analysis of the purpose of Internet use based on the subject background of the Users is given in Table 1.3.67

Table 1.3.66 Purpose of Internet Use - Library wise

Purpose Use of Internet	*KUL*	*MGUL*	*CUSATL*	*CUL*	*Total*
Study	35(21.47%)	31(17.32%)	19(14.07%)	9(8.91%)	94(16.26%)
Research	19(11.66%)	11(6.15%)	4(2.96%)	4(3.96%)	38(6.57%)
General	11(6.75%)	3(1.68%)	9(6.67%)	5(4.95%)	28(4.84%)
Recreational	2(1.23%)	0(0.00%)	0(0.00%)	1(0.99%)	3(0.52%)
Communication	4(2.45%)	5(2.79%)	0(0.00%)	8(7.92%)	17(2.94%)
Study and Research	14(8.59%)	11(6.15%)	5(3.7%)	7(6.93%)	37(6.4%)
Study and General	8(4.91%)	12(6.7%)	11(8.15%)	6(5.94%)	37(6.4%)
Study and Recreational	4(2.45%)	0(0.00%)	0(0.00%)	1(0.99%)	5(0.87%)
Study and Communication	3(1.84%)	15(8.38%)	12(8.89%)	5(4.95%)	35(6.06%)
Research and Communication	4(2.45%)	5(2.79%)	4(2.96%)	2(1.98%)	15(2.6%)
Communication and General	1(0.61%)	0(0.00%)	5(3.7%)	1(0.99%)	7(1.21%)
Study, Research and General	9(5.52%)	4(2.23%)	2(1.48%)	2(1.98%)	17(2.94%)
Study, Research and Recreational	3(1.84%)	5(2.79%)	1(0.74%)	1(0.99%)	10(0.99%)
Study, Research and Communication	13(7.98%)	11(6.15%)	9(6.67%)	5(4.95%)	38(6.57%)
Study, General and Recreational	5(3.07%)	3(1.68%)	1(0.74%)	1(0.99%)	10(1.73%)
Study, General and Communication	2(1.23%)	20(11.17%)	13(9.63%)	10(9.9%)	45(7.79%)
Study, Recreational and	1(0.61%)	3(1.68%)	2(1.48%)	2(1.98%)	8(1.38%)

Purpose Use of Internet	*KUL*	*MGUL*	*CUSATL*	*CUL*	*Total*
Commu-nication Research, General and Commun-ication	0(0.00%)	5(2.79%)	7(5.19%)	1(0.99%)	13(2.25%)
Study, Research, General and Commun-ication	13(7.98%)	20(11.2%)	10(7.41%)	8(7.92%)	51(8.82%)
Study, Gen-eral Recre-ational and Commu-nication	4(2.45%)	6(3.35%)	7(5.19%)	14(13.86%)	31(5.36%)
Study, Research, General Rec-reational and Communication	8(4.91%)	9(5.03%)	14(10.37%)	8(7.92%)	39(6.75%)

Table 1.3.67 Purpose of Internet Use - Subject wise

Purpose of Internet Use	*Social Science*	*Science*	*Total*
Study	37(20%)	57(14.50%)	94(16.26%)
Research	9(4.86%)	29(7.38%)	38(6.57%)
General	15(8.11%)	13(3.31%)	28(4.84%)
Recreational	0(0.00%)	3(0.76%)	3(0.52%)
Communication	5(2.70%)	12(3.05%)	17(2.94%)
Study and Research	19(10.27%)	18(4.58%)	37(6.4%)
Study and General	12(6.49%)	25(6.36%)	37(6.4%)
Study and Recreational	2(1.08%)	3(0.76%)	5(0.87%)
Study and Communication	7(3.78%)	28(7.12%)	35(6.06%)
Research and Communication	4(2.16%)	11(2.8%)	15(2.6%)
Communication and General	3(1.62%)	4(1.02%)	7(1.21%)
Study, Research and General	6(3.24%)	11(2.8%)	17(2.94%)
Study, Research and Recreational	6(3.24%)	4(1.02%)	10(0.99%)
Study, Research and Communication	9(4.86%)	29(7.38%)	38(6.57%)
Study, General and Recreational	2(1.08%)	8(2.04%)	10(1.73%)
Study, General and Communication	5(2.70%)	40(10.18%)	45(7.79%)
Study, Recreational and	0(0.00%)	8(2.04%)	8(1.38%)

Purpose of Internet Use	Social Science	Science	Total
Communication Research, General and Communication	4(2.16%)	9(2.29%)	13(2.25%)
Study, Research, General and Communication	19(10.27%)	32(8.14%)	51(8.82%)
Study, General Recreational and Communication	7(3.78%)	24(6.11%)	31(5.36%)
Study, Research, General Recreational and Communication	14(7.57%)	25(6.36%)	39(6.75%)

The percentage of users making use of Internet for study purpose alone found to be higher in Social Sciences (20%) while it is only 14.5% among Science users. But the use for Research purpose alone is found to be higher among those from Science subjects (7.38%) while it is only 4.86 per cent among users from Social Science background. Use of Internet for pure Recreational purpose was not found among Social Science users while a minority of 0.76 per cent from Science subjects found to be using Internet for mere Recreational purposes.

Status wise purpose of Internet use is given in Table 1.3.68

Table 1.3.68 Purpose of Internet Use - Status wise

Purpose of Internet Use	Students	Research Scholars	Teachers	All Groups
Study	88(21.00%)	2(2.13%)	4(6.15%)	94(16.26%)
Research	13(3.10%)	14(14.89%)	11(16.92%)	38(6.57%)
General	20(4.77%)	4(4.26%)	4(6.15%)	28(4.84%)
Recreational	2(0.48%)	1(1.06%)	0(0.00%)	3(0.52%)
Communication	16(3.82%)	1(1.06%)	0(0.00%)	17(2.94%)
Study and Research	19(4.53%)	10(10.64%)	8(12.31%)	37(6.40%)
Study and General	37(8.83%)	0(0.00%)	0(0.00%)	37(6.40%)
Study and Recreational	4(0.95%)	1(1.06%)	0(0.00%)	5(0.87%)
Study and Communication	32(7.64%)	1(1.06%)	2(3.08%)	35(6.06%)
Research and Communication	8(1.91%)	7(7.45%)	0(0.00%)	15(2.60%)
Communication and General	7(1.67%)	0(0.00%)	0(0.00%)	7(1.21%)

Purpose of Internet Use	*Students*	*Research Scholars*	*Teachers*	*All Groups*
Study, Research and General	8(1.91%)	4(4.26%)	5(7.69%)	17(2.94%)
Study, Research and Recreational	6(1.43%)	3(3.19%)	1(1.54%)	10(1.73%)
Study, Research and Communication	19(4.53%)	9(9.57%)	10(15.4%)	38(6.57%)
Study, General and Recreational	10(2.39%)	0(0.00%)	0(0.00%)	10(1.73%)
Study, General and Communication	44(10.50%)	1(1.06%)	0(0.00%)	45(7.79%)
Study, Recreational and Communication	8(1.91%)	0(0.00%)	0(0.00%)	8(1.38%)
Research, General and Communication	3(0.72%)	7(7.45%)	3(4.62%)	13(2.25%)
Study, Research, General and Communication	23(5.49%)	17(18.1%)	11(16.9%)	51(8.82%)
Study, General Recreational and Communication	31(7.40%)	0(0.00%)	0(0.00%)	31(5.36%)
Study, Research, General Recreational and Communication	21(5.01%)	12(12.77%)	6(9.23%)	39(6.75%)

An overall 83.52 per cent among Students, 63.84 per cent among Research Scholars and 72.30 per cent among Teachers found using Internet for Study purposes. Similarly, an overall 24.1 per cent among Students, 78.75 per cent among Research Scholars and 69.21 per cent among Teachers were found using Internet for their Research purpose while the use of Internet for purposes other than Study and Research were found among 10.74 per cent of Students, 6.38 per cent of Research Scholars and 6015 per cent of Teachers.

TRAINING IN THE USE OF INTERNET FACILITY

Internet is a very vast ocean of information and one has to navigate properly for collecting the required information from Internet. User should be conversant with right techniques and should be provided with right tools for getting the right information. He/She has to understand the potential of the technology and should be able in dealing with different hardware and software. Without proper training, no one can explore the full potential of Internet services. All the university libraries under study claimed to be providing training in the use of Internet. On observation it was found that the libraries are not conducting any training programme in an organized manner rather users are given instruction in the basics of browsing on the basis of their request made at the time of they first come to use Internet in the library.

Table 1.3.69 shows the library wise details of the users who got training in the use of Internet.The Table reveals that only around 30 per cent of the users were trained in the use of Internet and a majority of 70 per cent is using the facility without any orientation in making best use of the services. The MGUL has the highest rate of trained users 44.13 per cent while in CUSATL it is the lowest i.e. 24.44 per cent. But there is not much difference between KUL, CUSATL and CUL where almost only one fourth of the Internet users only received any training in the use of Internet. This is a serious handicap of the provision of services and adequate training need to be imparted to the users for enabling them to get better results out of their efforts. The Chi-square test also proved significant association between the university library and the number of users who got training in the use of Internet.

Table 1.3.69 Trained and Non-Trained Users of Internet - Library wise

Library	*Yes*	*%*	*No*	*%*	*Total*
KUL	42	25.77	121	74.23	163
MGUL	79	44.13	100	55.87	179
CUSATL	33	24.44	102	75.56	135
CUL	25	24.75	76	75.25	101
All Libs	179	30.97	399	69.03	578

Pearson Chi-square: 21.0895, df=3, p=.000101

Details of the users of Internet from Science as well as Social Science subjects who obtained training in the use are given in Table 1.3.70 given below.

Table 1.3.70 Trained and Non-Trained Users of Internet - Subject wise

Subject	Yes	%	No	%	Total
Social Science	43	23.24	142	76.76	185
Science	136	34.61	257	65.39	393
All Groups	179	30.97	399	69.03	578

Pearson Chi-square: 7.59631, df=1, p=.005852

Subject wise analysis showed that from Social Sciences, only 23.24 per cent have got training while in Science it is 34.61 per cent and Chi-square test also proved that there is significant difference between users from both subjects in the matter of training obtained in the use of Internet.

Status wise analysis showed that Research Scholars (37.23%) have the highest percentage among the users in the matter of training obtained while the lowest is among the teachers (18.46%). Among students 31.50 per cent have said that they received training in the use of Internet services. Chi-square test did not find any significant difference among the different status groups in obtaining training.

It is evident that majority of the users are using the Internet services without any training in the utilization of the service. Teachers are the least trained user group while Researchers are the most trained and Students stands in between the other groups. The graphical user interface features may enable one to navigate through many areas in the net. But to fetch the appropriate information one need to be familiar with various tools and techniques and one need to know the pattern of adopted by different leading websites in storing their valuable information.

Table 4.71 Trained and Non-Trained Users of Internet - Status wise

Status	Yes	%	No	%	Total
Students	132	31.50	287	68.50	419
Research Scholars	35	37.23	59	62.77	94
Teachers	12	18.46	53	81.54	65
All Groups	179	30.97	399	69.03	578

Pearson Chi-square: 6.53830, df=2, p=.038051

SATISFACTION OVER AVAILABILITY OF INFORMATION FROM INTERNET

Though training was not received by majority of the users, they claimed to be getting required information from the Internet. As Table 1.3.72 reveals much difference is not found among users from different universities. An overall 84.43 per cent responded that they are getting required information and the responses from different universities are not varying more than 4 per cent and this is evident in the p value of Chi-square test also.

Table 1.3.72 Satisfaction of Receipt of Required Information from Internet - Library wise

Library	*Yes*	*%*	*No*	*%*	*Total*
KUL	135	82.82	28	17.18	163
MGUL	157	87.71	22	12.29	179
CUSATL	114	84.44	21	15.56	135
CUL	82	81.19	19	18.81	101
All Libs	488	84.43	90	15.57	578

Pearson Chi-square: 2.59242, df=3, p=.458831

Users from MGUL found to be ahead of others in getting the required information and it was in MGUL the higher percent of trained users were also found.

Subject wise analysis proved that those from Science subjects are more satisfied on getting required information from Internet compared to those who belong to Social Science subjects. When 80.54 per cent Social Science persons claimed as getting the required information, the rate in Science subject is found to be a little higher with 86.26 per cent. Chi-square test did not prove any association between the subject backgrounds and getting required information from Internet.

Table 4.73 Satisfaction of Receipt of Required Information from Internet - Subject wise

Subject	*Yes*	*%*	*No*	*%*	*Total*
Social Science	149	80.54	36	19.46	185
Science	339	86.26	54	13.74	393
All Groups	488	84.43	90	15.57	578

Pearson Chi-square: 3.12947, df=1, p=.076898

In the Table heigher level of satisfaction is very clearly seen among the users with Science background.

In the status wise analysis given in Table 1.3.74 it is seen that Research Scholars (88.30%) are more satisfied with the information they are getting while the rate among teachers it is 73.85 per cent. The Chi-square test did not prove any significant association between the category of the user and the level of receiving information from Internet.

Table 1.3.74 Satisfaction of Receipt of Required Information from Internet - Status wise

Status	*Yes*	*%*	*No*	*%*	*Total*
Students	357	85.20	62	14.80	419
Research Scholars	83	88.30	11	11.70	94
Teachers	48	73.85	17	26.15	65
All Groups	488	84.43	90	15.57	578

Pearson Chi-square: 6.79860, df=2, p=.033409

The Table clearly indicates comparatively better level of satisfaction among Research Scholars over getting required information from net. Students are just behind the Research Scholars and Teachers found to be behind other two categories.

SPEED OF THE INTERNET CONNECTION

Different universities have different types of Internet connectivity with different bandwidth. Speed of the Internet connection depends upon many factors such as the bandwidth of the connection as well as the Internet traffic over the particular service provider. Likewise the processor speed of the machine used also contributes to the speed of Internet connection. Internet users found to be complaining against the low speed and difficulty in getting the required data due to poor bandwidth. Question was asked to indicate the satisfaction of the users with regard to the speed of the connection. Except in MGUL more than half of the respondents from all other universities are found to be dissatisfied with the speed of the connection. Table 1.3.75 gives the university wise details of the satisfaction over the speed of the connection.

Table 1.3.75 Speed of the Internet Connection - Library wise Responses

Library	***Yes***	***%***	***No***	***%***	***Total***
KUL	75	46.01	88	53.99	163
MGUL	97	54.19	82	45.81	179
CUSATL	51	37.78	84	62.22	135
CUL	43	42.57	58	57.43	101
All Libs	266	46.02	312	53.98	578

Pearson Chi-square: 8.98419, df=3, p=.029517

In KUL 53.99 per cent have of the opinion that the Internet connection is not fast enough while in CUL it is 57.43 per cent and in CUSATL it is 62.22 per cent. In the category wise analysis all the categories expressed almost the same opinion. Teachers found to be the most dissatisfied about the speed of the connection. Chi-square test showed that the association between the Library and speed of Internet connection is significant.

Table 1.3.76 Speed of the Internet Connection - Status wise Responses

Status	***Yes***	***%***	***No***	***%***	***Total***
Students	194	46.30	225	53.70	419
Research Scholars	43	45.74	51	54.26	94
Teachers	29	44.62	36	55.38	65
All Groups	266	46.02	312	53.98	578

Pearson Chi-square: .067783, df=2, p=.966676

Chi-square test did not prove any association between the status of the user and the their satisfaction over the speed of Internet connection. Irrespective of the status of the users, majority of the users find the speed of the Internet connection inadequate.

SATISFACTION OF INTERNET SERVICES PROVIDED BY THE LIBRARIES

Question was asked about the overall satisfaction of the users regarding the Internet services provided by the library. In MGUL 76.54 per cent of the respondents found to be satisfied with the existing provisions and did not want to suggest any other improvement over the existing facility. In KUL 69.94 per cent of the respondents were satisfied and in CUSATL 62.22 per cent responded the existing services sufficient to meet their requirements. But in CUL it was 57.43 per cent and the remaining 42.57 per cent are not satisfied and wanted improvement over the existing provisions. Table 1.3.77 gives library wise details of the respondents.

Table 1.3.77 Satisfaction of the Internet Services Provided - Library wise Responses

Library	*Yes*	*%*	*No*	*%*	*Total*
KUL	114	69.94	49	30.06	163
MGUL	137	76.54	42	23.46	179
CUSATL	84	62.22	51	37.78	135
CUL	58	57.43	43	42.57	101
All Libs	393	67.99	185	32.01	578

Pearson Chi-square: 13.5352, df=3, p=.003616

Chi-square test showed that the association between the University Library and the satisfaction of users over the Internet services provided is significant. The above Table has been graphically represented in the Figure 4.31 given below which clearly depicts the higher level of satisfaction among users in MGUL and lower level among users in CUL.

A subject wise analysis revealed that satisfaction over the existing facility is more among Social Science people compared to those from Science background. Table 1.3.78 gives details about the satisfaction of different subject groups.

Table 1.3.78 Satisfaction of the Internet Services Provided - Subject wise

Subject	*Yes*	*%*	*No*	*%*	*Total*
Social Science	130	70.27	55	29.73	185
Science	263	66.92	130	33.08	393
All Groups	393	67.99	185	32.01	578

Pearson Chi-square: .648332, df=1, p=.420716

70.27 per cent of the Social Science people found to be satisfied with the existing provisions of Internet while among Science people it is 66.92 per cent only. But the Chi-square test did not prove any association between the subject background and level of satisfaction over the Internet services provided.

Status wise analysis has shown that Students (72.55%) are more satisfied with the existing facility while Teachers (50.77%) are less satisfied. Among the Research scholars 59.57 per cent found to be satisfied with facilities provided at present. Table 1.3.79 provides the details.

Table 1.3.79 Satisfaction of the Internet Services Provided - Status wise

Status	*Yes*	*%*	*No*	*%*	*Total*
Students	304	72.55	115	27.45	419
Research Scholars	56	59.57	38	40.43	94
Teachers	33	50.77	32	49.23	65
All Groups	393	67.99	185	32.01	578

Pearson Chi-square: 15.9264, df=2, p=.000349

Chi-square test has proved significant association between the status of the user and the level of satisfaction over the Internet services provided.

Table 1.3.79 clearly shows the poor level of satisfaction among the faculty members over the Internet services provided by the university libraries.

IMPROVEMENT OVER INTERNET SERVICES / FACILITIES PROVIDED

In order to understand the shortcomings with regard to the Internet services provided, users of the Internet facilities were asked whether they find the Internet services provided by the library sufficient or do they feel need for any other facility with regard to the Internet services. This question was an open ended one as users may have different needs and views with regard to the improvement of the services. Out of the 578 users of Internet, 67.99 per cent responded that they find the services provided sufficient while the remaining 32.01 per cent respondents found to be dissatisfied with the facilities provided and wanted improvement over the facility. 49 of them were from KUL, 42 from MGUL, 51 from CUSATL and 43 from CUL. They were asked to mention their requirements hence they specified it. It was found that the highest demand made was for sufficient number of computers. A total of 58.38 per cent responded thus. Lack of sufficient E-resources has been reported by 6.49 per cent users and they wanted the respective libraries subscribe to more E-resources. Copying facility (both hard copy and soft copy) was demanded by 11.76 per cent of the respondents from CUSATL while in CUL no one has demanded this. Internet service without charging any fee was demanded by 6.12 per cent from KUL and 2.33 per cent from CUL. Extension of the Internet service to the departments were demanded by respondents from MGUL while in other three universities the Internet facility is available in many of the teaching departments and users found to be satisfied over it. Users also demand secrecy at the time of browsing and they account to 2.04 per cent from KUL and 4.77 per cent from MGUL. Other suggestions included extension of time duration allotted to users and many of them complained that by the time they locate required information their allotted time might be over and had to leave the place for the next person in waiting without downloading the information. Users also suggested instructors in the use of Internet as well as providing proper guidance in the use of facility.

Table 1.3.80 Other Internet Facilities and Services Needed - Library wise Responses

Other Services Needed	*KUL*	*MGUL*	*CUSATL*	*CUL*	*Total*
Copying Facility (Hard & Soft)	2(4.08%)	1(2.38%)	6(11.76%)	0(0.00%)	9(4.86%)
Adequate Machines	32 (65.31%)	26 (61.90%)	27 (52.94%)	23 (53.49%)	108 (58.38%)
Free Service	3(6.12%)	0(0.00%)	0(0.00%)	0(0.00%)	3(1.62%)
Secrecy	1(2.04%)	2(4.76%)	0(0.00%)	0(0.00%)	3(1.62%)
Adequate Machines, More E Resources	4(8.16%)	3(7.14%)	2(3.92%)	1(2.33%)	10(5.41%)
Free Service, Adequate Machines	2(4.08%)	0(0.00%)	0(0.00%)	1(2.33%)	3(1.62%)
Instructor/ Orientation, Adequate Machines	1(2.04%)	0(0.00%)	0(0.00%)	1(2.33%)	2(1.08%)

Other Services Needed	*KUL*	*MGUL*	*CUSATL*	*CUL*	*Total*
Sufficient Time Allocation	1(2.04%)	0(0.00%)	2(3.92%)	3(6.98%)	6(3.24%)
More E Resources	1(2.04%)	4(9.52%)	5(9.80%)	24.65%)	12(6.49%)
Instructor/ Orientation	1(2.04%)	0(0.00%)	0(0.00%)	0(0.00%)	1(0.54%)
Adequate Machines, Sufficient Time Allocation, More E Resources	1(2.04%)	0(0.00%)	0(0.00%)	0(0.00%)	1(0.54%)
Adequate Machines, Sufficient Time Allocation	0(0.00%)	1(2.38%)	5(9.80%)	3(6.98%)	9(4.86%)
Extension of Service to Department	0(0.00%)	3(7.14%)	1(1.96%)	0(0.00%)	4(2.16%)
Adequate Machines, Sufficient Time Allocation, Extension of Service to Department	0(0.00%)	2(4.76%)	0(0.00%)	0(0.00%)	2(1.08%)
Adequate Machines, Copying Facility (Hard & Soft)	0(0.00%)	0(0.00%)	3(5.88%)	2(4.65%)	5(2.70%)
Adequate Machines, Extension of Service to Department	0(0.00%)	0(0.00%)	0(0.00%)	1(2.33%)	1(0.54%)
Adequate Machines, Copying Facility (Hard & Soft), Sufficient Time Allocation	0(0.00%)	0(0.00%)	0(0.00%)	3(6.98%)	3(1.62%)
Instructor/ Orientation, Adequate Machines and Sufficient Time Allocation	0(0.00%)	0(0.00%)	0(0.00%)	1(2.33%)	1(0.54%)
Access to Other International Libraries	0(0.00%)	0(0.00%)	0(0.00%)	1(2.33%)	1(0.54%)
Free Service, Adequate Machines and More E Resources	0(0.00%)	0(0.00%)	0(0.00%)	1(2.33%)	1(0.54%)
All Groups	49	42	51	43	185

Table 1.3.81 gives the details of demand for other services and facilities with regard to Internet by Science and Social Science groups.

Table 1.3.81 Other Internet Facilities and Services Needed : Subject wise Responses

Other Services Needed	*SocialScience*	*Science*	*Totals*
Copying Facility (Hard & Soft)	4(7.27%)	5(3.85%)	9(4.86%)
Adequate Machines	38(69.09%)	70(53.85%)	108(58.38%)
Free Service	1(1.82%)	2(1.54%)	3(1.62%)
Secrecy	1(1.82%)	2(1.54%)	3(1.62%)
Adequate Machines, More E Resources	2(3.64%)	8(6.15%)	10(5.41%)
Free Service, Adequate Machines	0(0.00%)	3(2.13%)	3(1.62%)
Instructor/Orientation, Adequate Machines	0(0.00%)	2(1.54%)	2(1.08%)
Sufficient Time Allocation	1(1.82%)	5(3.85%)	6(3.24%)
More E Resources	1(1.82%)	11(8.46%)	12(6.49%)
Instructor/Orientation	0(0.00%)	1(0.77%)	1(0.54%)
Adequate Machines, Sufficient Time Allocation, More E Resources	0(0.00%)	1(0.77%)	1(0.54%)
Adequate Machines, Sufficient Time Allocation	2(3.64%)	7(5.38%)	9(4.86%)
Extension of Service to Department	0(0.00%)	4(3.08%)	4(2.16%)
Adequate Machines, Sufficient Time Allocation, Extension of Service to Department	0(0.00%)	2(1.54%)	2(1.08%)
Adequate Machines, Copying Facility (Hard & Soft)	2(3.64%)	3(2.31%)	5(2.70%)
Adequate Machines, Extension of Service to Department	0(0.00%)	1(0.77%)	1(0.54%)
Adequate Machines, Copying Facility (Hard & Soft), Sufficient Time Allocation	2(3.64%)	1(0.77%)	3(1.62%)
Instructor/Orientation, Adequate Machines and Sufficient Time Allocation.	0(0.00%)	1(0.77%)	1(0.54%)

Other Services Needed	*SocialScience*	*Science*	*Totals*
Access to Other International Libraries	1(1.82%)	0(0.00%)	1(0.54%)
Free Service, Adequate Machines and More E Resources	0(0.00%)	1(0.77%)	1(0.54%)
All Groups	55	130	185

It was found that users with Science background, compared to those who belong to Social Sciences demanded more E-resources.

What ever may be the combinations; higher percentage of users with Science background demanded more e-resources. This shows that they are not satisfied with the subject contents they receive through Internet and want the respective libraries subscribe to more E-Resources. Libraries need to take measures to procure more E resources in Science subjects on a consortia basis.

Table 1.3.82 provides Status wise demand of other Internet services and facilities. The percentage of faculty members who demand for adequate machines are found to be much higher compared to the other category of users. This shows that the teachers find it difficult to get sufficient nodes for browsing.

It is found in all the analysis regarding the other services/facilities needed that there is an acute shortage of adequate number of computers in proper working conditions in all the universities. The highest number of respondents demanded for sufficient computers and their need for more E-resources comes after this need only. Analysis on the available hardware in the libraries have proved that libraries are running with very old computers and the latest Pentium IV machines are very less and in some libraries it is not available also. Hence steps need to be taken to procure latest computers by making sufficient funds available for the purpose.

Table 1.3.82 Other Internet Facilities and Services Needed : - Status wise Responses

Other Services Needed	*Students*	*Research Scholars*	*Teachers*	*Totals*
Copying Facility (Hard & Soft)	8(6.96%)	1(2.63%)	0(0.00%)	9(4.86%)
Adequate Machines	68 (59.13%)	18 (47.37%)	22 (68.75%)	108 (58.38%)
Free Service	2(1.74%)	1(2.63%)	0(0.00%)	3(1.62%)
Secrecy	3(2.61%)	0(0.00%)	0(0.00%)	3(1.62%)
Adequate Machines, More E Resources	6(5.22%)	3(7.89%)	1(3.13%)	10(5.41%)
Free Service, Adequate Machines	2(1.74%)	1(2.63%)	0(0.00%)	3(1.62%)
Instructor/Orientation, Adequate Machines	1(0.87%)	1(2.63%)	0(0.00%)	2(1.08%)
Sufficient Time Allocation	5(4.35%)	1(2.63%)	0(0.00%)	6(3.24%)
More E Resources	4(3.48%)	7(18.42%)	1(3.13%)	12(6.49%)
Instructor/Orientation	0(0.00%)	1(2.63%)	0(0.00%)	1(0.54%)
Adequate Machines, Sufficient Time Allocation, More E Resources	0(0.00%)	0(0.00%)	1(3.13%)	1(0.54%)
Adequate Machines, Sufficient Time Allocation	7(6.09%)	2(5.26%)	0(0.00%)	9(4.86%)
Extension of Service to Department	1(0.87%)	0(0.00%)	3(9.38%)	4(2.16%)
Adequate Machines, Sufficient Time Allocation, Extension of Service to Department	0(0.00%)	0(0.00%)	2(6.25%)	2(1.08%)
Adeqµate Machines, Copying Facility (Hard & Soft)	5(4.35%)	0(0.00%)	0(0.00%)	5(2.70%)
Adequate Machines, Extension of Service to Dep.	1(0.87%)	0(0.00%)	0(0.00%)	1(0.54%)
Adequate Machines, Copying Facility (Hard & Soft), Sufficient Time Allocation	2(1.74%)	0(0.00%)	1(3.13%)	3(1.62%)
Instructor/Orientation, Adequate Machines and Sufficient Time Allocation	0(0.00%)	1(2.63%)	0(0.00%)	1(0.54%)
Access to Other International Libraries	0(0.00%)	1(2.63%)	0(0.00%)	1(0.54%)
Free Service, Adequate Machines & More E Resources	0(0.00%)	0(0.00%)	1(3.13%)	1(0.54%)
All Groups	115	38	32	185

DIGITIZATION OF DOCUMENTS

Our universities generate huge intellectual contents and these valuable contents are usually marketed and profit made out of it by outside publishers. Internal contents of each university include Theses and Dissertations, Research or Annual Reports and other publications, issued by the university. Similarly there may be research publications and proceedings of conferences hosted by the universities. Contents generated in-house by not-for-profit institutions can also be collected and hosted in a distributed fashion by different departments and institutions in the universities and made available at least for the use of the academics in the state.

No university library under study has made digitization of documents to any considerable extent. CUSATL has just made a beginning in this direction by attempting digitization of their Theses collection and it is in the infancy stage only. Kerala University Library has decided to digitize their archive collection under the Kerala Studies Section. Table 4.1 reveals that all the universities have a good collection of Theses that are unique sources of information hence very valuable also. Making it available in digital form will enhance its use and the same will help the libraries to preserve such unique sources without any damage in future. Digitization and sharing of the information will help to reduce duplication of studies conducted on local situations as well as in the regional literature. There should be concrete efforts to begin Electronic Thesis and Dissertation (ETD) projects and to digitize unique collections that do not come under the purview of copyright act.

SERVICES PROVIDED OVER INTERNET BY THE UNIVERSITY LIBRARIES

Out of the four University Libraries under study, KUL, CUSATL and CUL have their official web pages as part of the university website while MGUL has not yet hosted their web page though the official university web site is available over net and it is known that the site will be hosted soon. Services of the library can be extended beyond the library premises through the web sites reaching a wide range of users without geographical barriers. Libraries can provide their general as well as specialized services to remote users through their web site. It was observed as well as ascertained by examining the University Library websites that none of the library provides web based Reference Service and specialized services like CAS, SDI etc. through their websites. CUSATL is the only library that makes its catalogue available over the web while none of the others have this facility. All the three libraries provide their new additions list through their home page and are seen frequently updated and this is the single information service provided by all the libraries through their websites. The following Table 1.3.83 depicts the information provided and services rendered by the libraries through their web sites.

All the libraries provide general information about the library, collection and service details and information regarding attaining membership in the library. None of the libraries provide online membership registration facility. All the libraries have given library working-hours while CUL only lists the library holidays of the year. Similarly CUL only has provision for downloading the membership form from the site. None of the sites provides links to other University Libraries in the state. CUSATL has provided link to two sources of free journals while CUL has provided link to the INFLIBNET web site. Staff member details are not provided by any of the library and there is no facility for online renewal of borrowed items and online reservation of issued out documents. CUL and CUSATL have provision for notifying the events related with the library while KUL is seen ignored this. The sites under study found to be informative about the library activities while the information services provided through these sites are not remarkable.

CONCLUSION

The above analysis based on information collected from the university libraries of the state as well as the representative samples of users of these libraries has revealed the present state of affairs of computer applications in these libraries and

Table 1.3.83 Comparison of the Websites of the University libraries under study

Website Details	*KUL*	*CUSATL*	*CUL*
General Information	Yes	Yes	Yes
Library Collection details	Yes	Yes	Yes
Library Services details	Yes	Yes	Yes
Contact details (Email & telephone)	Yes	Yes	Yes
Library Working Hours	Yes	Yes	Yes
Library Holidays	No	No	Yes
Staff details	No	No	No
Membership attainment details	Yes	Yes	Yes
Downloadable membership application form	No	No	Yes
Online Registration of Membership	No	No	No
New Arrivals List	Yes	Yes	Yes
Online Catalogue Access	No	Yes	No
Online renewal of borrowed items	No	No	No
Online reservation of documents	No	No	No
Link to other libraries and institutions	Nil	2	1
Events Notifications	No	Yes	Yes

its level of reach to the users for whom it is intended and the aspirations and requirements of the users.

Having discussed the state of the art of computerisation in the University libraries under study along with the responses of the user in this chapter, the major findings of the study as well as certain suggestions for the improvement of the existing facilities are given in the succeeding chapter.

REFERENCE :

1. Kumbar, T S et.al. (2000). **Development of Union databases at INFLIBNET and role of University Libraries**. In *Information Services in a networked world.* Seventh National Convention for Automation of Libraries in Education and Research (CALIBER 2000), Chennai, India, 16 – 18 February 2000, Organized by University of Madras, Chennai and INFLIBNET Centre, Ahmedabad, edited by R Vengan, H R Mohan and K S Raghavan. Ahmedabad: INFLIBNET Centre. P. 3.43.

an iterative sequence. This sequence include :

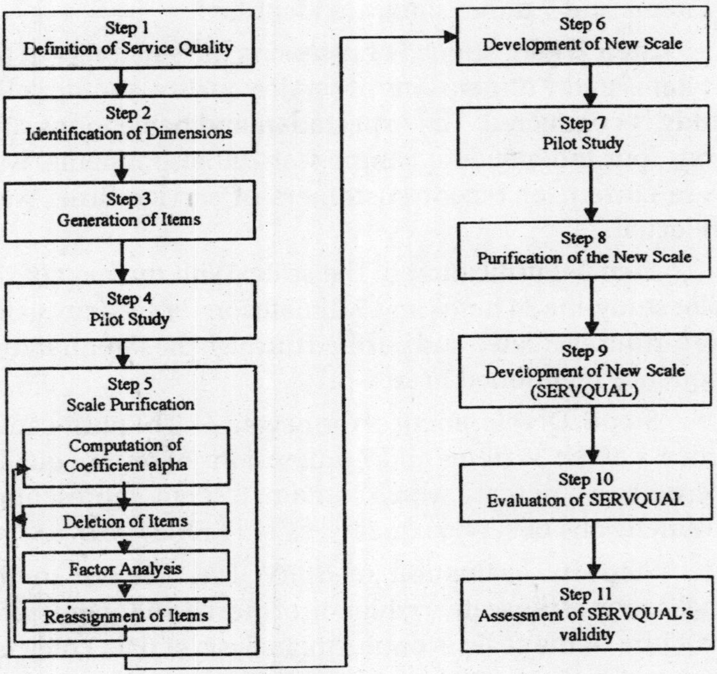

Figure 10.3. Steps for the Construction of SERVQUAL Scale

1. Computation of coefficient alpha and item-to-total correlations for each dimensions.
2. Deletion of items whose item-to total correlations were low and whose removal increased coefficient alpha
3. Factor analysis to verify the dimensionality of the overall scale.
4. Reassignment of items and re-structuring of dimensions wherever necessary
5. Repetition of the above 4 steps till the scale purification is complete.

Step 6. Development of purified scale: As a result of the purification process of the 97 items and the 10 dimensions of service quality, a modified scale containing 34 items and 7 dimensions are identified.

Step 7. Pilot study: For assessing the suitability of the 34 items and 7 dimensions of service quality, another pilot study is conducted. The expectation and perceptions data from four independent samples of 200 respondents, who were current or recent customers of service firms were collected.

Step 8. Purification of the scale: With the help of the pilot study, the 34 items and 7 dimensions of service quality are further evaluated and purified through the same iterative sequence mentioned in step 5.

Step 9. Development of the new scale: The purification process of the 34 items and 7 dimensions of service quality identified a new scale, which contains 22 items representing 5 dimensions of service quality, called SERVQUAL

Step 10. Evaluation of SERVQUAL. Before to the finalisation of the scale, evaluation of the reliability and factor structure of the scale is done. An analysis of data collected in step 4 is done to prove the SERVQUAL's reliability and factor structure.

Step 11. Assessment of SERVQUAL's validity. Research to assess the validity and applicability of the SERVQUAL instrument in different service environments.

The conceptual foundation for the SERVQUAL scale was derived from the works of researchers who examined the meaning of service quality and from a comprehensive qualitative research study that defined service quality precisely and identified the dimensions along which the customers perceive and evaluate service quality.

SERVQUAL scale measure perceived quality of a service firm or a specific service. Perceived quality is the consumers judgment about an entity's overall excellence or superiority. It is a form of attitude, related but no equivalent to satisfaction, results from the comparison of expectations with perceptions of performance.

SERVQUAL instrument uses 22 pairs of 7-point Likert scale statements to measure the five dimensions of service quality, namely Tangibles, Reliability, Responsiveness, Assurance and Empathy. The first 22 statements are designed to measure customer expectations while the remaining 22 are intended to measure the perceive level of service provided by a particular service firm. The level of service quality is determined by subtracting the perceived service score from the customers' expectation score for each of the statement. This method of determining service quality is called the GAP theory.

The SERVQUAL questionnaire is given as Appendix to this chapter.

Initially, the SERVQUAL study identified the criteria used by customers in assessing, service quality, called dimensions. These 10 dimensions identified are: tangibles, reliability, responsiveness, communication, credibility, security, competence, courtesy, understanding/knowing the customer and access. These 10 dimensions and their descriptions served as the basis of SERVQUAL scale. Then items representing these dimensions were generated. Accordingly 97 items were identified. Each of these item are recasted into two statements, one to measure expectations and the other to measure the perceptions of service quality. A seven point scale ranging form 'strongly agree' (7) to strongly disagree (1), with no verbal labels for scale points 2 through 6. The first half of the SERVQUAL instrument contains statements on expectations and the other contains statements on perceptions. The perceived service quality is derived on the basis of the principle 'Q = P - E' where Q = Perceived service quality, P = Perceptions and E = Expectations.

The reliability and factor structure of the SERVQUAL scale was evaluated and found that the reliabilities and factor structures are consistently high. The total-scale reliability was also found very high. The reliabilities and factor structures indicates that the final scale and its five dimensions have sound and stable psychometric properties. Therefore, SERVQUAL can be used in its original form to assess and compare service quality across a wide variety of service firms or units within a firm, or a particular service. Appropriate adaptation of the instrument for specific services or service firms is desirable. Items under each of the five dimensions can be suitably reworded or augment to the context in which the instrument is to be used.

As part of the assessment of SERQUAL's validity, the content validity and scale's validity (does the scale appear to measure what it is supposed to? and do the scale items capture key facets of the unobservable construct being measured?), are evaluated and found that it possess both content validity and scale's validity very well. Its validity was further assessed by examining whether the construct measured by it was empirically associated with measures of other conceptually related variables.

The instrument has been designed to be applicable across a broad spectrum of services. It provides a basic skeleton through its expectations/perceptions format encompassing statements for each of the five service quality dimensions. The skeleton can be adapted or supplemented to fit the characteristics or needs of a particular organization.

Applications of SERVQUAL are:

1. Understand the service expectations and perceptions of customers.
2. Understand service quality trends periodically
3. Assess firms quality along each of the five service dimensions

19. Large majority of the Computer Nodes available in the University Libraries in Kerala belongs to 486, Pentium I, Pentium II or Celron class machines that are very old and out dated models.
20. Pentium IV machines, the latest in the personal computer series, are not available in CUSATL and CUL. KUL have only 6 and MGUL only 5 Pentium IV computers. This reveals that the University Libraries under study mostly depend on old machines that are error prone and may put limitations on the users in using some of the applications especially in web related applications.
21. Laptop Computer that helps in conducting effective user education programmes both inside as well as out side the library is available only in CUL.
22. LCD projector, which is very essential for conducting effective training programmes and user education programmes is not available in any of the University Library under study.
23. Web Camera, equipment very much needed during Internet visual communication sessions is not available in any of the University Libraries.
24. Over-Head Scanner that is necessary for high volume digitization work is not available in the University Libraries in Kerala.
25. CUL does not have a CD Server which is very much needed for providing CD based Services.

SOFTWARE USED

26. All the libraries are using proprietary software. KUL and CUL use Libsys, costly commercial software, MGUL is using SOUL, which is comparatively cheaper, developed and marketed by INFLIBENT and CUSATL uses ADLIB, foreign costly commercial software

received as part of the foreign aid to the University. CUSATL only have a web-enabled software.

27. For word processing, spreadsheets and presentation purposes all the University Libraries under study are using Microsoft products.
28. Application of open source software in the University Libraries under study is limited to the use of Linux Operating System in CUL and KUL and Mozilla as well as Netscape Navigator as Internet Browsers in CUL.
29. Digital Library Software is available only in KUL and CUSATL.29. None of the University Library has Optical Character Recognition software that is needed for conversion of the digitized texts and images.

MANPOWER

30. Presently CUSATL only have a University Librarian. In other libraries the senior most professional is put in charge of the University Librarian.
31. Only CUSATL and CUL filled the post of Information Scientist sanctioned by UGC. Therefore KUL and MGUL have no qualified persons to look after the computerised activities and Assistant Librarians without any qualification in Computer Science / Application are put in charge of the Computer Sections.
32. University Libraries in Kerala in general are not equipped with adequate number of qualified staff to handle the computerised activities. In KUL, all the four staff, the Assistant Librarian, the Reference Assistant, the Technical Assistant and the Library Assistant working in the Computer Section possess MA and MLib.Sc. And the Technical Assistant additionally possesses Diploma in Computer Applications. In MGUL two Assistant Librarians with MLISc and two Reference Assistants one with MLISc and another with BLISc and PGDCA qualifications are working in the

Computer Section. In CUSATL one Information Scientist with M Tech. and in CUL one Information Scientist with MA MLib.Sc, PGDCA and PGDLAN and two Professional Assistants, one with MA BLISc and the other with MLISc are working in the Computer Section.

33. The persons in charge of Computer Sections in KUL, MGUL and CUL have obtained training on various aspects of library computerisation where as the person in charge of Computerisation in CUSATL has not obtained training on any aspects of library computerisation and has not attended any workshop/seminar related with library computerisation.

AREAS OF APPLICATIONS OF COMPUTERS

34. None of the University Library studied is totally computerised. They are yet to computerise some of their operations or services. KUL has not applied computers in Circulation procedure, Digitization of documents, Reference Service, Intra Library communications, Stock Verification, and Financial management. MGUL has not applied computer in Serials Control, Digitization of documents, Reference Service, Intra Library Communications, Stock Verification, and Financial Management. CUSATL has not applied computers in Stock Verification and Financial management and CUL has not applied in Digitization of documents, Reference Service, Intra Library Communications and Financial management.

35. Computerised CAS, SDI and User Education services are provided by MGUL and CUSATL only. All the University Libraries provide Computer assisted Circulation of Accession List, Online database, Full text services and Internet services. All the libraries except CUL provide multimedia services and CD/DVD based

services. None of the libraries provide Content Page Service. None of the libraries is using Smart Card for member identification, microchips for document identification, totally automated check-in/check-out systems and electronic theft detection systems.

36. Only CUL have computerised stock verification system and using barcodes for feeding the data of documents during stock verification.

37. Most of the modern applications of computers are totally absent in the University Libraries studied.

USER AWARENESS ABOUT COMPUTERISED SERVICES AND AVAILABILITY OF THE SERVICES

38. User awareness about various computerised library and information services was found to be very poor.

39. All the computerised services, except the Internet service are not reaching the target users properly. This handicap was reflected in the general awareness about the services also. It means that majority of the computerised services are not properly interpreted to the users. Though MGUL and CUSATL provided user education services, it is revealed that only 22.78 per cent got any orientation in the use of services provided by them. In case of the other two libraries no user education programmes are conducted and there is an urgent need for bringing the services to the notice of the users. But none of the libraries under study possess an LCD Projector. Without such a facility no university library in this era can properly educate the larger community of users about the use of various computerised services provided by them.

CURRENT AWARENESS SERVICE

40. An overall 51.9 per cent of users are aware about CAS. In KUL 50.23 percent, in MGUL 57.21 percent, in

CUSATL 59.75 percent and in CUL 41.58 per cent are aware about the service.

41. Majority of the users (51.05%) are not getting the Current Awareness Service where it is provided and KUL and CUL are not providing this service. In MGUL 45.27 per cent and in CUSATL 52.83 per cent only are getting the service.

SELECTIVE DISSEMINATION OF INFORMATION

42. Overall 25.36 per cent of awareness was found about this specialized service. In KUL it is 28.37 per cent, in MGUL 27.86 per cent in CUSATL 23.27 per cent and in CUL 21.05 per cent of users only are aware about the service.

43. The service is available to only 18.82 per cent of the users with 19.4 per cent in MGUL and 18.24 per cent in CUSATL

CIRCULATION OF NEW ADDITIONS LIST

44. Overall 34.77 per cent of users are aware about the service. In KUL 28.37 per cent, in MGUL 44.28 percent, in CUSATL 38.36 per cent and in CUL 28.95 per cent are aware about the service.

45. Overall availability of the service is 26.93 per cent only. In KUL 19.07 per cent, in MGUL 33.83 per cent, in CUSATL 32.08 per cent and in CUL 24.21 per cent are getting this service.

ONLINE DATABASE SERVICE

46. Overall 41.7 per cent of users are aware about Online Database Service. In KUL 41.86 per cent, in MGUL 46.27 per cent, in CUSATL 54.72 per cent and in CUL 25.79 per cent are aware about this service

47. Overall 30.72 per cent of the users are getting the service. In KUL 30.7 per cent, in MGUL 38.81 per cent, in CUSATL 43.40 per cent and in CUL only 11.58 per cent are getting online database services.

ONLINE FULL TEXT SERVICES

48. An overall 53.07 per cent of the users are found to be aware about full text services. In KUL 51.63 per cent, in MGUL 69.65 per cent, in CUSATL 55.97 per cent and in CUL 34.74 per cent are aware about the service.
49. Overall availability of the service is 40.39 per cent only with 34.88 per cent in KUL, 61.69 per cent in MGUL, 42.77 per cent in CUSATL and only 22.11 per cent in CUL.

CD / DVD BASED SERVICES

50. An overall 41.83 per cent awareness about the CD/ DVD based service is found among the users. In KUL 42.33 per cent, in MGUL 59.7 per cent, in CUSATL 43.4 per cent and in CUL 21.05 per cent are aware about this service.
51. The service is reaching only to an overall 33.04 per cent of the users in case of the libraries where it is provided with 20 per cent in KUL, 51.74 percent in MGUL, and 27.04 per cent in CUSATL.

INTERNET SERVICES

52. High rate of awareness of 93.2 per cent were found among the users with 88.84 per cent in KUL, 97.51 per cent in MGUL, 96.23 per cent in CUSATL and 91.05 per cent in CUL.
53. Overall 85.62 per cent of users are found really getting Internet services with 85.58 per cent in KUL, 94.53 per cent in MGUL93.08 per cent in CUSATL and 70 per cent in CUL.

USER EDUCATION SERVICES

54. Awareness about User Education services is found as 26.98 per cent in KUL, 31.84 per cent in MGUL, 37.74 per cent in CUSATL and 16.84 per cent in CUL

55. Only 19.9 per cent in MGUL and 26.42 per cent in CUSATL are getting this service.

COMPUTER APPLICATION IN VARIOUS OPERATIONS AND SERVICES : DATABASE CREATION

56. All the University Libraries have completed the retrospective conversion of their bibliographical records. Transliteration method is used for records other than in English language. Record structure adheres to ISO 2709 standard.
57. Different standards are used for Classification, Cataloguing and Subject descriptors by the University Libraries studied.
58. The University Libraries studied have taken adequate measures for securing the valuable data by taking backup of the data regularly using reliable medium for data storage.

ACQUISITION PROCEDURES

59. MGUL and CUL have applied computers in almost all the aspects of Acquisition procedures. CUSATL is not using it for Invoice processing and for Budget handling and KUL is not using for Budget handling.

CIRCULATION PROCEDURES

60. KUL has not computerised the circulation procedures. All other three University Libraries are using computer for almost all circulation procedures except that CUSATL is not using for overdue calculation.
61. User awareness about the circulation services provided found to be varying among University Libraries. In CUSATL awareness among users about computerised circulation services is low (76.73%) while in CUL it is high (92.11%).
62. All the services that are to be provided under the circulation module such as Issue/Return/Renewal,

Reservation, Fine collection and Enquiry are reaching to a minority of 10.28 per cent only. In CUSATL only 7.38 per cent claimed to be getting all the circulation services provided by the library and in MGUL it is 18.82 per cent and in CUL 4.57 per cent only.

63. It is found that majority (44.11%) of the users are getting the Issue / Return / Renewal of documents only under the circulation module.

64. Even after maintaining the traditional practices of circulation procedures as a security measure, users rated the computerised circulation procedure time saving. In MGUL 95.29 per cent, in CUSATL 84.43 per cent and in CUL 91.43 per cent found the present system time saving. A slightly lower rate is recorded in CUSATL due to the fact that the overdue collection is done in CUSATL manually.

65. It was found that the large majority of the users are satisfied with the existing circulation system and they do not want any more addition to this service. In MGUL 6.47 per cent, in CUSATL 13.11 per cent and in CUL 10.29 per cent only responded that they need other computerised circulation services. But a very few, were able to specify what other services are needed by them.

SERIALS CONTROL

66 None of the University Library is found making total utilization of computers in the Serials Control System.

67. In KUL and MGUL the applications in Serials module are too limited. KUL is making use of the module for article indexing only while MGUL is using it for Ordering and making entry of the receipt of the journal. CUSATL is making use of the system for Ordering, making receipt of the journal issue, sending reminders, budget handling, invoice processing, accessioning and Current Awareness Service. CUL is using computers

for Ordering, making receipt of the journal issue, sending reminders, budget handling, invoice processing, accessioning, sending for bindery and article indexing. CUSATL is not making use of the system for Routing of periodicals, sending for bindery, article indexing, SDI and check in/check out. CUL is not using Routing, CAS, SDI, and check in/check out. In a nutshell, KUL and MGUL do not make use of the Serials module up to any considerable extent while CUSATL and CUL use it for limited operations.

68. Use of computers in the Serials module in the University Libraries under study is more confined to the housekeeping operations and its use in the provisions of services to the clientele is found very limited.

OPAC

69. It was observed that apart from OPAC, libraries are maintaining the traditional card catalogue also.
70. All the libraries provide access to Books database and MGUL, CUSATL and CUL provide access to Journals and Theses database also. CUSATL provides access to Audio Visual Material database also.
71. All the libraries found providing access points such as Author, Title, Subject and Words in title. Except CUSATL, all others are providing access through class number and publisher. Access through Place of publication is given by CUSATL and CUL only. Access through Series is given by MGUL only. Access through Year of publication is given by CUSATL only. All the libraries provide Boolean search facility and truncation facility. Word proximity search is permitted by only KUL and CUL.
72. No University Library studied entertains reservation of issued out document through OPAC. All the library OPACs entertain knowing the status of the document.

73. OPAC of KUL only permits suggestion of new titles for procurement.
74. Only in CUSATL the OPAC is available over the campus LAN and Internet.
75. KUL has provided a single OPAC terminal to the users while MGUL and CUL have two each and CUSATL has 4 terminals.
76. In MGUL, CUSATL and CUL higher level of awareness about OPAC is found among the users while in KUL the awareness among users about OPAC is 72.09 per cent only.
77. Users from Science subjects are more aware about OPAC than those from Social Science subjects. Teachers are more aware about OPAC compared to Students and Research Scholars.
78. It was found that OPAC is being made use by an overall 82.88 per cent of the users. CUL has the highest rate of OPAC users with 93.68 per cent using it while KUL has the lowest rate of OPAC use with only 61.86 per cent.
79. Compared to Social Science subjects, users from Science subjects are found to be making more use of OPAC.
80. Among the users Teachers are making more use of OPAC followed by the Students and the Research Scholars.
81. It was found that the mostly used access point is the name of the Author and is followed by Title and Subject. Words in title was also found to be made use by many users while the usage of other points are very limited. In general the access points used are not different from that of the traditional card catalogue.
82. None from Researchers found to be using Truncation and Word Proximity Searches. Teachers are also not found to be using Truncation Search.

83. The access points used by Students, Research Scholars and Teachers are almost the same and it was observed that in the traditional catalogue almost the same access points are found used.

84. The peculiar features of electronic catalogue such as Boolean Search, Truncation Search, and Word Proximity Search have not been made use by any groups of users to any considerable extent.

85. Users from all the libraries irrespective of subject background and status found to be highly satisfied over the access points provided in the OPAC.

86. It was found that some users only got orientation in the use of OPAC. In MGUL the highest percentage (45.36%) got the orientation while in CUL the lowest percentage (24.16%) got orientation in the use of OPAC.

87. Trial and error method and learning from friends found to be the favourate methods adopted by the users for learning use of OPAC.

88. There are shortages of adequate number of terminals to browse OPAC in the University Libraries studied. In CUL 69.66 per cent, in MGUL 66.67 per cent and in KUL 58.65 per cent and in CUSATL 45.71 per cent of users expressed that they had to wait for their turn to use the OPAC.

INFLIBNET SUPPORT

89. All the University Libraries received financial aid from INFLIBNET according to its priorities. KUL, being an old university, got 52 Lakhs Rupees while the other three University Libraries received Rs. 6.5 Lakh each.

90. CUSATL and CUL only have utilized the support provided to appoint Information Scientist.

91. INFLIBNET provided manpower training for library computerisation to all the University Libraries studied.

92. All the libraries have got the UGC Infonet facility with 1 Mbps bandwidth connection and E-Resources are made available to the libraries through this. CUL is yet to make proper utilization of the facility due to shortage of adequate infrastructure.

PARTICIPATION IN INFLIBNET ACTIVITIES

93. All the University Libraries have contributed their records to the INFLIBNET union catalogue database. Yet a good amount of records are still to be sent by these libraries.

94. All the University Libraries except CUSATL conducted the IRTPLA programme helping library professionals from universities and affiliated colleges to gain knowledge in computerisation and the use of SOUL software.

NETWORK INFRASTRUCTURE

95. All the University Libraries have a LAN within the library. But only CUSATL and KUL have a campus LAN and the library LAN of CUSATL only is accessible through campus LAN as well as Internet. LANs connected to Internet are protected through Firewall.

96. All the libraries participate in the INFLIBNET while MGUL and CUSATL participate in the DELNET also. MGUL has membership in AIRC (American Information Resource Centre) network also.

97. CUSATL and CUL have Router installed in the library and the library network is protected through firewall implementation.

INTERNET

98. All the libraries have Internet connection with 1 Mbps bandwidth and are providing Internet services to the academic community.

99. The University Libraries impart training to the users in the use of Internet Services.

100. Provision of terminals for using Internet in the University Libraries is very meager. KUL and CUSATL provide only 12 computer nodes each and MGUL and CUL provide only 10 computer nodes each to the users of the entire University community. This numbers are too less to meet the demand from users.

101. MGUL, CUSATL and CUL are providing Internet services to Students, Research Scholars and Teachers while KUL provides to the public also.

102. KUL charges fee from users of Internet on hourly basis where as CUL charges on yearly basis. The fee charged by CUL is very high. MGUL and CUSATL do not charge any fee from Internet users.

103. MGUL has got the highest rate (89.05 % of users) of Internet usage followed by CUSATL (84.91%) and KUL (75.81%). CUL has the lowest (53.16%) rate of Internet usage.

104. The users with Science background are found making more use of Internet than those with Social Science background.

105. Almost similar level of usage habit is found among various categories of users and Teachers use Internet services more followed by Research Scholars and Students.

106. In the use of Internet, Browsing, Communication and obtaining E-Resources are found to be the priority of the majority of the users.

107. Users from Science subjects found to be using Internet for serious purposes than those from Social Science subjects.

108. Study and Research were found to be the main purposes

of Internet usage among the users of Internet in the University Libraries of Kerala. The majority of Students used Internet for Study purpose and the majority of Research Scholars and Teachers used Internet for Research purpose.

109. Training in the use of Internet services is received by 30 per cent of the users only. Highest percentage of trained users was found in MGUL and the lowest percentage is in CUSATL.

110. Among different status groups of users Research Scholars got the highest rate of training followed by Students and Teachers.

111. The majority of the users are using Internet services without any training in the use of the service.

112. Users from all the Universities have almost same level of satisfaction over getting information from Internet. In KUL 82.82 per cent, in MGUL 87.71 per cent, in CUSATL 84.44 per cent and in CUL 81.19 per ccnt claimed that they are getting the required information from Internet.

113. Internet users from Science subjects are more satisfied on getting required information from Internet than those from Social Science subjects.

114. Research Scholars are more satisfied with the information they are getting followed by the Students and the Teachers have the least satisfaction.

115. Majority of the users from all the Universities is not satisfied with the speed of the Internet connection.

116. Teachers found to be the most dissatisfied about the speed of the connection followed by Research Scholars and Students.

117. Users from MGUL have the highest satisfaction over the Internet services provided followed by KUL and CUSATL. The users of CUL have the least satisfaction.

118. Satisfaction over the existing Internet facility is more among Social Science people compared to those from Science background.
119. Students are more satisfied with the existing Internet facilities in the University Libraries while Teachers are least satisfied
120. Majority of the users from all the University Libraries demanded adequate number of machines for their use.
121. Science users demanded more E-Resources than the Social Sciences users.
122. The proportion of Teachers who ask for adequate machines are much higher compared to other category of users.

DIGITIZATION

123. None of the University Library has seriously started digitization though these libraries have good collection of Theses and Dissertations.

UNIVERSITY WEBSITES

124. All the University Libraries studied, except MGUL have their website as part of the University website and only CUSATL have the web OPAC.
125. Websites of the University Libraries are not providing many of the services needed by the users like online renewal of documents borrowed as their computerised systems are not web enabled.
126. University Libraries studied have not taken seriously the need for providing information services through their websites. None of the library provides general services like Reference Service and specialized service like CAS, SDI through Internet.

SUGGESTIONS FOR IMPROVING THE COMPUTERISED UNIVERSITY LIBRARY SYSTEM

On the basis of the findings unveiled by the study certain suggestions are put forwarded here for the improvement of the computerisation process of the University Libraries in Kerala.

1. Collections of the University Libraries should be developed in a balanced manner giving due share to digital resources also. KUL should properly record the collection clearly distinguishing the type of various materials.
2. All the University Libraries should make subscriptions to online journals and databases after ascertaining the requirements of the user community.
3. All the University Libraries in Kerala should follow uniform international standards for the technical processing of the collection as well as for their database creation.
4. Adequate funds should be made available to the University Libraries for procuring necessary hardware and software from time to time and sufficient budgetary provisions on regular basis should be made to maintain the computerised system.
5. Sufficient number of latest computers should be procured for the use in various Sections as well as for the users to make use of OPAC and Internet. Necessary hardware like LCD, Web Camera, CD Server, Laptop Computers etc. should be procured by all the University Libraries.
6. There should be adequate equipments and tools available for conducting video conferencing among the University Libraries in the state for creating an effective communication channel between the libraries in higher education in the state and a Virtual Private Network

should be established through the existing 1 Mbps Leased Line Asianet Internet connection for Resource Sharing among the University Libraries in Kerala.

7. All the University Libraries should procure software capable of meeting the library as well as user requirements. It was observed that all the libraries are facing one or the other problem related with the software they are using. Since all the libraries have almost similar requirements, a cooperative venture should be initiated to develop software for the use of all the University Libraries in the state. Open sources should be utilized to the maximum possible extent.

8. KUL and MGUL should take steps to appoint qualified professionals to manage the computerised library system and adequate training on periodic basis should be imparted to the staff of all the universities working in the computer section so that they are able to cope with the tremendous changes taking place in the field of Information Technology. Library services are becoming more net based now days and library professionals should be trained in the development and use of net-based services and digital library applications.

9. All the University Libraries should provide computerised User Education Programmes, Current Awareness Service, Selective Dissemination of Information, Reference Service, Content Page Service, Multi Media Service and CD/DVD based service.

10. All the University Libraries should make computer application in all the areas in Acquisition procedures, Technical processing, Serials Control, Circulation procedures and Stock verification to the maximum possible extent.

11. All the library and information services should be re evaluated so as to automate them properly so that users

are able to get the service without much staff intervention. Totally automated systems like self check-in/check-out should be introduced.

12. User Education on regular basis should be conducted with the help of computers to properly interpret the IT based services to the users. Adequate facilities like an air-conditioned hall with sufficient seating capacity and sound and light arrangements should be provided for presentation purposes. The equipments should include multimedia computers, LCD Projectors and library network as well as Internet connections. Proper user education programmes have to be chalked out, presentation packages with multimedia support should be prepared and demonstrated to the users and comprehensive brochures and hand outs should be given to the users at the time of membership registration in the library and at the time of conducting user education prgorammes. The graphical user interface features may enable the users of Internet to navigate through many areas in the net. But to fetch the appropriate information the Internet user need to be familiar with various tools and techniques and they need to know the pattern adopted by different leading websites in storing their valuable information. So Database and E Journal vendors should be invited to interpret the usage of their respective products properly to the users.

13. All the University Libraries in the state should make available their complete bibliographical records to the Union Database hosted by INFLIBENT. The University Libraries should promote information services provided by INFLIBNET like Document Delivery Service.

14. MGUL and CUL should take initiative to establish a campus LAN in the respective university campuses

and all the University Libraries should make their information services available over the Intranet and Internet and their computerised library system should be made web enabled so as to enable the users to make online renewal, reservation of documents etc.

15. The University Library websites should provide information services like CAS and SDI to the users. Similarly old question papers and syllabi of various courses conducted by the respective university should be made available through the websites.
16. All the University Libraries should procure necessary hardware and software like Over Head Scanner and OCR software for digitizing their potential collection.
17. A consortia of the University Libraries in the state should be formed so as to mutually benefit in the collection development, provision of information, manpower development etc.

CONCLUSION

It is hoped that the present study has provided for understanding the computerisation scenario in the University Libraries in Kerala, with respect to its coverage and limitations. Any automated system has a life cycle and it is to be re analysed after the system has been put in to use for certain period and if any short comings are found they are to be rectified and the system is to be redesigned to solve the lacunas in it. It is believed that the assessment made here, a little earlier though, on the level of reach of various computerised services to the targeted users will enable the University Libraries in the state to review the process and re design it in to a form that is more user oriented and contributory to the widening of the horizon of the knowledge.

Bibliography

Adam, Alison. (2001). **Computer ethics in a different voice.** *Information and Organization.* **11:** pp. 235–261.

Aiken, Milam. et. al. (2003). **College student Internet use**. *Campus-Wide Information Systems.* **20** (5): pp. 182-185.

Alemna, A.A. and Antwi, I.K. (2002). **A review of consortia building among university libraries in Africa**. *Library Management.* **23** (4/5): pp. 234-238.

Antonuccia, Robert V. and Cronin, Joseph M. (2001). **Creating an online university**. *The Journal of Academic Librarianship.* **27** (1): pp. 20-23.

Arant, Wendi and Payne, Leila. (2001). **The common user interface in academic libraries: myth or reality?**. *Library Hi Tech.* **19** (1): pp. 63-76.

Austen, Gaynor, Schmidt, Janine and Calvert, Philip. (2002) **Australian university libraries and the new educational environment**. *The Journal of Academic Librarianship.* **28** (1-2): pp. 63-67.

Averya, G.C. and Baker, E. (2002). **Reframing the infomated household-**workplace". *Information and Organization.* 12: pp. 109–134.

Babini, Dominique. (2004). Training virtual library network's staff using the Internet: the experience of the Latin American and the Caribbean Social Science Virtual Library online course. *Library Management.*25(1/2): pp72-78.

Bar-Ilan, Judit, Peritza, Bluma C. and Wolman, Yecheskel. (2003). **A survey** on the use of electronic databases and electronic journals accessed **through the web by the**

academic staff of Israeli universities. *The Journal of Academic Librarianship*. **29** (6): pp 346-361.

Barton, Jane. (2004). **Measurement, management and the digital library**. *Library Review*. **53** (3): pp. 138-141.

Battleson, Brenda, Boothb, Austin and Jane Weintrop. (2001). **Usability testing of an academic library Web site: a case study**. *The Journal of Academic Librarianship*. **27** (3): 188-198.

Bennett, Scott. (2001). **The Golden Age of libraries**. *The Journal of Academic Librarianship*. **27** (4): pp. 256-259.

Bevis, Mary D. and Graham, John-Bauer. (2003). **The evolution of an integrated electronic journals collection**. *The Journal of Academic Librarianship*. **29** (2): pp. 115-119.

Bose, Kabita. (2003). **An e-learning experience - a written analysis based on my experience in an e-learning pilot project**. *Campus-Wide Information Systems*. **20** (5): pp. 193-199.

Bostick, Sharon L. (2001). **The history and development of academic library consortia in the United States: an overview**. *The Journal of Academic Librarianship*. **27** (2): pp. 128-130.

Cain, Mark. (2003). **Managing technology: Being a library of record in a digital age**. *The Journal of Academic Librarianship*. **29** (6): pp. 405-410.

Cain, Mark. (2003). **Cybertheft, network security, and the library without walls**. *The Journal of Academic Librarianship*. **29** (4): pp. 245-248.

Chandra, Smita. (2002). **Information in a NetworkedWorld: the Indian Perspective**. *International Information & Library Review*. **34:** pp. 235-246.

Chávez-Villa, Micaela and Perezrul, Abelardo Herrero. (2003). **Library systems without systems librarians: the Mexican experience**. *Library Hi Tech*. **21** (3): pp. 309-316.

Ching, Steve H., Poon, Paul W. T. and Huang, Ken L. (2003). **Managing the effectiveness of the library consortium: a core values perspective on Taiwan e-book Net**. *The Journal of Academic Librarianship*. 29 (5): pp. 304-315.

Chowdhury, Gobinda G. (2002). **Digital libraries and reference services: present and future.** *Journal of Documentation*. 58 (3): pp. 258-283.

Christiansen, Lars, Stombler, Mindy and Thaxton, Lyn. (2004). **A Report on Librarian-Faculty Relations from a Sociological Perspective**. *The Journal of Academic Librarianship*. **30** (2): pp. 116-121.

Church, Jennifer. et. al. (2002). **The Information Commons at Lied Library**. *Library Hi Tech*. **20** (1): pp. 58-70.

Cockrell, Barbara J. and Jayne, Elaine Anderson. **How do I find an article? Insights from a web usability study**. *The Journal of Academic Librarianship*. **28** (3): pp. 122-132.

Cogan, Sarah and Bullard, Rita. (2000). **The automated retrieval collection at Bruce T. Halle Library**. *Library Hi Tech* **18** (2): pp. 142-143.

Courtney, Nancy. (2001) **Barbarians at the gates: a half-century of unaffiliated users in academic libraries**. *The Journal of Academic Librarianship*. **27** (6): pp. 473-480.

Cowgill, Allison, Beam, Joan and Wess, Lindsey. (2001). **Implementing an information commons in a university library**. *The Journal of Academic Librarianship*. **27** (6): pp. 432-439.

Croneis, Karen S. and Henderson, Pat. **Electronic and digital librarian positions: A content analysis of announcements from 1990 through 2000**. *The Journal of Academic Librarianship*. **28** (4): pp. 232-237.

Crowley, Gwyneth H. et. al. (2002). **User perceptions of the library's web pages: A focus group study at Texas A&M University**. *The Journal of Academic Librarianship*. **28** (4): pp. 205-210.

D'Esposito, Joann E. and Gardnerb, Rachel M. (1999). **University students' perceptions of the Internet: an exploratory study**. *The Journal of Academic Librarianship*. **25** (6): pp. 456-461.

Darch, Colin, Rapp, Joan and Underwood Peter G. (1999). **Academic library consortia in contemporary South Africa**. *Library Consortium Management: An International Journal*. **1** (1/2): pp. 23-32.

Diedrichs, Carol Pitts. (1998). **Using Automation in Technical Services to Foster Innovation**. *The Journal of Academic Librarianship*. **24** (2)

Dillon, Dennis. (2001). **E-books: the University of Texas experience, part 1**. *Library Hi Tech*. **19** (2): pp. 113-125.

Dillon, Dennis. (2001). **E-books: the University of Texas experience, part 2**. *Library Hi Tech*. **19** (4): pp. 350-362.

Dong, Xi Aoying. (2003). **Searching Information and Evaluation of Internet: A Chinese Academic User Survey**. *International Information & Library Review*. **35:** pp. 163-187.

Dugan, Robert E. (2001). **Managing laptops and the wireless network at the Mildred F. Sawyer library"**. *The Journal of Academic Librarianship*. **27** (4): pp. 295-298.

Dugan, Robert E. (2002). **Information technology budgets and costs: Do you know what your information technology costs each year?**. *The Journal of Academic Librarianship*. **28** (4): pp. 238-243.

Dugan, Robert E. (2002). **Information technology plans**. *The Journal of Academic Librarianship*. **28** (3): pp. 152-156.

Dugan, Robert E. and Ou, Carol. (2002). **Keeping me awake at night: Some issues and questions about managing technology**. *The Journal of Academic Librarianship*. **28** (6): pp 406-409.

Dunn, Kathleen. (2000). **Assessing Information Literacy**

Skills in the California State University: A Progress Report. *The Journal of Academic Librarianship*. **28**. (1): pp. 26–35.

Elkington, Nancy E. and Massie, Dennis. (2000) **The changing nature of international resource sharing: Risks and benefits of collaboration**. *Library Consortium Management: An International Journal*. **2** (5/6): pp. 95-103.

Fabbi, Jennifer L, Watson, Sidney D and Marks, Kenneth E. (2002). **Implementation of the 3M[tm] Digital Identification System at the UNLV libraries**. *Library Hi Tech*. **20** (1): pp. 104-110.

Frank, Donald G. et. al. (2001). **Information consulting: The key to success in academic libraries**. *The Journal of Academic Librarianship*. **27** (2): pp. 90-96.

Gaur, Ramesh C. **Rethinking the Indian Digital Divide: The Present State of Digitization in Indian Management Libraries**. *International Information & Library Review*. **35**: pp. 189-203.

Goddard, Lisa. (2003). **The integrated librarian: IT in the systems office**. *Library Hi Tech*. **21** (3): pp. 280-288.

Górski, Marek M. (2002). **Around the world to Cracow University of Technology Library: Taking the chances of Polish transitions**. *Library Hi Tech News incorporating Online and CD Notes*. **19** (10).

Graham, Rebecca A. (2002). **Wireless use in libraries**. *Library Hi Tech*. **20** (2): pp. 237-240.

Gregory, David and Nixon, William J. (2003). **The Instruction Commons: an information literacy initiative at Iowa State University**. *Library Review*. **52** (9): pp. 422-432

Guinea, Janet. (2003). **Building bridges: the role of the systems librarian in a university library**. *Library Hi Tech*. **21** (3): pp. 325-332.

Haslam, Michaelyn. et. al. (2002). **The automated storage and retrieval system (ASRS) in Lied Library**. *Library Hi Tech.* **20** (1): pp. 71-89.

Herring, Susan Davis. (2001). **Using the World Wide Web for research: are faculty satisfied?**. *The Journal of Academic Librarianship.* **27** (3): pp. 213-219.

Hirshon, Arnold. (1999). **The development of library client service programs and the role of library consortia.** *Library Consortium Management: An International Journal.* **1** (3/4): pp. 59-75.

Ho, Jeannette and Crowley, Gwyneth H.. (2003). **User perceptions of the "reliability" of library services at Texas A&M University: A focus group study**. *The Journal of Academic Librarianship.* **29** (2): 82-87.

Hunter, Karen. (2003). **The future of digital libraries**. *The Journal of Academic Librarianship.* **29** (5): p. 275.

Hurst, Leslie. (2003). **The special library on campus: A model for library orientations aimed at academic administration, faculty, and support staff**. *The Journal of Academic Librarianship.* **29** (4): pp 231-236.

Innocentawasom. (2003). **Digital Libraries in the Central African Sub-region: A Case Study of Cameroon.** *International Information & Library Review.* **35:** pp. 149-155.

Introna, Lucas D. (2002). **The (im)possibility of ethics in the information age**. *Information and Organization* **12:** pp. 71–84.

Jackson, Mary E. and Preece, Barbara G. (2002). **Consortia and the portal challenge**. *The Journal of Academic Librarianship.* **28** (3): pp 160-162.

Jain, P.K. (2003). **Indian Council of Social Science Research (ICSSR) Maintained Research Institutes' Libraries in India: Towards Digitization and Networking.**

International Information & Library Review. **35:** pp. 217-232.

Jankowska, Maria Anna. (2004). **Identifying University Professors' Information Needs in the Challenging Environment of Information and Communication Technologies**. *The Journal of Academic Librarianship*. **30** (1): pp. 51-66.

Jeevan. V.K.J. (2000). **Kharagpur Electronic Library on the Internet (KELNET)**. *Library Hi Tech*. **18** (3): pp. 272-278.

Jilovsky, Cathie. (2003). **Systems librarianship in Australia: a historical perspective**. *Library Hi Tech*. **21** (3): pp. 297-308.

Jirojwong, Sansnee and Wallin, Margie. (2002). **Use of formal and informal methods to gain information among faculty at an Australian regional university**. *The Journal of Academic Librarianship*. **28** (1-2): 68-73.

Jordan, Mark (2003). **The self-education of systems librarians.** *Library Hi Tech*. **21** (3): pp. 273-279.

Kalra, H.P.S. (2001). **Efforts Towards Digitization of Libraries in India: Problems and Prospects.** *International Information & Library Review*. 33: pp. 197-204.

Kavulya, Joseph Muema. (2003). **Challenges facing information literacy efforts in Kenya: a case study of selected university libraries in Kenya**. *Library Management*. 24 (4/5): pp. 216-222.

Keating III, John J. and Hafner, Arthur W. (2002). **Supporting individual library patrons with information technologies: emerging one-to-one library services on the college or university campus**. *The Journal of Academic Librarianship*. **28** (6): pp. 426-429.

Kirby, Steven. (2000). **Free to choose: the real power of Linux.** *Library Hi Tech*. **18** (1): pp. 85-88.

Kolovos, Filippos, Papargeris, Stella and Tsanaktsidou,

Elisabeth. (2004). **An Electronic Online Access Showroom for the New Acquisitions of the Library of the University of Macedonia.** *Library Hi Tech News.* **21** (1) : pp. 22-29.

Liao, Jing. (2004). **A Historical Perspective: The Root Cause for the Underdevelopment of User Services in Chinese Academic Libraries.** *The Journal of Academic Librarianship.* **30** (2): pp. 109-115.

Lonsdale, Ray and Armstrong, Chris. (2001). **Electronic books: challenges for academic libraries.** *Library Hi Tech.* **19** (4): pp. 332-339.

Lundy, Mack. (2003). **Changing roles of the systems librarian at the College of William and Mary: the explosion of technology and position of the systems librarian.** *Library Hi Tech.* **21** (3): pp. 333-339.

Lynch, Clifford. (2003). **Digital library opportunities.** *The Journal of Academic Librarianship.* **29** (5): pp. 286-289.

Mambo, Henry L. (2001). **Tanzania: An Overview of Information Communications Technology (ICT) Development in Libraries and Information Services.** *International Information & Library Review.* **33:** pp. 89-96.

Manifold, Alan. (2000). **A principled approach to selecting an automated library system.** *Library Hi Tech.* **18** (2): pp. 119-130.

Marcum, Deanna. (2003). **Requirements for the future digital library.** *The Journal of Academic Librarianship.* **29** (5): pp. 276-279.

Mark Cain. **"The two cultures? librarians and technologists".** *The Journal of Academic Librarianship.* **29** (3): pp. 177-181.

Martey, A.K. (2004). **The Future Library Consortium in Ghana.** *Library Hi Tech News.* **21** (2): pp. 15-19.

McCabe, Jennifer. (2004). **Getting started with PDAs: A Library-driven Project at James Madison University.**

Library Hi Tech News. **21** (1): pp. 30-32.

McLaren, Scott. (2000). **Linux: a viable alternative or desert mirage?**. *Library Hi Tech*. **18** (1): pp. 82-84.

Miller, Rush G. (2002). **Shaping digital library content**. *The Journal of Academic Librarianship*. **28** (3): pp. 97-103.

Morghn, Steve. (2001). **Change in university libraries: don't forget the people**. *Library Management*. **22** (1/2): pp. 58-61.

Mozenter, Frada, Sanders, Bridgette T. and Bellamy, Carol. (2003). **Cross-training public service staff in the electronic age: I have to learn to do what?!**. *The Journal of Academic Librarianship*. **29** (6): pp 399-404.

Munshi, Ushamujoo. (2003). **Building Digital Resources: Creating Facilities at INSA**. *International Information & Library Review*. **35:** pp. 281-309.

Nitecki, Danuta A. (2000). **Measuring service quality at Yale University's libraries**. *The Journal of Academic Librarianship*. **26** (4): pp. 259-273.

Omoniyi, Joseph O. (2001). **The security of computer and other electronic installations in Nigerian university libraries**. *Library Management*. **22** (6/7): pp. 272-277.

Orji, Ozioma Ijeoma. (2002). **Information in a Networked World: the Nigerian Perspective**. *International Information & Library Review*. **34:** pp. 271-277.

Papadakis, Ioannis, Karakoidas, Vassileios and Chrissikopoulos, Vassileios. (2002). **DocML: a digital library of university data**. *Library Hi Tech*. **20** (3): pp. 378-387.

Parikha, Mihir. And Verma, Sameer. (2002). **Utilizing Internet technologies to support learning: an empirical analysis**. *International Journal of Information Management* **22:** pp. 27–46

Peterman, Thomas W. (2000). **Elements of success at a traditional/virtual university: lessons learned from three years of growth in cyberspace.** *The Journal of Academic Librarianship.* **26**, (1): pp. 27-32.

Peters, Thomas A. (2003). **Consortia and their discontents.** *The Journal of Academic Librarianship.* **29** (2): pp. 111-114.

Pilston, Anna Klump and Hart, Richard L. (2002). **Student response to a new electronic reserves system.** *The Journal of Academic Librarianship.* **28** (3): pp. 147-151.

Pomerantz, Je. Rey et. al. **The current state of digital reference: validation of a general digital reference model through a survey of digital reference services.** *Information Processing and Management.* **40:** pp. 347- 363.

Pors, Niels Ole. (2003). **Managing change in Danish libraries.** *The Journal of Academic Librarianship.* **29** (6): pp. 411-415.

Pupeliene, Janina. (2004). **LITHUANIA: The Changing Image of Academic Libraries.** *The Journal of Academic Librarianship.* **30** (1): pp. 80-84.

Ratchatavorn, Phandao. (2002). **Development of Electronic Resources across Networks in Thailand"**. *International Information & Library Review.* **34:** pp. 279-287.

Ren, Wen-Hua. (2000). **Library instruction and college student self-efficacy in electronic information searching.** *The Journal of Academic Librarianship.* **26** (5): pp. 323-328.

Rhyno, Arthur. (2003). **From library systems to mainstream software: how Web technologies are changing the role of the systems librarian.** *Library Hi Tech.* **21** (3): pp. 289-296.

Richards, Sylvie L.F. (2002). **Innovative library uses of handheld devices.** *Library Hi Tech News incorporating Online and CD Notes.* **19** (9)

Ross, Mary and Marmion, Dan. (2000). **Systems librarians**

and the client/server environment. *Library Hi Tech*. **18** (2): pp. 151-157.

Sanville, Tom. (1999). **Use levels and new models for consortial purchasing of electronic journals**. *Library Consortium Management: An International Journal*. **1** (3/4): pp. 47-58.

Schwartz, Candy. (2000). **Digital libraries: an overview. The Journal of Academic Librarianship**. **26** (6): pp. 385-393.

Schwarz, G.M. (2002). **Organizational hierarchy adaptation and information technology**. *Information and Organization*. **12:** pp. 153–182.

Seadle, Michael. (2004). **Copyright in a networked world: ethics and infringement.** *Library Hi Tech*. **22** (1): pp. 106-110.

Shaw, Elizabeth J. (2000). **Building a digital library: a technology manager's point of view**. *The Journal of Academic Librarianship*. **26** (6): pp. 394-398.

Shkolnikov, Tanya. (2002). **To link or not to link: how to avoid copyright traps on the Internet**. *The Journal of Academic Librarianship*. **28** (3): pp. 133-140.

Shuler, John A. (2001). **Beyond the depository library concept**. *The Journal of Academic Librarianship*. **27**(4): pp. 299-301.

Shuler, John. (2004). **INFORMATION POLICY: Ask Not for whom the bells toll**. *The Journal of Academic Librarianship*. **30** (1): pp. 77-79.

Smith, Erin T. (2003). **Changes in faculty reading behaviors: the impact of electronic journals on the University of Georgia**. *The Journal of Academic Librarianship*. **29** (3): pp. 162-168.

Stallings, Dees. (2001). **The virtual university: organizing to survive in the 21st Century**. *The Journal of Academic Librarianship*. **27** (1): pp. 3-14.

Stallings, Dees. (2002) **Measuring success in the virtual university**. *The Journal of Academic Librarianship*. **28** (1-2): pp. 47-53.

Stierna, Eric J. and Rowe, Neil C. (2003). **Applying information-retrieval methods to software reuse: a case study**. *Information Processing and Management* **39**: pp. 67–74.

Susana Romanos de Tiratel. (2000). **Assessing information use by humanists and social scientists: A study at the Universidad de Buenos Aires, Argentina**. *The Journal of Academic Librarianship*. 26 (5): pp.346-354.

Tam, Lawrence W.H. and Robertson, Averil C. (2002). **Managing change: libraries and information services in the digital age.** *Library Management*. 23 (8/9): pp. 369-377.

Thomas, Mary Augusta. (2000). **Redefining library space: managing the co- existence of books, computers, and readers**. *The Journal of Academic Librarianship*. **26** (6): pp. 408-415.

Tyson, Lisa. (2003). **Library systems teams - more than just peripherals**. *Library Hi Tech*. **21** (3): pp. 317-324.

Von Elm, Catherine and Trump, Judith F. (2001). **Maintaining the mission in the hybrid library**. *The Journal of Academic Librarianship*. **27** (1): pp. 33-35.

Wade, Rona. (1999). **The very model of a modern library consortium**. *Library Consortium Management: An International Journal*. **1** (1/2): pp. 5-18.

Waldhart, Thomas J., Millera, Joseph B. and Chana, Lois Mai. (2000). **Provision of local assisted access to selected internet information resources by ARL academic libraries**. *The Journal of Academic Librarianship*. **26** (2): pp 100 - 109.

Warnken, Paula. (2004). **The Impact of Technology on**

Information Literacy Education in Libraries. *The Journal of Academic Librarianship*. **30** (2): pp. 151-156.

Webster, Janet and Middleton, Cheryl. (1999). **Paying for technology: student fees and libraries**. *The Journal of Academic Librarianship*. **25** (6): pp. 462-472.

White, Marilyn Domas. (2001). **Diffusion of an innovation: digital reference service in Carnegie Foundation master's (comprehensive) academic institution libraries**. *The Journal of Academic Librarianship*. **27** (3): pp. 173-187.

Wu, Jianzhong and Huang, Ruhua. (2003). **The academic library development in China**. *The Journal of Academic Librarianship*. **29** (4): pp. 249-253.

Appendix A

QUESTIONNAIRE

(To the Person in Charge of the University Library)

This questionnaire is intended to collect data regarding the computerisation of University Libraries in Kerala in connection with a research undertaken by me under the guidance of Prof. M Bavakutty. I seek your valuable co-operation and help in obtaining necessary information. I request you to kindly fill up the questionnaire with care and accuracy.

MUHAMMED SALIH T.K.
CHMK LIBRARY
UNIVERSITY OF CALICUT

PART I

A. General

1. Name of the University:
2. Year of establishment of the University:
3. Address of the University:
4. URL of the University:
5. Name of the University Library:
6. URL of the University Library, if any:
7. Year of establishment of the University Library:
8. Name of the Person holding charge of the University Library:
9. Designation:

B. **Library Collections** (Please specify the collections as on 31/3/2004)

Type of document	*Number*	*Type of document*	*Number*
Books/Monographs		Audio Cassettes	
Bound Vol. of Journals		Video Cassettes	
Theses		Microfiches	
Dissertations		CDs	
Reports		DVDs	
Patents		Any other (please specify)	
Standards			
Number of Journals subscribed:		Journals received as Gift :	
Foreign Journals		Indian Journals	
Online databases subscribed			

C. **Membership** (Please specify categories of membership and the total numbers)

Category	*Number*	*Category*	*Number*
Under graduates		Public	
Post Graduates		Others (please specify)	
Researchers			
Teachers			
Non teaching staff		Total	

D. **Technical Processing of documents**

1. Classification Scheme used (with Edition)

   a). CC ☐ b).UDC ☐

   c). DDC ☐

   d). Any other (specify) ....

   Are you satisfied with the Classification Scheme followed? Yes/No

   If no, what standard would you prefer instead: ....

2. Cataloguing Rules (with Edition) followed:

   a). CCC ☐ b).AACR ☐

   c). Any other (please specify): ....

   Are you satisfied with the existing Cataloguing Rules followed? Yes/No

   If no, what standard would you prefer instead: ....

3. Standard used for assigning Keywords:

   a). Chain Procedure ☐ b). Sear's List ☐

   c). LC Subject Headings ☐

   d). Any other (please specify): ....

   Are you satisfied with the existing standard for keywords? Yes/No

   If no, what standard would you prefer instead: ....

E. Library and Information Services

Please ✓ mark the Library and Information services provided by your library

Book Lending	Y	N
Inter Library Loan	Y	N
Reprographic Services	Y	N
Reference service	Y	N
Selective Dissemination of Information	Y	N
Current Awareness Service	Y	N
Circulation of Accession List	Y	N
Routing of Periodicals	Y	N
Content page service	Y	N
User Education	Y	N
Compilation of Bibliographies	Y	N
Translation Services	Y	N
Local abstracting/indexing service	Y	N
Other (Specify)	Y	

F. Staff Strength

1. Professional

Designation	*No. of persons*	*Designation*	*No. of persons*
Deputy Librarian		Junior Librarian	
Asst Librarian Sr Scale		Reference Assistant	
Asst Librarian Sel Grade		Professional Assistant Gr I	
Asst Librarian		Professional Assistant Gr II	
Assistant Librarian Gr I		Technical Assistant	
Assistant Librarian Gr II		Library Assistant	

2. Non Professionals

Designation	*No. of persons*	*Designation*	*No. of persons*
Library Assistant		Peons	
Attender			

PART II

A. General

1. Please specify the status of computerisation of your library:
   a). Fully computerized ☐
   b). Partially computerised ☐
   c). Not computerized ☐
2. How long you have been using computers in your library? :......years ......months
3. What are the application softwares used in your library? (Please specify along with the platform on which it is used)

Items	*Name of the Software*	*Platform*
Housekeeping operation		
Word Processing		
Spreadsheets		
Presentation Softwares		
DTP		
Digital Library software		
OCR (Optical Character Recognition)		
Any Other		

4. Is Your computerised library system web enabled? Yes/No

5. Please specify the areas of application of computer in your library (Please ümark)
   - a). Database creation ☐
   - b). Information Retrieval ☐
   - c). Circulation Procedures ☐
   - d). Acquisition Procedures ☐
   - e). Serials Control ☐
   - f). Cataloguing ☐
   - g). OPAC ☐
   - h). Digitization of documents ☐
   - i). Reference services ☐
   - j). Inter Office communication ☐
   - k) Intra Library Communication ☐
   - l). Financial Management ☐
   - m) Office file works ☐
   - n) Stock Verification ☐
   - o). Other (Please specify): ....

6. Did your library conduct a formal system analysis prior to the computerisation? Yes/No

7. Do you get support from INFLIBNET for computerisation? Yes/No

8. Does the library professionals from your library got training from INFLIBENT? Yes/No

   If yes, How many persons were trained by INFLIBNET? Please give the number: ....

   Type of training received (please specify the name of the training programme and its period)

Name of training programme	*No. of persons*	*Duration*

9). Please provide the number of bibliographical records sent to the INFLIBNET database

   a). Books: ....

   b). Serials: ....

   c). Theses: ....

   d). Any Other (please specify): ....

10). Do you come under the UGC Infonet Project? Yes/No

   If Yes, please ✓ mark the mode of connectivity?

   a). SCPC VSAT Link ☐

   b). Radio Link ☐

   c). Leased Line ☐

   d). Any Other (Please specify) ....

11). Which is the service providing agency? Please ü mark

a). ERNET ☐

b). Asianet ☐

c). Others specify: ....

12). What is the bandwidth of the connection?

13). How many machines are provided to access the Infonet in the Library?

14). Have you extended the Infonet connection to outside the library? Yes/No

15). Please specify the category of users getting the Infonet service?

a). Student ☐

b). Research Scholar ☐

c). Teacher ☐

d). Non-teaching staff ☐

e). Others (please specify): ....

16). Do you charge any fee from the users for the use of Infonet

If yes kindly give the fee structure: ....

Category	*Amount*	*Duration*
Teachers		
Research Scholars		
Students		
Others(Please specify)		

Database Creation

1). Have you done retrospective conversion of the bibliographic items in your library? Yes/No

2). Number of records converted so far:

3). Please ✓ mark the appropriate data source used for conversion

a). Accession Register ☐
b). Catalogue Cards ☐
c). Data input sheets ☐
d). From databases in CDs ☐
e). Databases of other institutions ☐
f). Direct from document ☐
g). Any other (Please specify)

4). Please ✓ mark the nature of database creation
a). In-house ☐
b). By external agency ☐

5). If in-house, by whom the database is created? (Please ü mark)
a). Staff members ☐
b). Data entry operators ☐

6). Please specify the number of persons engaged in the database creation:

7). What method you have adopted for data entry of documents in languages other than English?
a). Transliteration ☐
b). Using GIST cards ☐
c). Any other method (Please specify) :.....

8). Please ü mark the duration taken for database creation
a). Up to six months ☐
b). 6 months to one year ☐
c). One year to two years ☐
d). More than two years ☐

9). Have you taken in to consideration any national or international standards in database creation?

Yes/No

If yes, specify the standard:

a). ISO 2709 ☐

b) CCF ☐

c) UNIMARC ☐

d)Any other (specify)............................

10) Classification Scheme followed in the database:

a). DDC ☐

b). CC ☐

c). UDC ☐

d). LC ☐

e) Any other (Please Specify) ....

11). Cataloguing Rules followed in the database:

a). AACR I ☐

b). AACR II ☐

c). CCC ☐

d). Any other (Please specify) ....

12). Standard used for assigning key words in the database

a). LC Subject Headings ☐

b). Sear's List ☐

c). Chain Indexing ☐

d). Any other (Please specify) ....

13). How often you take the back up of your database? :

a). Daily ☐

b). Once in two days ☐

c). Weekly ☐

d). Fortnightly ☐

e). Any other (Specify) ....

14). What is the medium used for taking backup?

a). Cartridge ☐

b). DAT Drive ☐

c). CD ☐

d). Harddisc ☐

e). Any other (Please Specify):............

15). Do you have any automatic backup mechanism like mirroring of hard disc? Yes/No

If yes, Please specify:

16). Do you have a standby Server to use during emergency? Yes/No

Acquisition Module

Please ✓ mark areas of application

a). Duplication Checking ☐

b). Ordering ☐

c). Receipt of Docur ıent ☐

d). Accessioning ☐

e). Invoice Processing ☐

f). Budget Handling ☐

g). Any other areas (Please specify) ....

1). Do you use Internet as an aid in your Acquisition work

Circulation Module

Please ✓ mark areas of application

a). Membership Management ☐

b). Check out/Check in ☐

c). Renewal ☐

d). Reservation of documents ☐

e). Renewal ☐

f). Fine collection ☐

g). Sending reminders ☐

1). Do you use barcode facility for check in/check out operations? Yes/No

Serials Control

Please ✓ mark areas of application

a). Ordering ☐

b). Receipt ☐

c). Reminders ☐

d). Budget Handling ☐

e). Invoice Processing ☐

f). Routing ☐

g). Sending for Bindery ☐

h). Accessioning ☐

i). Article Indexing ☐

j). Current Awareness Service ☐

k). Selective Dissemination of Information ☐

l) Check in/Check out ☐

1). Do you use Internet as an aid in your Serials Control work

OPAC (Online Public Access Catalogue)

1). Please specify the number of terminals provided for users to browse OPAC:

2). Access points provided in the OPAC (Please ü mark)

a). Author ☐

b). Title ☐

c). Words in Title ☐

d). Subject ☐

e). Class Number ☐

f). Place ☐

g). Publisher ☐

h). Series ☐

i). Boolean search ☐

j). Truncation ☐

k). Word Proximityo l) Any other (Please specify) .....

3. Have you given the provision for members to suggest new titles for procurement through OPAC? Yes/No

4. Is there a provision in OPAC to know the status (like on the shelf, issued out, in bindery etc.) of a particular document? Yes/No

5. Is the OPAC accessible over the campus LAN? Yes/No

6. Is the OPAC accessible over Internet (webOPAC)? Yes/No

G). Other Services and Operations Using Computers

Please ✓ mark your option regarding services provided and operations carried out using computers

Services

Current Awareness Services	Yes/No
SDI Service	Yes/No
Circulation of New Additions List	Yes/No
Content Page Service	Yes/No
Multimedia Service	Yes/No
Internet Services	Yes/No
CDROM/DVD Based Service	Yes/No
Online Full Text Service	Yes/No
Online database services	Yes/No
User Education programmes	Yes/No

Operations

Computerised stock verification	Yes/No
Bar code for stock verification	Yes/No
Smart Card for member identification	Yes/No
Microchips for document identification	Yes/No
Totally automated check in/Check out	Yes/No

Electronic theft detection systems Yes/No

H). Networks

1). Do you have a Local Area Network in your library?
Yes/No

If yes what is the physical medium of transmission

a) UTP Cable ☐
b) Coaxial cable ☐
c) OFC ☐
d) Wireless ☐
e) Other specify ....

Please specify the baud rate of the medium of transmission

2). Do you have a Campus LAN in your University?
Yes/No

3). Do you have link with any regional, national or international networks? Yes/No

If yes, please specify the names of the network you participate

a). INFLIBNET ☐
b). DELNET ☐
c). OTHER (Please specify): ....

4). Do you use email facility for communication between various sections? Yes/No

5). Do you use email facility for communication with other offices and libraries? Yes/No

6). Do you have Router? Yes/No

If yes, have you configured it to protect your database?
Yes/No

7). Have you implemented Firewall for protection of your databases Yes/No

If yes, how you have implemented it? ....

a). Through hardware ☐

b). Through software ☐

I. Internet Facility

1). Please ✓ mark the type of Internet connectivity you have and specify the bandwidth

ISP	*PSTN Dial up*	*ISDN Dial up*	*VSAT*	*Leased Line*	*Radio Link*	*Band-width*
BSNL						
ERNET						
NICNET						
Dishnet						
Asianet						
Satyam online						
Others Pl. specify						

2). How many terminals are provided for the users? Specify the number :................

3). Please ✓ mark the type of services provided?

a). Browsing ☐

b). Email only ☐

c). Database Access ☐

d). Full text access ☐

e). Other (Please specify) ....

4). Please specify the category of members who are given the facility

a). Students ☐

b). Research Scholars ☐

c). Teachers ☐

d). Others (Please specify) ....

5). Do you charge any fee from the users of Internet?

Yes/No

If yes, Kindly give the present fee structure for various category of users:

J. Digitization of Documents

1). Have you identified the collection for digitization?

Yes/No

If yes, please ✓ mark the collections you have selected for digitization

Theses	Manuscripts	Books
Dissertations	Pamphlets	Reports
Question Papers	Syllabus	

2). Have you digitized any of the library collection?

Yes/No

If yes, Please specify the number of various collections you have digitized so far

Collection	*Number*	*Collection*	*Number*	*Collection*	*Number*
Theses		Manuscripts		Books	
Dissertations		Pamphlets		Reports	
Question Papers		Syllabus		Other (specify)	

K. Sources of Finance

1). Sources of Finance for the Library (Please ✓ mark)

a). Govt. ☐

b). UGC ☐

c). Endowment ☐

d). Any other (Specify).........

2). Please specify the sources of finance received for Computerisation of the Library

Name of the Agency	*Amount*	*Year*
INFLIBNET, UGC		
State Govt.		
Endowment		
Any other (Specify)		

3). Please specify the amount allocated for various purposes in the Library budget for the last three financial years (2001-02, 2002-03, 2003-04)

Purpose	*2002-03*	*2003-04*	*2004-05*
Total amount allotted for the library			
Staff Salary			
Books and Journals			
Online subscription (journals, databases etc.)			
Procurement of Computer Hardware and Software			
Recurring charges like Internet subscription			
AMC charges for Hardware			
AMC charges for software			

4). Do you find the funds available sufficient for the computerisation process Yes/No.

L. Personnel Engaged in the Library Computerisation

Designation	*Qualifications (General)*	*Qualification in Computer Science/IT*

M. Hardware Available (Please provide the number of computers and other equipments available in your library in the space provided below. Please use a separate sheet if necessary)

Item	*No.*	*Item*	*No.*
Server Class machines		Flat Bed Scanners	
Laptop Computers		Over Head Scanners	
Pentium I		Barcode Scanners	
Pentium II		Modems	
Pentium III		Hubs	
Pentium IV		Switches	
Celron		Router	
Dot Matrix Printers		LCD Projector	
Inkjet Printers		Web Camera	
Laser Printers		UPS	
Heavy Duty Network Printer		Other items specify	
CD Server			
CD ROM Tower			
Systems with DVD Drives			
Barcode Printer			

Date: Signature:

Appendix B

QUESTIONNAIRE

(To the Person in charge of the Computer Section of the Library)

This questionnaire is intended to collect data regarding the computerisation of University Libraries in Kerala in connection with a research undertaken by me under the guidance of Prof. M Bavakutty. I seek your valuable co-operation and help in obtaining necessary information. I request you to kindly fill up the questionnaire with care and accuracy.

MUHAMMED SALIH T.K.
CHMK LIBRARY
UNIVERSITY OF CALICUT

1) Name of the Person:
2) Designation:
3) Qualifications in general:
4) Qualifications in Computer Science:
5) Date of joining the service:
6) Scale of Pay:
7) Training obtained in Computer Applications in Libraries

Training Programme	*Agency*	*Duration*	*Course content*

8) Do you get guidance from your superior(s) regarding your work Yes/No

9) Do you get enough encouragement from your superior officers Yes/No

10) Do you get assistance from your colleagues in your work Yes/No

11) Do you communicate with your counterparts in other Universities Yes/No

12) Do you share your problems with other people in the profession elsewhere Yes/No

13) Do you attend any Conference/Seminar/Workshop/ User group meet? Yes/No

If yes specify the events you have attended:

Event	*Topic*	*Place*	*Year*

14) Do you get any valuable information/suggestions in improving your work through such participation Yes/No

15) Do you have enough systems and peripherals to support your work? Yes/No

16) Do you have enough manuals and reference sources to support your work? Yes/No

17) Do you get immediate attention from vendors or service contractors? Yes/No

18) Do you have enough freedom to incorporate your own ideas in to your work? Yes/No

19) Are you provided with enough physical facility to work? Yes/No

If no, please mention further facilities required: ....

....

20) Please ü mark your duties and responsibilities as the chief person in the Computer Section

Over all Management of the Section	*Communicating with Vendors*
Database Administration	Planning future Programmes/ Services
Training the Library Staff	File Works
Training the Users	Hardware Maintenance
Software Development	Software Maintenance
Providing Services to Users	Network Management
Any Other (specify)	

Date: Signature

Appendix C

QUESTIONNAIRE

(To the users of the Library)

This questionnaire is intended to collect data regarding the computerisation of University Libraries in Kerala in connection with a research undertaken by me under the guidance of Prof. M Bavakutty. I seek your valuable co-operation and help in obtaining necessary information. I request you to kindly fill up the questionnaire with care and accuracy.

MUHAMMED SALIH T.K.
CHMK LIBRARY
UNIVERSITY OF CALICUT

SECTION A

1) Name:
2) Type of membership you have in library (Please ü mark):
   a) Student ☐
   b) Research Scholar ☐
   c) Teacher ☐
3) Faculty of Study/Teaching:
   a) Science ☐
   b) Social Science ☐
4) Purpose of Library use (Please ü mark):
   a) Study ☐
   b) Research ☐
   c) Official ☐
   d) Recreational ☐

e) Any Other (Please specify):....................

5) Frequency of library visit (Please ✓ mark):

a) Daily ☐

b) Alternative days ☐

c) Once in three days ☐

d) Once in a week ☐

e) Rarely ☐

6) Average time spent in the library on a visit (Please ✓ mark):

a) Less than 30 minutes ☐

b) Between 30 minutes and 2 hours ☐

c) Between 2 and 5 hours ☐

d) More than 5 hours ☐

SECTION B

Are you aware of the following **Computer aided Library and Information Services** and please ü mark to indicate whether you get this service from your library or not.

Computer aided Services	*Are you aware about this service?*	*Do you get this Service?*
Current Awareness Service	Yes/No	Yes/No
Selective Dissemination of Information	Yes/No	Yes/No
Circulation of New Additions List	Yes/No	Yes/No
Online Database Services	Yes/No	Yes/No
Online Full Text (E – Journals)	Yes/No	Yes/No
CD ROM / DVD based Services	Yes/No	Yes/No
Internet Services	Yes/No	Yes/No
User Education	Yes/No	Yes/No

SECTION C

1) Do you have online catalogue in your library? Yes/No

   If yes, What are the access points through which you search?

   a) Author ☐
   b) Title ☐
   c) Words in Title ☐
   d) Subject ☐
   e) Class Number ☐
   f) Place ☐
   g) Publisher ☐
   h) Series ☐
   i) Boolean search ☐
   j) Truncation ☐
   k) Word Proximity ☐
   l) Any other (Please specify) ....

2) Do you find the access points provided sufficient? Yes/No

   If no, what other access points you need? Please specify:

   ....

3) Did you get any orientation in the use of Online catalogue? Yes/No

   If no, how did you come to know about searching techniques/strategies in the online catalogue (Please ✓ mark)

   a) Through trail and error ☐
   b) By observing others browse the catalogue ☐
   c) From your friends ☐
   d) Any other (Please specify): ....

4) Do you spend time waiting (while some one is making search) for searching the online catalogue? Yes/No

5) Do you get computerized book circulation facilities?

Yes/No

If yes, what are services available?(please ü mark)

a) Issue/Return ☐

b) Document Reservation ☐

c) Fine Collection ☐

d) Enquiry ☐

e) Any other (Please specify): ....

6) Do you find the computer based circulation procedure time saving ? Yes/No

7) Do you feel the need for any other computer based circulation services? Yes/No

If yes, Please specify

8) Do you use Internet facility in your library? Yes/No

If yes, Please indicate the services you use in Internet

a) Web browsing ☐

b) Email ☐

c) Chatting ☐

d) Newsgroups ☐

e) Discussion Groups ☐

f) Searching Databases ☐

g) Accessing E Journals ☐

h) Accessing Reference sources ☐

i) To access the Catalogues and databases of other libraries ☐

j) Other purposes Please specify: ....

9) Please specify the purposes of your Internet usage

a) Study ☐

b) Research ☐

c) To collect general information ☐

d) Recreational ☐

e) Communication ☐

f) Any Other (please specify):..........................

10) Have you got any formal training in the use of Internet facility? Yes/No

11) Do you receive required information through Internet? Yes/No

12) Do you find the speed of the Internet connection sufficient to meet your requirements? Yes/No

13) Do you find the Internet services provided by the library sufficient? Yes/No

If no, what else you expect with regard to Internet facility? Please specify:

....

....

....

....

Date: Signature

Part II

Muhammed Haneefa K

Application of Information and Communication Technologies in Special Libraries

2.1
Introduction

Technology may be regarded as the application of science to useful ends. During the passage of years several types of technologies have evolved. Information and Communication Technology (ICT) is the biggest achievement in the evolution of mankind. ICT is any system designed to gather, process, or distribute information or it is the science and skill of all aspects of computing, data storage, and communication. ICT may be any combination of tools and procedures that facilitate the generation, acquisition, storage, organisation, retrieval, searching, viewing, updating and transmission of information using electronic means. The tools used in ICT include purpose-built computer programs, databases, communication networks, analysis and design methods, programming languages, artificial intelligence, robotics, knowledge bases, etc. ICT has long standing influence in almost all areas of human activity. It acts as a catalyst in all spheres of science and technology.

The availability of information at right time and in the right form is of utmost importance in the development of knowledge as well as in all the developmental activities. It has become very difficult to manage the information manually due to the explosive growth of knowledge. Knowledge in almost all fields is increasing tremendously in a multidimensional way. There is a need for proper organisation and management of knowledge. The advent of digital computers, advances in telecommunication technology, widespread use of networking, explosive growth of Internet, world wide packet networks, optical discs and other mass storage media, interactive video technology, image technology, computer graphic technology, virtual reality and the growth of public and private databases have opened up new possibilities in dealing with the collection, organisation and dissemination of information. Now information can not only be stored, retrieved, communicated and broadcasted electronically in enormous quantities at phenomenal speed, but can also be rearranged, selected and transformed.

Over the past two decades, libraries have become increasingly aware of the revolutionary impact of developments in Information and Communication Technology on their key functions. Information and Communication Technologies are now diminishing the central role of traditional libraries. With limited budgets or reduced budgets and escalating cost of publications, individual libraries are unable to satisfy their users' diverse needs. Access to other library collections is no longer a mere convenience; it is a matter of urgent necessity in view of the large amount of information being produced every year and the costs to acquire and organise it. This necessitates co-operation and resource sharing among libraries and information centres. Resource sharing is successful only through computer and telecommunication networking and to participate in such network, the application of ICT is very essential. Owing to the interdisciplinary nature of learning, the information seeking behaviour of users is also changing. The traditional methods of information handling have become almost ineffective to provide pinpointed, expeditious and exhaustive information at the right time to the right user. The application of ICT facilitates easy and instantaneous access to information. It provides opportunities for libraries and information centres to widen the scope of their resources and services and to increase their significance within the organization they serve. The increasing availability of information in machine readable form allows many information needs to be satisfied with decreased involvement of libraries and librarians. Information is generated too faster that the libraries with traditional technologies are unable to handle it. There are several reasons for the application of ICT in libraries and information centres. The following are the important among them:

* Explosive growth of information
* Wastage of time in handling routine and repetitive library operations.
* Advantages like speed, accuracy and reliability in the process of information handling.
* Widespread availability of digital information.
* Multi and simultaneous use of digital information
* Facility to access resources and services of a library without visiting the library.
* Saving of library or information centre.
* Facility to accommodate increased work load of library professionals
* Provision of an effective control over the entire library resources, services and operations
* Improvement of the existing resources and services as well as the introduction of new resources and services.
* Facility to share the resources and services among various libraries and information centres through library networking and library consortia.
* Avoidance of duplication of resources and services.

The Information and Communication Technologies have brought many benefits in library and information systems and services. The application of computers in storage, retrieval and dissemination of information has brought new possibilities of automatic indexing and free text searching. Computerized acquisition helps processing purchase requests, pre-order searching, approval process, placement of orders, receiving and accessioning documents, invoice processing and payment arrangement, order follow-up, online enquiries and preparation of reports, etc. In this process, computers enable libraries in making use of the same data available in different files without entering it again each time. Computerised catalogue is the most efficient tool in retrieving information about the documents in a library easily and quickly. Computerised serial control helps in creating a database of journals, processing new subscriptions, renewal of subscriptions, order placing and invoice processing, receiving and recording issues, claiming missing issues, bindery management, maintenance of list of periodicals, serials holdings, etc. Circulation procedure in a conventional system is very lengthy and consumes much of the staff time in repetitive works. The use of technological devices such as computers, barcode scanners, smart cards, etc in circulation helps in performing routine operations easily and quickly. It saves lot of time for the staff as well as users. Computerised library can provide information quickly on various library management activities required by the management for budgetary control, preparation of accounts, maintenance of records, library statistics, etc. Once the computerisation activities are well progressed, information retrieval and database management activities, including the Internet based information services can be strengthened. A wide variety of advantages can be derived by the appropriate use of ICT. Following are some of the benefits of using ICT in libraries:

* To help the library professionals to free from routine, repetitive and uninteresting jobs which can be done

using computer and telecommunication technology

* To avoid or eliminate duplication of library resources, services and operations
* To facilitate cooperation and resource sharing through library networks and library consortia.
* To introduce new resources and services and revitalise existing ones.
* To allow easy integration of various library systems and operations
* To facilitate faster information communication
* To help to increase the quality and range of services
* To facilitate easy and wider access to all kinds of information sources
* To help to increase efficiency and effectiveness in library operations
* To save time, space, energy and resources
* To provide online search and access of information.
* To develop/upgrade the skills and abilities of library professionals
* To facilitate digitisation of information for preservation and for space saving
* To improve the cost-effectiveness of library resources and services
* To provide marketing opportunity of library services
* To provide remote access to users
* To provide round-the-clock access to users
* To provide access to unlimited information from different sources
* To provide more upto date information
* To provide information flexibility to be used by any

individual according to his or her requirements

* To facilitate the reformatting and combining of data from different sources; and
* To save and/or generate money

ICT has immense potential for a variety of applications in libraries. It helps libraries and information centres in creating databases of their collections and making them available for easy access to users inside as well as outside library through computer networks. In an automated library, once databases are developed in the computer, many services like bibliographic service, indexing service, current awareness service, selective dissemination of information service, etc. will be automatically generated and users can have direct access to them. Networking has enabled libraries to share their resources and services more effectively, especially in the present days of increasing document prices and decreasing budgets. The use of ICT with its immense capabilities of acquiring, storing, processing, retrieving and disseminating information with high speed and accuracy has made a tremendous impact on the overall functioning of libraries and information centres.

Though ICT has potential for modernising the library activities, there is a wide gap between what is told and what has been achieved. It is estimated that a large per cent of library professionals in India are not aware of the proper use of ICT in libraries. The problems in the application of ICT in libraries or for its slow progress are many. The following may be considered important among them:

* Insufficient funds
* Inadequate ICT infrastructure
* Inadequately trained library professionals
* Lack of initiative on the part of the library professionals

* Lack of support from higher authorities
* Lack of awareness among library professionals about the potential of ICT
* Lack of co-ordination among library professionals
* Lack of ICT knowledge on the part of users
* Lack of interest on the part of users
* Lack of long-term approach towards ICT application
* Inadequate publicity for ICT based resources and services
* Discouraging attitude of library professionals towards their users

The application of Information and Communication Technologies in different types of libraries in India has gained much momentum. New and emerging technologies such as Wireless Networking, Radio Frequency Identification technology, multimedia technology, graphical user interfaces, etc have immense possibilities for libraries. Although the use of ICT in libraries in India at present is quite low, it is expected to go up in the coming years with continued reduction in the prices of the hardware and software. The extent of use of ICT in the libraries, which are already using it, will increase substantially. Libraries will use expert systems and artificial intelligence systems. Remote browsing of databases and tele-delivery of documents will increase. Packet-switched networks will be common. Use of CD-ROM and DVD-ROM will increase further. The World Wide Web is going to be more interactive and multidimensional, incorporating multimedia presentations.

SPECIAL LIBRARIES

Any attempt at a clear definition of a special library poses a significant challenge, since the community of special libraries is best characterised by its diversity. Special libraries are very large or very small; government-supported or privately funded; open to the public or closed to public access; serve non-profit institutions or for-profit organizations. Special libraries cater to specific professional or academic groups whose information needs are defined by a particular subject or activity. Special libraries, sometimes referred to as information centers, are located in a multitude of settings, including large corporations, government agencies, health institutions, print and electronic media organisations, law firms, not-for-profit organisations, and college campuses. Given the diversity and the fact that many special libraries are not accessible to the general public, special libraries are the least familiar of the four major categories of libraries. A special library delivers services that are tailored to the mission of the organization or institution it services. Usually these services are defined by subject area and delivered to specific clientele. The clientele of the special libraries recognise the value of and rely upon library services to be successful in their work. The clientele is often very well educated and reasonably sophisticated in their use of libraries and information services. Staffs in special libraries develop significant subject expertise in order to enhance services. Within their subject areas, special libraries constitute invaluable sources of information and service.

Special libraries are different from other libraries in a number of ways. First, as already stated, special libraries are created to serve the information needs of a specific audience. Usually, but not always, special libraries are used by professionals working in the area of knowledge that the library collects materials on. The main focus of the special library is not on creating and managing a large, diverse collection of materials. Rather, the focus is on actively providing a specialized information service to the users. Special librarians often develop user profiles, and create what is called an "alerting service." In an alerting service, special librarians try to anticipate the specific information needs of individual users, and collecting relevant information from such sources as journals, newspapers, books, web sites, electronic databases, or the internal correspondence. All the above factors and features are considered in the following statements, i.e a library is special when[1]:

1. It is organized around a special collection;
2. It serves a special clientele;
3. It specialises in a particular form of material;
4. The services organized by it are of a special nature;
5. It gives emphasis in providing information contained in different media rather than providing documents themselves;
6. It is established in non-traditional setting; and
7. It is subservient to a parent organization.

The resources and services of special libraries vary, reflecting the values, services and mandate of the parent organization. In addition to offering traditional library services, special libraries offer value-added services such as research and publication of various types of reports. Special libraries are always in the forefront of the application of Information and Communication Technologies in information handling activities. They are now routinely using ICT like online databases, CD-ROM products, World Wide Web, electronic journals, E-mail and Intranets for information handling activities. ICT offers variety of services and facilities for special libraries. Internet resources are available for acquisition, order processing, cataloguing, and serials management. Publishers and vendors can be located via their web pages and orders can be placed using e-mail. Resource sharing, co-operative cataloguing, co-operative information retrieval and access to central authority files are procedures that can more easily be streamlined using online resources. Special libraries can access directories, bibliographies, catalogues, reviews, table of contents through online. Enquiries can be taken and answered via e-mail, reducing delays for urgently required information. The Internet provides a convenient tool for retrieving information for a whole range of queries. Electronic document delivery services offer an efficient and speedy alternative to traditional interlibrary loan. Electronic journals are a good example of the kind of multimedia products likely to feature more prominently in the special libraries and information centres. Electronic publishing offers enormous potential for information delivery. It provides search facilities and the inclusion of hypertext links to external sources. It can transform an electronic journal into a data warehouse of navigable information. Following are some of the areas of key concern of a special library where librarian can play vital role to keep pace with the changing ICT environment[2]:

* Library automation: automating library house keeping operations
* Progressive automation of reference services
* Library management: classification, cataloguing, indexing, database creation
* Access to local and wide area networks
* Reprography: photography, microfilms, microfiche, audio and videotapes, printing, optical discs etc.
* Technical communication: technical writing, editing, publishing, etc.
* Need for bibliographical instructions, orientation and training in the field of latest information technology
* Collection development in different storage media-

paper as well as other non paper media like optical and electronic resources

* Developing skills to navigate internet
* Human Resource Development

SPECIAL LIBRARIES IN KERALA

Kerala lies on the southwest coast of the Indian Peninsula, stretching 360 miles along what is known as the Malabar Coast. The political state of Kerala was formed on November 1st, 1956 with the joining of the Travancore-Cochin State and Malabar. Its area of 15,000 square miles comprises just over one percent of the total land area of India, though its 29 million population accounts for 3.5% of the Indian population. The state is bordered by Karnataka to the north and Tamil Nadu to the east, but Kerala is physically separated from neighboring states by the Western Ghat mountain range.

There are about one hundred special libraries in Kerala. These include Science and Technology institution libraries, Social Science institution libraries, Industrial and Commercial institution libraries, Government Departmental libraries, etc. Depending upon the parent body, these libraries can be classified into three: libraries coming under the purview of Government of India institutions, those attached to State Government institutions and private institutions.

CENTRAL GOVERNMENT ORGANISATION LIBRARIES

This category includes both Central Government institution libraries and libraries of autonomous institutions coming under Government of India. Most of these libraries come under different councils and ministries or departments. Therefore these libraries can further be classified according to their affiliation:

Indian Council Agricultural Research (ICAR): This Council comes under the Ministry of Agriculture. It is an autonomous body and all research institutions coming under ICAR are autonomous in nature. In Kerala, there are five major research institutions under ICAR.

The major ICAR institution libraries are:

* Central Marine Fisheries Research Institute (CMFRI) Library, established in 1947 by the Govt. of India under the Ministry of Food and Agriculture in Cochin
* Central Plantation Crops Research Institute (CPCRI) established in 1970 as one of the agricultural research institutes in the National Agricultural Research System under the ICAR, in Kasaragod
* Central Institute of Fisheries Technology (CIFT), Cochin in 1957
* Central Tuber Crops Research Institute (CTCRI), Thiruvananthapuram in 1963
* Indian Institute of Spices Research (IISR), established in 1975 as the erstwhile Regional Station of Central Plantation Crops Research Institute, in Calicut

Council of Scientific and Industrial Research (CSIR): Regional Research Laboratory (RRL), one among the 38 national laboratories of the CSIR, is a multidisciplinary research laboratory nucleated in Thiruvananthapuram in 1976. It has a very good library and it is participating in a consortium for electronic journal subscription.

Department of Science and Technology: Sree Chithira Tirunal Institute of Medical Science and Technology (SCTIMSCT), Thiruvananthapuram comes under this category. It has a Biomedical Wing and a Hospital Wing and both have well established and automated libraries.

Indian Space Research Organisation (ISRO): The major institution of ISRO is Vikram Sarabhai Space Centre (VSSC) established in 1963 in Thiruvananthapuram. It has a very good library with all modern ICT facilities and it is considered the biggest special library in Kerala. Another important institution coming under ISRO is Liquid Propulsion System Centre (LPSC), the youngest Centre of ISRO established in Thiruvananthapuram in 1987, has been contributing substantially towards the successful space missions of India. It also has a well-equipped automated library. The PSLV and GSLV projects also have separate collections.

Defence Research Development Organisation (DRDO): This institution comes under the Department of Defence. Naval Physical Oceanographic Laboratory (NPOL) established in 1952 in Cochin form part of this organisation. It has a very good automated library.

Department of Electronics : There are two major institutions under this department. Centre for Development of Advanced Computing (C-DAC) in Thiruvananthapuram and DOEACC (Department of Electronics Accredited Computer Courses) Centre in Calicut. Both have libraries, which are heavily used by students of engineering colleges in Kerala as well as IT professionals.

Ministry of Commerce and Industry: The major institutions coming under this ministry are Spices Board in Cochin and Rubber Board in Kottayam. Rubber Research Institute of India (RRII) established in 1955 in Kottayam functions under Rubber Board. RRII is the best library of its kind in Asia and has services like documentation list, Rubber Alerts, New Additions List, and Current List of Periodical Publications, and literature searches from AGRIS, HORTCD and RAPRA CD. Indian Cardamom Research Institute (ICRI) established in Idukki is the R&D wing of Spices Board. All these institutions have libraries, but the use is comparatively less, especially electronic information resources and services.

The Marine Products Export Development Authority (MPEDA), a nodal agency established in 1972 in Cochin is the lone centre under this category. This authority has a well-equipped library. Another institute is National Institute of Oceanography (NIO) Regional Centre, Cochin established in 1971. This institute has a very good library. It is also participating in consortia for electronic journals.

PUBLIC SECTOR INSTITUTIONS/ORGANISATIONS

Public Sector Institutions/Organisations fall under various departments. Most of these institutions have very good libraries. But they lagg behind in automation as well as ICT application. Important Public Sector Institutions/ Organisations in Kerala are:

* FACT Engineering Design Organisation (FEDO) established in 1964 in Cochin
* Kochi Refineries Limited (KRL) in Cochin
* Cochin Shipyard (CS) in Cochin
* Hindustan Machine Tools (HMT) Kalamassery, Cochin, established in 1966
* News print factory established in Velloor in 1978
* Fluid Control Research Institute (FCRI) established in 1989 in Palakkad

MEDIA LIBRARIES

The two major radio stations in Kerala, namely AIR Thiruvananthapuram and Kozhikode and the library of Doordarshan Kendra, Thiruvananthapuram belong to this category.

STATE GOVERNMENT INSTITUTION LIBRARIES

Special libraries under State Government institutions can be categorised as research institution libraries, industrial and commercial institution libraries, government departmental libraries, etc.

RESEARCH INSTITUTION LIBRARIES

The nineteen seventies witnessed the emergence of a number of research institutions in Kerala, which can be considered as the golden period in the development history of special libraries in Kerala. The major ones are:

Center for Development Studies (CDS) was established in 1971 in Thiruvananthapuram. CDS has accorded high priority for building up a good library in social sciences. It is now one of the leading professional research and reference libraries in the country with a rich collection of books, journals, publications of other research institutions, and publications by the government.

Kerala Forest Research Institute (KFRI) established under the science and technology umbrella of Kerala in Peechi, in 1975. KFRI has one of the best scientific libraries in Kerala with about 13000 books, 6000 back volumes of journals, and 7000 reprints of scientific papers covering all disciplines related to forestry.

Center for Earth Science Studies (CESS) was established in Thiruvananthapuram in 1978, as an autonomous multi-disciplinary research institute by the Government of Kerala in accordance with its science and technology policy.

Center for Water Resource Development and Management (CWRDM) was established in 1978 in Calicut.

Tropical Botanical Garden and Research Institute (TBGRI) is an autonomous orgnisation established in Thiruvananthapuram in 1979.

Centre for Management Development (CMD) was established in 1980 in Thiruvananthapuram.

Institute for Management in Government (IMG) was established in 1987 in Thiruvananthapuram,

Kerala Institute of Local Administration (KILA) was

established in 1990 under the initiative of the Department of Local Self Government of the Government of Kerala, is a nodal institutions for training, research, documentation and consultancy in area of local governance in Thrissur.

Other research institutions which has good library facilities are National Transportation Planning and Research Centre (NATPAC), Thiruvananthapuram; Regional Cancer Centre (RCC), Thiruvananthapuram and Agency for Non-Conventional Energy and Rural Technology (ANERT), Thiruvananthapuram.

INDUSTRIAL AND COMMERCIAL INSTITUTION LIBRARIES

There are a number of Industrial and Commercial Institution Libraries in Kerala. Kerala State Industrial Development Corporation (KSIDC) established in 1961, Thiruvananthapuram, and Kerala Industrial Technical Consultancy Organisation (KITCO) established in 1972, Cochin are the most prominent among them. Even though a number of industries are there in Kerala and libraries are attached to most of them, they are not generally well established except in few firms. One of the notable libraries in this are is that of Technopark, Thiruvananthapuram.

GOVERNMENT DEPARTMENT LIBRARIES

Major Government Department Libraries include libraries of Directorate of Economics and Statistics, Thiruvananthapuram (1951); State Planning Board, Thiruvananthapuram (1968) and Kerala State Pollution Control Board, Thiruvananthapuram (1974). Apart from these there are libraries attached to Kerala Secretariat, Kerala Legislative Assembly and Government Departments like Bureau of Economics and Statistics, Thiruvananthapuram; Bureau of Health Intelligence, Thiruvananthapuram; Directorate of Agriculture, Thiruvananthapuram; Directorate of Animal Husbandary, Thiruvananthapuram; Directorate of Fisheries, Thiruvananthapuram; Directorate of Industries and Commerce, Thiruvananthapuram; Directorate of National Employment Service, Thiruvananthapuram; Directorate of Public Instruction, Thiruvananthapuram; Public Service Commission, Thiruvananthapuram etc.[3] Most of these departments have libraries and some have fulltime librarians. But the use of these libraries is very less compared to other special libraries.

LIBRARIES OF PRIVATE INSTITUTIONS

The prominent libraries in this category belong to the newspapers and TV channels. Leading Malayalam dailies like Malayala Manorama, Kottyam, Mathrubhumi, Kozhikode, Kerala Kaumudi, Thiruvanathapuram have excellent library facilities. The major TV channel libraries are that of Asianet, Thiruvanathapuram, Kairali, Thiruvanathapuram and India Vision, Kochi.

As far as Kerala is concerned, special libraries are much ahead of academic and public libraries in services and facilities. Among them, the libraries attached to the Central Government autonomous institutions are better of. There is no study about the current state-of-the-art application of ICT in these libraries. One major drawback of special library system in Kerala is that each one of these libraries function as independent units and there is no effective cooperation among these libraries so far. Different types of library networks and consortia are emerging in the different parts of India. Kerala is practically remaining aloof from these initiatives. A well-planned network or consortia of these libraries can function more effectively.

SIGNIFICANCE OF THE STUDY

All over the world, including developing countries like India, there is a shift in the library operations and services. In India libraries are shifting towards automation and ICT application. This is more prominent in the case of special libraries. Generally, special libraries are positive towards automation and the application of Information and Communication Technologies in library operations and services. Special libraries in India are no exception to this trend. They are the centres of scientific information, which is very essential for the development of a nation. Application of ICT helps to provide more advanced, effective and efficient services in special libraries. Special libraries are using advanced Information and Communication Technologies for accessing and retrieving information. They are getting bibliographic and full text databases through online. The introduction of CD-ROM technology has made immence possibilities in the storage, retrieval and dissemination of information in special libraries. Now a variety of databases like multimedia databases, image databases, etc are available in CD-ROM and a library can provide this information through CD-Net Server or CD Tower. The explosive growth of Internet and widespread acceptance of networking has made possible to access any type of information anywhere in the world. There are different tools/services/utilities in Internet to get information. E-mail, WWW, Ftp, Telnet, Newsgroups, etc are some of them. The introduction of online journals and databases had revolutioned the information handling capacities of special libraries.

Even after a decade of application of ICT in special libraries in India, it has not reached to the expectations of the user community. Therefore, it is the right time to assess the various issues and find out solutions to accelerate the use of ICT in libraries and information centres in India. In this context this study is very important and useful as far as special libraries in developing countries like India are concerned. The application of ICT in the special library sector in India is less well documented. The special library sector in India is still a relatively neglected area for research, particularly the research and development institutions libraries. In the process, many libraries are facing different kinds of problems. There exists no detailed account of the state of special libraries and their problems in ICT application. Though some studies have been made by few scholars, they are either restricted to particular region or few selected libraries attached to research oriented institutions. There is no research study conducted about the application of Information and Communication Technologies in special libraries in Kerala. It is very relevant and essential to know what is the status/position of special libraries in the Kerala state. Hence, the need is felt to study in detail the application of ICT in special libraries in Kerala and the problems relating to ICT application.

This study provides current state-of-the-art as well as gives an indication of future application of Information and Communication Technologies in special libraries in Kerala. It also identifies the reasons that promoted or hindered the application of ICT, the ICT skills and expertise of the library staff and the attitude of librarians and users towards the application of ICT in Special Libraries in Kerala. This study also reveals the implications of the state-of-the-art-technology on libraries and library profession. The present study provides information for the effective application of ICT in special libraries in India. It shows the present conditions of special libraries in Kerala and possible solutions for the effective and efficient implementation of ICT in Special Libraries in India.

The study provides useful information for librarians and other information managers in India and other developing countries to develop sustainable automated, ICT based library system that may enhance their services and resources. It provides the information on the availability of ICT related infrastructure and it may help in planning and improvement of information services in libraries. Understanding the benefits and potential of ICT will help in improving the existing infrastructure for providing quality information services and resources. Finding out the current status and the level of training and re-orientation needed for the library staff in using the ICT resources and services will greatly facilitate to take necessary steps in meeting these requirements in a systematic and effective way. Many libraries are taking steps to switch over from their traditional roles into technology enabled service-centered roles; in this context the findings of this study is very useful for these libraries to plan and develop a well automated, ICT enabled library system.

SCOPE AND LIMITATIONS OF THE STUDY

This study assesses in detail the application of Information and Communication Technologies in Special Libraries in Kerala. It aims to pinpoint the need for development and application of ICT in Special Libraries in Kerala. The universe of the present study is the special libraries of national importance such as libraries of premier academic institutions, scientific and technological research centres (comprising institutions of Council of Scientific and Industrial Research/ Department of Science and Technology, Defence Research and Development Organisation, Indian Council of Agricultural Research, and Indian Space Research Organisation) and research and development units of industrial organizations in Kerala. Since the use of Information and Communication Technologies require certain minimum infrastructure and qualified fulltime library professional and also ICT resources and related equipments require substantial financial commitment by libraries, government departmental libraries were excluded from the study.

The present investigation focuses on the Special Libraries in Kerala. Only the automated special libraries of national importance such as premier scientific and research institutions, and research and development units of industrial organizations in Kerala are selected for the study. A study of this kind at the national level is not feasible in a country like India. This study also did not take into account other types of libraries such as academic and public libraries. The tools used for data collection are structured questionnaires, semi-structured interviews and personal observations. Neverthless, these tools have their own limitations to investigate a problem like the present study.

CONCLUSION

This study has provided detailed information about the current state-of-the-art application of Information and Communication Technologies in Special Libraries in Kerala. Application of ICT in special libraries has become inevitable in an era of information explosion and widespread use of digital information resources. Effective application of ICT in libraries helps in performing their operations and services most efficiently. In Kerala many libraries have been applying ICT for providing efficient services and resouces. In an era when large number of useful information products is only available in digital format, the gap between so-called 'information rich' and 'information poor' countries is widening further. Rather information poor countries are now under the threat of 'information starvation'. To overcome this unfortunate situation, library management in developing countries need to review their policies and, instead of heavily depending on traditional information resources, should set apart adequate ICT based resources for collecting digital information. They also need to give priority to staff training, and user education in regard to ICT based resources and services.

REFERENCES

1. Vijayakumar, K.P. (1999) Special library scene in India: a conspectus. IN: Devarajan, G. ed. **50 Years of Indian Librarianship**. New Delhi, Ess Ess Publications, p. 76.
2. Sumati Sharma. (1999) Information technology in special library environment. **DESIDOC Bulletin of Information Technology,** 19 (6) November, p. 19.
3. Hemachandran Nair, G. (1996) **Government department libraries of Kerala: an investigative study based on Thiruvananthapuram.** M.L.I.Sc. Dissertation, University of Kerala.

2.2 Applications of ICT in Libraries

Information is a dynamic and unending resource that affects all disciplines and all walks of life. It supports education, research and development. Technology in its broad sense is the main factor determining the development of information. Information and Communication Technologies (ICT) facilitate transfer of electronic data or information from one place to another, one person to another and from one library to another library. ICT is a key phrase to indicate the dynamism that can be achieved with the convergence of computing and telecommunications. ICT is the electronic means of capturing, processing, storing and communicating information. It covers any product that will store, retrieve, manipulate, transmit or receive information electronically in a digital form. It encompasses an array of hardware, software, businesses, services and networks that enable access to online technology. ICT infrastructure is considered as the most dominant paradigm of development in the recent years. ICT have become dramatically and strategically important in modern civilisation. These technologies are inexorably integrated, creating new intellectual capabilities by assisting the human brain and thus changing most aspects of daily life[1]. During the past decade or more, several developing countries and regions of the world have been adopting, adapting and applying components of ICTs, in ways that facilitate information access and exchange to assist R&D,

decision making, problem solving, management, and so on, in the public and private sectors, in such areas as science and technology, education, industry, trade, social and cultural development, etc.

ICT has immense possibilities in library services, operations and resources. The main functions of a library are to acquire information from various sources and arrange, process, disseminate them to satisfy the needs of the users in the right form and at the right time. The libraries have found it very difficult to acquire, arrange, process and disseminate information in traditional ways. So, librarians are compelled to plan, organise and communicate the huge information according to the needs of users with the help of Information and CommunicationTechnologies. The application of ICT facilitates innovation, free flow of information, creative expression, and effective management. The use of ICT in libraries has tremendously increased because it provides enhanced user satisfaction, cost effectiveness, faster and simpler programmes, rapid responses, and easier operational procedures. Electronic information resources are available in static physical forms such as CD-ROMs, floppies or in a fluid form like the Internet. Libraries need to adopt a renewed approach for managing and accessing various retrieval tools available. It needs a good understanding and assessment of users needs as well as evaluation of electronic information resources. The value of electronic information is that it can be easily shared, distributed, updated, manipulated and rapidly searched. A feature of the current electronic environment is the apparently seamless way in which resources are networked and accessed across different computing platforms, and a substantial research and development effort is being concentrated in this direction. The World Wide Web currently represents the single most important common interface from which to access a diverse and disparate range of information.

It is the desire of a modern library to apply and enjoy the benefits of up-to-date technologies in its every day functioning and future development. Developments in Information and Communication Technology have had a major impact in all types of libraries and information centres over the last two decades. The challenges for libraries arise from the advent of computer and the proliferation of cheaper, faster, and more efficient means of accessing information. These challenges are profound and have a wide reach in the library world. The ability of computer to store and process vast amount of information coupled with the ability of communication technology to transmit this information from one location to another has revolutionised storage, retrieval and dissemination of information in libraries. The systems of Information and Communication Technology constitute several things. Following is an attempt to show some of the major components of ICT in the domain of library and information science.

The computers are being increasingly used in library and information services for processing and repackaging of information and on improving products and services of library and information centers. Computers have made possible the availability of information and have brought many benefits in library and information systems and services. The computers' application to the information storage, retrieval and dissemination are the inevitable consequences of the information explosion/overload. The application of computers to information storage and retrieval has brought new possibilities of automatic indexing and free text searching for the words or phrases on the subject, which is likely to occur in any document, and the computer is set to read entire document for the appropriate words or phrases. The development of digital representation of information has made the computer an effective tool for data processing. The computers are of great significance with the advancement of telecommunication and reprography technologies in the library automation.

Using computers to assist in information processing began experimentally in the 1960s. In the 1970s most libraries used the computer of the parent body, or a mainframe system over which they had no direct control. The 1970s saw the growth of cooperative services and resource sharing among libraries. The significant drop in prices and impressive increase in power for microcomputers made microcomputer-based systems became feasible by the mid-1980s. Automation in the nineties is an increasingly divergent issue, in terms of resources, skills, and abilities. Over the past few years, library automation has undergone a dramatic shift in direction. Library automation began with the in-house processing of traditional tasks and grew to include the use of computing and telecommunications tools. Now there is a "library without walls" which uses technology to expand services, resources, and relationships between libraries and resources around the world. Digital libraries necessitate a move toward automation, in that to get access to the library resources, a user has to have access to a networked computer. The future of library automation systems will include Information Kiosks, where people with no computer experience can access information easily. Information scientists will create the human-computer interfaces and library scientists will manage the resources. Current trends in library automation reflect the dynamic nature of library automation. Library automation will continue to change and evolve in the future.

ONLINE PUBLIC ACCESS CATALOGUES (OPACS)

The ALA Glossary defines online public access catalogue as 'a computer-based and supported library catalogue (bibliographic database) designed to be accessed via terminals so that library users may directly and effectively search for and retrieve bibliographic records without the assistance of a human intermediary such as a specially trained member of the library staff'[2]. Online catalogues were developed in the late 1970s and since then have become widely accepted as the contemporary form of catalogue in the developed world. An online catalogue database normally consists of bibliographic records. The ability to search by keyword liberates the user from the need to have full author or title information. OPAC allows searching by name, title, subject and keywords and offers online access through terminals. One of the major advantages of an online catalogue is that if linked to an automated circulation system it can indicate the current status of an item.

The concept of WebOPAC is recent origin and it is serving as a gateway to the resources not only held by the respective library but also to the holdings of other participating libraries without limiting to local collection but going beyond further to regional, national and international levels[3]. It allows users to interact with documents stored on computers all over the world and makes easier access to catalogue data in the form of bibliographic records. It becomes another search engine referred as 'Web Cats' and as an 'Information Gateway'. It can support protocols such as telnet, http, ftp and Gopher and can support files and documents like Portable Document Format (PDF), Hypertext Mark-up Language (HTML) and Standard Generalised Mark-up Language (SGML). Some of the disadvantages of WebOPAC are: 1) Some WebOPACs, even though the link is available on the Web page or the telnet address is given, are restricted to a particular user community and requires the use of appropriate login names and passwords, 2) Some WebOPACs do not provide links through authors or subjects, 3) Displays in most of the WebOPACs failed to provide access to online help and 4) Some of the WebOPACs do not display the database being searched, the search strategy/query and the call number[4].

STORAGE TECHNOLOGIES

For centuries paper has been considered as the appropriate medium for storing of information. But now the new technologies have succeeded in storing information on various media. Mass storage is necessary to meet the following needs[5]:

* Providing large-volume digital storage for archival management;
* Providing users with immediate access to the rapidly growing volume of data and information that is stored in digital information system and is likely to be distributed on optical media in the future;
* Providing users with access to multimedia information quickly and interactively through the integration of technologies; and
* Transferring large volumes of data and/or files from one system to another.

Libraries have been using microfilm, microfiche and ultra-fiche, which help to store large volumes of data in a comparatively lesser space than the print media. Computer-based mass storage technologies are becoming the major storage technologies in libraries and information centres. Computer storage technologies can be grouped into magnetic and non-magnetic technologies. The magnetic storage technologies include magnetic tape, magnetic disc, cartridge tape and digital audiotape. The optical disc storage technologies include read-only, write once read many and erasable/rewritable media.

CD-ROM (COMPACT DISC-READ ONLY MEMORY)

CD-ROM was developed[6] in 1985. The growth of multimedia titles, games, entertainment and cheap availability of videodiscs, and the latest trend in software distribution through CDs made CD-ROM discs and drives more popular. The CD-ROM, as 12-cm and 1.2 mm thick disc can hold approximately 650-700 million characters (650-700 MB) equal to about 2, 70,000 pages of plain text or about 60,000 suitably compressed images. The advantages of CD-ROM are its huge storage capacity, durability, transportability, light weight, easy and fast access to and non-corruptibility of stored information, immunity to magnetic fields and amenability for parallel searching by multiple users in a Local Area Network (LAN) or Wide Area Network (WAN) environment. CD-ROMs can be used to store abstracts, databases, full-length articles, images, audio and software. The uses of CD-ROM databases are given below[7]:

1. Facilitate collection development, evaluation, print purchase orders, produce card catalogue and quantitative/citation studies as databases like Books-in-Print Plus with about 2 million records and a number of indexes offer such flexibility;
2. Serve as reference tools;
3. Support current awareness service and selective dissemination of information as it is possible to provide contents, abstracts, full text etc and also facilitate information retrieval by a specific journal name;
4. Allow expanded quality of services, enhanced number of users, exhaustive coverage of information at little or no extra cost or time;
5. Are viable and cost effective alternatives to online searching though not as current as online databases;
6. Facilitate library automation, retro conversion of bibliographic data as well as cataloguing since many OPACs of individual or groups of libraries are available on CD-ROMs;
7. Amenable for retrospective searching as back files are also available in many cases;
8. Facilitate networking, library cooperation, searching

by multi and remotely located users, and resource sharing;

9. Help in saving of resources as less-used journals can be discontinued if they are included in bibliographic databases and only those articles needed from such journals can be procured based on CAS and SDI services;
10. Involve lesser transit delays and provide more current information than print media;
11. Enhance the image of the library and serve as excellent public relation tools, especially in the present environment of marketing of information products;
12. Allow exchange of bibliographic data, software, etc; and
13. Are ideal for archival purposes of gray literature like internal reports, newspapers, reports, standards and patents.

Increasing availability of numerous databases such as abstracting journals, dictionaries and encyclopaedia on CDs is proving a cost-effective solution for libraries. With multimedia extensions, the CDs are seen as provider of interactive reading and viewing material.

CD-ROM networking is the technology that allows workstations on a Local Area Network (LAN) to access CD-ROM drives on another computer functioning as a CD-ROM server. This enables sharing of information available on the CDs within the organisation. The CD-ROMs centrally stored can be connected to an existing network and there is no limit to the number of users that can access them at any time. The different types of CD-ROM drives are: CD-Changers, CD-Tower, and CD-ROM Arrays. Many libraries depend more on CD-ROM databases than the online systems because CD-ROM needs only a fixed annual charge and there is no need to rely upon telecommunications networks. Online searches are used just to supplement the information obtained from CD-ROMs.

The popularity of some CD-ROM databases and the presence of Local or Wide Area Networks in many organisations along with the increasing availability of networking solutions have provided librarians with an impetus for exploring the feasibility of simultaneous multi-user access.

DVD (DIGITAL VIDEO DISC OR DIGITAL VERSATILE DISC)

Digital Video Disc or Digital Versatile Disc is an optical storage medium looks like a CD but with high storage capacity. DVD facilitates greater data density by making the pits smaller and the spiral tighter, small recording pits, more closely-spaced tracks, and backward compatibility with CD-ROM. For reading these tightly packed discs lasers that produce a shorter wavelength bean of light are required. DVD technology provides data capacity that is atleast 6 to 7 times greater than CD-ROM. Various form of DVDs are available, some of them are DVD-Video or DVD-V, DVD-ROM, DVD-R, DVD-RAM and DVD-RW. High storage capacity is achieved by compression technology and storing data on multi-layer sides. The DVDs are developed in four forms: the single-side single-layer (SSSL), single-side double-layer (SSDL), double-side single-layer (DSSL), and double-side double-layer (DSDL). A single sided-single layer DVD can store 4.7 GB of data and two-layer DVD can store 8.5 GB of data. A double sided-single layer DVD can store 9.4 GB of data and double-sided double layer DVD can store 17 GB of data. CD-ROM drives can upgrade to DVD-ROM drives. One can play a CD-ROM on a DVD drive, but DVD discs cannot be played on CD-ROM drives and also DVD-Video cannot be able to play a DVD-ROM. The application of DVD-RAM and DVD-RW include data archiving, software development, video and audio editing, and recording one's own optical discs [8].

Some of the benefits of DVD are [9]:

1. To represent more multimedia elements and to integrate many reference sources on a single DVD disc.
2. Its use as a single interchange standard to provide unification for computer, consumer electronics and entertainment industry;
3. Its backward read compatibility with existing CDs, and future compatibility with read/write and WORM discs;
4. Its utility as a single file system for all disc types;
5. Its low cost;
6. DVD can deliver the data at a higher rate than CD-ROM;
7. It does not need for mandatory containers for playing discs;
8. Its reliability in data storage and retrieval including error correction capability for ROMs and rewritable discs;
9. Its high online capacity of 8.5 GB on a single side or 17 GB on both sides;
10. DVD drives can read both CD-ROMs and DVD-ROMs;
11. Better security of data; and
12. Its high performance for sequential and non-sequential data.

High Density CD (HDCD) and DVD are the latest trend in storage technology. Hybrid jukeboxes can accept CDs, optical discs or digital linear tapes to provide storage capacities of the order of a few Terabytes (TB) are being developed. With enhanced data transfer rates and a few GB online capacity, DVD is being seen as a replacement to VCR. A DVD recorder may be used to record programmes digitally. Optical medium have long-term archival standard and it can be used for both online and archival applications. Optical medium claim a shelf life of more than 100 years. Another technology expected to play a vital role in storage applications is magneto-optic technology.

Fluorescent Multi-layered (FM) technology is the latest storage technology. FMD-ROM (Fluorescent Multi-layering Disc-Read Only Memory) can store 140 GB of data on a single disc. It is based on 3-D florescence of chemicals in the pits and grooves.

DATABASE AND DATABASE MANAGEMENT SYSTEMS

A database is a collection of logically related pieces of electronic information (known as data) that have been organised into categories (known as fields) and grouped into units (known as records). Databases are created so that stored information can be found when needed. It is designed, built, and populated to take in information and information sources acquired for the specific purpose of serving user groups. It has an intended group of users and some preconceived applications in which these users are interested. The selection of information and other sources is based on the objective of serving them.

DBMS (Database Management System) is the software used to manipulate and access data stored in a database. It provides facilities that allow users to deal with data without needing to know how that data is actually stored or retrieved. DBMS acts as an interface between the user and the data. The maturation of DBMS technology has coincided with significant developments in distributed computing results the emergence of Distributed Database Management Systems (DDBMS). A distributed database management system is a database management system capable of supporting and manipulating distributed databases. Distributed database is a logical database that is physically divided among computers at several sites on a network. The basic motivation for distributed databases is improved performance, increased availability, shareability, expandability and access facility.

Distributed database management system manges applications based on data access from different sources at multiple locations.

DATA WAREHOUSING AND DATA MINING

Data Warehousing involves integrating the data from a number of source databases into one target resource centre, the data Warehouse. The Data Warehouse provides the required resource for informational purposes, and is analysis and decision support oriented, not operational or transaction oriented. The data warehouse is relatively non-volatile because the data are updated at fixed periodicity and not any time in between. Warehouse generation, data management and data access tools are the three distinct aspects in the implementation of data warehousing [10].

Planning, forecasting, organisation and management decisions can be made on information obtained from the warehouse by Data Mining. Data Mining is the process of extraction of previously unknown potentially useful information from the database. Various Data Mining algorithms exist which can extract various association rules, classification rules or can cluster the data. The single distinguishing characteristic of the data mining algorithms, which differentiates it from the traditional algorithms, is that it works on extremely large data set. Predictive modelling (using statistical clustering techniques), link analysis (using association theory) and deviation detection (filtering techniques) are the major operations involved in data mining process [11].

LIBRARY NETWORKING

A computer network is created when several computers and terminal devices are connected together by data communication systems. Networks offer two resources. First, they offer access to the people who use computers on the network, by means of e-mail, conferencing, chat facilities, etc. Second, networks permit the use of files (text, graphics, sounds and video), software, databases and peripherals (like printers or fax machines) stored on, or attached to, computers on the network.

Library networking is meant to promote and facilitate sharing of the resources available within a group of libraries in order to provide maximum information to users, lower operational costs and also make optimum use of national resources [12]. They have grown mostly during the last thirty years in different geographical environments in order to cater to the specific needs of users. In the United States, there has been a proliferation of them. Library networks in other countries are also growing. Several models have emerged that provide specific services. Numerous library networks have been in place, and are still in existence, throughout the world. Networks can be divided into two categories [13]: 1) Infrastructural networks, which provide the hardware, software and protocols for the flow of information. I-NET, NICNET, ERNET and INDONET are examples of this category. 2) Application networks which are set up by or for a specific community or for serving well-defined end-users. Networks like OCLC, INFLIBNET, DELNET, CALIBNET and MALIBNET are examples of this category.

LIBRARY CONSORTIA

A library consortium is a formal association of libraries not under the same institutional control, but usually restricted to a geographical area, number of libraries, type of materials, or subject interest established to develop resource sharing among members. It is a group of libraries that agree to pool their resources by allowing the users of each institution, either through interlibrary loan or borrowing privileges. The objective of library consortia is to control and reduce information costs, to improve resource sharing, to develop a network information environment and share licensing issues with each other [14]. Although cooperation among libraries has been an international tradition for decades, the phenomenal growth of consortia over the past decade clearly has been fueled by the rapid transformation made possible through Information and Communication Technologies. For several years, libraries of developed countries formed consortia for many different reasons such as sharing the same system, sharing common databases, sharing electronic journals, etc. Though there have been many cooperative efforts for resource sharing among the libraries of India in the last two decades, it is hard to find one successful programme that could be used as a benchmark to replicate in other libraries. The main factors that affect these kinds of efforts are more human and attitudinal than technological or economical. The information environment today is very much conducive enough to tackle the problems faced earlier. With the advent of the Internet and World Wide Web, it is possible to provide instantaneous access to the sources available not only within the organisation, but other institutions that participate in the consortia programme.

CONSORTIA BASED SUBSCRIPTION

Shared subscription to electronic resources is the main activity of a library consortium and it can be a viable solution in order to increase the access to electronic resources across institutions at a lower cost. Shared subscription means a strategic planning through which number of institutions having more or less the same information needs and requirements for fostering the library and information services to their readers agreeing to participate in a collective and collaborative efforts to subscribe electronic information resources for their mutual benefits. The consortia-based subscription can be successfully deployed to meet the pressures such as diminishing budget, increased user's demand and rising cost of electronic resouces. The collective strength of consortia members facilitates the libraries to get the benefit of wider access to electronic resources at affordable cost and at the best terms and conditions. The Committee of Experts on Consortia-based Subscription to Electronic Resources for Technical Education System in India listed the following benefits [15]:

1. Consortia-based subscription to electronic resources would provide access to wider number of electronic resources at substantially lower cost.
2. The consortia, with its collective strength of participating institutions, have attracted lower rates of subscription with most favourable terms of agreement.
3. The research productivity of all institutions is expected to improve with increased access to international databases and full-text resources.
4. The consortia is expected to trigger remarkable increase in sharing of both print and electronic resources amongst participating library through J-Gate Custom Contents for Consortia proposed for subscription by the committee.
5. The consortia is proposed to be an open-ended venture where other institutions can join and get the benefit of not only the lower subscription rates but also the favorable terms and conditions.
6. Consortia members will also have the benefit of cap on the annual increase in the rates of subscription.
7. The consortia have been offered better terms of agreement for use, archival access and preservation of subscribed electronic resources, which would not have been possible for any single institutions.
8. Since the subscribed resources would be accessible online in electronic format, the beneficiary institutions would have less pressure on space requirement for storing and managing print-based library resources. Moreover, all problems associated with print media such as their wear and tear, location, shelving, binding,

1.4
Summary of the Findings and Suggestions

The summary of the findings of the rearch study and suggestions for improving the computerised University Library System in the state of Kerala are discussed in this chapter.

SUMMARY OF THE FINDINGS

A number of findings are derived from the analysis of the data, a summary of which is given below:

LIBRARY COLLECTIONS

1. Library collections of University Libraries in Kerala were found mostly print based and the share of digital resources in the collection is very limited. KUL has a total collection of 286155 documents including Books, Bound Volumes of Journals, Theses and Dissertations, Approximately 150 Video Cassettes, 1500 Microfiches, 3000 CDs and 2 DVDs. MGUL has 33379 Books, 2881 Bound volumes of Journals, 428 Theses and Dissertations and 150 CDs. CUSATL has 55882 Books, 20798 Bound Volumes of Journals, 573 Theses and Dissertations, 1891 Patents and 168 CDs. CUL has 89568 Books, 2105 Bound Volumes of Journals, 3005 Theses and Dissertations, Audio and Video Cassettes one each, 250 Microfiches and 140 CDs. The share of digital collection in KUL, MGUL, CUSATL and CUL are only 1.03 per cent, 0.4 per cent, 0.21 per cent and 0.15 per cent

respectively of their total collection of documents.

2. KUL has not properly recorded the library collection and even after completion of complete retro-conversion KUL is not able to provide the exact data regarding various types of documents available in the library collections.

JOURNALS

3. KUL subscribes to a total of 294 Journals, MGUL to 269, CUSATL to 220 and CUL to 197 Journals. Out of these, 56 in KUL, 107 in MGUL, 122 in CUSATL and 36 in CUL are foreign Journals and 238 in KUL, 162 in MGUL, 98 in CUSATL and 161 in CUL are Indian Journals.
4. Subscription to online database by the University Libraries in Kerala is awfully less and KUL and MGUL have subscribed to two online databases each while CUSATL and CUL have not subscribed any.

TECHNICAL PROCESSING

5. University Libraries in Kerala follow different standards for Technical processing of documents
6. MGUL and CUL follow Dewey Decimal Classification, Anglo American Cataloguing Rules II and Library of Congress Subject Headings that are the standards internationally well accepted for technical processing of documents while KUL follows Colon Classification, Classified Catalogue Code and Chain Indexing which are not in wider use, and CUSATL follows AACR II, for Cataloguing rules and Universal Decimal Classification and Sears List of Subject Headings for classification and assigning subject heading respectively.

LIBRARY SERVICES

7. It was found that University Libraries differ on traditional library and information services provided to the users. KUL provide 6, MGUL 8, CUSATL 7 and

CUL 5 total number of services to their users. All the University Libraries provide Book Lending, Reference Service and Reprographic Service. None of the libraries provide Content Page Service, Local Indexing/ Abstracting Services, Routing of Periodicals and Translation Services. MGUL and CUSATL provide Current Awareness Service, Selective Dissemination of Information, Inter Library Loan Services and User Education Programmes. KUL and CUL provide Circulation of Accession List. Compilation of Bibliographies is provided by KUL, MGUL and CUL.

UTILIZATION OF THE LIBRARY

8. The analysis on frequency of visit by the users, purpose of library visit and time spent on a visit revealed that the academic community uses the University Libraries in Kerala mainly for Study and Research purposes. Majority of the users usually makes regular visit to the library on daily or alternative days. They are heavily depended on their respective libraries for satisfying their information requirements with regard to their higher education purposes.

FINANCIAL ASSISTANCE

9. There are disparities with regard to financial assistance received for computerisation purposes from various agencies by the University Libraries in Kerala.
10. INFLIBNET provided Rs. 52 Lakhs to KUL and Rs. 6.5 Lakhs each to other three libraries. KUL got Rs. 8 Lakhs while MGUL got Rs. 33 Lakhs and CUL Rs. 10 Lakhs and CUSATL got nil as financial assistance from the State Government annual plan fund for Computerisation purpose.
11. CUSATL got Rs. 2 Crores from MHO project Netherlands while no other library received any such huge amount from external source.

12. Substantial portion of the budget of the University Libraries studied are set apart for staff salary and purchase of books and journals while computer application related aspects are over looked in the university budgets.
13. During the last three financial years, KUL spent an average of 52.89 per cent, MGUL spent 47.45 per cent, CUSATL spent 45.84 per cent and CUL spent 79.98 per cent of their respective budget for their staff salary. KUL, MGUL, CUSATL and CUL spent an average of 21.48 per cent, 38.8 per cent, 50.58 per cent and 8.76 per cent respectively of their budget allocations for purchase of Books and Journals. On the other hand, for computerisation related matters the allocation of KUL, MGUL, CUSATL and CUL were 0.7 per cent, 8.12 per cent, 4.01 per cent and 5.73 per cent respectively.
14. MGUL and CUSATL have made budgetary provisions for the procurement of computer hardware and software while KUL and CUL have not made any provision towards the procurement of hardware and software.
15. MGUL and CUL have financial provision towards Recurring Charges related with computer applications whereas KUL and CUSATL have not made provision for this.
16. All the libraries except CUSATL have budgetary provision for AMC of Computer Hardware.
17. The meager budgetary provision made for computerisation in the university budgets reveals that the university authorities have not properly taken into consideration the expenditure towards the application of computers in libraries.

HARDWARE AVAILABLE

18. All the University Libraries studied found to be having adequate Server Class machines.

enhance researchers' ability to collaborate and conduct experiments.

* Demonstrate enhanced delivery of education and other services (e.g., health care, environmental monitoring) by taking advantage of "virtual proximity" created by an advanced communications infrastructure.
* Support development and adoption of advanced applications by providing middleware and development tools.
* Facilitate development, deployment, and operation of an affordable communications infrastructure, capable of supporting differentiated quality of service based on applications requirements of the R & E community.
* Promote experimentation with the next generation of communications technologies.
* Coordinate adoption of agreed working standards and common practices among participating institutions to ensure end-to end quality of service and interoperability.
* Catalyze partnerships with governmental and private sector organisations.
* Encourage transfer of technology from Internet 2 to the rest of the Internet.
* Study impact of new infrastructure, services, and applications on higher education and the Internet community in general.

IMPORTANCE OF INTERNET TO LIBRARIES

With more and more documents getting published electronically and Internet resources growing at 18% a month, libraries of 21st century will have to shift towards electronic means of acquiring, processing and disseminating information[19]. As the libraries are going web based more and more libraries are accessible via Internet. Web accessible

OPAC allows a user to browse through the documents of a library from any where in the world. The libraries can develop individual library web sites, bulleting board services, ready reference services and online acquisition of documents. Now a days almost every library have there own webpage and it is very helpful to promote library services at wider level. Institute can use library webpage as a platform to explore library services to users as well as community in concerned subject and it definitely help end users to know about library activity. A library can also disseminate information through e-mail, voice chatting, video-conferencing etc. and can access various remote databases through online [20].

Internet has made simple and speedy purchase of information sources/documents like books, journals, electronic publications, etc. Most of the publishers and booksellers have web sites and place regular catalogue and leaflets of new publications. Librarian can prepare standard catalogue with the help of Internet. Librarian can also check the catalogues with other libraries and confirm the information required for a record, which can be easily ascertained from the original document. Library users with Internet connection at home or anywhere can browse the catalogue with the help of WebOPAC and reserve the books sitting right at their offices or at home. According to Schmidt[21], "access to OPAC will be increasing from outside the library. The boundaries between the cataloguing of libraries holding and cataloguing of information will be more difficult than today, in my opinion they will vanish completely when networks have reached a certain technical capacity".

The Internet can be successfully utilised for providing reference service because various primary and secondary sources of information are available online from many sites. Internet can be useful in finding certain type of information such as computers and the people who use them; scientific and technical information, popular culture and entertainment,

historical and humanities information. Libraries can use Internet to communicate with publishers, booksellers and vendors. Librarian can also use Newsgroups for getting information. Through the Internet a librarian can access the resources of other libraries and through the Web OPAC he can browse the entire collection of a library and can make a request for a document through e-mail.

INTRANET AND EXTRANET

An Intranet is a private network with the Internet technology used as the underlying architecture. It uses TCP/IP protocols for communication as well as Internet resources such as the World Wide Web, E-mail, Telnet, and Ftp. The protocol can run in a variety of network hardware and can also co-exist with other network protocols such as IPX. An Intranet is separated from the rest of the Internet by a firewall- a hardware and software combination that prohibits unauthorized access to the Intranet. Intranets allow people to work together more easily and more efficiently. Intranet can be built using components that allow the extremely high bandwidth required for transferring such information. Often an Intranet is composed of different networks inside the corporation that all communicate with one another via TCP/IP. These separate networks are often referred to as Subnets. The information is sent across the Intranet using routers. Which examine each TCP/IP packet for the IP address and determine the packet destination. The benefits of an Intranet are: 1) Powerful data management, 2) Ease to use, 3) Cost efficiency and 4) Dynamic workgroup exchange.

For many organisations, the electronic information infrastructure is being build around groupware products or around the intranet. The appeal of intranets is that they provide a single central information store and encourage communication flows throughout the organisation. There is the potential to link every desktop in the organisation irrespective of which computing systems are in use. As intranet technologies mature, the focus is moving away from the technical aspects of implementation and development to consideration of the management of information and end-user applications. Information professionals are becoming Webmasters and intranet coordinators, combining technical expertise with information management ability.

An Extranet or Extended Internet is basically an Intranet lined up with some other organisation's Intranet or network of several co-operating organisations' Intranet. It uses existing Internet interactive infrastructure including standard servers, e-mail, web browsers etc. Extranet is considered as the 'Third wave' whereas Intranet as the 'Second wave' of Internet concept. A typical extranet site is divided into open and secure segments. Access security is the foundation of extranet concept. The Internet is wide open to anybody, an Intranet is private held behind the corporate firewall and an Extranet is a hybrid of the two in that it restricts access to the information but it extends beyond the protection of the firewall to allow suppliers, customers, vendors, partners etc. In a fully functional Extranet, transactional data are usually stored in a powerful database engine. The Extranet members to directly input or to retrieve a record or to initiate an automatic transaction could use special forms. A typical Extranet offers a private Discussion Area, which permits the members to exchange ideas and to share information.

WIRELESS TECHNOLOGIES

Over the last several years, wireless technologies have progressed and achieved success in various fields like healthcare, education, manufacturing, etc. Wireless technology has been around libraries for some years. But now only the libraries have realised its benefits for information services and library management activities. A number of libraries in western countries are using this technology. Wireless technology is very fast, reliable and highly flexible.

Its major benefit is the immediate access to digital resources. It enables users to simply and easily connect a wide range of computing and telecommunications devices without the need to buy, carry, or connect cables. It uses a variety of devices such as laptop and notebook computers, tablets, personal digital assistants (PDAs), email-only devices, handheld computers, etc. Wireless technology allows users to access the Internet without the constraints of cables, data lines, phone jacks, or even walls. Wireless data-translation protocols allow disparate devices to use the information from all sources effectively.

WIRELESS NETWORKING

Wireless networks use high-frequency electromagnetic waves, either infrared (IR) or radio frequency (RF) to transmit information from one point to another without relying on any physical connections. RF is expected to be of more practical use in library networking than IR, because it is not limited by line-of-sight transmission; radio waves travel through wall and windows. Data and voice traffic is superimposed or modulated, onto the radio waves or careers, and extracted at the receiving end. Multiple radio careers can exist in the same space at the same time without interfering with each other by transmitting at different frequencies. There are a large number of different technologies that can be used in wireless library network applications. Following are some of the technologies for wireless networking.

BLUETOOTH

Bluetooth is a global de facto standard for wireless connectivity and is based on a low-cost, low-power, short-range radio link for mobile devices and for Wide Area Network/Local Area Network access points. It offers fast and reliable transmissions of both voice and data over the globally available 2.4 GHz ISM (Industrial, Scientific and Medical) band[22]. Bluetooth will enable users to connect to a wide range of computing and telecommunication devices without the need to buy, carry, or connect cables. And because Bluetooth utilizes a radio-based link, it doesn't require a line-of-sight connection in order to communicate. When two Bluetooth equipped devices come within 10 metres of each other, they can establish a connection.

Bluetooth uses a radio link to connect devices instead of a cable and it can handle raw data of 1 Mbps with a peak asymmetric asynchronous throughput of 721 Kbps or three symmetric voice channels of 64 Kbps[22]. Bluetooth has sufficient in built encryption and authentication. Bluetooth eliminates the need for numerous cable attachments for connecting practically any kind of communication devices. The range of each radio is approximately 10 metres, but it can be extended to around 100 metres with an optional amplifier. Up to eight devices can be connected together wirelessly in a network called a 'picone '. A master unit is the device in a piconet whose clock and frequency hopping sequence are used to synchronise all other devices in the piconet. There is one master unit per piconet. Slaveunits are all devices in a piconet that are not the master. The slaves receive frequency-hopping sequences from the master and rely on the master's clock for the timing of the piconet. Up to 10 piconets can come together to form a 'scatternet' resulting in a total of 80 devices that are able to communicate through the network.

INFRARED

IrDA is a wireless technology that uses infrared, a faster wave frequency that is closer to visible light. It is a cable replacement technology similar to Bluetooth wireless technology. It has a short transmission range, 15 feet to 5 metres. Two devices must have an almost direct line-of-sight to connect. It transmits data in a point-to-point configuration. IrDA technologies did not develop with interoperability and industry standardisation as a primary goal, as did Bluetooth.

HIPERLAN TECHNOLOGY

High Performance Radio Local Area Network type 2 (HIPERLAN/2) provides high-speed multimedia communications between different broadband core networks and mobile terminals. HIPERLAN/2 relies on cellular networking topology combined with and adhoc networking capability. It supports two basic modes of operation: centralised mode and direct mode. The centralised mode is used in the cellular networking topology where each radio cell is controlled by an access point covering a certain geographical area. In this mode, a mobile terminal communicates with other mobile terminals or with the core network via an access point. The direct mode is used in the adhoc networking topology, where a radio cell covers the whole serving area.

WIRELESS LAN

A Wireless Local Area Network (WLAN) is a flexible data communication system implemented as an extension to, or as an alternative for, a wired LAN. It uses a high speed, radio-frequency (RF) network access technology to transmit data. It links computers to each other or to networks for shared access and Internet based information. The Institute of Electrical and Electronic Engineers (IEEE) established the 802.11b standard for wireless networks, and the Wireless Compatibility Ethernet Alliance (WECA), assures that Wireless LAN products are interoperable from manufacturer to manufacturer[23]. Wireless LANs have a range of technologies and each technology comes with its own set of advantages and limitations. The important technologies are Narrowband Technology, Spread Spectrum Technology and Infrared Technology.

A narrowband radio system transmits and receives information on a specific radio frequency. Narrowband radio keeps the radio signal frequency as narrow as possible just to pass the information. Undesirable cross talk between communication channels is avoided by carefully coordinating different users on different channel frequencies.

Spread Spectrum Technology is a wideband radio frequency technique developed to use in reliable, secure, mission-critical communications systems. It is designed to trade off bandwidth efficiency for reliability, integrity and security. There are two types of spread spectrum radio: Frequency Hopping Spread Spectrum Technology and Direct Sequence Spread Spectrum Technology. Frequency Hopping Spread Spectrum (FHSS) uses a narrowband career that changes frequency in a pattern known to both transmitter and receiver. Properly synchronized, the net effect is to maintain a single logical channel. To an unintended receiver, FHSS appears to be short duration impulse noise. Direct Sequence Spread Spectrum (DSSS) generates a redundant bit pattern for each bit to be transmitted. This bit pattern is called a chip (or chipping code). The longer the chip, the greater the probability the original data can be recovered. Even if one of more bits in the chip is damaged during transmission, statistical techniques embedded in the radio can recover the original data without the need for retransmission.

Infrared (IR) systems use very high frequencies, just below visible light in the electromagnetic spectrum to carry data. Like light, IR cannot penetrate opaque objects; it is either directed (line-of-sight) or diffuse technology. Inexpensive directed systems provide very limited range and typically used for personal area networks but occasionally used in specific wireless LAN applications.

WIRELESS NETWORKING IN LIBRARIES

Wireless networking help users to access digital information without connecting physically, and system administrators can set up or extend networks without installing wires. Mobility is the most attractive feature of wireless networking. It is more flexible than wired networking. It provides all the functionality of wired networking, without the physical constraints of the wire. Wireless networking can be used to access the library network, library resources and Internet without plug in by wires and cables. Wireless networking will allow users with devices like laptops, notebooks, simputers, PDAs, tablet PCs, etc to move freely in the library while remaining connected to the library network. Wireless networking is an excellent solution for libraries with historic buildings or older buildings where the installation of wired networking is either impossible or very expensive. Libraries can be saved from the constant wiring and rewiring by installing wireless networks. Libraries can get lot of space by wireless networking. Installation of wireless network is very easy because there are no wires. Wireless network components can be set up anywhere in the library. Wireless networking makes it easy to move computers and other devices without the need to reconfigure the network.

Here are some of the benefits of wireless networking in libraries [24]:

* A library wireless network provides access to multiple computers, databases, the Internet and library OPAC throughout the library or outside the library.
* It provides faster access to information for library users, resulting in better service and improved user satisfaction, location independent access for network administrators for easier on-site-trouble-shooting and support.
* Using laptop computers library users can access electronic media and also be physically near whatever printed material they want.
* Sharing of peripherals, files, multimedia resources and databases are easier.
* Improved database access.
* Simplified network configuration.

* Wireless networking permit quick connectivity to the network.
* Wireless networking is an excellent solution for libraries with historic buildings or older buildings, which make the installation of wired networking either impossible or very expensive.

There are some issues to be considered while installing wireless networks in libraries.

* It should be simple to install, set up, use and manage.
* It should be reliable and easy to expand as the library network grows.
* It should be compatible with other network devices.
* It should be built by reputable, experienced companies that know the complexities of wireless networking.
* It should be backed by easily accessible, sound technical support.
* Interference in wireless environment should be avoided.
* Wireless technologies should meet the prescribed standards for safety.

WIRELESS INTERNET ACCESS IN LIBRARIES

Wireless technology allows users to access the Internet without the constraints of cables, data lines, phone jacks, or even walls. When connected to library wireless network, users can use their laptops, notebooks, simputers, handheld devices, or web-enabled pagers or phones to check e-mail or to surf the web without a physical connection. Each device connected to a wireless library network allows users to e-mail, or surf the Internet. Notebook computers and simputers are becoming more affordable and portable. Users can use this facility for reading E-mails and newsgroups, accessing online library catalogues, searching information through web, and live online reference.

MOBILE TECHNOLOGIES

Mobile technologies provide wide coverage to access information from networks. There are several mobile technologies. Here are some of the most used mobile technologies.

WIRELESS APPLICATION PROTOCOL (WAP)

Wireless Application Protocol is a protocol for wireless access to information resources and services from mobile devices. It is the de-facto-standard for the presentation and delivery of wireless information on mobile devices. WAP can be used to access Internet without a PC or modem. Mobile devices contain specifically designed WAP enabled microbrowser to display the information from Internet. Microbrowser is software built into a wireless device that allows users to access and display specially formatted Internet content. But in order to display the information on the screen of mobile devices, websites should be written in specifically designed Wireless Markup Language (WML). WML is a markup language developed for mobile devices. It is based on Extensible Markup Language (XML) and created to address the display, bandwidth and memory limitations of mobile and wireless devices. WML supports text and images and manages navigation and command execution. Websites written in Hypertext Markup Language (HTML) should be transferred to WML. The WAP gateway facilitates the delivery of WML contents to wireless devices. WAP technology can be used to send information to users' mobile devices. It can be used to provide reference services for specific information.

GENERAL PACKET RADIO SERVICE (GPRS)

The General Packet Radio Service is a service that allows mobile phones to be used for sending and receiving data over an Internet Protocol based network. GPRS enables wireless access to Internet, enabling users to access E-mail and other Internet applications using mobile phones. As in Internet,

GPRS data is also handled as a series of "packets" that can be routed over several paths through the network. GPRS enables any service that is used over the Internet like File Transfer Protocol (FTP), web browsing, chat, E-mail, and telnet. It allows information to be transmitted more quickly and efficiently and facilitates instant connections whereby information can be sent or received immediately as the need arises. To use GPRS, users need a mobile phone or terminal that supports GPRS and a subscription to a mobile telephone network that supports GPRS. Users should know how to send and receive GPRS information using the mobile devices.

UNIVERSAL MOBILE TELECOMMUNICATIONS SYSTEM (UMTS)

Universal Mobile Telecommunications System uses ATM based switching network architecture. UMTS aims to provide services for mobile and fixed subscribers by common call processing procedures. It will provide at least 144 kbps for full mobility, 384 kbps for limited and 2048 mbps for low mobility applications[25]. It can deliver low-cost, high capacity mobile communications offering data rates upto 2Mbis/sec with global roaming and other advanced capabilities. UMTS can deliver pictures, graphics, video communications and other wide-band information as well as voice and data. It will extend the capability of mobile technologies by providing increased capacity, data capability and a far greater range of services using an innovative radio access scheme and an enhanced network.

DIGITAL LIBRARY

The widespread use of Internet and the wide availability of affordable computing equipments have created tremendous interest in digital libraries. Digital libraries are a set of electronic resources and associated technical capabilities for creating, searching and using information. They are an extension, enhancement and integration of variety of information institutions where resources are selected, collected, organised, preserved and accessed in support of user community. Digital Library Federation defines digital libraries as 'organisations that provide the resources, including the specialised staff, to select, structure, offer intellectual access to, interpret, distribute, preserve the integrity of, and ensure the persistence over time of collections of digital works so that they are readily and economically available for use by a defined community or set of communities'[26]. Digital libraries differ from their counterparts in significant ways: storage is digital, remote access is quick and easy, and materials are copied from a master version. Furthermore keeping extra copies on hands is easy and not hampered by budget and storage restriction, which are major problems in traditional libraries. A digital library collection may include two types of information resource. One type comprises the "digital original resources, which are sometimes referred to as resources, which are "born digitally". The other type comprises "digital surrogates", which are created from traditional information resources through format conversion. Digital information presently exists in a variety of formats: OPACs, library networks, CD-ROMs, local databases, online commercial databases, the World Wide Web, image libraries, audio libraries, digital video libraries and so on and so forth. The concept of a digital library cannot be reduced merely to a digitised collection with information handling tools. It is to be viewed as a mechanism for providing information services, because its inherent design combines end-user needs with technology that has the ability to handle vast amounts of complex data. The emergence of Internet2 offers very high bandwidth, which allows digital libraries to provide real-time information services and also offer opportunities to enrich and extend the current state-of-the-art in information access and retrieval.

VIRTUAL LIBRARY

Virtual Library or in simple words the Internet based digital library is defined as 'a library with little or no physical plant of books, periodicals, reading space or support staff but one that disseminates selective information directly to distributed library customers, usually electronically' [27]. The concept is that any person who has a computer by which he can make connection to the library network(s) can access not only the resources of that library but also access variety of information that is available nationally and internationally through networks, like internet, intranet, without being physically present in library. It is an amalgamation of the three basic things viz: computer network, telecommunication media and reading materials in electronic format [28]. The service of a Virtual Library is far better than a traditional one, since a user could retrieve information in a short span of time without visiting the library. The virtual library has unique content or should provide content more readily than any other source of information. User will raise their hands if they have the opportunity to get something quicker, easier or more reliably through a good virtual library. Sherwell describes characteristics of virtual library as [29]:

* There is no corresponding physical collection
* Information will be available in electronic formats
* Information are not stored in any location
* Documents can be accessed from any terminal which have a net presence
* Documents are retrieved and delivered as and when required and
* Effective search and browse facilities are available.

MULTIMEDIA

Multimedia means the integration or combination of various medias like texts, graphics, animation, video and sound files into an electronic environment. It provides the interactive and attractive environment for the presentation of data using user-friendly interfaces and hypertext links. Video conferencing, voice chatting, computer animation, desktop publishing are some of the finest testimonies of the growing importance of multimedia. Multimedia technologies are designed to enable users to integrate and manipulate data from diverse sources on a single hardware platform.

The application of multimedia for collection, and dissemination of information has a lot of influence and it acts as a vital catalyst to extend improved services in the library. Its impact can be traced in various areas like: 1) it allows the users to browse and navigate quickly and type of complex information; 2) multimedia enhances resource sharing and networking, 3) it gives maximum freedom to the user, 4) it can be on both a single stand-alone system or multi user system, 5) it creates 3-D effects of an object in a variety of ways, 6) it makes the programme interesting, excellent, easy and quick to understand, 7) multimedia can have management technique by using management information system, decision support system, export system etc and 8) for library operations, the computers can be integrated to enhances the operations efficiency of the library or information centres.

ELECTRONIC JOURNALS

Electronic journal may be defined broadly as any journal, magazine, e-zine, webzine, newsletter or type of electronic serial publication which is available over the internet and can be accessed using different technologies such as World Wide Web, Gopher, ftp, telnet, e-mail or listserv. In some cases, print equivalents exist; in some cases, not. Some electronic journals are freely available; other has charging mechanisms of different types. Following are the worth mention advantages of the e-journals:

1. Speed of access to the latest information

2. Ability to implement multimedia elements
3. Quick searching
4. Linking from and to other resources
5. Security
6. Single user or location restrictions do not apply
7. Downloading an article to a personal computer for later use or printing is easier than photocopying or scanning.

Access for a particular article or a journal is not bounded with time/period and place/geographic constraints, in case of e-journals. Besides the traditional plain text, tables, figures and graphics other innovative ways of presenting research results can be supported by multimedia capabilities. Also a large amount of supporting data can be linked to from the article if the reader wanted to look more deeply into the results. Hypertext and hyper media enable linkage among sections within an article and among articles in journals and other electronic resources.

EMERGING TECHNOLOGIES:

ARTIFICIAL INTELLIGENCE

Artificial Intelligence is the science and engineering of making intelligent machines, especially intelligent computer programs. It is 'concerned with the study and creation of computer systems that exhibit some form of intelligence: systems that learn new concepts and tasks, systems that can reason and draw useful conclusions about the world around us, systems that can understand a natural language or perceive and comprehend a visual scene, and systems that perform other types of feats that require human types of intelligence'[30]. It is a branch of science, which deals with helping machines, finds solutions to complex problems in a more human-like fashion. This generally involves borrowing characteristics from human intelligence, and applying them as algorithms in a computer friendly way. It is an interdisciplinary field making use of concepts from various fields like Cybernetics, Information theory, Psychology, Linguistics, Logic, etc. It can use to stimulate human behaviour and for Computer Aided Instruction, Expert Systems, Robotics and for Natural Language Processing (NLP). It can also use for Intelligent Retrieval from databases.

The application of Artificial Intelligence to information and library work is relatively recent and has been mostly in the expert-systems field [31]. Natural language processing can use to search relevant information from databases, indexing and to reduce language barrier. In information retrieval process the user can state his information requirement in natural language making the searching more easy and fruitful. This allows users to state complex query statements without knowing the complex retrieval languages.

EXPERT SYSTEMS

Expert systems are meant to solve real problems, which normally would require a specialised human expert. Building an expert system first involves extracting the relevant knowledge from the human expert. Such knowledge is often heuristic in nature. Expert systems have been used to solve a wide range of problems in domains such as medicine, mathematics, engineering, geology, computer science, business, law, defence, education, etc. Within each domain, they have been used to solve problems of different types. As a practical implementation of research into artificial intelligence, expert systems also described as knowledge-based systems, have been developed as an attempt to propagate, via a computer program, the knowledge and skills of experts who are engaged in tasks such as diagnosis, interpretation, prediction, instruction, design and monitoring. Through the development of such systems, organisations seek improved and consistent performance at places where relevant expertise is not otherwise accessible.

Many activities in the provision of library and information services involve expertise, and thus provide applications where expert systems techniques and technology promise to improve performance. An analysis of the literature on the applications of expert systems in LIS yields the following application areas [32]:

* Intelligent interfaces, in particular interfaces for online information retrieval systems
* Subject analysis and representation, including classification, indexing and abstracting services
* Information storage and retrieval systems in general
* Reference and referral systems
* Hypertext and hypermedia
* Collection development.

SMART CARD

Similar in look and size to a credit card, a smart card has an embedded microprocessor or memory chip, or both, instead of magnetic strip commonly found on credit and debit cards. It provides not only memory capacity, but computational capacity as well. The self-containment of smart card makes it resistant to attack, as it does not need to depend upon potentially vulnerable external resources. This technology will have several applications in identification, authentication, access control, healthcare, finance, administration, etc. Application of smart card in library delivers increased efficiency by providing a means of regularly updating the library's inventory and maintaining an accurate control of borrowing records.

RFID TECHNOLOGY

RFID stands for Radio Frequency Identification, use radio waves to uniquely identify an object by transmitting a stored code from a chip to a reader [33]. It is a form of automatic identification and data capture technology. It has a combination of radio frequency and microchip technology. It stores and retrieves data from computer chips using radio frequency transmission. It does not require line of sight contact and it can be used anywhere that needed a unique identification. It is an emerging, more effective, convenient, and cost efficient technology in library automation and security. It has been around libraries for more than two decades. Libraries began using this technology in the late 1990s[34]. Several libraries around the world, especially in U.S, Canada, and Singapore are using this technology for library functions.

RFID technology has many advantages. As far as a library or information center is concerned it will increase the speed of charging and discharging of documents, RFID tags can detect and read much faster and it can read several documents at the same time. Library users can charge several documents simultaneously using special self-charging stations and return documents in the special boxes or book-drops making circulation faster and easier. Library staff can relive from repetitive and clerical tasks and they can concentrate on more demanding personalised information services. RFID can sort documents automatically and library staff can shelve documents very easily. Library staff can use portable hand held readers for electronic inventorying by passing them rapidly along the shelves to read all the documents. There is no need of handling each document individually. They can report the lost, hidden or unordered documents more easily using these portable readers.

RFID tags have greater storage capacity and can hold large amount of information about a document. Its microchips are read/write with update flexibility. It can be used for status control as well as for security checks. It can be placed anywhere in the documents since it does not need a line of sight contact. For example it can be placed inside the documents and this will provide protection to the tags from damage or destruction during rough handling of documents. The tags can stand up in harsh environments. Several tags can read simultaneously even through the hard document covers.

Security is a major concern in an electronic environment. RFID will provide improved security without staff intervention. Its tags have an advanced security bit and it will detect uncharged documents while passing through the security gate. The tags have an interface between the readers in the exit and the circulation system to detect and identify items moving through the exit. The same tag can be used for detecting materials and also for security.

RFID technology has few drawbacks. As far as the libraries in developing country like India is concerned, cost is a major concern. For implementing and maintaining RFID system, a substantial amount is needed. It may cost around $50,000 for a library with 40,000 documents. A comprehensive RFID system for 100,000 documents with self-charging station, book-drop unit and automatic book sorting system ranges from $100,000 to $200,000 [35]. But recent advancements in hardware and software have boosted the potential of this technology and shortly libraries are going to implement RFID technology for their functions.

Another drawback is that the radio waves cannot pass through metal and liquid at certain frequencies. But this is not a major drawback, that RFID is far better than the barcode technology. Lack of standard is another disadvantage of RFID. This may be due to the limited use of RFID technology. A uniform standard is necessary to bring interoperability to libraries using RFID. This condition may change and RFID readers can read any tags. It is also possible to compromise an RFID system by placing two items against one another to cancel out the signals.

SKILL AND EXPERTISE OF LIBRARY PROFESSIONALS IN THE ELECTRONIC ENVIRONMENT

There have been many attempts to define the core skills or competencies of information professionals in the future and many of these analyses of information skills highlight the need for both professional and organisational/personal competencies. A professional is a person with determined training and skills, who concentrates his energy and expertise being up to date, gaining day-by-day knowledge and with a multi disciplinary vision of society's demands. The shape of an information professional with those abilities and skills to affront being consultant information worker, information manager, information researcher, information specialist, knowledge engineer, database manager, database programmer, hypertext specialist, thesaurus constructor. Today's information professional requires a number of new skills in order to deal properly with the influx of Information and Communication Technology. The information professional must know about new technologies and being an expert in the application of these, have to understand the library as a social system, to develop user instruction programs and to train to retrieve information.

Skill is defined as the knowledge and ability that enables one to do something. In other worlds, skill is an acquired ability to perform a task efficiently and effectively. Knowledge of a subject without relevant skills can be of some use like teaching, providing information and advising some one in that area. But skills without appropriate background knowledge can reduce a professional task to the level of an occupation. As part of professional skills the new library professionals need to develop extraordinary access skills. In other words, gaining access to sources of information and managing a knowledge base is likely to become very fundamental activity in future. Library professionals must have technical skills, ICT skills and managerial skills. The other skills, which are likely to be emphasised in future are skills reuired to analyse, synthesise, assimilate, interpret and reformulate the information accessed and retrieved. The depth and breadth of skills required as complimentary to library professional skills for this purpose vary very widely.

ICT has virtually unlimited potential for variety of applications in libraries. Library professionals have undergone a drastic change, which had not been seen ever before. The challenges posed by ICT in the storing and transferring of information has profoundly altered the roles and services of library and library professionals. Libraries ushered into an era in which professionals of all levels from top to bottom shared the common responsibility of providing access to information "just in time". The use of ICT in libraries has changed the services into an attractive and user friendly and at the same time making a feeling of status to the information professionals. The library professional responsible for the implementation of ICT in libraries should combine ICT and library or information science qualifications, skills, competencies and experience. During this period of library automation and ICT application it was widely felt that library personnel lack requistite level of working knowledge and skills of ICT. Such working knowledge and skills were essential to prepare library staff both mentally and technically for modernisation of library services in the new electronic environment. There are different levels of skills required by new library professionals in the electronic environment. Firstly library professionals should have skills required for handling ICT products, particularly, operating system, software, physical handling of gadgets, telecommunication products, DBMS, data and file management, DTP, word processing, generation of reports, etc. The next level of skills include skills required to apply ICT for service management in general and information processing, search and retrieval in particular. This involves collection and organisation of data in electronic form, indexing techniques, selection and evaluation of sources, searching techniques, updation techniques, etc. Information retrieval skills include online searching as well as searching CD-ROM databases. This level should incorporate skills required for query formulations as well as query interpretation.

The library professionals should also have Internet skills and skills required for accessing networked resources as well as marketing of electronic information. A lot more can be said about skills expected for electronic publishing, electronic commerce and electronic marketing. Yet another area in which skills are likely to be expected is document management and management of data archives. Preservation and archiving of data in electronic medium not only require administrative skills but also knowledge of data fields, which a system analyst knows better. The other advanced skills which are less likely to be needed by library professionals unless they become part of ICT are programming skills, system administration, hardware maintenance and own trouble shooting, networking, system migration, etc.

The managerial skills expected to library professionals are quite vast. Library professionals need to have managerial skills required for information management in teams. Another important area of managerial skills library professionals have to develop is marketing of services and particularly marketing themselves and their skills. Skill relating to systems analysis, self-development, creativity analysis and negotiation are also necessary. Yet another set of important skills is communication skills, i.e., skill to communicate orally and in written form.

As ICT itself is changing at a fast rate, any prediction of skills required by library professionals beyond few years is difficult and become absurd. Yet it is interesting to note some of the broad trends and projections for future e-world and librarianship. Firstly, the amount of information transacted in electronic form is steadily increasing and in future, a substantial part of information will be received only in electronic form. Secondly, librarianship is going to have much wider sphere of operation than what it is today. Thirdly, publishers and information providers are increasingly targeting their services directly to individual customers and not through intermediaries. Consequently, the intermediaries may have to seek more and more opportunities with end users in interpreting and repackaging the sources directly received by them.

The electronic information environment is changing rapidly and many information professionals are struggling with the fear that end-user access to the Internet (and other electronic media) will adversely affect their jobs. The information environment is quickly changing and it is essential that library professionals change with it. Librarians need to prove and publicise that they are information specialists who can still provide valuable assistance with their clients' research needs. Internet technology provides an avenue for information specialists to show they are professionals who have adapted to the new technology and have much to contribute to any project because they wear many hats-problem solver, computer user, librarian, researcher, trainer, marketer, writer, database developer-the list is endless. In this age of ICT, there have been so many opportunities for the librarians for involvement in an information-based society including electronic and multimedia pubishing, internet based-information services, global networking, web based digital resources, etc.

CONCLUSION

The advances in Information and Communication Technology will no doubt drive library movements in the new millennium. A process of moving from e-presence to e-commerce to e-transact to e-transform is envisaged in most of the sectors and library too would undergo similar transformation in the future. ICT provides an excellent opportunity for library professionals to manage themselves better. Application of ICT have made a great impact on libraries and information centres, and the computers and associated facilities have come to be recognised as indispensable for accurate storage, processing, retrieval and dissemination of information. All librarians should be perfectly familiar with the benefits of modern technology and perform efficiently. The challenge is to design library services and to manage operations exploiting the advantages offered by ICT. To that end it is pertinent to understand the process of technology development and technology diffusion in general and ICT in particular.

Today libraries are using web technology extensively for user services to provide dynamic services to the remote users. Web technology currently available is helping the libraries to achieve their purposes. There is a need for librarians to get extensive exposure with the Information and Communication Technology in general and web technology specifically. Lot of innovation and developments in the fields of Information and Communication technologies has taken place in the last decade. India has been able to achieve moderate success in making computer networks operational for communication; libraries and information; in spite of various inadequacies. Few networks still remain undeveloped, although existing networks have to be interconnected to achieve the desired goals. India aims to catch up with advanced countries through the application of modern technology, and reliance on local industry for hardware and software. The total communication scenario is bound to change in next decade. Optical networks, portable networking, wireless libraries will emerge on the scene. Web based e-education will be used for educating the masses. For exploration and processing of data from distributed databases, a concept of virtual data warehousing is emerging. The trends in the ICT field, expected to emerge in next decade, look very exciting and promising.

REFERENCES

1. De Horowitz, G. (1993) Literacy and development in the third world: could librarianship make a difference. **IFLA Journal,** 19 (2) p.172.
2. **The ALA Glossary of Library and Information Science**. (1983) Chicago, American Library Association.
3. Ramesh Babu, B. (2000) **The emergence of web OPACs in the 21st century: challenge for Indian libraries**. IN: Proceedings the Seventh National Convention for Automation of Libraries in Education and Research (CALIBER 2000). Ahmedabad, INFLIBNET Centre. p. 1.186.
4. Cherry, Joan M. (1998) Bibliographic displays in OPACs and web catalogs: how well do they comply with display guidelines. **Information Technology and Libraries,** 17 (3) September, pp.124-137.
5. Chen, Ching-Chin. (1997) **Multimedia technologies**. World Information Report 1997/98. Paris, UNESCO, pp.206-225.
6. Vijayakumar, J.K. & Manju Das. (2000) CD-ROM to DVD-ROM: a new era in electronic publishing of databases and multimedia reference sources. **IASLIC Bulletin,** 45 (2), p. 49.
7. Moorthy, A.L. & Karisiddappa, C.R. (2000) Mass storage technologies for libraries and information centres. **BESIDOC Bulletin of Information Technology,** 20(5) September, p. 9.
8. Shakkarwar, Rajesh. (1998) Host-based DVD: arriving on PC platforms today. **Intelinsight** [Internet] 2(1), pp.8-19. Available from: <*http://developer.intel.com/solutions.tech/dvd/dvdpr10.pdf*> [Accessed April 3rd 2004].
9. Moorthy, A.L. & Karisiddappa, C.R. op. cit. p. 13.
10. Inmon, W. & Hackathorn, R. (1994) **Using the data warehouse**. New York, Wiley.

11. Berry, M.J.A. & Linoff, G. (1999) **Mastering data mining.** New York, Wiley.
12. Kaul, H.K. (1998) **From printed bibliographies to online databases: role of library networks.** IN: 50 Years Library and Information Services in India. Jain, M.K, ed. Delhi, Shipra Publications.
13. Haravu, L.J. (1993) Library automation and networking in India: an overview of recent developments. **Annals of Library Science and Documentation,** 40 (1), pp.32-40.
14. Hirshon, A. (1998) Academic library consortia [Internet] Available from: <*http://www.leigh.edu/~arth5/arh5.html*> [Accessed April 16th 2004].
15. **Ministry of Human Resource and Development Committee of Experts on Consortia-based Subscription to Electronic Resources for Technical Education System in India.** (2002) New Delhi, MHRD, pp. 9-10.
16. Satyanarayana, Pattnaik & Saravanan, A. (1999) Internet in India: an overview. **Yojna,** April, p.44.
17. Premchand, Cmde & Jubali, Praveen M. (2000) IT training requirements for the year 2000 and beyond. **DESIDOC Bulletin of Information Technology,** 20 (1-2), p. 63.
18. Saunders-McMaster, Laverna. (1997) Internet 2: an overview of the next generation of the internet. **Computers in Libraries,** March, p. 57.
19. Jitendra Sharma. (1999) **Coping up with the challenges of information technology to the library profession.** IN: Proceedings of the 45th All India Library Conference on Library vision 2010 Indian Libraries and Librarianship in Retrospect and Prospect, Hisar. Delhi, ILA.
20. Neena Singh. (2001) Internet: importance and usage for

library and information professionals. **DESIDOC Bulletin of Information Technology,** 21 (3) May, p. 18.

21. Schmidt, Ronald M. (1997) **Libraries bibliographic utilities and library networking: looking ahead**. IN:Proceedings of the 19th International Essen Symposium. Essen, Universitatsbibliothek Essen. p.197.
22. Mohamed Haneefa, K. & Bavakutty, M. (2002) **Wireless networking in libraries: a conceptual introduction.** IN: Proceedings of the National Seminar on Library Co-operation in a Networked World, 25-26 May, University of Calicut. New Delhi, Ess Ess Publications. p. 133.
23. Bhartiya, Chandra Shekhar. (2001) Wireless LANs a cost benefit analysis. **Information Technology,** 10 (7) May, p. 80.
24. Mohamed Haneefa. K. (2004) **Application of wireless technologies in libraries.** IN: Proceedings of the Second International CALIBER on Road Map to New Generation of Libraries Using Emerging Technologies, Feb. 11-13, New Delhi. Ahmedabad, INFLIBNET Centre. p. 367.
25. Ashwani Kush & Chauhan, R.K. (2003) Wirelss media: a new paradigm. **DESIDOC Bulletin of Information Technology,** 23 (3) May, p. 4.
26. **A working definition of digital library**. (2001) Digital Library Federation [Internet] Available from: <http://www.diolib.org/pubs/ar9899p1.html> [Accessed March 3rd 2003].
27. Powell, Alan. (1994) Management models and measurements in the virtual library. **Special Libraries,** 85 (4), pp. 260-263.
28. Khan, A.A.Abbas. (2000) **Virtual libraries: real or virtual**. IN: Proceedings of the Seventh National Convention for Automation of Libraries in Education

and Research (CALIBER 2000). Ahmedabad, INFLIBNET Centre. pp.1.97-1.99.

29. Sherwell, John. (1997) Building virtual library: the case of Smithkine Beachem. **Aslib Managing Information,** 4 (5), pp.35-36.
30. Patterson, D.W. (1990) **Introduction to artificial intelligence and expert systems**. London, Prentice Hall.
31. Kumbargoudar, Praveen Kumar. (1999) Application of artificial intelligence techniques to library and information science. **ILA Bulletin,** 34 (3-4), pp. 55-59.
32. Gibb, F. (1992) Bibliography on the application of expert systems, knowledge-based systems, artificial intelligence and natural language processing in the library and information sciences, 1978-1992. **Expert Systems for Information Management,** 4(3), pp.143-220.
33. Jones, Peter. et al. (2004) Radio frequency identification in the UK: opportunities and challenges. **International Journal of Retail & Distribution Management** [Internet] 32(3), pp.164-171. Available from: <*http://juno.emeraldinsight.com/vl=3706277/cl=47/nw=1/rpsv/~1081/v32n3/s4/p164*> [Accessed October 4th 2004].
34. Kern, Christian. (2004) Radio-frequency-identification for security and media circulation in libraries. **The Electronic Library** [Internet] 22 (4), pp.317-324. Available from: *http://juno.emeraldinsight.com/vl=3706277/cl=47/nw=1/rpsv/~1091/v22n4/s2/p317*> [Accessed October 4th 2004].
35. Indira Koneru. (2004) **RFID technology: a revolution in library management**. IN: Proceedings of the Second International CALIBER on Road Map to New Generation of Libraries using Emerging Technologies, Feb. 11-13, New Delhi. Ahmedabad, INFLIBNET Centre, p. 414.

2.3
Research Methodology

The methodology used for the investigation has been described in this chapter. The major objective of the present study was to assess the current state-of-the-art Information and Communication Technology infrastructure and application in Special Libraries in Kerala. Developments in Information and Communication Technologies have revolutionised the modes and methods of information handling. The advent of digital computers, advances in telecommunication technology, widespread use of networking, explosive growth of Internet, world wide packet networks, optical discs and other mass storage media, interactive video technology, image technology, computer graphic technology, virtual reality and the growth of public and private databases have opened up new possibilities in dealing with the collection, organisation and dissemination of information. Today information can not only be stored, retrieved, communicated and broadcasted electronically in enormous quantities at phenomenal speed, but can also be rearranged, selected and transformed. But any operation on information can be carried out without further human intervention or supervision.

This chapter includes research aim and objectives, hypotheses of the study, research design and data analysis techniques.

OBJECTIVES OF THE STUDY

The aim of the research study is to investigate the application of Information and Communication Technologies in Special Libraries in Kerala. However, the specific objectives identified are:

1. To assess the current state-of-the-art Information and Communication Technology Infrastructure in Special Libraries in Kerala.
2. To identify and evaluate contemporary application of Information and Communication Technologies in Special Libraries in Kerala.
3. To compare the Information and Communication Technology status among the Special Libraries in Kerala.
4. To identify and analyse the specific factors that promoted or hindered application of Information and Communication Technologies in Special Libraries in Kerala.
5. To assess to what extent users are satisfied with Information and Communication Technology resources and services and what factors affect their use in Special Libraries in Kerala.
6. To ascertain the ICT skills and expertise of the library professionals and examine its application in information handling process.
7. To study the facilities of training in Information and Communication Technologies in Special Libraries in Kerala.
8. To assess the attitude of the librarians and users towards the application of Information and Communication Technologies in Special Libraries in Kerala.
9. To suggest measures for improvement of existing resources and services and implementation of Information and Communication Technologies.

HYPOTHESES

The following are the major hypotheses of the study:

1. The application of Information and Communication

Technologies in Special Libraries in Kerala is not satisfactory.

2. Among the Special Libraries in Kerala, libraries of Central Government autonomous institutions are in better position in the application of Information and Communication Technologies.
3. Lack of funds/financial support hinders full application of Information and Communication Technologies in Special Libraries in Kerala.
4. Users are not fully satisfied with the present application of Information and Communication Technologies in Special Libraries in Kerala.
5. The electronic information resources and services of Special Libraries in Kerala are inadequate to meet the information needs of users.
6. The skills and expertise of library professionals in Special Libraries in Kerala are inadequate to provide Information and Communication Technology based resources and services.
7. Special Libraries in Kerala are providing adequate training in ICT based operations and services to their professionals.
8. Librarians and users of Special Libraries in Kerala have a positive attitude towards the application of Information and Communication Technologies.

RESEARCH DESIGN

As mentioned, the present study is designed to assess the contemporary application of Information and Communication Technologies in Special Libraries in Kerala and to help plot future directions for implementing Information and Communication Technologies. To meet the specific objectives of the present investigation, a combination of quantitative and qualitative research methodologies along with a comprehensive literature review has been employed

DATA COLLECTION METHODS

In order to accomplish the objectives of the study, four main methods have been employed in data collection: review of related studies, questionnaire surveys of librarians and library users, semi-structured interviews with librarians and observation of the libraries.

REVIEW OF RELATED STUDIES

To start with, the investigator began literature search and collected selected documents on the topic of research and related fields. For this purpose, LISA database was used as source of information. Other reference sources consulted include 'Bibliography of Doctoral Dissertations accepted by Indian Universities' published by Association of Indian Universities, 'Bibliography of Research in Library and Information Science in India' compiled by Pathak and L.S.Ramaih, 'Research in Library and Information Science in India: A Bibliography of PhD., MPhil, and MLISc. Dissertations' compiled by P.S.G. Kumar, et. al. and 'University News' published by Association of Indian Universities. Having studied the literature on ICT application and library automation and such other related topics, a state-of-the-art current development was prepared. The review of related literature helped the investigator to identify previous and present research studies on the same or similar topics and assisted the researcher to properly understand the issues involved in the present study in the right perspective. It provided reasons why the topic is of sufficient importance for it to be researched.

QUESTIONNAIRE SURVEY

Structured questionnaires were prepared and administered to chief librarians and users/clients of the libraries **(Appendices A and B).** Structured questionnaires are simple to administer and relatively inexpensive to analyse. These questionnaires were pre-tested before the final application. The purpose of questionnaire targeted to librarians was to obtain data regarding the state-of-the-art Information and Communication Technology infrastructure, and contemporary application of ICT, to identify and analyse the specific factors that promoted or hindered application of Information and Communication Technologies, to assess librarians attitude towards application of Information and Communication Technologies and to investigate the skills and expertise of the library professionals. This questionnaire was distributed to chief librarians with a covering letter indicating the significance of the study and the intended plans for the results.

The purpose of the questionnaire targeted to users/ clients was to assess the use of Information and Communication Technology based resources and services, to know what extent they were satisfied with ICT resources and services, to assess what factors affect the use and to assess the users attitude towards ICT application.

SEMI-STRUCTURED INTERVIEWS

The method of collecting information through personal interviews is usually carried out in a structured way. This is called structured interviews. Such interviews involve the use of a set of predetermined questions and of highly standardized techniques of recording. Semi-structured interviews provide some flexibility from predetermined questions and standardised techniques of recording information.

For the present study, both telephone and face-to-face interviews were conducted with chief librarians using a semi-structured interview schedule **(Appendix C)**. The purpose of the interviews was to complement the quantitative information obtained by the questionnaire with more detailed qualitative information. This method provided the interviewer with the opportunity to clarify some questions of which respondent wss unclear. The interviews were directly addressed the application of Information and Communication Technologies in special libraries and called for a more personal response than the questionnaire.

OBSERVATION OF LIBRARIES

Observation becomes a scientific tool and method of data collection for the researcher, when it serves a formulated research purpose, is systematically planned and recorded and is subjected to check and controls on validity and reliability.

For the present study, observational visits were conducted in the libraries to collect information about the current state-of-the-art ICT facilities, resources and functions, to ascertain the ICT skill and expertise of the library professionals and examine its application in information handling process and to assess the degree of the utilisation of ICT based facilities and services for storage, retrieval and dissemination of information.

RESEARCH SAMPLE

The universe of the present study was the special libraries of national importance such as libraries of premier scientific and technological research institutions (comprising institutions of Council of Scientific and Industrial Research/ Department of Science and Technology, Defence Research and Development Organisation, Indian Council of Agricultural Research, and Indian Space Research Organisation) and research and development units of industrial organisations in Kerala. The Directory of Libraries in India[1], Directory of Scientific and Technical Libraries in India[2] and Directory of Libraries in Kerala[3] were used to identify the names, administrative status and address of libraries for the study. Since the directories were dated, information was verified telephonically and through personal visits. All the libraries of the above mentioned categories that were using Information and Communication Technologies were selected for the present study. Since the use of Information and Communication Technologies require certain minimum infrastructure and qualified fulltime library professional and also ICT resources and related equipments require substantial financial commitment by libraries, government departmental libraries were excluded from the study. The investigator identified 31 libraries with various stages of ICT application and library automation. But after several attempts one library did not grant permission to collect data, hence, it has been excluded from the list. Finally, 30 libraries were selected for the study. Among these 13 libraries are from Central Government Autonomous Institutions, 8 libraries are from Central Government Institutions, 7 are from State Government Autonomous Institutions and 2 libraries are from State Government Institutions. One library was from public sector; it was included in the State Government Autonomous Institutions category. These libraries were selected out of more than 100 existing special libraries in Kerala on the basis of the following criteria: 1. All these libraries represented the categories explained above, and 2. All of these libraries were automated and they were in the different stages of automation and ICT application. List of these libraries is given as Appendix E

Pilot study was conducted in five libraries prior to the survey proper, in order to elicit any possible criticism of the questionnaire or ambiguity in phrasing of the questions. Data was collected from the librarians of the all selected libraries through a questionnaire. The questionnaire comprised fourteen sections and was completely structured, including spaces for open-ended comments. The data collection was started during September 2003 and all the completed questionnaires were received by the end of April 2004, thus, achieving a 100 per cent response rate. The information from the questionnaire survey was updated through semi-structured interviews with chief librarians and observational visits to the library. Data was also collected from the users of these libraries with the help of a structured questionnaire. These questionnaires were distributed randomly to all categories of users to get a representative sample. A total of 1431 questionnaires were distributed to users at various times during the months of September 2003 to March 2004. 1017 filled in questionnaires were received back. From these, 889 questionnaires were found to be usable, which comes to an overall response rate of 62.1 per cent. Table 2.3.1 gives the response rate of users per organisation. The table shows that the total population of library users is 10387. Among these 2304 (22.2 per cent) users are from the Central Government institutions, 6453 (62.1 per cent) users are from Central Government autonomous institutions, 250 (2.4 per cent) are from State Government institutions and 1380 (13.3 per cent) are from State Government autonomous institutions. The data were treated confidentially and were processed by using the Excel and SPSS Software.

Table 2.3.1 Details of the Sample users taken

Organisation type	***Sample Population***	***% of Sample Population***	***Sample Size***
Central Government	2304	22.2	460
Central Government autonomous	6453	62.1	645
State Government	250	2.4	50
State Government autonomous	1380	13.3	276
Total	10387	100	1431

DATA ANALYSIS TECHNIQUES

The data collected were analysed and inferences were made using standard statistical methods. Analysis of the questionnaires, interview schedules and observation data using both quantitative and qualitative measures provided the researcher an in-depth interpretation of the ten research objectives. The objectives and hypotheses of the present study demand the use of the following major statistical techniques:

PERCENTAGE ANALYSIS

Simple percentage analysis was undertaken to study the current state-of-the-art, infrastructure, application of Information and Communication Technologies in Special Libraries in Kerala. This was done for the libraries and library users in different categories as well as for relevant sub-samples formed on the basis of sex, age, designation, etc.

CHI-SQUARE TEST

The Chi-Square (c^2) test is one of the simplest and most widely used non-parametric tests in statistical analysis. Chi-Square is a measure of actual divergence of the observed and expected frequencies (or values). If there is no difference between actual and observed frequencies, the value of the Chi-Square is zero. The greater the discrepancy between observed and expected frequencies, the greater is the value of c^2. If the calculated value of chi-square is less than the table value, it indicates that the difference between actual and observed frequencies may have arisen due to chance of fluctuations and can be ignored. The quantity c^2 is defined as

$$\chi^2 = \Sigma\,(O-E)^2 / E$$

Where O refers to the observed frequencies and E refers to the expected frequencies. Steps to determine the value of c^2 are:

1. Calculate the expected frequencies
2. Take the difference between observed and expected frequencies and obtain the square of these differences i.e, obtain the value of $(O-E)^2$.
3. Divide the quantity $(O-E)^2$ obtained in step (ii) by the expected frequency and obtain the sum over all cells $\Sigma\,(O-E)^2 / E$.

This gives the value of χ^2 and is compared with the table value of χ^2 for given degree of freedom at a certain specified level of significance. If the calculated value of χ^2 is more than table value of χ^2 the difference between theory and observation is considered to be significant, i.e, it could not have arisen due to fluctuations of simple sampling. If, on the other hand, the calculated value of χ^2 is less than the table value, the difference between theory and observation is not considered as significant. i.e., it is regarded as due to fluctuations of simple sampling and hence ignored.

For the present study Chi Square test was employed to test the association between two categories whenever necessary. For this, a two way table of observed frequencies for the two categories were obtained first and then chi square value corresponding to each cell of the two way table were computed and sum of these chi square values were calculated. If the computed value is greater than table value it indicates that there is an association (dependency) between two categories. Otherwise the two categories are independent.

CLUSTER ANALYSIS

The cluster analysis is one of the methods of grouping large sums of data. It is a classificatory procedure. The objective is to group either the data units or the variables into clusters so that the elements within a cluster have a high degree of 'natural association' among themselves, while the clusters are 'relatively distinct' from one another. According to Aldemderfer and Blashfied a clustering method is a multivariable statistical procedure that starts with data set containing information about a sample of entities and attempts to reorganize these entities into relatively homogenous groups[4].

The first phase of any clustering technique is to work out the relationships among the *n* samples expressed in terms of some distance measure obtained between every pair of samples. The distance measure used may depend on the scale of measurement. Usually Euclidean distance or correlation coefficients are used with interval scale. Association coefficients are used with nominal scale. The method then consists of a way of sorting the samples that determines clusters for a series of increased distance thresholds. This analysis using weighted arithmetic average method, groups the variable or observations into pairs of clusters. If correlation coefficient is the basis for combining such pair, then the pairs having high correlation are clustered. If, on the other hand, distance coefficient is the basis, then the pairs having small differences (distances) are combined in clusters.

The cluster is done on the basis of such similarity as may be indicated by the small distance coefficients or high correlation coefficients. The coefficients are used in the construction of tree diagram or dendrogram or linkage tree. This diagram is based to reduce hierarchy. Basically the variables or cases are clustered on the basis of correlation coefficient or like measures of association or Euclidean distance. Though there are various similarity measures available, Euclidean distance is generally preferred for cluster analysis.

For the present study cluster analysis was employed to study the attitude of librarians and users towards ICT application and to study the barriers of ICT application in Special Libraries in Kerala.

SUMMARY OF THE METHODOLOGY

The methodology adopted in the present research study is summarised in Fig 2.3.1 for clarity and easy reference.

REFERENCES

1. Gupta, K.R. (2001) **Directory of Libraries in India**. New Delhi, Atlantic Publishers and Distributors.
2. Kalia, D.R. & Surinder Kumar ed. (1998) **Directory of Scientific and Technical Libraries in India**. New Delhi, Reliance Publishing.

3. **Directory of Libraries in Kerala**. (1976) IN: National Library Week Souvenir. Trivandrum, Kerala Library Association, pp. C1-C16.

4. Aldenderfer, Marks. & Marks, Roger K. (1994) **Cluster analysis**. London, Sage Publications, P.7.

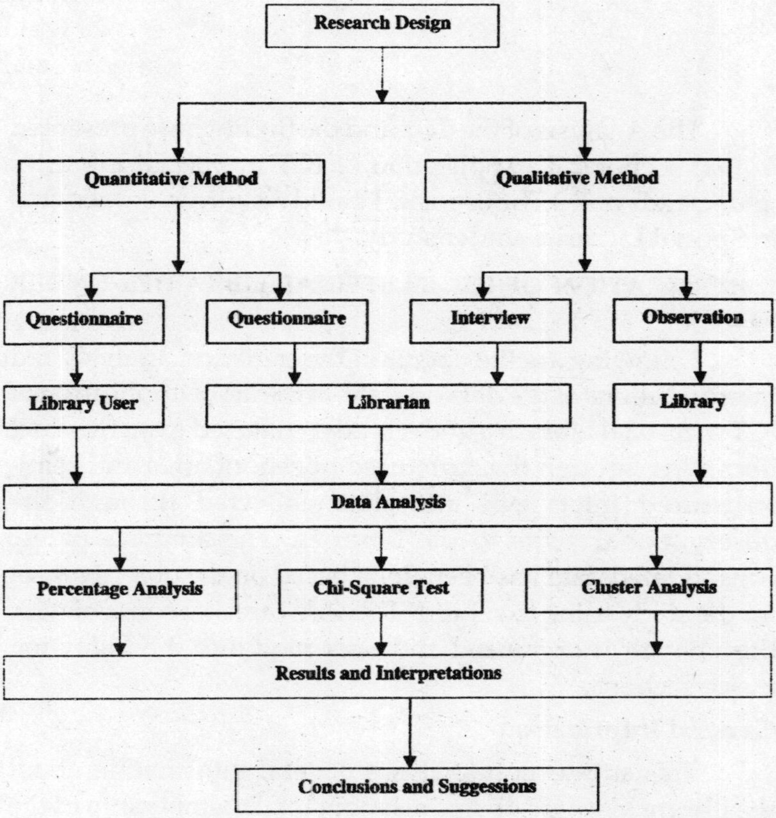

Figure 2.3.1. Summary of Research Methodology

2.4
Analysis of the Data and Interpretations

The Analysis of the data and the findings are presented in two sections: 1. Application of ICT in Special Libraries under study and 2. The use of ICT based resources and services in Special Libraries under study.

1. APPLICATION OF ICT IN SPECIAL LIBRARIES UNDER STUDY

Following are the details of the statistical analysis and interpretations of the data on state-of the art of application of ICT in Special Libraries under study, collected from the chief librarians through the structured questionnaires and semi-structured interviews and data collected through the observational visits to the libraries. The analysis of the consolidated data has been done based on the objectives set for the study using Excel and SPSS software. For convenience, this chapter is organized and presented into the following major sections.

General Information

This sub-section analyses general information about the library like type of organisation, total membership of the library and library budget in different financial years, etc..

Type of Parent Organisations

Although nearly 100 special libraries exist in Kerala, about 31 special libraries only have the application of Information and Communication Technologies. After several attempts one institution is not allowed to collect data from its library and library users, therefore it is excluded from the list of institutions. Finally, the questionnaires were administered to the remaining 30 institutions and responses have been received from all the libraries with 100 per cent response rate. Table 2.4.1 presents the data pertaining to the type of institutions and number of libraries.

Table 2.4.1 Types of parent organisations of the Libraries

Organisation type	*Number of Libraries*
Central Government	8 (26.7 %)
Central Government Autonomous	13 (43.3 %)
State Government	2 (6.7 %)
State Government Autonomous	7 (23.3 %)
Total	30 (100 %)

It is seen from the Table that among the 30 libraries selected, 8 (26.7 per cent) libraries belong to Central Government institutions, 13 (43.3 per cent) libraries are attached to Central Government autonomous institutions, 2 (6.7 per cent) belong to State Government institutions and 7 (23.3 per cent) libraries come under State Government autonomous institutions category. A good number of libraries are from Central Government autonomous institutions and these institutions have more computerized and automated libraries than other types of Special Libraries under study. They have good financial assistance, so they have comparatively better ICT infrastructure and electronic resources. All the worth mentioned Special Libraries in Kerala are attached to the Central Government autonomous institutions.

As one of the criteria for selection of libraries for this study is library automation and ICT application, it is observed that libraries of Central Government autonomous institutions have gone far ahead in computerization and automation compared to the libraries of other categories of institutions.

MEMBERSHIP OF THE LIBRARIES

Usually membership of special libraries will be comparatively less than other types of libraries, but the users' information needs and demands will be more pinpointed and exhaustive. Total membership of the libraries were collected and analysed. Table 2.4.2 shows the details.

Table 2.4.2 Membership of the Libraries/Information Centres

Organisation type	*Total membership*			
	<200	*Between 200 and 500*	*>500*	*Total*
Central Government	3(37.5 %)	4(50 %)	1(12.5 %)	8(100 %)
Central Government autonomous	8(61.5 %)	4(30.8 %)	1(7.7 %)	13(100 %)
State Government	2(100 %)	-	-	2(100 %)
State Government autonomous	4(57.1 %)	2(28.6 %)	1(14.3 %)	7(100 %)
Total	17(56.7 %)	10(33.3 %)	3(10 %)	30(100 %)

The table indicates that the total membership of the 50 per cent libraries of Central Government institutions is between 200 and 500. All the libraries of State Government institutions, majority of Central Government autonomous institutions (62 per cent) and State Government autonomous institutions (57 per cent) have below 200 members.

It is found that the total membership of the majority of the libraries is below 200. A few libraries have between 200 and 500 members. There are three libraries with membership greater than 500.

LIBRARY BUDGET

Annual budget is an important indicator of the financial commitment of any library. The main purpose for inclusion of budget allocation in the questionnaire was to identify the potential abilities of the libraries to acquire ICT infrastructure, electronic information resources including databases and electronic journals

Table 2.4.3 Average Library Budget in the Financial Years 2001- 02 to 2003 – 04

Budget	*Central Government*	*Central Government Autonomous*	*State Government*	*State Government Autonomous*	*Grand Total*
No Response	1(12.5 %)	2(15.4 %)	-	4(57.1 %)	7(23.3 %)
150000	-	-	1(50 %)	-	1(3.3 %)
366667	1(12.5 %)	-	-	-	1(3.3 %)
500000	2(25 %)	2(15.4 %)	-	-	4(13.3 %)
533333	1(12.5 %)	-	-	-	1(3.3 %)
600000	1(12.5 %)	1(7.7 %)	-	-	2(6.7 %)
633333	-	-	-	1(14.3 %)	1(3.3 %)
1000000	-	1(7.7 %)	-	-	1(3.3 %)
1100000	-	-	-	1(14.3 %)	1(3.3 %)
2133333	-	1(7.7 %)	-	-	1(3.3 %)
2400000	-	-	1(50 %)	-	1(3.3 %)
2500000	1(12.5 %)	1(7.7 %)	-	-	2(6.7 %)
2506037	-	1(7.7 %)	-	-	1(3.3 %)
2833333	1(12.5 %)	-	-	-	1(3.3 %)
3216667	-	-	-	1(14.3 %)	1(3.3 %)
3933333	-	1(7.7 %)	-	-	1(3.3 %)
5000000	-	1(7.7 %)	-	-	1(3.3 %)
5066667	-	1(7.7 %)	-	-	1(3.3 %)
250000000	-	1(7.7 %)	-	-	1(3.3 %)
Grand Total	8(100 %)	13(100 %)	2(100 %)	7(100 %)	30(100 %)

Annual budget of libraries in three financial years from 2001 to 2004 were collected and analysed. Table 2.4.3 shows the average budget of special libraries in Kerala in the financial years 2001-02 to 2003-04. Seven (23.3 per cent) librarians have not responded to this question. Some times they may not have a separate annual budget or they were not willing to disclose the financial status of their libraries. A good number

(33.3 per cent) of libraries have below 10 lakhs of average annual budget. Majority of the Central Government institutions (62.5 per cent) and 50 per cent of State Government institutions have below 10 lakhs of average library budget. Two (6.7 per cent) libraries have 25 lakhs of annual budget and 4 (13.3 per cent) libraries have 25 to 40 lakhs of annual budget. Libraries of Central Government Autonomous institutions have substantial annual budget compared to the libraries of other categories of institutions. Majority of them have above 10 lakhs of average annual budget and three of them have above 50 lakhs of average annual budget. Libraries of RRL and SCTIMST have around 50 lakhs of average annual budget. VSSC library has 2.5 crores of average annual budget. It is found that a good number of the Special Libraries under study have below 10 lakhs of average annual budget. Libraries of Central Government Autonomous institutions have substantial annual budget compared to the libraries of other categories of institutions. Majority of them have above 10 lakhs of average annual budget and three of them have above 50 lakhs of average annual budget. Libraries of RRL and SCTIMST have around 50 lakhs of average annual budget. VSSC library has 2.5 crores of average annual budget.

The analysis of the responses received from the chief librarians collected through semi-structured interviews shows that about half of the Special Libraries under study do not have enough budgets for their needs. They are struggling to introduce ICT based library resource and services. In order to provide more advanced library and information services more financial assistance is required. Due to limited budgets they are not able to subscribe to sufficient number of foreign journals and electronic databases. Only three libraries are participating in consortia based subscription, therefore these they are better in providing more full text electronic journals. About 40 per cent of librarians responded that they get financial assistance from their parent institution according to their needs. But most of them are not able to provide more advanced ICT based services and resources like full text electronic journals and databases.

DOCUMENTS COLLECTIONS OF SPECIAL LIBRARIES UNDER STUDY

Library collection forms a sound foundation for efficient services. The type and quantum of collection in the selected libraries has been presented in the Tables 3.4 to 3.15. Table 2.4.4 presents the availability of different types of documents in the selected libraries. It is observed that all the libraries have books and except one or two, most of them have Indian, foreign and gratis journals. Most of them are also have back volumes of journals. Very few (26.7 per cent) of them have online journals and full text databases. Majority of the libraries have bibliographic databases (80 per cent), and CD-ROM databases (66.6 per cent). About 50 per cent of libraries have theses, standards and technical reports. Very few libraries have dissertations, patents, reprints, audiocassettes, videocassettes, VCDs, and microforms. Only one (3.3 per cent) library has DVD at the time of data collection. Few libraries are accessing electronic resources like online journals and databases and most of them are attached to Central Government autonomous institutions.

Table 2.4.4 Documents Collections of Special Libraries under study

Document	*Central Government*	*Central Government Autonomous*	*State Government*	*State Government Autonomous*	*Grand Total*
Books	8(100 %)	13(100 %)	2(100 %)	7(100 %)	30(100 %)
Foreign journals	7(87.5 %)	13(100 %)	2(100 %)	7(100 %)	29(96.7 %)
Indian Journals	7(87.5 %)	13(100 %)	1(50 %)	7(100 %)	28(93.3 %)
Gift Journals	4(50 %)	12(92.3 %)	2(100 %)	5(71.4 %)	23(76.7 %)
Online/E-journals	1(12.5 %)	4(30.8 %)	1(50 %)	2(28.6 %)	8(26.7 %)
Back volumes	8(100 %)	13(100 %)	1(50 %)	7(100 %)	29(96.7 %)

Document	*Central Govern-ment*	*Central Government Autonomous*	*State Gover-nment*	*State Government Autonomous*	*Grand Total*
of Journals					
Theses	4(50 %)	8(61.5 %)	-	3(42.9 %)	15(50 %)
Dissertations	2(25 %)	5(38. 5 %)	-	1(14.3 %)	8(26.7 %)
Standards	4(50 %)	6(46.1 %)	1(50 %)	2(28.6 %)	13(43.3 %)
Patents	1(12.5 %)	2(15.4 %)	-	-	3(10 %)
Technical Reports	4(50 %)	8(61.5 %)	1(50 %)	-	16(53.3 %)
Reprints	1(12.5 %)	1(7.7 %)	1(50 %)	1(14.3 %)	3(10 %)
Audio cassettes	-	2(15.4 %)	1(50 %)	2(28.6 %)	5(16.7 %)
Video cassettes	1(12.5 %)	4(30.8 %)	-	4(57.1 %)	9(30 %)
Microforms	-	5(38. 5 %)	-	2(28.6 %)	7(23.3 %)
Bibliographic databases	4(50 %)	13(100 %)	2(100 %)	5(71.4 %)	24(80 %)
Full text databases	-	5(38. 5 %)	1(50 %)	2(28.6 %)	8(26.7 %)
CD-ROM databases	5(62.5 %)	11(84.6 %)	1(50 %)	3(42.9 %)	20(66.6 %)
CD_ROMs	7(87.5 %)	12(92.3 %)	2(100 %)	6(85.7 %)	27(90 %)
DVDs	-	-	1(50 %)	-	1(3.3 %)
VCDs	-	1(7.7 %)	1(50 %)	1(14.3 %)	3(10 %)

This may be due to the fact that the Central Government autonomous institutions have comparatively good financial assistance than any other types of institutions. It is found that most of the libraries have different types of collections like books, journals, bound volumes of journals, etc. A very few of them have subscribed to online journals and full text databases. Majority of them have bibliographic databases and CD-ROM databases.

BOOK COLLECTION

Table 2.4.5 exhibits the quantum of books available in Special Libraries under study. It is found that majority (70 per cent) of Special Libraries under study have below 10000 volumes of books.

Table 2.4.5 Book Collection in Special Libraries under study

Number of books	*Central Government*	*Central Government autonomous*	*State Government*	*State Government autonomous*	*Grand Total*
<= 5000	5(62.5 %)	3(23 %)	1(50 %)	2(28.6 %)	11(36.7 %)
5000 - 10000	1(12.5 %)	6(46.1 %)	-	3(42.9 %)	10(33.3 %)
10000-50000	2(25 %)	3(23 %)	1(50 %)	1(14.3 %)	7(23.3 %)
>50000	-	1(7.7 %)	-	1(14.3 %)	2(6.7 %)
Total	8(100 %)	13(100 %)	2(100 %)	7(100 %)	30(100 %)

It is also found that about 30 per cent of libraries have greater than 10000 volumes of books. Among these, two (6.7 per cent) of them have greater than 50000 volumes of books. 36.7 per cent of libraries have less than or equal to 5000 volumes of books and about 33.3 per cent libraries have a collection ranging between 5000-10000 volumes. Majority (62.5 per cent) of the libraries of Central Government institutions have less than or equal to 5000 volumes of books. A good number (46.1 per cent) of the libraries of Central Government autonomous institutions have book collection ranging 5000-10000 volumes.

The maority of Special Libraries under study have below 10000 volumes of books. A few libraries have greater than 10000 volumes of books. Two of them have greater than 50000 volumes of books and they are attached to the Central Government autonomous and State Government autonomous institutions category.

SUBSCRIPTION OF FOREIGN JOURNALS

Table 2.4.6 presents the distribution of libraries according to the number of foreign journals being subscribed.

Table 2.4.6 Foreign Journals Subscribed in Special Libraries under study

Number of Foriegn Journals	*Central Govern-ment*	*Central Govern-ment autonomous*	*State Govern-ment*	*State Govern-ment autonomous*	*Grand Total*
<25	4(50 %)	2(15.4 %)	2(100 %)	2(28.6 %)	10(33.3 %)
25-50	2(25 %)	3(23 %)	-	1(14.3 %)	6(20 %)
50-100	1(12.5 %)	6(46.1 %)	-	3(42.9 %)	10(33.3 %)
>100	-	2(15.4 %)	-	1(14.3 %)	3(10 %)
Total	7(87.5 %)	13(100 %)	2(100 %)	7(100 %)	29(96.7 %)

The majority (86 per cent) of libraries have below 100 foreign journals. Among these 33.3 per cent of them have below 25 foreign journals and 20 per cent of them subscribes between 25 and 50 titles. It is found that 33.3 per cent libraries are subscribing about 50-100 foreign journals. There are only 3 (10 per cent) libraries subscribing more than 100 foreign journals. Central Government autonomous institutions are subscribing more foreign journals than any other types of Special Libraries under study. This may due to the improved financial assistance and strong demands from the users of these libraries, but it will be very useful to assess the use and cost effectiveness of these journals.

The majority of libraries are subscribing less than 100 foreign journals. A few libraries are subscribing 50-100 foreign journals. It is also found that only 3 libraries are subscribing more than 100 foreign journals and they are attached to the Central Government autonomous and State Government autonomous institutions category.

SUBSCRIPTION OF INDIAN JOURNALS

Table 2.4.7 provides distribution of libraries according the number of Indian journals being subscribed. It is found that majority (80 per cent) of Special Libraries under study are subscribing below 100 Indian journals. About 33.3 per cent of them are subscribing 25-50 Indian journals and 26.7 per cent are subscribing 50-100 Indian Journals. The Indian journal subscriptions of 20 per cent of them are below 25 titles. It is also found that 4 (13.3 per cent) libraries are subscribing more than 100 titles.

Table 2.4.7 Indian Journals Subscribed in Special Libraries under study

Number of Indian Journals	*Central Government*	*Central Government autonomous*	*State Government*	*State Government autonomous*	*Grand Total*
<25	1(12.5 %)	2(15.4 %)	-	3(42.9 %)	6(20 %)
25-50	3(37.5 %)	5(38. 5 %)	-	2(28.6 %)	10(33.3 %)
50-100	2(25 %)	5(38. 5 %)	-	1(14.3 %)	8(26.7 %)
>100	1(12.5 %)	1(7.7 %)	1(50 %)	1(14.3 %)	4(13.3 %)
Total	7(87.5 %)	13(100 %)	1(50 %)	7(100 %)	28(93.3 %)

It is revealed that majority of libraries are subscribing below 100 Indian journals. Few of them are subscribing less than 25 Indian journals and four libraries are subscribing more than 100 Indian journals.

It is found that majority of libraries are receiving less than 50 gratis journals and a very few libraries are receiving greater than 50 gratis journals. Three of them are receiving more than 100 gratis journals.

SUBSCRIPTION OF ONLINE/ELECTRONIC JOURNALS

The number of electronic and online journals as well as the value of digital information is steadily growing. More and more libraries are embracing electronic journals, and slowly marching towards using online journals, which provide a number of advantages. Table 2.4.8 exhibits the distribution of libraries according to the number of electronic /online journals being subscribed. The table reflects that a few (26.7 per cent) libraries are subscribing electronic/online journals. 30.8 per cent libraries of Central Government autonomous institutions are subscribing electronic journals. Only the libraries of IIITMK, NIO, and RRL are subscribing or getting more than 1000 electronic/online journals. This condition may be due to the limited budgets of libraries or lack of awareness and knowledge of library staff and users about the potential use of online journals.

Table 2.4.8 Online/Electronic Journals Subscribed in Special Libraries under study

Number of online E-Journals	*Central Government*	*Central Government autonomous*	*State Government*	*State Government autonomous*	*Grand Total*
6	-	1(7.7 %)	-	-	1(3.3 %)
22	-	-	-	1(14.3 %)	1(3.3 %)
35	-	-	-	1(14.3 %)	1(3.3 %)
50	-	1(7.7 %)	-	-	1(3.3 %)
75	-	1(7.7 %)	-	-	1(3.3 %)
1000 >	1(12.5 %)	1(7.7 %)	1(50 %)	-	3(10 %)
Total	1(12.5 %)	4(30.8 %)	1(50 %)	2(28.6 %)	8(26.7 %)

It is found that a few libraries are subscribing or receiving online/electronic journals and about half of them are attached to the Central Government autonomous institutions. It is also found that only the libraries of IIITMK, NIO, and RRL are subscribing or getting more than 1000 electronic/online journals.

BACK VOLUMES OF JOURNALS

Table 2.4.9 shows the distribution of libraries by size of the back volumes of journals holdings. It is seen that majority (63.3 per cent) of libraries have back volumes of journals in their libraries. It is found that the libraries of majority of Central Government institutions (62.5 per cent) and Central Government autonomous institutions (76.9 per cent) have back volumes of journals. The back volume collections of about 23.3 per cent of libraries are below 1000. It is also found that 4 (13.3 per cent) libraries have 1000-5000 back volumes and another 4 libraries have 5000-20000 back volumes. Four libraries have more than 20000 back volumes of journals.

Table 2.4.9 Back Volumes of Journals in Special Libraries under study

Number of Back volumes of Journals	*Central Government*	*Central Government autonomous*	*State Government*	*State Government autonomous*	*Grand Total*
<1000	3(37.5 %)	2(15.4 %)	1(50 %)	1(14.3 %)	7(23.3 %)
1000-5000	1(12.5 %)	3(23 %)	-	-	4(13.3 %)
5000-20000	-	3(23 %)	-	1(14.3 %)	4(13.3 %)
>20000	1(12.5 %)	2(15.4 %)	-	1(14.3 %)	4(13.3 %)
Total	5(62.5 %)	10(76.9 %)	1(50 %)	3(42.9 %)	19(63.3 %)

It is found that majority of the institutions have back volumes of journals in their libraries. Libraries of majority of Central Government institutions and Central Government autonomous institutions have back volumes of journals. Four libraries have more than 20000 back volumes of journals.

THESES COLLECTION

Table 2.4.10 shows the distribution of libraries according to the size of theses holding. It is observed that 50 per cent of libraries have thesis collection and about 23.3 per cent of libraries' thesis collection is below 25. Majority (61.5 per cent) of the libraries of Central Government autonomous institutions have thesis collection. It is found that four (13.3 per cent) libraries have 25-100 theses collection and another 4 have more than 100 theses.

Table 2.4.10 Theses Collection in Special Libraries under study

Number of theses	*Central Government*	*Central Government autonomous*	*State Government*	*State Government autonomous*	*Grand Total*
<25	3(37.5 %)	3(23 %)	-	1(14.3 %)	7(23.3 %)
25-100	1(12.5 %)	2(15.4 %)	-	1(14.3 %)	4(13.3 %)
>100	-	3(23 %)	-	1(14.3 %)	4(13.3 %)
Total	4(50 %)	8(61.5 %)	-	3(42.9 %)	15(50 %)

It is found that about half of the libraries have theses collection and majority of them have less than 100 theses. Majority of Central Government autonomous institutions have theses collection. It is also found that four libraries have more than 100 theses.

DISSERTATIONS / PROJECT REPORTS

Table 2.4.11 provides the distribution of libraries by the number of dissertations / project reports holdings.

Table 2.4.11 Dissertation/Project Reports in Special Libraries under study

Number of Dissertation	*Central Government*	*Central Government autonomous*	*State Government*	*State Government autonomous*	*Grand Total*
<50	-	1(7.7 %)	-	1(14.3 %)	2(6.7 %)
50-100	-	3(23 %)	-	-	3(10 %)
>100	2(25 %)	1(7.7 %)	-	-	3(10 %)
Total	2(25 %)	5(38. 5 %)	-	1(14.3 %)	8(26.7 %)

It shows that few (26.7 per cent) libraries have dissertations / project reports. 38.5 per cent libraries of Central Government autonomous institutions have dissertation collection. Only 3 (10 per cent) libraries have more than 100 dissertations / project reports.

It is revealed that few libraries have dissertations/ project reports. It is also revealed that 3 libraries have more than 100 dissertations/project reports

STANDARDS COLLECTION

Table 2.4.12 shows the size of standards present in Special Libraries under study. It is revealed that about 43.3 per cent of libraries have standards and majority of them have less than 1000 standards. Fifty percent Central Government institutions and 46.1 per cent Central Government autonomous institutions have standards in their libraries. Only 2 (6.7 per cent) libraries have more than 5000 standards.

Table 2.4.12 Standards in Special Libraries under study

Number of Standards	*Central Govern-ment*	*Central Govern-ment autonomous*	*State Govern-ment*	*State Govern-ment autonomous*	*Grand Total*
<1000	2(25 %)	4(30.8 %)	-	2(28.6 %)	8(26.7 %)
1000-5000	1(12.5 %)	1(7.7 %)	1(50 %)	-	3(10 %)
>5000	1(12.5 %)	1(7.7 %)	-	-	2(6.7 %)
Total	4(50 %)	6(46.1 %)	1(50 %)	2(28.6 %)	13(43.3 %)

It is found that a good number of Special Libraries under study have standards. Majority of them have less than 1000 standards. It is also found that 2 libraries have more than 5000 standards.

TECHNICAL REPORTS COLLECTION

Table 2.4.13 presents the distribution of libraries according to the number of technical reports. It is revealed that 53.3 per cent of libraries have technical reports and majority of them have less than 1000 technical reports.

Table 2.4.13 Technical Report in Special Libraries under study

Number of Technical report	*Central Government*	*Central Government autonomous*	*State Government*	*State Government autonomous*	*Grand Total*
<1000	3(37.5 %)	6(46.1 %)	1(50 %)	2(28.6 %)	12(40 %)
1000-5000	1(12.5 %)	1(7.7 %)	-	1(14.3 %)	3(10 %)
>5000	-	1(7.7 %)	-	-	1(3.3 %)
Total	4(50 %)	8(61.5 %)	1(50 %)	3(42.9 %)	16(53.3 %)

Libraries of majority (61.5 per cent) of Central Government autonomous institutions have technical reports and one (3 per cent) of them have more than 5000 technical reports.

It is found that about half of the libraries have technical reports in their collection and majority of these libraries have less than 1000 technical reports. Only one library has more than 5000 technical reports.

CD-ROM COLLECTION

Table 2.4.14 presents the distribution of libraries according to the number of CD-ROMs holding. The table indicates that 90 per cent of libraries have CD-ROMs. Majority (66.7 per cent) of libraries have less than 100 CD-ROMs.

Table 2.4.14 CD-ROMs in Special Libraries under study

Number of CD-ROMs	*Central Government*	*Central Government autonomous*	*State Government*	*State Government autonomous*	*Grand Total*
<100	6(75 %)	8(61.5 %)	-	6(85.7 %)	20(66.7 %)
100-500	-	3(23 %)	2(100 %)	-	5(16.7 %)
>500	1(12.5 %)	1(7.7 %)	-	-	2(6.7 %)
Total	7(87.5 %)	12(92.3 %)	2(100 %)	6(85.7 %)	27(90 %)

The analysis revealed that a few (16.7 per cent) libraries have 100-500 CD-ROMs and 2 (6.7 per cent) libraries have more than 500 CD-ROMs. Libraries of majority of Central Government institutions (75 per cent), Central Government autonomous institutions (61.5 per cent), and State Government autonomous institutions (865.7 per cent) have less than 100 CD-ROMs.

It is found that most of the Special Libraries under study have CD-ROM collection and majority of them have less than 100 CD-ROMs. It is also found that a few libraries have 100-500 CD-ROMs and 2 libraries have more than 500 CD-ROMs.

CD-ROM DATABASES

The massive storage capacity of CD-ROM databases has enabled libraries to access instantly, easily, and conveniently a substantial amount of relatively current and retrospective information at a reasonable cost. Table 2.4.15 shows the number of CD-ROM databases present in Special Libraries under study. The Table shows that 50 per cent libraries have less than 5 CD-ROM databases. Three (10 per cent) libraries have 5-10 CD-ROM databases and only 2 (6.7 per cent) libraries have more than 10 CD-ROM databases. It is found that the libraries of majority of Central Government institutions (62.5 per cent) and Central Government autonomous institutions (61.5 per cent) have less than 5 CD-ROM databases. Majority (84.6 per cent) of libraries of Central Government autonomous institutions have CD-ROM databases.

Table 2.4.15 CD-ROM Databases in Special Libraries under study

Number of CD-ROM Database	*Central Government*	*Central Government autonomous*	*State Government*	*State Government autonomous*	*Grand Total*
<5	5(62.5 %)	8(61.5 %)	1(50 %)	1(14.3 %)	15(50 %)
5-10	-	2(15.4 %)	-	1(14.3 %)	3(10 %)
>10	-	1(7.7 %)	-	1(14.3 %)	2(6.7 %)
Total	5(62.5 %)	11(84.6 %)	1(50 %)	3(42.9 %)	20(66.7 %)

The majority of Central Government institutions (62.5 per cent) and Central Government autonomous institutions (61.5 per cent) and libraries of 50 per cent State Government institutions have less than 5 CD-ROM databases. Few libraries of Central Government autonomous institutions (15.4 per cent) and State Government autonomous institutions (14.3 per cent) have 5 to 10 CD-ROM databases.

It is found that majority of libraries have CD-ROM databases, and majority of them are belong to the Central Government autonomous institutions. It is also found that about half of the libraries have less than 5 CD-ROM databases and three libraries have 5-10 CD-ROM databases. Only two libraries have more than 10 CD-ROM databases.

It is found from the interview with chief librarians that about half of the libraries are poor in electronic resources. Among the libraries, Central Government autonomous institutions libraries are better in electronic resources. In most of the cases the libraries have their bibliographic databases in electronic form and one or two CD-ROM databases. A few libraries have medium collection and a very few libraries have good electronic resources.

LIBRARY PROFESSIONALS

Human resources play a prominent role for the successful management of any library. The details of library professionals/staff available in Special Libraries under study are presented in Tables 2.4.16 to 2.4.18.

STRENGTH OF THE LIBRARY PROFESSIONALS

Table 2.4.16 shows the strength of professionals in different type of Special Libraries under study. It is observed that 87.5 per cent of Central Government institutions, 53.8 per cent of Central Government autonomous institutions, all the State Government institutions and 57.1 per cent of State Government institutions have 1 to 4 number of library professionals in their libraries. Six institutions have more than 9 library professionals. Out of which 5 (38.5 per cent) of them belong to Central Government autonomous institutions.

Table 2.4.16 Library Professionals in Special Libraries under study

Organisation type	*1 to 4 staff*	*5 to 9 staff*	*10+ staff*
Central Government	7(87.5 %)	1(12.5 %)	-
Central Government Autonomous	7(53.8 %)	1(7.7 %)	5(38. 5 %)
State Government	2(100 %)		-
State Government Autonomous	4(57.1 %)	2(28.6 %)	1(14.3 %)

All the libraries of State Government institutions and majority of Central Government institutions, Central Government autonomous institutions, and State Government autonomous institutions have 1 to 4 number of library staff. 38.5 per cent libraries of Central Government autonomous institutions have more than 10 number of library staff.

It is revealed that majority of libraries in all the category of institutions have 1 to 4 number of library professionals. Six libraries have more than 9 numbers of library professionals and five of these libraries are attached to the Central Government autonomous institutions category.

QUALIFICATIONS OF THE LIBRARY PROFESSIONALS

Table 2.4.17 shows the qualifications of library professionals in different category of institutions. A slight majority (53 per cent) of library professionals in Special Libraries under study are postgraduates. Majority of library professionals of Central Government autonomous institutions (56 per cent) and State Government autonomous institutions (52 per cent) and a good number (46 per cent) of library professionals of Central Government institutions are postgraduates. The data collected revealed that there are three library professionals who hold a PhD in librarianship.

Table 2.4.17 Qualifications of Library Professionals in Special Libraries under study

Organisation type	*Qualifications*					
	Below Graduation	*Graduation*	*Post Graduation*	*Ph. D*	*Not mentioned*	*Total*
Central Government	-	9(38 %)	11(46 %)	-	4(17 %)	24(100 %)
Central Government Autonomous	7(8 %)	11(12 %)	52(56 %)	3(3 %)	20(22 %)	93(100 %)
State Government	-	2(67 %)	1(33 %)	-	-	3(100 %)
State Government Autonomous	1(2 %)	3(7 %)	22(52 %)	-	16(38 %)	42(100 %)
Total	8(5 %)	25(15 %)	86(53 %)	3(2 %)	40(25 %)	162(100 %)

It is found that a slight majority of library professionals in different category of institutions are Postgraduates and three of them hold a Ph.D. Degree in librarianship

AGE OF THE LIBRARY PROFESSIONALS

Table 2.4.18 provides the ages of library professionals in Special Libraries under study. Majority of library professionals of Central Government institutions (54 per cent), Central Government autonomous institutions (55 per cent) are greater than 45 years of age. It is found that 51 per cent of the library professionals have greater than 45 years of age.

The table also shows that 33 (35 per cent) library professionals of Central Government autonomous institutions and 17 (40 per cent) library professionals of State Government autonomous institutions are between 35 and 40 years of age. Library professionals below 35 years of age are seen in Central Government autonomous institutions (10 per cent) and State Government autonomous institutions (40 per cent). Majority of the library staffs are above 45 years of age and this indicates that fresh appointments in Special Libraries under study is less.

Table 2.4.18 Library Professionals in Different Age Groups in Special Libraries under study

Organisation type	*Age group*			
	<35	*Between 35 and 45*	*>45*	*Total*
Central Government	2(8 %)	9(38 %)	13(54 %)	24(100 %)
Central Government Autonomous	9(10 %)	33(35 %)	51(55 %)	93(100 %)
State Government	1(33 %)	1(33 %)	1(33 %)	3(100 %)
State Government Autonomous	8(19 %)	17(40 %)	17(40 %)	42(100 %)
Total	20(12 %)	60(37 %)	82(51 %)	162(100 %)

The adequate numbers of library professionals are very essential for the successful application of Information and Communication Technologies in libraries. It is clear from the analysis that majority of library professionals are above 45 years of age. Libraries of autonomous institutions have comparatively younger workforce. This may be due to the privilege of autonomous institutions to conduct appointments according to their needs or the presence of more number of professionals in these institutions.

SKILL AND EXPERTISE OF LIBRARY STAFF

It is found in the responses received from the interviews with chief librarians that library professionals of majority of Special Libraries under study have adequate skill and expertise in ICT based library resources and services. But it is also found that in majority of libraries the ICT based library resources and services are managing by a single library professional. Most of them need more qualified library professionals to handle ICT based resources and services. In most cases the library professionals are not trained in ICT based resources and services. Librarians of about 40 per cent of the special libraries indicated that the skill and expertise of their library professionals are inadequate. Most of the libraries are getting support from the computer professionals of the institute or libraries depend them for rectifying any problem in the hardware, software or networking.

Even though majority of librarians responded that the skill and expertise of their professionals are adequate, the investigator observed that the skill and expertise of library professionals in ICT based library resources and services in Special Libraries under study are inadequate, the main problem of the libraries is lack of qualified library professionals in Information and Communication Technologies. Library professionals need to improve their skill and expertise in Information and Communication Technologies by attending workshops, seminars, short-term course or undergoing refresher courses or any other means like deputing professionals to other institutions, etc. Libraries should be provided career advancement facilities to improve and extend the knowledge, skill and expertise of library professionals in ICT.

INFORMATION AND COMMUNICATION TECHNOLOGY INFRASTRUCTURE

ICT infrastructure is usually considered with respect to its main areas, which are: hardware, software, telecommunication and humanware. The infrastructure remains the main bottleneck to the development of ICT in libraries. Sufficient infrastructure is very essential for the successful implementation of advanced information services and resources. Tables 2.4.19 to 2.4.24 provide information about the Information and Communication Technology infrastructure in Special Libraries under study.

HARDWARE

Table 2.4.19 provides information about the hardware available in Special Libraries under study.

Table 2.4.19 Use of Hardware in Special Libraries under study

Hardware	*Central Govern-ment*	*Central Govern-ment autonomous*	*State Govern-ment*	*State Govern-ment autonomous*	*Grand Total*
Server	3(37.5 %)	12(92.3 %)	-	5(71.4 %)	20(66.7 %)
Clients/ Computer Workstations	8(100 %)	13(100 %)	2(100 %)	7(100 %)	30(100 %)
Dot Matrix Printer	7(87.5 %)	12(92.3 %)	-	4(57.1 %)	23(76.7 %)
Ink Jet Printer	3(37.5 %)	5(38. 5 %)	-	3(42.9 %)	11(36.7 %)
Laser Printer	2(25 %)	10(76.9 %)	1(50 %)	4(57.1 %)	17(56.7 %)
Barcode Printer	-	4(30.8 %)	-	-	4(13.3 %)
Scanner	-	7(53.8 %)	-	3(42.9 %)	10(33.3 %)
Barcode Scanner	-	6(46.1 %)	-	-	6(20 %)
CD-Net Server	-	4(30.8 %)	1(50 %)	2(28.6 %)	7(23.3 %)
CD-ROM Tower	1(12.5 %)	5(38. 5 %)	-	-	6(20 %)
Systems with DVDs	-	3(23 %)	-	-	3(10 %)
Back up Device	-	7(53.8 %)	1(50 %)	2(28.6 %)	10(33.3 %)
LCD Projector	-	1(7.7 %)	1(50 %)	1(14.3 %)	3(10 %)
CD-Writer	-	8(61.5 %)	1(50 %)	6(85.7 %)	15(50 %)
UPS	5(62.5 %)	11(84.6 %)	1(50 %)	6(85.7 %)	23(76.7 %)
Others (Please specify)	-	3(23 %)	1(50 %)	-	4(13.3 %)

The analysis reveals that most of the (92.3 per cent) libraries of Central Government autonomous institutions and 71.4 per cent of State Government autonomous institutions have server in the library. All the libraries of different categories of institutions have computer nodes or workstations. Majority (76.7 per cent) of libraries except State Government institutions have Dot Matrix Printer. A few (36.7

per cent) libraries except State Government institution libraries have inkjet printer. Majority of libraries of Central Government autonomous institutions (76.9 per cent) and State Government autonomous institutions (57.1 per cent) have laser printer. Only the Central Government autonomous institution libraries have Barcode printer (30.8 per cent), and Barcode Scanner (46.1 per cent). Central Government autonomous institutions have CD-Net Server (30.8 per cent) and CD-ROM Tower (38.5 per cent) in their libraries. Majority of institutions except Central Government institutions have backup devices, and CD Writer in their libraries, but Central Government autonomous institutions are predominant with this hardware. Majority (76.7 per cent) of libraries in all the categories of institutions have UPS. Four (13.3 per cent) libraries have some other hardware like Data Capturing Unit, Digital Camera, Planetary Scanner, Portable Barcode Reader, Network Laser Printer, etc.

It is found that majority of the Special Libraries under study have basic hardware facilities like servers, computers, printers, etc. However in the majority of the cases it was underutilised. The libraries of Central Government autonomous institutions have more better hardware facilities including scanner, barcode printer, barcode scanner, Net Server, CD-ROM Tower, CD-Writer, etc. It is observed that most of the library professionals are not aware of the operations of hardware properly, so they are underutilised. A good number (33 per cent) of the libraries need more computer terminals and devices like printers to provide ICT based resources and services. Seven libraries (23.3 per cent) have very poor hardware; it is not at all adequate for library automation and ICT application. It is very essential to have sufficient hardware for providing ICT based services and resources. The cost of hardware is decreasing day by day and it will boost the ICT application in Special Libraries under study.

SOFTWARE

To bring the hardware establishment into activation, proper software facilities are required by the special libraries to serve up-to-date information to the clientele. Table 2.4.20 gives the availability of software in Special Libraries under study. The analysis shows that all the libraries of Central Government autonomous and State Government institutions, 85.7 per cent of State Government autonomous and 50 per cent of Central Government institutions have Network Operating System. All the libraries of different category of institutions have Library Management Software, whether it is commercially prepared or in house prepared. A few (20 per cent) of them have digital library software like greenstone. A few (23.3 per cent) of them have CD-Net Management Software, 5 (38.5 per cent) of them belong to Central Government autonomous institutions. Majority of institutions have DTP Software like MS Office in their libraries. The presence of DBMS or RDBMS is not satisfactory and it is found that about 62.5 per cent of Central Government institutions, 38.5 per cent of Central Government autonomous institutions, 50 per cent of State Government institutions and 28.6 per cent of State Government autonomous institutions have DBMS/ RDBMS. Majority of Libraries are using Norton Antivirus Software. Few of them also have other software like Winspiris, Adobe Acrobat reader, Photoshop, DSpace, etc.

Table 2.4.20 Use of Software in Special Libraries under study

Software	*Central Government*	*Central Government autonomous*	*State Government*	*State Government autonomous*	*Grand Total*
Network Operating System	4(50 %)	13(100 %)	2(100 %)	6(85.7 %)	25(83.3 %)
Library Management Software	8(100 %)	13(100 %)	2(100 %)	7(100 %)	30(100 %)
Digital Library Software	-	4(30.8 %)	1(50 %)	1(14.3 %)	6(20 %)
CD-Net Management Software	-	5(38. 5 %)	1(50 %)	1(14.3 %)	7(23.3 %)
DTP Software	6(75 %)	11(84.6 %)	1(50 %)	6(85.7 %)	24(80 %)
DBMS/ RDBMS	5(62.5 %)	5(38. 5 %)	1(50 %)	2(28.6 %)	13(43.3 %)
Antivirus Software	5(62.5 %)	11(84.6 %)	1(50 %)	4(57.1 %)	21(70 %)
Others (Please specify)	1(12.5 %)	2(15.4 %)	1(50 %)	-	4(13.3 %)

It is revealed that all the libraries have library management software, majority of them have commercially prepared. Majority of them have Network Operating System, DTP Software and Anti Virus Software, but a few of them have digital library software, CD Net Management Software and DBMS/RDBMS.

USE OF NETWORK OPERATING SYSTEM

Table 2.4.21 shows the different type of Network Operating Systems (NOS) used in Special Libraries under study. It is revealed that libraries of 37.5 per cent of Central Government institutions, 53.8 per cent of Central Government autonomous institutions, 50 per cent of State Government institutions and 42.9 per cent of State Government autonomous institutions are using Windows NT as their NOS. It is also found that libraries of about 25 per cent of Central Government institutions, 30.8 per cent of Central Government autonomous institutions, 50 per cent of State Government institutions and 28.6 per cent of State Government autonomous institutions are using Linux as their NOS. Other Networking Operating Systems used are Unix (3.3 per cent), Novel Netware (3.3 per cent) and Windows 98/2000/XP (16.7 per cent).

Table 2.4.21 Use of Network Operating System in Special Libraries under study

Network Operating Systems	*Central Govern-ment*	*Central Govern-ment autonomous*	*State Govern-ment*	*State Govern-ment autonomous*	*Grand Total*
Linux	2(25 %)	4(30.8 %)	1(50 %)	2(28.6 %)	9(30 %)
Unix	-	1(7.7 %)	-	-	1(3.3 %)
Windows NT	3(37.5 %)	7(53.8 %)	1(50 %)	3(42.9 %)	14(46.7 %)
Novel Netware	-	1(7.7 %)	-	-	1(3.3 %)
Windows 98/2000/XP	-	3(23 %)	1(50 %)	1(14.3 %)	5(16.7 %)

A good number (46.7 per cent) of Special Libraries under study are using Windows NT as their Networking Operating System. Linux is the distant second NOS with 30 per cent libraries. It is revealed that Windows NT and Linux are the major Network Operating Systems used in Special Libraries under study. It is observed that Windows NT is used more libraries as Network Operating System, followed by Linux.

USE OF LIBRARY MANAGEMENT SOFTWARE

Library Management Software package plays a key role for the success of library automation. There are a number of library automation software packages in use in India.

Responses indicate that the organisations surveyed use a wealth of different software packages depending upon particular application. Table 2.4.22 shows the different library management software used in Special Libraries under study. The analysis shows that Special Libraries under study are more interested in commercial software packages. There are 11 software preferred by 23 (77 per cent) libraries. It is found that CDS/ISIS is used more in libraries (23.3 per cent) than any other software. Libsys software is a distant second with 16.7 per cent of libraries, 30.8 per cent of them from Central Government autonomous institutions category. Two (28.6 per cent) libraries of State Government autonomous institutions are using Libsoft software. Seven (23.3 per cent) libraries reported to have developed the library management software in-house. The other software used are Alice for Windows, SLIM++, Winisis, Winsoft, Winlis, Chronicles 2001, E-grandhalaya, and LibsuitASP+.

It is seen that Special Libraries under study are using a number of library management software, and still today CDS\ISIS is used more number of libraries. Few libraries are using Libsys library management software and few libraries have developed the library management software in-house.

The analysis revealed that all the special libraries have library management software. CDS/ISIS is the more used software and Libsys is the second. Central Government autonomous institutions are better in library management software as most of them are using good library management software. Seven libraries reported to have developed the library management software in-house.

USE OF DBMS/RDBMS

Table 2.4.23 provides the type of DBMS/RDBMS used in Special Libraries under study. It shows that libraries of 50 per cent of Central Government institutions, 15.4 per cent of Central Government autonomous institutions, and 14.3 per

Table 2.4.22 Use of Library Management Software in Special Libraries under study

Library Management Software	*Central Government*	*Central Government autonomous*	*State Government*	*State Government autonomous*	*Grand Total*
CDS/ISIS	4(50 %)	2(15.4 %)	-	1(14.3 %)	7(23.3 %)
Libsys	-	4(30.8 %)	-	1(14.3 %)	5(16.7 %)
Alice for Windows	-	1(7.7 %)	-	1(14.3 %)	2(6.7 %)
SLIM++	-	1(7.7 %)	-	-	1(3.3 %)
WINISIS	-	1(7.7 %)	-	-	1(3.3 %)
Winsoft	1(12.5 %)	-	-	-	1(3.3 %)
WinLis	1(12.5 %)	-	-	-	1(3.3 %)
Chronicles 2001	1(12.5 %)	-	-	-	1(3.3 %)
Egrandhalaya	-	1(7.7 %)	-	-	1(3.3 %)
Libsoft	-	-	-	2(28.6 %)	2(6.7 %)
LibsuitASP+	-	1(7.7 %)	-	-	1(3.3 %)
In house prepared	1(12.5 %)	2(15.4 %)	2(100 %)	2(28.6 %)	7(23.3 %)
Grand Total	8(100 %)	13(100 %)	2(100 %)	7(100 %)	30(100 %)

cent of State Government institutions are using CDS/ISIS for their database management activities. It is also found that libraries of about 15.4 per cent of Central Government autonomous institutions and 50 per cent of State Government institutions are using ORACLE as their DBMS. The other RDBMS/DBMS used are dBase (6.7 per cent), FoxPro (6.7 per cent), MS Access (16.7 per cent) and WINISIS (6.7 per cent).

Table 2.4.23 Use of DBMS/RDBMS in Special Libraries under study

BDMS/ RDBMS used	*Central Govern-ment*	*Central Govern-ment autonomous*	*State Govern-ment*	*State Govern-ment autonomous*	*Grand Total*
dBase	-	1(7.7 %)	-	1(14.3 %)	2(6.7 %)
FoxPro	-	1(7.7 %)	-	1(14.3 %)	2(6.7 %)
MS Access	1(12.5 %)	1(7.7 %)	-	3(42.9 %)	5(16.7 %)
CDS\ISIS	4(50 %)	2(15.4 %)	-	1(14.3 %)	7(23.3 %)
WINISIS	-	2(15.4 %)	-	-	2(6.7 %)
ORACLE	-	2(15.4 %)	1(50 %)	-	3(10 %)

It is clear from the table that the use of DBMS/RDBMS in Special Libraries under study are very less. CDS/ISIS and ORACLE are the two successfully used software.

USE OF DIGITAL LIBRARY/DTP/ANTIVIRUS SOFTWARE

Libraries are also using different software like digital library software, DTP software, Antivirus software, etc. Table 2.4.24 shows the use of these software in the libraries of different organisations. The analysis shows that 6 (20 per cent) libraries are using digital library software, among these, 5 (16.7 per cent) libraries are using Greenstone Digital Library Software and one (3.3 per cent) library is using ACADO Software. As far as the DTP software are concerned 66.7 per cent libraries are using MS Office software, 3 (10 per cent) libraries are using Page Maker Software and only one (3.3 per cent) library is using Coral Draw software. Norton is the most favored Antivirus software with a percentage of sixty. Two (6.7 per cent) libraries are using PC Cellin software and one (3.3 per cent) library is using AVG Software. It is also found that Central Government autonomous institutions are comparatively good in these software, four (30.8 per cent) of them are using Greenstone, and 8 (61.5 per cent) are using MS Office and Norton Antivirus.

It is found that very few libraries are using digital library software and majority of libraries are using MS Office and Norton Antivirus software.

The analysis of the data received from the interviews of the chief librarians reveals that most of the libraries have library management software but majority of them are not successful in using the software or their software are not sufficient for complete automation and ICT application in their libraries. Few libraries indicated that their library management software are good. On observation it is found that about 40 per cent libraries have somewhat good software, including library management software and other software like MS Office, DBMS, etc., but in this case also except few libraries most of them are not completely utilised their software properly, some modules are not utilised or library professionals do not know how to use them properly.

Table 2.4.24 Use of Digital Library/DTP/Antivirus Software in Special Libraries under study

Software	*Central Government*	*Central Government autonomous*	*State Government*	*State Government autonomous*	*Grand Total*
Digital Library Software					
ACADO	-	-	1(50 %)	-	1(3.3 %)
Greenstone	-	4(30.8 %)	-	1(14.3 %)	5(16.7 %)
DTP Software					
MS Office	6(75 %)	8(61.5 %)	1(50 %)	5(71.4 %)	20(66.7 %)
Page Maker	-	2(15.4 %)	-	1(14.3 %)	3(10 %)
Coral Draw	-	1(7.7 %)	-	-	1(3.3 %)
Antivirus Software					
Norton	5(62.5 %)	8(61.5 %)	1(50 %)	4(57.1 %)	18(60 %)
AVG	-	1(7.7 %)	-	-	1(3.3 %)
PC Cellin	-	2(15.4 %)	-	-	2(6.7 %)

COMPUTER APPLICATIONS

This section of the survey sought to identify the diversity of computerised system in use, and the combinations in which they can be found in Special Libraries under study. Questions in this section pertained to library automation, library management software, databases, digital libraries, etc.

YEAR OF LIBRARY AUTOMATION

Table 2.4.25 shows the year of commencement of library automation in Special Libraries under study. From the analysis it is evident that library automation largely commenced during the period 1990-2000. The analysis shows that all the libraries of Central government organisation are automated before the year 2000. Majority of them (88 per cent) automated in between 1990 and 2000. Among Central Government Autonomous institutions 46.1 per cent institutions are automated before 1990 and equal number (46.1 per cent) of institutions are automated in between 1990 and 2000. All the State Government institutions surveyed are automated after 1990. Majority of State Government autonomous institutions are automated in between 1990 and 2000.

Table 2.4.25 Year of Automation in Special Libraries under study

Organisation type	*Year of Automation*		
	<=1990	***Between 1990 and 2000***	***>2000***
Central Government	1(12.5 %)	7(87.5 %)	-
Central Government Autonomous	6(46.1 %)	6(46.1 %)	1(7.7 %)
State Government	-	1(50 %)	1(50 %)
State Government Autonomous	1(14.3 %)	4(57.1 %)	2(28.6 %)

$$\lambda^2 = 9.46$$

Chi-square test was carried out to test the association between the organisation type and year of automation. The hypothesis tested was year of automation is independent of the type of organisation. The computed value of χ^2 is 9.46, which is less than table value (9.49) at 4 degrees of freedom and 5 per cent level of significance. Hence it can be conclude that year of automation and organisation types are independent.

The majority of the libraries of Central Government institutions (87.5 per cent) and State Government autonomous institutions (57.1 per cent) and a good number of Central Government autonomous institutions (46.1 per cent) and State Government institutions (50 per cent) are automated in between 1990 and 2000.

It is found that library automation in Special Libraries under study largely commenced during the period 1990-2000. All the libraries of the Central government organisation are automated before the year 2000. A good number of libraries Central Government Autonomous institutions are automated before 1990. All the State Government institutions surveyed are automated after 1990. Majority of the State Government autonomous institutions are automated in between 1990 and 2000. Chi-square test also indicates that there is no association between year of automation and type of organisation.

FEATURES OF LIBRARY MANAGEMENT SOFTWARE

Table 2.4.26 shows the different features of library management software used in Special Libraries under study. Majority of the libraries have network version of library management software and have OPAC and Online help facilities. It is revealed that the Library Management Software of 71.4 per cent State Government Institutions, 69.2 per cent Central Government institutions are network version. The Library Management Software of majority of the Central Government autonomous institutions (84.6 per cent) and State Government autonomous institutions (71 .4 per cent) have online help for users. The Library Management Software of all the State Government institutions, majority of Central

Government autonomous institutions (84.6 per cent) and State Government autonomous institutions have OPAC facility. It is also found that the Library Management Software of 53.8 per cent of Central Government autonomous institutions, 50 per cent of State Government institutions, and 57.1 per cent of State Government autonomous institutions have WebOPAC facility.

Table 2.4.26 Features of Library Management Software in Special Libraries under study

Organisation type	*Network Version*	*Online help for users*	*OPAC Facility*	*WebOPAC Facility*
Central Government	2(25 %)	3(37.5 %)	4(50 %)	2(25 %)
Central Government Autonomous	9(69.2 %)	11(84.6 %)	11(84.6 %)	7(53.8 %)
State Government	1(50 %)	1(50 %)	2(100 %)	1(50 %)
State Government Autonomous	5(71.4 %)	5(71.4 %)	6(85.7 %)	4(57.1 %)

It is found that majority of Library Management Software are good and most of them are network version and have online help and OPAC facilities.

PRESENT STATUS OF LIBRARY AUTOMATION

Almost all the operations in a library can be computerized to achieve more efficient and effective functioning and for providing excellent library and information services. Librarians were asked to indicate the library housekeeping operations they have automated. Table 2.4.27 shows the status of library automation in Special Libraries under study. The library catalogue found to be the most popular area for automation- 93.3 per cent of them computerized their catalogue or different stages of computerisation. This was followed by the circulation system (60 per cent).

Table 2.4.27 Areas of Automation in Special Libraries under study

Library Functions/ Services	*Central Government*	*Central Government autonomous*	*State Government*	*State Government autonomous*	*Grand Total*
Acquisition	1(12.5 %)	6(46.1 %)	1(50 %)	2(28.6 %)	10(33.3 %)
Cataloguing	8(100 %)	13(100 %)	2(100 %)	5(71.4 %)	28(93.3 %)
Circulation	5(62.5 %)	8(61.5 %)	1(50 %)	4(57.1 %)	18(60 %)
Serial control	4(50 %)	6(46.1 %)	1(50 %)	4(57.1 %)	15(50 %)
OPAC	3(37.5 %)	9(69.2 %)	1(50 %)	4(57.1 %)	17(56.7 %)
Annual Stock verification	1(12.5 %)	4(30.8 %)	-	-	5(16.7 %)
Budget control	-	2(15.4 %)	-	1(14.3 %)	3(10 %)

Few libraries of Central Government institutions (37.5 per cent) and majority of the libraries of Central Government autonomous institutions (69.2 per cent), State Government institutions (50 per cent), and State Government autonomous institutions (57.1 per cent) have OPAC facility. One library of Central Government institutions (12.5 per cent) and a few libraries of Central Government autonomous institutions (30.8 per cent) used computer for annual stock verification. Only two libraries of Central Government autonomous institutions (15.4 per cent) control the budget using library management software.

It is seen that all the libraries of Central Government institutions, Central Government autonomous institutions, State Government institutions and majority of State Government autonomous institutions (71.4 per cent) have computerised their cataloguing work. It revealed that about 46.1 per cent of the libraries of Central Government autonomous institutions, 50 per cent of State Government institutions, and few (28.6 per cent) of State Government autonomous institutions do acquisition work using computer. Majority of the libraries of Central Government institutions

(62.5 per cent), Central Government autonomous institutions (61.5 per cent), State Government institutions (50 per cent) and State Government autonomous institutions (57.1 per cent) have computerised the circulation system.

It is found that the library catalogue proved to be the most popular area for automation; this was followed by the circulation system. All the libraries of Central Government institutions, Central Government autonomous institutions, State Government institutions and majority of State Government autonomous institutions have computerised their cataloguing work. Majority of the libraries have computerised circulation systems. Few libraries of Central Government institutions and majority of the libraries of Central Government autonomous institutions, State Government institutions and State Government autonomous institutions have OPAC facility. Only two libraries of the Central Government autonomous institutions are doing budget control using library management software. It is also found that Central Government autonomous institutions are better in library automation compared to the libraries of other categories of institutions.

ACQUISITION

This area of activity is normally treated as indoor activity of a library but it is very important for library managers to know financial status at any time. Automating acquisition reduces repetitive and clerical tasks and library staff can devote more time to information activities. According to the responses received through interview and observation, it is found that majority (60 per cent) of libraries' acquisition process is purely manual. Even though majority of them have library management software and computers, they are doing acquisition work manually. It is revealed that this is due to the lack of well-accepted library management software, or the library professionals are not aware of the complete process of acquisition work using the computer and library management software. The acquisition process of about 40 per cent of the libraries is semi-automated. They are using library management software, computer, Internet, etc for the acquisition work, but they are not fully automated, they are doing some aspects manually, for example budget control, preparation of letters, etc.

CATALOGUING

The analysis of the responses received through interview with chief librarians indicates that majority of libraries are in the different stages of automation of their cataloguing work. About 33 per cent of the libraries studied have automated their cataloguing work and few them are providing OPAC facility. Most of them are attached to the Central Government autonomous institutions. About 27 per cent of the libraries have automated their cataloging work in part and the retrospective conversion process is in progress. About 40 per cent of libraries cataloguing works are still manual. However, the investigator observed that about half of the Special Libraries under study are semi-automated their cataloguing work and a few libraries have fully automated cataloguing system with OPAC facility. Majority of them are attached to the Central Government autonomous institutions.

CLASSIFICATION

The analysis of the data received through interview and observation shows that the classification work is purely manual in all Special Libraries under study. These may due to the intellectual aspect of the classification work and due to the lack of well-accepted software for automated classification work. Automated classification is possible in a limited manner.

CIRCULATION

It is found that a few (16.7 per cent) Special Libraries under study are fully automated in their circulation work. They are attached to the Central Government autonomous institutions and all are using barcode technology in circulation process. It is also found that about 43.3 per cent libraries are doing their circulation work manually. There are several reasons for this situation like, lack of sufficient infrastructure, lack of well-accepted library automation software, lack of qualified library professionals, etc. About 40 per cent of the libraries have not completed automation of their circulation work, even though they are using computer and library management software, they are not fully automated. Majority of them need well-accepted library management software, barcode technology, etc. The above findings are confirmed by the data collected through personnel observation. It is observed that majority (56.7 per cent) of the libraries are doing their circulation work manually.

SERIAL CONTROL

Serials or periodicals are backbone of any special library. Therefore, automated serials management gives quickest information access to users even in the absence of library professionals. It is found through the interview with chief librarians and through observational visits to the libraries that majority (56.7 per cent) of Special Libraries under study are purely manual in their serial control and about 36.7 per cent libraries are in the process of automating their serials control. Even though most of these libraries are semi-automated, they are not successful in their computerised serial control. There are several reasons for this like lack of well accepted library management software, lack of computer infrastructure, lack of qualified library professionals, or library professionals are not trained in computerised serial control. Only 2 (6.6 per cent) libraries of Central Government autonomous institutions are automated their serial control, but they also doing some aspect of serial control manually.

OPAC

The analysis of the data received through interview and observational visits shows that about half of the Special

Libraries under study have no OPAC. A few (33.3 per cent) libraries have good OPACs, some are excellent in their performance. Most of them are attached to the Central Government autonomous institutions.

SYSTEM ADMINISTRATION

The interview and observational visits provide information about the system administration in Special Libraries under study. It is found that majority (56.7 per cent) of the libraries are getting help and support from the computer professionals of the parent institute. Majority of them are attached to the Central Government autonomous institutions. It is also found that the system administrations of good number (43.3 per cent) of libraries are by their library professionals alone. The analysis reveals that skill and expertise of library professionals are inadequate to manage and administer ICT based resources and services. Library professionals should acquire needed skills and expertise in system administration and database management operations and networking.

USE OF BARCODE TECHNOLOGY

Barcodes is used in many forms of automated library circulation systems, as well as in stock verification. Table 2.4.28 shows the use of barcode technology in Special Libraries under study. The analysis revealed that 30.8 per cent of the libraries of Central Government autonomous institutions using barcode technology for both annual stock verification and circulation of documents. All other libraries except one (12.5 per cent) Central Government institutions are not using this technology. It is seen that a very few libraries are using barcode technology in the library. It may be due to the lack of finance and manpower. Special libraries usually have less hardcopy collection; this may also be a reason for not implementing the barcode technology. But barcode or smart card technology is very essential to fully computerize the circulation process.

Table 2.4.28 Use of Barcode Technology in Special Libraries under study

Organisation type	*Circulation*	*Circulation and Annual stock verification*	*Not Using*
Central Government	1(12.5 %)	-	7(87.5 %)
Central Government autonomous	1(7.7 %)	4(30.8 %)	8(61.5 %)
State Government	-	-	2(100 %)
State Government autonomous	-	-	7(100 %)
Total	2(6.7 %)	4(13.3 %)	24(80 %)

It is found that only a few Special Libraries under study are using barcode technology for circulation and stock verification of documents. Four libraries of Central Government autonomous institutions are using it for both circulation and stock verification.

USE OF SMART CARDS

No library is introduced smart card technology but one Central Government autonomous institution is going to introduce this technology in the library.

Use of Database for Information Retrieval and the Nature of Information Retrieved Electronic databases form sound foundation for providing efficient information services in special libraries. In recent years the demands for database services are increasing, because most of the latest information is available in online databases. Further some of the information are available only on CD-ROM format. Image databases and multimedia databases are also becomes predominant. Similarly personnel reference databases and internal records enrich the knowledge of the users. Librarians were asked to indicate the types of databases and the nature of information retrieved, that is, bibliographic information or full text with choices ranging from commercial online databases to those containing internally generated records. Librarians were also asked to list the "search software" in use. Tables 2.4.29 to 2.4.31 provide information pertaining to the availability of databases in Special Libraries under study.

COMMERCIAL ONLINE DATABASES

Table 2.4.29 shows the use of Commercial Online Databases in Special Libraries under study.

Table 2.4.29 Use of Commercial Online Databases and the Nature of Information Retrieved in Special Libraries under study

Organisation type	*Bibliographical information*	*Full text*	*Both*	*Not Using*
Central Government	-	-	1(12.5 %)	7(87.5 %)
Central Government autonomous	3(23 %)	-	1(7.7 %)	9(69.2 %)
State Government	-	1(50 %)	-	1(50 %)
State Government autonomous	-	-	-	7(100 %)
Total	3(10 %)	1(3.3 %)	2(6.7 %)	24(80 %)

The analysis revealed that few (20 per cent) libraries are using commercial online databases, both bibliographic and full text. Majority of them belong to central Government autonomous institutions. One (12.5 per cent) library of Central Government institutions and another (7.7 per cent) of Central Government autonomous institutions are using both bibliographical and full text databases.

It is found that only a few libraries are using Commercial Online Databases and four of them belong to Central Government autonomous institutions.

CD-ROM DATABASES

Table 2.4.30 shows the use of CD-ROM databases in Special Libraries under study. The analysis revealed that nearly 57 per cent libraries are using CD-ROM databases.

Libraries of 25 per cent of Central Government institutions, 53.8 per cent of Central Government autonomous institutions and 14.3 per cent of State Government autonomous institutions are using it for retrieving bibliographical information. A few libraries of State Government autonomous institutions (28.6 per cent), Central Government institutions (12.5 per cent) and Central Government autonomous institutions (23 per cent) are using it for retrieving both full text and bibliographical information

Table 2.4.30 Use of CD-ROM Databases and the Nature of Information Retrieved in Special Libraries under study

Organisation type	Bibliographical information	Full text	Both	Not Using
Central Government	2(25 %)	-	1(12.5 %)	5(62.5 %)
Central Government autonomous	7(53.8 %)	-	3(23 %)	3(23 %)
State Government	-	1(50 %)	-	1(50 %)
State Government autonomous	1(14.3 %)	-	2(28.6 %)	4(57.1 %)
Total	10(33.3 %)	1(3.3 %)	6(20 %)	13(43.3 %)

It is found that majority of special libraries are using CD-ROM databases, but a very few of them are accessing full text databases. Majority of them are attached to the Central Government autonomous institutions.

DATABASES OF INTERNAL RECORDS

Here databases of internal records mean databases containing library specific information like bibliographic details. Table 2.4.31 shows the use of databases of internal records in Special Libraries under study. The analysis revealed that very few libraries are using databases of internal records. One library (50 per cent) of State Government institutions and two (28.6 per cent) libraries of State Government autonomous institutions are using databases for storing bibliographical information. One (7.7 per cent) library of Central Government autonomous institutions and another (14.3 per cent) library of State Government autonomous institutions are using databases for storing full text information.

Table 2.4.31 Use of Databases of Internal Records and the Nature of Information Retrieved in Special Libraries under study

Organisation type	*Bibliographical information*	*Full text*	*Both*	*Not Using*
Central Government	-	-	1(12.5 %)	7(87.5 %)
Central Government autonomous	-	1(7.7 %)	-	12(92.3 %)
State Government	1(50 %)	-	-	1(50 %)
State Government autonomous	2(28.6 %)	1(14.3 %)	-	4(57.1 %)
Total	3(10 %)	2(6.7 %)	1(3.3 %)	24(80 %)

It is observed that a very few libraries are using databases for storing internal records and two of them are using it for storing full text information.

EXTENT OF END-USER ACCESS TO DATABASES

This section of the survey sought to identify the prevalence of access to electronic databases by end users. Librarians were asked to indicate which database types could be accessed from within the library, and also whether access was available either via terminals situated elsewhere within the organisation premises or from offsite using telecommunication links (remote access). The following are the details.

COMMERCIAL ONLINE DATABASES

Table 2.4.32 shows the extent of end user access to Commercial Online Databases in different Special Libraries under study. The analysis shows that very few libraries are using Commercial Online Databases and it is accessible both via terminals situated in the library and outside the library. Three (10 per cent) of them are accessing commercial databases through terminals situated in the library and one (3.3 per cent) library is providing access to databases through remote terminals. Three (10 per cent) libraries are providing access to databases through terminals situated in the library and through remote terminals outside the library.

Table 2.4.32 Extent of End-User Access to Commercial Online Databases in Special Libraries under study

Organisation type	***Via terminals situated in the library***	***Via terminals situated outside the library***	***Both***	***Not Using***
Central Government	-	1(12.5 %)	-	7(87.5 %)
Central Government autonomous	2(15.4 %)	-	1(7.7 %)	10(76.9 %)
State Government	-	-	1(50 %)	1(50 %)
State Government autonomous	1(14.3 %)	-	1(14.3 %)	5(71.4 %)
Total	3(10 %)	1(3.3 %)	3(10 %)	23(76.7 %)

It is found that very few libraries are using commercial online databases and it is accessible through terminals situated both in the library and outside the library.

CD-ROM DATABASES

Table 2.4.33 shows the extent of end user access to CD-ROM databases in libraries of different organisations. The analysis shows that about half of the institute libraries are accessing CD-ROM databases. About 20 per cent of them are accessing the databases through terminals situated in the library and 30 per cent of them are accessing the databases through remote terminals situated outside the library. 38.5 per cent of the libraries of Central Government autonomous institutions and 50 per cent of State Government institutions are accessing CD-ROM databases through terminals situated outside the library. 23 per cent of the Central Government autonomous institutions and 28.6 per cent of the State Government autonomous institutions are accessing databases through terminals situated in the library.

Table 2.4.33 Extent of End-User Access to CD-ROM Databases in Special Libraries under study

Organisation type	***Via terminals situated in the library***	***Via terminals situated outside the library***	***Not Using***
Central Government	1(12.5 %)	2(25 %)	5(62.5 %)
Central Government autonomous	3(23 %)	5(38. 5 %)	5(38.5 %)
State Government	-	1(50 %)	1(50 %)
State Government autonomous	2(28.6 %)	1(14.3 %)	4(57.1 %)
Total	6(20 %)	9(30 %)	15(50 %)

It is revealed that about half of the Special Libraries under study are accessing CD-ROM databases and it is accessed through terminals situated inside the library and through remote terminals situated outside the library. It is also found that majority of them are belong to the Central Government autonomous institutions.

DIGITAL LIBRARY

The developments in the mass storage, computers and communications technologies have resulted in many projects and initiatives for the creation and establishment of digital libraries. Table 2.4.34 shows the distribution of libraries according to the presence of digital library or digital library initiatives. It is revealed that only two (6.7 per cent) libraries have a separate digital library and a few (36.7 per cent) libraries have digital library initiatives and they are started creation and digitization of some of their collections. Majority (56.7

per cent) of the libraries have no digital library or no digital library initiatives. Even though a few libraries have Greenstone Digital Library Software, nobody is using it properly. Library staff should have adequate knowledge to build a good digital collection and manage it properly.

Table 2.4.34 Digital Library initiatives in Special Libraries under study

Organisation type	*Digital library*			
	Present	*Initiative*	*Not Present*	*Total*
Central Government	-	3(37.5 %)	5(62.5 %)	8(100 %)
Central Government autonomous	1(7.7 %)	5(38. 5 %)	7(53.8 %)	13(100 %)
State Government	1(50 %)	-	1(50 %)	2(100 %)
State Government autonomous	-	3(42.9 %)	4(57.1 %)	7(100 %)
Total	2(6.7 %)	11(36.7 %)	17(56.7 %)	30(100 %)

It is found that only two libraries have a separate digital library and a few libraries have digital library initiatives and they are started creation and digitization of some of their collections.

It is observed that majority of Special Libraries under study have no digital library or digital library initiatives. A few libraries have started to develop a digital library or started digitization of some of their collection or digital library initiatives. It is found that 2 libraries have separate digital libraries, but these are not organised in a proper manner and they are in the beginning stage. It is also observed that the main components of these digital libraries include electronic databases, full text e-journals through Science Direct, Emerald, etc., publications of the institute research community, e-books, CD-ROM databases, discussion groups, online news, in house databases, publication databases, etc. A few libraries have Greenstone Digital Library Software and IIITMK library has Acado software, VSSC library has very good hardware for digital library development, but not systematic in the digitation process. They lack proper guidance, and qualified library professionals in the digitisation and digital library development process. This can be avoided by providing training facilities in digital libraries to the library professionals and appointing trained and qualified library professionals for digital library development and digitisation of collections.

TELECOMMUNICATION AND NETWORKING

The transmission of data especially digital data from one point to a remote point is very essential. Libraries of all over the world are using telecommunication and networking technology for transmitting digitised data of all kinds. Data on the telecommunication facilities available in Special Libraries under study are ascertained.

USE OF TELEPHONE AND FAX

Table 2.4.35 shows the availability of telephone and fax facilities in the Special Libraries under study.

Table 2.4.35 Use of Telephone and Fax in Special Libraries under study

Organisation type	*Telephone*	*Telephone and Fax*	*None*
Central Government	8(100 %)	-	-
Central Government autonomous	12(92.3 %)	1(7.7 %)	-
State Government	-	1(50 %)	1(50 %)
State Government autonomous	4(57.1 %)	2(28.6 %)	1(14.3 %)
Total	24(80 %)	4(13.3 %)	2(6.7 %)

It is found that large majority (80 per cent) of the libraries have telephone facility, but a very few (13.3 per cent) of them have both telephone and fax facility. The analysis shows that all the libraries of Central Government institutions, most (92.3 per cent) of the Central Government autonomous institutions and majority (57.1 per cent) of State Government autonomous institutions have telephone facility. One (7.7 per cent) library of Central Government autonomous institutions and State Government institutions (50 per cent) and two (28.6 per cent) libraries of State Government autonomous institutions have both telephone and fax facility. Telephone or fax facilities are not available in two libraries.

It is found that large majority of Special Libraries under study have telephone facility and very few of them have both telephone and fax facility.

STATE OF LIBRARY NETWORK

Table 2.4.36 shows that whether the library network is independent or part of the institute network. It is found that most (90 per cent) of the libraries are part of the institute network or Intranet and about 47 per cent of libraries have independent network.

Table 2.4.36 State of Library Network in Special Libraries under study

Organisation type	*Independent Network*	*Part of institute Network*
Central Government	2(25 %)	7(87.5 %)
Central Government autonomous	9(69.2 %)	11(84.6 %)
State Government	-	2(100 %)
State Government autonomous	3(42.9 %)	7(100 %)
Total	14(46.7 %)	27(90 %)

The analysis shows that libraries of 87.5 per cent of Central Government institutions, 84.6 per cent of Central Government autonomous institutions and all the State Government and State Government autonomous institutions are part of the institute network or Intranet. About 69.2 per cent of the Central Government autonomous institutions, 42.9 per cent of State Government autonomous institutions and two (25 per cent) libraries of Central Government institutions have independent library network and few of them are connected to the institute network or Intranet also.

It is found that a large majority of Special Libraries under study are part of the institute network or Intranet and majority of Central Government automatons institutions have independent library network.

However, it is observed that about half of the Special Libraries under study have separate library network. Majority of them are attached to the Central Government autonomous institutions category. It is revealed that about 50 per cent libraries have no separate network and machines or computer terminals are connected to the Institute's LAN or intranet. It is preferred to have separate library network and connection to the institute LAN or intranet. In majority of the cases only one terminal in the library is connected to the institute LAN or intranet for accessing the network for services like Internet. It is also found that a few (10 per cent) libraries have no separate network and not connected to the institute LAN and they are working with standalone machines. They have one or two terminals. This is not suitable for providing advanced ICT based services like Internet and access to online databases and electronic journals.

USE OF CD-NET/CD-ROM SERVER/CD TOWER

CD-Net/CD-ROM Server/CD Tower has several advantages, especially in a special library environment. This facility will be helpful to provide access to CD-ROM databases and other CD based information resources. Library users can access this facility through the intranet and they can access the same resources simultaneously. Table 2.4.37 shows the use of CD-Net/ CD-ROM Server/CD Tower in Special Libraries under study. The analysis revealed that 76.9 per cent of Central Government autonomous institutions and 50 per cent of State Government institutions have CD-Net/CD-ROM Server/CD Tower.

Table 2.4.37 Use of CD-Net/CD-ROM Server/CD Tower in Special Libraries under study

Organisation type	***Libraries having CD-Net/ CD-ROM Server/CD Tower***
Central Government	1(12.5 %)
Central Government autonomous	10(76.9 %)
State Government	1(50 %)
State Government autonomous	2(28.6 %)
Total	14(46.7 %)

It is found that good a number of the Special Libraries under study have CD-Net/ CD-ROM Server / CD Tower and majority of them are attached to the Central Government autonomous institutions.

LIBRARY CONSORTIA

The main reason for forming a library consortium is to improve information resources and services to the library users and to gain financial benefits. The standardized policy in collection development and bargaining power of a consortium can help to reduce costs of documents. Presently only three Special Libraries under study are participating in consortium. IIITMK library is participating in INDEST consortia. This library is accessing e-journals through this consortium. NIO library is also participating in consortia. Main activity of this consortium is also E-journal subscription. RRL library is also participating in consortia, CSIR Consortium on e-journals. By participating in this consortium this library has launched the e-journal access facility by subscribing to the Science Direct. Search and retrieval including full text of 1080 journal titles covering five year back up was possible. No Special Libraries under study have sufficient digital information resources, but only three libraries are participating in consortia.

It is found that only three Special Libraries under study

are participating in library consortia and this is for accessing electronic journals.

INTERNET

The Internet has become an indispensable resource for special libraries worldwide to enhance the collection and improve services and operations. Librarians were asked to indicate the extent of use of Internet in the library. The analyses of the data are summarised in the tables 2.4.38 to 2.4.45. All the institutions under study have the Internet connectivity in the library or information center. Majority (63.3 per cent) of the Special Libraries under study have leased line connection, and a few (36.7 per cent) libraries are accessing Internet through dialup connection.

INTERNET SERVICE PROVIDERS

Librarians are asked to provide their Internet Service Provider (ISP), the details of which are given in Table 2.4.38. The analysis shows that majority (73.3 per cent) of the libraries are accessing Internet through VSNL. It is found that 62.5 per cent of Central Government institutions, 84.6 per cent of Central Government autonomous institutions, and 85.7 per cent of State Government autonomous institutions are using VSNL. Asianet is the Internet Service Provider of all the libraries of State Government institutions. Other ISPs are NICNET (13.3 per cent), Sathyam (3.3 per cent) and BSNL (10 per cent).

Table 2.4.38 Internet Service Providers (ISP) in Special Libraries under study

Organisation type	*VSNL*	*NICNET*	*ASIANET*	*Sathyam*	*BSNL*
Central Government	5(62.5 %)	-	1(12.5 %)	1(12.5 %)	1(12.5 %)
Central Government autonomous	11(84.6 %)	4(30.8 %)	-	-	1(7.7 %)
State Government	-	-	2(100 %)	-	-
State Government autonomous	6(85.7 %)	-	-	-	1(14.3 %)
Total	22(73.3 %)	4(13.3 %)	3(10 %)	1(3.3 %)	3(10 %)

The analysis of the data reveals that there are five Internet Service Providers in Special Libraries under study, namely VSNL, NICNET, ASIANET, Sathyam and BSNL and majority of them are accessing Internet through the VSNL.

TYPE OF INTERNET CONNECTION

Internet can be accessed through different kinds of connections, but majority of libraries in Kerala prefer leased line connections. Table 2.4.39 indicates the type of Internet connection in Special Libraries under study. The analysis revealed that majority (56.7 per cent) of the libraries have leased line connections and a few (20 per cent) libraries have ordinary dialup connections. It is found that majority (75 per cent) of the libraries of Central Government institutions, good number of libraries of Central Government autonomous institutions (46.1 per cent), State Government autonomous institutions (42.9 per cent) and all the State Government institutions have the leased line connection. It is also seen that 23 per cent of Central Government autonomous institutions have VSAT connection. The other types of Internet connections are leased line and ordinary dialup (3.3 per cent), leased line and VSAT (3.3 per cent), and ISDN dialup (6.7 per cent).

It is found that the majority of the libraries have leased line connections and a few libraries have ordinary dialup and VSAT connections.

INTERNET ACCESS THROUGH LIBRARY NETWORKS

Internet access through library networks or through institute LAN or Intranet is very important. It will provide full time Internet connection into the library and library professionals can access Internet from any workstations in the library. The data in Table 2.4.40 shows the availability of Internet access through library networks or institute LAN/ Intranet.

Table 2.4.39 Type of Internet Connection in Special Libraries in Kerala

Organisation type	*Leased line*	*Leased line and Ordinary dialup*	*Leased line and VSAT*	*Ordinary dialup*	*ISDN dial up*	*VSAT*	*Grand Total*
Central Government	6(75 %)	1(12.5 %)	-	1(12.5 %)	-	-	8(100 %)
Central Government autonomous	6(46.1 %)	-	1(7.7 %)	2(15.4 %)	1(7.7 %)	3(23 %)	13(100 %)
State Government	2(100 %)	-	-	-	-	-	2(100 %)
State Government autonomous	3(42.9 %)	-	-	3(42.9 %)	1(14.3 %)	-	7(100 %)
Total	17(56.7 %)	1(3.3 %)	1(3.3 %)	6(20 %)	2(6.7 %)	3(10 %)	30(100 %)

Table 2.4.40 Internet Access through Library Networks in Special Libraries under study

Organisation type	*Internet access through network*
Central Government	7 (87.5 %)
Central Government autonomous	11 (84.6 %)
State Government	2 (100 %)
State Government autonomous	7 (100 %)
Total	27 (90 %)

The analysis shows that all the libraries of State Government institutions and State Government autonomous institutions and large majority of the Central Government institutions (87.5 per cent) and Central Government autonomous institutions (84.6 per cent) have access to Internet through the institute's or library network.

It is found that large majority of the libraries have access to Internet through institute's or library network.

COMPUTER WORKSTATIONS FOR INTERNET ACCESS

Sufficient computer nodes or workstations are very essential for providing quality Internet based services and resources. Distribution of libraries according to the number of workstations provided for Internet facilities are given in Table 2.4.41.

It is seen that a good number (43.3 per cent) of the libraries have only one computer node with Internet connection. Libraries of 62.5 per cent of the Central Government institutions, 23 per cent of Central Government autonomous institutions, 50 per cent of State Government institutions and 57.1 per cent of State Government autonomous institutions have only one node with Internet access. It is found that VSSC (7.7 per cent) library has 30 computer nodes with Internet access and SCTIMST-HW library have 13 nodes with Internet access.

Table 2.4.41 Number of Internet Access Nodes in Special Libraries under study

Number of nodes	*Central Government*	*Central Government Autonomous*	*State Government*	*State Government Autonomous*	*Grand Total*
0	1(12.5 %)	2(15.4 %)	-	-	3(10 %)
1	5(62.5 %)	3(23 %)	1(50 %)	4(57.1 %)	13(43.3 %)
2	1(12.5 %)	1(7.7 %)	-	1(14.3 %)	3(10 %)
3	1(12.5 %)	1(7.7 %)	1(50 %)	2(28.6 %)	5(16.7 %)
4	-	1(7.7 %)	-	-	1(3.3 %)
5	-	2(15.4 %)	-	-	2(6.7 %)
6	-	1(7.7 %)	-	-	1(3.3 %)
13	-	1(7.7 %)	-	-	1(3.3 %)
30	-	1(7.7 %)	-	-	1(3.3 %)
Grand Total	8(100 %)	13(100 %)	2(100 %)	7(100 %)	30(100 %)

It is found that a good number of the libraries have only one computer node with Internet access and the Central Government autonomous institutions have more terminals with Internet access.

INTERNET BROWSERS

Table 2.4.42 highlights the details of the Internet browsers being used in the Special Libraries under study.

Table 2.4.42 Internet Browsers Available in Special Libraries under study

Organisation type	*Netscape*	*Internet Explorer*	*Netscape and Internet Explorer*	*Netscape, Internet Explorer and Opera*	*Grand Total*
Central Government	2(25 %)	5(62.5 %)	1(12.5 %)	-	8(100 %)
Central Government autonomous	1(7.7 %)	7(53.8 %)	4(30.8 %)	1(7.7 %)	13(100 %)
State Government	-	1(50 %)	-	1(50 %)	2(100 %)
State Government autonomous	1(14.3 %)	4(57.1 %)	2(28.6 %)	-	7(100 %)
Total	4(13.3 %)	17(56.7 %)	7(23.3 %)	2(6.7 %)	30(100 %)

It is found that 56.7 per cent libraries are using Internet Explorer as their browser software whilst 13.3 per cent used Netscape Navigator. It is also found that libraries of 62.5 per cent Central Government institutions, 53.8 per cent Central Government autonomous institutions, 50 per cent State Government institutions, and 57.1 per cent State Government autonomous institutions are using Internet Explorer as their Internet navigator. It is found that a few (23.3 per cent) libraries are using both Internet Explorer and Netscape Navigator. Two (6.7 per cent) libraries are using Opera in addition to Internet Explorer and Netscape Navigator.

It is revealed that majority of libraries are using Internet Explorer as their Internet browser software and a few libraries are using Netscape Navigator for browsing Internet.

PRESENCE OF LIBRARY WEBSITE OR LINK IN THE INSTITUTE'S HOMEPAGE

Library website or a link for library in the institute home page is very essential to provide various types of information through Internet. Library users can access various types of digital information like WebOPAC through this website.

Table 2.4.43 shows the distribution of libraries according to the presence of library website or a link in the institute's home page.

Table 2.4.43 Presence of Library Website or Link in the Institute's Homepage

Organisation type	*Libraries having separate web sites or link in the institute's home page*
Central Government	5(62.5 %)
Central Government autonomous	13(100 %)
State Government	2(100 %)
State Government autonomous	6(85.7 %)
Total	26(86.7 %)

Table 2.4.43 shows that majority (86.7 per cent) of libraries have a website or at least a link in the home page of the parent institute. It is found that all the libraries of Central Government autonomous institutions and State Government institutions and majority of Central Government (62.5 per cent) and State Government autonomous (86.7 per cent) institutions have website or link in the homepage of the parent institute. But it is observed that all these websites or links are not informative and these are created without any plan or intention to provide any type of information. Majority of them provides general information about the library.

It is found that majority of libraries have a website or at least a link in the home page of the parent institute.

COMPONENTS OF THE WEBSITE OR LINK

A library website can provide lot of services to its users like an interface for selected online journals and databases, online catalogue, digital library, online reference service, e-mail, chat, newsgroups, etc. Table 2.4.44 shows the components of the website or link in libraries of different type of organisations.

Table 2.4.44 The Components of the Website or Link in the Institutes Homepage

Components of the Website/Link	*Central Government*	*Central Government Autonomous*	*State Government*	*State Government Autonomous*	*Grand Total*
Library profile	2(25 %)	8(61.5 %)	2(100 %)	2(28.6 %)	14(46.7 %)
Web OPAC	-	4(30.8 %)	-	1(14.3 %)	5(16.7 %)
Online databases	-	1(7.7 %)	1(50 %)	1(14.3 %)	3(10 %)
Audio/ Video	-	-	1(50 %)	-	1(3.3 %)

A good number (46.7 per cent) of libraries are providing their profile using website or link and a few (16.7 per cent) libraries are providing OPAC. It is revealed that only 3 (10 per cent) libraries are providing online databases and one (3.3 per cent) library is providing audio/video clippings. It is observed that Central Government autonomous institutions have more informative websites or links in the homepage of parent institute.

It is found that about half of the libraries are providing their profile through websites or links. Very few libraries are providing online catalogue and databases.

INTERNET BASED LIBRARY OPERATIONS AND SERVICES

Internet has made simple and speedy purchase of information sources/documents like books, journals, electronic publications, etc. The Internet can be successfully utilised for providing reference service because various primary and secondary sources of information are available online from many sites. Libraries can use Internet to communicate with publishers, booksellers and vendors. Librarian can also use Newsgroups for getting information. Through the Internet a librarian can access the resources of other libraries and through the Web OPAC it is possible to browse the entire collection of a library and can make a request for a document through e-mail. Table 2.4.45 describes the use of Internet for various library operations and services.

Table 2.4.45 Use of Internet for various Operations and Services in Special Libraries under study

Library Operations/ Services	*Central Government*	*Central Government Autonomous*	*State Government*	*State Government Autonomous*	*Grand Total*
Acquisition	2(25 %)	8(61.5 %)	-	2(28.6 %)	12(40 %)
Cataloguing	1(12.5 %)	-	-	-	1(3.3 %)
Classification	1(12.5 %)	-	-	-	1(3.3 %)
Bibliographic databases	2(25 %)	6(46.1 %)	1(50 %)	3(42.9 %)	12(40 %)
SDI	2(25 %)	7(53.8 %)	2(100 %)	4(57.1 %)	15(50 %)
CAS	1(12.5 %)	5(38. 5 %)	2(100 %)	4(57.1 %)	12(40 %)

The analysis of the data revealed that about 40 per cent of libraries are using Internet for acquisition work, for accessing bibliographic databases and for current awareness services. Majority (61.5 per cent) of libraries of Central Government autonomous institutions are using Internet for acquisition work. All the libraries of State Government institutions and majority (53.8 per cent) of the Central Government autonomous institutions and State Government autonomous institutions (57.1 per cent) are using Internet for SDI services. All the libraries of State Government institutions and majority (57.1 per cent) of the State Government autonomous institutions are using Internet for current awareness service.

All the libraries of State Government institutions and majority (53.8 per cent) of the Central Government autonomous institutions and State Government autonomous institutions (57.1 per cent) are using Internet for SDI services.

Majority (61.5 per cent) of the libraries of Central Government autonomous institutions are using Internet for acquisition work. All the libraries of State Government institutions and majority (57.1 per cent) of the State Government autonomous institutions are using Internet for current awareness service.

The use of Internet for library and information services is found to be very less. Majority of the Central Government autonomous institutions are using Internet for acquisition work and SDI services and all the State Government institutions and majority of State Government autonomous institutions are using Internet for CAS and SDI services. This may be due to the lack of awareness about the potential possibilities of Internet as an information resource or library professionals may not know how to use them effectively.

ICT BASED LIBRARY SERVICES

User is the kingpin of the library. So the main purpose of ICT application is to provide better services and facilities to users. Table 2.4.46 portraits the provision of various types of ICT based services provided in Special Libraries under study.

The analysis shows that all the libraries are providing Current Awareness Services using different methods and majority of them are providing access to bibliographical databases (86.7 per cent), OPAC (56.7 per cent), and SDI Services (86.7 per cent). It is clear that nearly 38.5 per cent of libraries of Central Government autonomous institutions are providing access to full text databases. All the Central Government and Central Government autonomous institutions and majority (57.1 per cent) of the State Government autonomous institutions are providing access to bibliographical databases. Majority of the libraries of Central Government autonomous institutions (69.2 per cent) and State Government autonomous institutions (57.1 per cent) are providing OPAC facility. The analysis also revealed that

Table 2.4.46 Services Provided Using Information and Communication Technologies in Special Libraries under study

Types of Services	*Central Govern-ment*	*Central Government Autonomous*	*State Govern-ment*	*State Government Autonomous*	*Grand Total*
Access to full text databases	2(25 %)	5(38. 5 %)	1(50 %)	2(28.6 %)	10(33.3 %)
Access to bibliogra-phical databases	8(100 %)	13(100 %)	1(50 %)	4(57.1 %)	26(86.7 %)
OPAC	3(37.5 %)	9(69.2 %)	1(50 %)	4(57.1 %)	17(56.7 %)
Web OPAC		4(30.8 %)	-	1(14.3 %)	5(16.7 %)
Multimedia Service	1(12.5 %)	2(15.4 %)	1(50 %)	2(28.6 %)	6(20 %)
Automated indexing service	1(12.5 %)	2(15.4 %)	1(50 %)	2(28.6 %)	6(20 %)
Automated reference service	2(25 %)	5(38. 5 %)	1(50 %)	3(42.9 %)	11(36.7 %)
CAS	8(100 %)	13(100 %)	2(100 %)	7(100 %)	30(100 %)
SDI	8(100 %)	11(84.6 %)	2(100 %)	5(71.4 %)	26(86.7 %)
Scanning of documents and forwarding	1(12.5 %)	7(53.8 %)	1(50 %)	1(14.3 %)	10(33.3 %)
E-journals	2(25 %)	9(69.2 %))	1(50 %)	3(42.9 %)	20(50 %)
e-books	1(12.5 %)	2(15.4 %)	1(50 %)	-	4(13.3 %)

the libraries of all the Central Government and State Government institutions and majority of the Central Government autonomous institutions (84.6 per cent) and State

Government autonomous institutions (71.4 per cent) are providing SDI services. The other services provided are WebOPAC (16.7 per cent), Multimedia Services, and automated Indexing Services (20 per cent), automated Reference Service (36.7 per cent) Scanning of Documents and Forwarding (33.3 per cent) and E-books (13.3 per cent).

It is found that all the Special Libraries under study are providing Current Awareness Services using different methods and majority of them are providing access to bibliographical databases, OPAC, SDI Service. The other services provided are access to e-journals WebOPAC, multimedia service, and automated indexing service, scanning of documents and forwarding, and e-books. It is also found that libraries of Central Government autonomous institutions are better in providing ICT based services.

The analysis of the data received through interview and observation reveals that the ICT based resources and services of majority (63.3 per cent) of Special Libraries under study are very poor and not adequate. They are providing a few services like bibliographic searching, Internet browsing, etc and this too not in a successful manner. Most of them lack proper infrastructure and qualified library professionals. A few (36.7 per cent) of them are providing different services like electronic database service, online databases services, online journals services, SDI, CAS, content service, internet services, etc. Central Government autonomous institutions libraries are better in this regard. Some of them have separate sections for services like Internet and digital library and some have CD-Net based services, some are participating consortia based subscription for accessing bibliographic and full-text online journals.

INTERNET SERVICES PROVIDED IN SPECIAL LIBRARIES UNDER STUDY

Table 2.4.47 elucidates the availability of various Internet based services/facilities in Special Libraries under study. The analysis revealed that all the libraries are providing E-mail and World Wide Web facilities and majority of the libraries of Central Government autonomous institutions are providing Ftp, Telnet, ListServe (53.8 per cent) and Usenet/ Newsgroups (61.5 per cent) services.

Table 2.4.47 Internet Services Provided in Special Libraries under study

Internet Services	*Central Govern-ment*	*Central Government Autonomous*	*State Govern-ment*	*State Government Autonomous*	*Grand Total*
E-mail	8(100 %)	13(100 %)	2(100 %)	7(100 %)	30(100 %)
Ftp	-	7(53.8 %)	-	-	7(23.3 %)
Telnet	-	7(53.8 %)	-	1(14.3 %)	8(26.7 %)
ListServe	-	7(53.8 %)	-	1(14.3 %)	8(26.7 %)
Usenet/ Newsgroups	1(12.5 %)	8(61.5 %)	-	1(14.3 %)	10(33.3 %)
WWW	8(100 %)	13(100 %)	2(100 %)	7(100 %)	30(100 %)

All the libraries are providing e-mail and www facility. Majority of the libraries of Central Government autonomous institutions are providing Ftp, Telnet, ListServe and Usenet/ Newsgroups services.

It is revealed that all the Special Libraries under study are providing E-mail and World Wide Web facilities and majority of the libraries of Central Government autonomous institutions are providing Ftp, Telnet, ListServe and Usenet/ Newsgroups services. It is also found that libraries of Central Government autonomous institutions are better in Internet based services or facilities than other categories of libraries.

TRAINING IN ICT BASED SERVICES AND OPERATIONS

Training is an integral component of staff development and well-organized institutions have staff development as a central hub in their personal policies. Training makes an important method of professional development in an organisation, which enables an organisation to prepare its people for various operations. Training is expected to bridge the performance gap. Training in ICT based services and operations are very important that enable the library professionals to provide value added services to their users. Preparation of future information professionals through formal and information means, poses a serious challenge to those responsible for their education and training.

TRAINING FOR LIBRARY PROFESSIONALS

Table 2.4.48 shows the facilities of training in ICT in Special Libraries under study. The analyses revealed that majority (60 per cent) of the libraries are providing training to their professionals in ICT based services and resources.

Table 2.4.48 Training for the Library Professionals

Organisation Type	*Trained*	*Not Trained*	*Grand Total*
Central Government	4(50 %)	4(50 %)	8(100 %)
Central Government autonomous	8(61.5 %)	5(38. 5 %)	13(100 %)
State Government	1(50 %)	1(50 %)	2(100 %)
State Government autonomous	5(71.4 %)	2(28.6 %)	7(100 %)
Grand Total	18(60 %)	12(40 %)	30(100 %)

The majority of the libraries of Central Government autonomous institutions (61.5 per cent) and State Government autonomous institutions (71.4 per cent) and about 50 per cent of the Central Government and State Government institutions are providing training to their professionals.

It is found that majority of Special Libraries under study are providing training to their professionals and large majority of these libraries are attached to the autonomous institutions.

TRAINING METHODS

Library professionals were asked about the training methods used for learning about ICT based services and operations. It was found that the library professionals are using a variety of learning methods. The Table 2.4.49 shows the training methods using in Special Libraries under study for training the library professionals.

Table 2.4.49 Methods of Training Used

Training Methods	*Central Government*	*Central Government Autonomous*	*State Government*	*State Government Autonomous*	*Grand Total*
Self-learning through reading manuals/ documentation	4(50 %)	9(69.2 %)	1(50 %)	5(71.4 %)	19(63.3 %)
Through trial and error	4(50 %)	5(38. 5 %)	1(50 %)	4(57.1 %)	14(46.7 %)
Through attending short term courses	1(12.5 %)	8(61.5 %)	1(50 %)	3(42.9 %)	13(43.3 %)
Staff attach-ment with institutions already using ICT	1(12.5 %)	2(15.4 %)	-	-	3(10 %)
Individua-lized training by coworker	1(12.5 %)	3(23 %)	1(50 %)	1(14.3 %)	6(20 %)
In-house workshops	2(25 %)	9(69.2 %)	1(50 %)	5(71.4 %)	17(56.7 %)
Individu-alized training by supervisor	1(12.5 %)	2(15.4 %)	-	2(28.6 %)	5(16.7 %)
Outside workshops	3(37.5 %)	7(53.8 %)	1(50 %)	4(57.1 %)	15(50 %)
Vendor workshops	1(12.5 %)	6(46.1 %)	1(50 %)	1(14.3 %)	9(30 %)

For all types of training methods, Self-learning through reading manuals/ documentation (63.3 per cent) and In-house workshops (56.7 per cent) are the most common training methods used. About half of the libraries responded outside workshops as the training method. A good number of libraries indicated that through trial and error (46.7 per cent) and through attending short training courses (43.3 per cent) as the training methods. The other training methods reported are vendor workshops (30 per cent), individualized training by coworker (20 per cent), individualized training by supervisor (16.7 per cent) and staff attachment with institutions already using ICT (10 per cent). It is also found that the libraries of majority of Central Government autonomous institutions (69.2 per cent) and State Government autonomous institutions (71.4 per cent) reported that self-learning through reading manuals/documentation and in-house workshops as the major training methods. About 61.5 per cent of Central Government autonomous institutions are reported through attending short training courses as a training method.

Although a variety of training methods are used, the most frequently used methods are self-learning and in house workshops. A good number of libraries are responded that outside workshops, through trial and error and through attending short training courses as the training methods. Majority of them are attached to the Central Government autonomous and State Government autonomous institutions.

CAREER ADVANCEMENT FACILITIES

The analysis of responses received through interviews with chief librarians found that a large majority (80 per cent) of Special Libraries under study are providing various facilities for career advancement and knowledge improvement to their library professionals like facilities for attending workshops, seminars, short-term courses and some of them are encouraging higher studies like Ph.D. But the major finding is that most of the library professionals are not using these facilities properly. A few (20 per cent) libraries are not providing any such facilities for their professionals.

USER EDUCATION / ORIENTATION IN ICT

Table 2.4.50 shows the user education/orientation facilities in ICT in Special Libraries under study.

Table 2.4.50 User Education/Orientation in ICT

Organisation Type	*User Education / Orientation*		*Total*
	Provided	*Not Provided*	
Central Government	4(50 %)	4(50 %)	8(100 %)
Central Government autonomous	11(84.6 %)	2(15.4 %)	13(100 %)
State Government	2(100 %)	-	2(100 %)
State Government autonomous	5(71.4 %)	2(28.6 %)	7(100 %)
Grand Total	22(73.3 %)	8(26.7 %)	30(100 %)

The analysis revealed that majority (73.3 per cent) of libraries are providing user education/orientation in ICT.

The libraries of all the State Government institutions, a large majority of Central Government autonomous institutions (84.6 per cent) and State Government autonomous institutions (71.4 per cent) and about half of the Central Government institutions are providing user education/orientation in ICT.

It is found that majority of the Special Libraries under study are providing user education/orientation in ICT.

MODULES IN USER EDUCATION / ORIENTATION PROGRAM

Table 2.4.51 shows the different modules used for user education in ICT in Special Libraries under study. The analysis shows that majority (56.7 per cent) of the libraries are giving user education in library management software and CD-ROM searching and 46.7 per cent of libraries providing user education in Internet services/tools/utilities. A few (23.3 per cent) of them are providing user education in computer network fundamentals.

Table 2.4.51 Modules Included in the User Education in ICT

Modules	*Central Govern-ment*	*Central Government Autonomous*	*State Govern-ment*	*State Government Autonomous*	*Grand Total*
Computer Network Fundaments	1(12.5 %)	4(30.8 %)	1(50 %)	1(14.3 %)	7(23.3 %)
Library Management Software	2(25 %)	10(76.9 %)	2(100 %)	3(42.9 %)	17(56.7 %)
Internet Services/ Tools/Utilities	2(25 %)	8(61.5 %)	2(100 %)	2(28.6 %)	14(46.7 %)
CD-ROM Searching	3(37.5 %)	9(69.2 %)	2(100 %)	3(42.9 %)	17(56.7 %)

It is also found that all the libraries of State Government institutions are providing user education in library management software, CD-ROM searching and Internet services/tools/utilities. Central Government autonomous institutions libraries are also providing user education in library management software (76.9 per cent), CD-ROM searching (69.2 per cent) and Internet services/tools/utilities (61.5 per cent).

It is found that majority of Special Libraries under study provide user education in library management software, CD-ROM searching and Internet services/tools/utilities. Majority of them are attached to the Central Government autonomous institutions.

The analysis of the responses from the interviews with chief librarians indicates that about 40 per cent of libraries are conducting training to their library professionals. But the major finding is that the training and user orientation programmes are not systematic and not in a useful manner.

OBJECTIVES OF INFORMATION AND COMMUNICATION TECHNOLOGY APPLICATION

In order to identify the objectives of ICT application in libraries, 11 most important objectives were offered with an additional 'others' option. Table 2.4.52 shows the major objectives of ICT application in Special Libraries under study.

Table 2.4.52 Objectives of ICT Application in Special Libraries under study

Objectives	***Central Government***	***Central Government Autonomous***	***State Government***	***State Government Autonomous***	***Grand Total***
To modernise the library activities	8 (100 %)	13 (100 %)	2 (100 %)	6 (85.7 %)	29 (96.7 %)
To render effective services to the user community	8 (100 %)	13 (100 %)	2 (100 %)	7 (100 %)	30 (100 %)
To keep the users up to date in their fields	8 (100 %)	13 (100 %)	2 (100 %)	7 (100 %)	30 (100 %)
To improve access to library collection	7 (87.5 %)	10 (77 %)	2 (100 %)	5 (71.4 %)	24 (80 %)
To improve the quality of existing services	8 (100 %)	12 (92.3 %)	2 (100 %)	7 (100 %)	29 (96.7 %)
To reduce routine and time consuming clerical works	5 (62.5 %)	11 (84.6 %)	2 (100 %)	5 (71.4 %)	23 (76.7 %)

Objectives	*Central Govern-ment*	*Central Government Autonomous*	*State Govern-ment*	*State Government Autonomous*	*Grand Total*
To improve cooperation and resource sharing among libraries	3 (37.5 %)	7 (53.8 %)	1 (50 %)	3 (42.9 %)	14 (46.7 %)
To easily participate and utilise national and international computer networks	1 (12.5 %)	4 (30.8 %)	1 (50 %)	3 (42.9 %)	9 (30 %)
To reduce the number of library staff required	1 (12.5 %)	5 (38. 5 %)	1 (50 %)	1 (14.3 %)	8 (26.7 %)
To improve prestige and visibility of library	6 (75 %)	7 (53.8 %)	2 (100 %)	5 (71.4 %)	20 (66.7 %)
To provide competitive and strategic information needed for research and development	2 (25 %)	6 (46.1 %)	2 (100 %)	4 (57.1 %)	14 (46.7 %)

The most important objectives of ICT application rated by respondents are to render effective services to the user community and to keep the users up to date in their fields. Another major objective stated by all the libraries of Central Government institutions, Central Government autonomous institutions, State Government institutions and majority (85.7 per cent) of State Government autonomous institutions is to modernise the library activities. The other major objectives stated by the libraries are to improve access to library collection (80 per cent), to improve the quality of existing services (96.7 per cent), to reduce routine and time consuming clerical works (76.7 per cent), to improve prestige and visibility of library (66.7 per cent), to improve cooperation and resource sharing among libraries (46.7 per cent), to provide competitive and strategic information needed for research and development (46.7 per cent), to easily participate and utilise national and international computer networks (30 per cent), and to reduce the number of library staff required (26.7 per cent).

It is found that the major objectives of ICT application in Special Libraries under study are to render effective services to the user community, to keep the users up to date in their fields, to modernise the library activities, to improve access to library collection, to improve the quality of existing services and to reduce routine and time consuming clerical works.

FACTORS INFLUENCING THE PROVISION OF ICT BASED LIBRARY RESOURCES AND SERVICES

It is very important to identify and analyse the specific factors that promoted or hindered the ICT application in libraries. Librarians were provided five specific factors plus an 'other' option. Percentage and Chi-square tests were carried out to analyse these factors. The analyses of the responses are presented below.

ALLOCATION OF BUDGET

Table 2.4.53 gives the opinion about 'Allocation of Budget' as a factor influencing the provision of ICT application in Special Libraries under study. The analysis revealed that about 40 per cent of the libraries stated that budget allocation is satisfactory and only one (3.3 per cent) library stated that budget allocation is excellent. A few (23.3 per cent) libraries stated that budget allocation is very good and 33.3 per cent stated that it is good.

Table 2.4.53 'Allocation of Budget' as a Factor Influencing the Provision of ICT Application

Organisation Type	*Excellent*	*Very Good*	*Good*	*Satisfactory*
Central Government	-	1(12.5 %)	4(50 %)	3(37.5 %)
Central Government autonomous	1(7.7 %)	5(38. 5 %)	3(23 %)	4(30.8 %)
State Government	-	1(50 %)	-	1(50 %)
State Government autonomous	-	-	3(42.9 %)	4(57.1 %)
Grand Total	1(3.3 %)	7(23.3 %)	10(33.3 %)	12(40 %)

λ^2 = 8.016ns

The Chi Square value computed for testing the association between the type of organisation and the opinion about the allocation of budget is 8.016. This value is less than the table value (16.9) at 9 degrees of freedom and at 5 per cent level of significance. Hence it can be concluded that there is no association in the allocation of budget among different type of organization.

It is seen that 50 per cent of Central Government institutions havd stated that budget allocation is good and about 38.5 per cent of Central Government autonomous institutions and 50 per cent of State Government institutions are stated that budget allocation is very good. Majority (57.1 per cent) of the libraries of State Government autonomous institutions stated that budget allocation is satisfactory. A good number of Special Libraries under study have not enough annual budget and this is a major barrier for the application of ICT in these libraries.

It is found that in good number of Special Libraries under study the budget allocation is either good or satisfactory. It is also found that the budget allocations to majority of the libraries are not adequate. It is observed that there is no association in the allocation of budget among different type of organisations.

ICT SKILL AND EXPERTISE OF LIBRARY STAFF

Table 2.4.54 shows the opinion about 'ICT skill and expertise of library staff' as a factor influencing the provision of ICT application in Special Libraries under study. It is found that majority (53.3 per cent) of the libraries are stated that the ICT skill and expertise of library staff are satisfactory and a substantial number (43.3 per cent) of libraries are stated that the skill and expertise of library staff are good.

Table 2.4.54 'ICT Skill and Expertise of Library Staff' as a Factor Influencing the Provision of ICT Application

Organisation Type	*Excellent*	*Good*	*Satisfactory*
Central Government	-	3(37.5 %)	5(62.5 %)
Central Government autonomous	-	6(46.1 %)	7(53.8 %)
State Government	1(50 %)	-	1(50 %)
State Government autonomous	-	4(57.1 %)	3(42.9 %)
Grand Total	1(14.3 %)	13(43.3 %)	16(53.3 %)

$\lambda^2 = 15.536$ **

The association about opinion about ICT skill and expertise of library staff among different type of organisation was tested using Chi-Square test. The computed value of Chi Square is 15.536, which is greater than the table value (12.6) at 6 degrees of freedom and at 5 per cent level of significance. Hence reject the hypothesis that there is no association and conclude that opinion about ICT skill and expertise of library staff depends on the type of organisation. 62.5 per cent of the libraries of Central Government institutions have the opinion that ICT skill and expertise of library staff are satisfactory. Only 37.5 per cent responded that ICT skill and expertise of library staff are good. In the Central Government autonomous institutions 53.8 per cent have the opinion satisfactory and 46.2 per cent have the opinion that it is good whereas in the State Government autonomous institutions 57.1 per cent have responded that ICT skill and expertise of library staff are good and 42.9 per cent have the opinion that it is satisfactory.

The majority (57.1 per cent) of libraries of State Government autonomous institutions stated that skill and expertise of staff are good. Majority of the libraries of Central Government institutions (62.5 per cent) and Central Government autonomous institutions (53.8 per cent) are stated ICT skill and expertise of library staff are only satisfactory. It is found that lack of skill and expertise is a barrier for ICT application in Special Libraries under study.

It is found that in majority of Special Libraries under study the ICT skill and expertise of library staff are just satisfactory and in majority of State Government autonomous institutions and about half of Central Government autonomous institutions the skill and expertise of staff are good. It is also found that ICT skill and expertise of library staff depends on the type of organisation.

ICT AWARENESS OF LIBRARY USERS

Table 2.4.55 shows the opinion about 'ICT awareness of library users' as a factor influencing the provision of ICT application in Special Libraries under study. It is found that majority (53.3 per cent) of libraries stated that ICT awareness of library users is good and 40 per cent of them stated that it is only satisfactory.

Table 2.4.55 'ICT Awareness of Library Users' as a Factor Influencing the Provision of ICT Application

Organisation Type	*Very Good*	*Good*	*Satisfactory*
Central Government	-	3(37.5 %)	5(62.5 %)
Central Government autonomous	-	10(76.9 %)	3(23 %)
State Government	1(50 %)	-	1(50 %)
State Government autonomous	1(14.3 %)	3(42.9 %)	3(42.9 %)
Grand Total	2(6.7 %)	16(53.3 %)	12(40 %)

$\lambda^2 = 12.594$ns

Opinion about the ICT awareness of library users among the different organisation types were tested using Chi Square test. The hypothesis tested was independent of the type of organisation. The computed values of Chi Square (12.594) was found to be non significant at 5 per cent level of significance and at 6 degrees of freedom. Hence it can be concluded that opinion is independent of type of organisation.

The majority (76.9 per cent) of libraries of Central Government autonomous institutions are stated that the ICT awareness of library users is good but majority (62.5 per cent) of the libraries of Central Government institutions stated that it is only satisfactory.

It is found that in majority of Special Libraries under study the ICT awareness of library users is good and most of them are attached to the Central Government autonomous institutions. It is also found that there is no association with the ICT awareness of library users and type of organisation, i.e., it is independent of type of organisation.

ICT TRAINING

Table 2.4.56 shows the opinion about 'ICT training' as a factor influencing the provision of ICT application in Special Libraries under study. The analysis revealed that large majority (90 per cent) of libraries stated that the training in ICT is only satisfactory. It is found that only two (15.4 per cent) libraries of Central Government autonomous institutions are stated that training in ICT is good and one (50 per cent) library of State Government institutions stated that training in ICT is very good.

Table 2.4.56 'ICT Training' as a Factor Influencing the Provision of ICT Application

Organisation Type	Very Good	Good	Satisfactory
Central Government	-	-	8(100 %)
Central Government autonomous	-	2(15.4 %)	11(84.6 %)
State Government	1(50 %)	-	1(50 %)
State Government autonomous	-	-	7(100 %)
Grand Total	1(3.3 %)	2(6.7 %)	27(90 %)

λ^2 = 17.179 **

Chi Square test was found significant indicating that opinion about the ICT training depends on the type of organisation. All the libraries in Central Government and State Government autonomous institutions have the opinion that ICT training is only satisfactory. Only two (15.4 per cent) libraries of Central Government autonomous institutions have the opinion that ICT training is good.

All the libraries of Central Government institutions and State Government autonomous institutions and a large majority (84.6 per cent) of Central Government autonomous institutions training in ICT is only satisfactory. Most of the libraries are not systematic in the training and this is hindered the application of ICT in Special Libraries under study.

It is found that in large majority of Special Libraries under study training in ICT is only satisfactory or it is inadequate. It is also found that ICT training depends on the type of organisation.

ICT INFRASTRUCTURE

Table 2.4.57 shows the opinion about 'ICT infrastructure' as a factor influencing the provision of ICT application in Special Libraries under study. The analysis revealed that majority (70 per cent) of the libraries stated ICT infrastructure is only satisfactory. It is also revealed that 38.5

per cent libraries of Central Government autonomous institutions and one (14.3 per cent) library of State Government autonomous institutions are stated that ICT infrastructure is good. It is found that 2 (15.4 per cent) libraries of the Central Government autonomous institutions and one (50 per cent) library of the State Government institutions are stated that ICT infrastructure is very good.

Table 2.4.57 'ICT Infrastructure' as a Factor Influencing the Provision of ICT Application

Organisation Type	*Very Good*	*Good*	*Satisfactory*
Central Government	-	-	8(100 %)
Central Government autonomous	2(15.4 %)	5(38. 5 %)	6(46.1 %)
State Government	1(50 %)		1(50 %)
State Government autonomous	-	1(14.3 %)	6(85.7 %)
Grand Total	3(10 %)	6(20 %)	21(70 %)

λ^2 = 11.852 ns

Opinion about the infrastructure was tested using Chi-Square and it is found that there is no association between the opinion and type of organisation. The computed value of Chi-Square is 11.852, which is less than the table value at 6 degrees of freedom. Hence accept the hypothesis and conclude that opinion about the infrastructure is independent on the type of organisation.

All the libraries of Central Government institutions and a large majority (85.7 per cent) of the State Government autonomous institutions indicated that the ICT infrastructure of the library is only satisfactory. A few (38.5 per cent) libraries of Central Government autonomous institutions and a very few (14.3 per cent) libraries of State Government autonomous institutions indicated that the ICT infrastructure is good. It is found that about 70 per cent of the libraries have poor in ICT infrastructure, but one reason for this may be due to the limited budget or lack of initiation from the library staff.

It is found that in majority of Special Libraries under study the ICT infrastructure is only satisfactory or it is inadequate. A few libraries of Central Government autonomous institutions have good ICT infrastructure. It is also found that the ICT infrastructure is independent on the type of organisation.

BARRIERS OF ICT APPLICATION IN SPECIAL LIBRARIES UNDER STUDY

It is very important to identify the barriers of ICT application in libraries. So, 15 main barriers were identified. An opinion of librarians of Special Libraries under study were obtained and analysed. The summarised opinions are given in Table 2.4.58.

Table 2.4.58 Barriers of ICT Application in Special Libraries under study

Sl. No	*Variable Description*	*Variable Code*	*Agree*	*Disagree*
1	Insufficient funds	BA1	19	11
2	Inadequate ICT infrastructure	BA2	24	6
3	Library professionals are not interested in ICT adoption in the library	BA3	10	20
4	Inadequately trained library professionals	BA4	27	3
5	Lack of initiative on the part of the library professionals	BA5	12	18
6	Lack of awareness among library professionals about the potential of ICT	BA6	13	17
7	Lack of ICT knowledge on the part of users	BA7	19	11
8	ICT operational cost is exceeding year by year	BA8	5	25
9	Inability to absorb recurring costs	BA9	4	26
10	Increasing costs of procuring hardware and software	BA10	6	24

Sl. No	*Variable Description*	*Variable Code*	*Agree*	*Disagree*
11	Political and administrative changes	BA11	3	27
12	Lack of well accepted & standard library management software package	BA12	17	13
13	Lack of official/policy guidelines	BA13	7	23
14	Non availability of less expensive library management software	BA14	7	23
15	Non availability of consultancy services	BA15	2	28

HIERARCHICAL CLUSTER ANALYSIS

Dendrogram using Average Linkage (Between Groups)

Rescaled Distance Cluster Combine

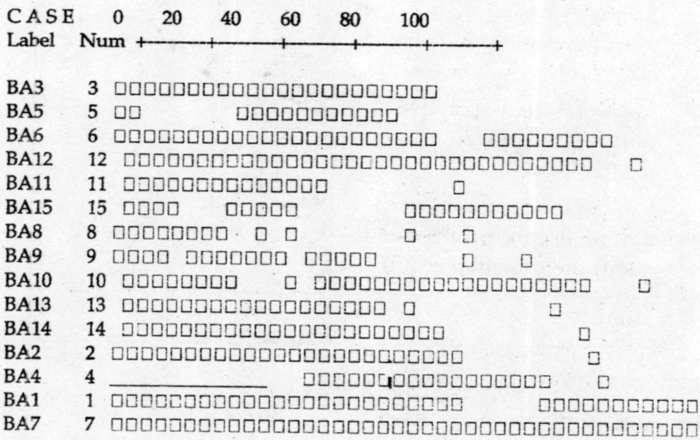

Figure 2.4.1 Dendrogram - Barriers of ICT Application in Special Libraries under study

In Figure 2.4.1 the dendrogram at the 60 per cent distance level 5 clusters are formed. The cluster formation table 2.4.59 has been given below.

Table 2.4.59 Clusters Formed

Clusters	*Member Variables in Clusters*
1	BA3, BA5, BA 6
2	BA 12,
3	BA11, BA15, BA8, BA9, BA10, BA13, BA14
4	BA2, BA4, BA1
5	BA7

Table 2.4.60 shows the cluster 1. It is named as "Lack of Awareness, Interest and Initiation of Library Professionals towards ICT Application in the Library"

Table 2.4.60 Cluster 1: Lack of Awareness, Interest and Initiation of Library Professionals towards ICT Application in the Library

Sl. No		*Variable Description*	*Variable Code*	*Agree Disagree*
3	Library professionals are not interested in ICT adoption in the library	BA3	10	20
5	Lack of initiative on the part of the library professionals	BA5	12	18
6	Lack of awareness among library professionals about the potential of ICT	BA6	13	17
	Total		35	45

Agreement Ratio = $\overline{A}$ = 35/30 = 1.2

Disagreement Ratio = 45 / 30 = 1.5

Cluster Centre : (1.2 : 1.5)

Agreement and Disagreement Ratio (4:5)

This cluster has been formed with three variables. The agreement and disagreement ratio of the cluster is 4:5. This indicates that majority of the librarians did not agree that lack of awareness, interest and initiation of library professionals towards ICT application in the library are the barriers of ICT application in the Special Libraries under study.

Table 2.4.61 gives the second cluster. It is named as "Lack of Well-accepted & Standard Library Management Software Package".

Table 2.4.61 Cluster 2: Lack of Well-accepted and Standard Library Management Software Package

Sl. No	*Variable Description*	*Variable code*	*Agree*	*Disagree*
12	Lack of well accepted & standard library management software package	BA12	17	13

Agreement and Disagreement Ratio (17:13)

This cluster has been formed with only one variable. The agreement and disagreement ratio of the cluster is 17:13. This indicates that a good number of librarians feel that lack of well accepted and standard library management software package is a barrier towards the ICT application in Special Libraries under study.

The third cluster is named as 'Negative Barriers Towards ICT Application in the Library' and is given in Table 2.4.62.

Table 2.4.62 Cluster 3: Negative Barriers Towards the ICT Application in the Library

Sl. No	*Variable Description*	*Variable Code*	*Agree*	*Disagree*
8	ICT operational cost is exceeding year by year	BA8	5	25
9	Inability to absorb recurring costs	BA9	4	26
10	Increasing costs of procuring hardware and software	BA10	6	24
11	Political and administrative changes	BA11	3	27

Sl. No	Variable Description	Variable Code	Agree	Disagree
13	Lack of official/policy guidelines	BA13	7	23
14	Non availability of less expensive library management software	BA14	7	23
	Total		**32**	**148**

Agreement Ratio = $\overline{A}$ = 32/30 = 1.1

Disagreement Ratio = 148/30 = 2.4.9

Cluster Centre: (1.1 : 2.4.9)

Agreement and Disagreement Ratio (1:5)

This cluster has been formed with six variables. The agreement and disagreement ratio of the cluster is 1:5. This indicates that a large majority of the librarians are negatively responded to these barriers. These barriers are ICT operational cost is exceeding year by year, Inability to absorb recurring costs, Increasing costs of procuring hardware and software, Political and administrative changes, Lack of official/policy guidelines, and Non availability of less expensive library management software.

Table 2.4.63 shows the 4th cluster. It is named as "Insufficient Fund, Infrastructure and Trained Manpower".

Table 2.4.63 Cluster 4: Insufficient Fund, Infrastructure and Trained Manpower

Sl. No	Variable Description	Variable Code	Agree	Disagree
1	Insufficient funds	BA1	19	11
2	Inadequate ICT infrastructure	BA2	24	6
4	Inadequately trained library professionals	BA4	27	3
	Total		**70**	**20**

Agreement Ratio = $\overline{A}$ = 70/30 = 2.3

Disagreement ratio = 20/30 = 0.7

Cluster Cenre : (2.3 : 0.7)

Agreement and Disagreement Ratio (23:7)

This cluster has been formed with three variables. The agreement and disagreement ratio of the cluster is 23:7. This indicates that about three fourth of the librarians feels that the main barriers of ICT application in Special Libraries under study are inadequately trained library professionals, inadequate ICT infrastructure and insufficient funds.

Fifth cluster is named as "Lack of ICT Knowledge on the Part of Users" and it is presented in Table 2.4.64.

Table 2.4.64 Cluster 5: Lack of ICT Knowledge on the Part of Users

Sl. No	*Variable Description*	*Variable Code*	*Agree*	*Disagree*
7	Lack of ICT knowledge on the part of users	BA7	19	11

Agreement and Disagreement Ratio (19:11)

This cluster has been formed with only one variable. The agreement and disagreement ratio of the cluster is 19:11. This indicates that majority of the librarians feels that lack of ICT knowledge on the part of users is a barriers towards the successful application of ICT in Special Libraries under study.

The clusters shows that about three fourth of the librarians feels that the main barriers of ICT application in Special Libraries under study are inadequately trained library professionals, inadequate ICT infrastructure and insufficient fund. Majority of them feels that lack of ICT knowledge on the part of users is a barrier towards the successful application of ICT and a good number of them also feel that lack of well accepted and standard library management software package is a barrier towards the ICT application in Special Libraries under study.

It is also observed that majority of the librarians did not agree that lack of awareness, interest and initiation of library professionals towards ICT application in the library are the barriers of ICT application and a large majority of them have negatively responded to the barriers like ICT operational cost is exceeding year by year, inability to absorb recurring costs, increasing costs of procuring hardware and software, political and administrative changes, lack of official/policy guidelines, and non availability of less expensive library management software.

The analysis of the data received through the observation and interview show a clear picture about the barriers of ICT application in Special Libraries under study. It reveals that insufficient funds/finance and lack of qualified library professionals in ICT application are the main barrier for the successful application of ICT in Special Libraries under study. Lack of appropriate computer infrastructure including well-accepted library management software, lack of initiative on the part of librarian, lack of support from the authorities, lack of professional and career advancement facilities, and lack of ICT knowledge on the part of users are the other barriers for ICT application in Special Libraries under study. Librarian of ICRI has reported that power failure is the main problem, because this institute is located in a remote hilly region and librarian of technopark has reported that the availability of web based resources is the main barrier of ICT application in the park center library.

LIBRARIANS' ATTITUDE TOWARDS ICT APPLICATION IN LIBRARIES

It is very relevant to assess the attitude of librarians towards the ICT application in the libraries. Therefore, the attitudes were formed into 13 variables. Responses of librarians belongs to Special Libraries under study were obtained and the same was analysed. The summarised responses are given in Table 2.4.65.

Table 2.4.65 Librarians' Attitude Towards ICT Application in Libraries

Sl. No.	*Variable Description*	*Variable Code*	*Agree*	*Disagree*
1	ICT applications are to improve the quality of the library services	ATQUAL	30	0
2	ICT application improve the efficiency of the library	ATEFFI	30	0
3	ICT application enhance the knowledge and expertise	ATKNOW	30	0
4	ICT application makes an integration within the organisation	ATINTE	24	6
5	ICT application are essential to improve the communication facilities	ATCOMM	30	0
6	ICT application improves the status of the library	ATSTAT	29	1
7	ICT use often disturb the routine work of the library	ATROUT	1	29
8	ICT reduces the work load of the library professionals	ATWORK	16	14
9	ICT takes over the traditional way of information handling in the library	ATTRAD	5	25
10	ICT application will spoil the image of the library	ATSPOIL	0	30
11	ICT applications will increase the number of supporting staff	ATSUPP	3	27
12	ICT affects regular budgeting provision	ATBUDG	2	28
13	ICT takes major share from the library	ATMAJOR	5	25

HIERARCHICAL CLUSTER ANALYSIS
Dendrogram using Average Linkage (Between Groups)
Rescaled Distance Cluster Combine

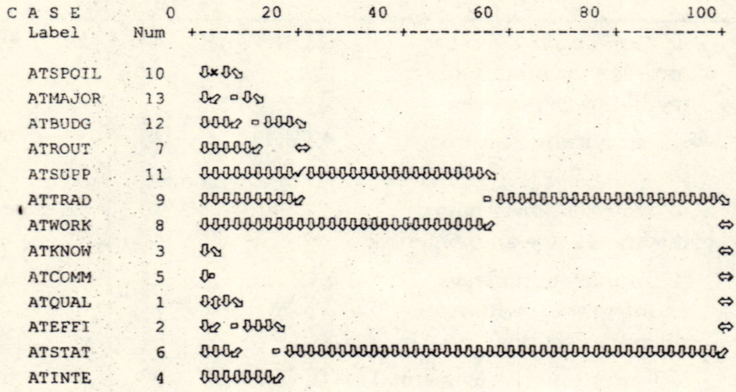

Figure 2.4.2 Dendrogram- Librarians' Attitude Towards ICT Application in Libraries

As seen in Figure 2.4.2 dendrogram shows that at 60 per cent distance level, two interpretable clusters have been formed. The first cluster consists of seven variables and the second cluster consists of 6 variables. The clusters formed are given in Table 2.4.66.

Table 2.4.66 Clusters Formed

Cluster 1	*Cluster 2*
7	1
8	2
9	3
10	4
11	5
12	6
13	

Table 2.4.67 gives the first cluster and it is named as 'ICT Application Creates Problems to the Resources and Services of the Library'.

Table 2.4.67 Cluster 1. ICT Application Creates Problems to the Resources and Services of the Library

Sl.No.	Variable Description	Variable Code	Agree	Disagree
7	ICT use often disturb the routine work of the library	ATROUT	1	29
8	ICT reduces the work load of the library professionals	ATWORK	16	14
9	ICT takes over the traditional way of information handling in the library	ATTRAD	5	25
10	ICT application will spoil the image of the library	ATSPOIL	0	30
11	ICT applications will increase the number of supporting staff	ATSUPP	3	27
12	ICT affects regular budgeting provision	ATBUDG	2	28
13	ICT takes major share from the library	ATMAJOR	5	25
	TOTAL		32	178

Agreement Ratio = $\overline{A}$ = 32/30 = 1.07

Disagreement Ratio = 178/30 = 5.93

Cluster Cenre : (1.07 : 5.93)

Agreement and Disagreement Ratio (1:6)

About 7 variables have been grouped for this cluster. The agreement and disagreement ration is 1:6. The analysis shows that the negative aspects hold in the variables are not agreed by the librarians of Special Libraries under study. Most of them have the attitude that ICT applications never create any problems to the services and resources of the library.

The second cluster is given in Table 2.4.68. It is named as 'ICT Application Improves the Quality and Efficiency of the Library Resources and Services.'

Table 2.4.68 Cluster 2. ICT Application Improves the Quality and Efficiency of the Library Resources and Services

Sl.No.	Variable description	Variable Code	Agree	Disagree
1	ICT applications are to improve the quality of the library services	ATQUAL	30	0
2	ICT application improve the efficiency of the library	ATEFFI	30	0
3	ICT application enhance the knowledge and expertise	ATKNOW	30	0
4	ICT application makes an integration within the organisation	ATINTE	24	6
5	ICT application are essential to improve the communication facilities	ATCOMM	30	0
6	ICT application improves the status of the library	ATSTAT	29	1
	TOTAL		**173**	**7**

Agreement Ratio = $\overline{A}$ = 173/30 = 5.8

Disagreement Ratio = 7/30 = 0.2

Cluster Centre : (5.8 : 0.2)

Agreement and Disagreement Ratio (30:1)

In the second cluster about 6 variables have been grouped. The agreement and disagreement ratio for these variables are 30:1. This shows that librarians have overwhelming positive attitude towards the application of Information and Communication Technologies in the Special Libraries under study. Most of them have the attitude that ICT application would improve the status of the library by improving the quality and efficiency of the library services and resources.

The librarians have overwhelming positive attitude towards the application of Information and Communication

Technologies in the Special Libraries under study. Most of them have the attitude that ICT application would improve the status of the library by improving the quality and efficiency of the services and resources. It is also observed that the negative aspects hold in the variables are not agreed by the librarians of Special Libraries under study. Most of them have the attitude that ICT applications never create any problems to the services and resources of the library.

FUTURE PLANS

This section of the questionnaire focused on future ICT application plans. Librarians' were asked for details of their future plans with regard to either extending their current ICT applications in the library or implementing new ICT based library resources and services. Table 2.4.69 shows the different future plans towards ICT application in Special Libraries under study.

Table 2.4.69 Future Plans Towards ICT application

Future Plans	***Central Government***	***Central Government Autonomous***	***State Government***	***State Government Autonomous***	***Grand Total***
Intranet	2(25 %)	1(7.7 %)	-	1(14.3 %)	4(13.3 %)
CD-ROM database	4(50 %)	3(23 %)	1(50 %)	3(42.9 %)	11(36.7%)
Multimedia system	2(25 %)	3(23 %)	-	3(42.9 %)	8(26.7 %)
CD-Net working	3(37.5 %)	4(30.8 %)	-	3(42.9 %)	10(33.3 %)
Barcoding	2(25 %)	5(38. 5 %)	-	1(14.3 %)	8(26.7 %)
Smart Cards	-	7(53.8 %)	1(50 %)	1(14.3 %)	9(30 %)
Web based administration & management	1(12.5 %)	4(30.8 %)	1(50 %)	3(42.9 %)	9(30 %)
Digital Library	6(75 %)	9(69.2 %)	-	6(85.7 %)	21(70 %)

The analysis revealed that majority (70 per cent) of the librarians indicated their enthusiastic future plan as to set up a digital library. The other plans stated were subscription of CD-ROM databases (36.7 per cent), establishment of CD-Networking (33.3 per cent), introduction of smart cards and web based administration & management (30 per cent), introduction of multimedia system and bar-coding (26.7 per cent), and setting up of Intranet (13.3 per cent). It is found that majority of the libraries of Central Government institutions (75 per cent), Central Government autonomous institutions (69.2 per cent) and State Government autonomous institutions (85.7 per cent) were stated digital library as their future plan. 53.8 per cent libraries of Central Government autonomous institutions are stated introduction of smart cards in the library as their future plans.

It is revealed that majority of librarians have digital library as their future plan. A few of them stated subscription of CD-ROM databases, establishment of CD-Networking, web based administration & management, introduction of multimedia systems, smart cards and bar coding, and setting up of intranet as their future plans.

LIBRARIANS' COMMENTS AND SUGGESTIONS

The comments and suggestions given by the librarians in response to the open-ended question about the state-of-the-art application of ICT in their libraries are categorised and analysed. A total of 23 librarians responded to this question. Of these 23 suggestions and comments, 8 librarians (35 per cent) pointed out that they are using the ICT based library resources and services like, access to electronic journals, databases including CD-ROM and full text databases, internet, OPAC and other utilities and devices for the storage, retrieval and dissemination of information like printer, scanner, CD-Net server, etc. They expressed that ICT made lot of advantages to their library management activities and it is very useful to provide value added services to users. They pointed out that ICT is very essential to provide up-to-data information. They also pointed out that lack of fund, lack of infrastructure and lack of support from the higher authority are the major barriers to the application of ICT in their libraries. They expressed the need to setup a digital library and access to more e-journals and electronic, bibliographic and full text databases.

From the expressions and suggestions of 7 librarians (30 per cent), it is clear that they are not successful in library automation and ICT application. Even though they are automated, they lack well-accepted library management software, sufficient hardware and network facilities. They are providing few e-journals and database facilities. Some are planning to automate their circulation system with barcode facility. They lack finance, infrastructure, support, qualified library staff and library management software. They also pointed out that ICT is very essential and useful for providing quality information. They expressed the need to acquire good software, hardware and electronic resources like e-journals and full text databases. Suggestions and comments of eight librarians (35 per cent) reveal that they are in the beginning stage of library automation and ICT application. Few libraries are doing retrospective conversion. They lack sufficient hardware and have one or two computer terminals. They also indicated that ICT is very important for storing, retrieving and dissemination information efficiently. They wanted e-journals, databases, increased bandwidth of Internet, sufficient hardware and software and qualified library professionals. They expressed the need to set up a digital library. These librarians also pointed out that lack fund, hardware, software, qualified library professionals and lack of interest on the part of users are the major barriers of automation and ICT application in their libraries.

The library survey has provided a useful summary of current state-of-the-art application of ICT in Special Libraries under study. Though most of the Special Libraries under study have hardware and software facilities to some extent, but the resources and services are not reaching the users community to the expected extent. Most of them are struggling to introduce ICT based resources and services. It is found that about half of the Special Libraries under study are poor in computer hardware and electronic resources. The skill and expertise of library staff in ICT based resources and services are not adequate. Majority of them have commercially prepared library management software. A few of them are using commercial online databases and majority of libraries are using CD-ROM databases. Majority of them have no digital library or digital library initiatives. Only three Special Libraries under study are participating in library consortia and this is for accessing electronic journals. The use of Internet for library and information services is found to be very less. ICT based resources and services of majority of libraries are very poor and not adequate. Majority of libraries are providing training to their staff and library users. The main barriers of ICT application are inadequately trained library professionals, inadequate ICT infrastructure and insufficient funds. The librarians have overwhelming positive attitude towards the application of ICT. Application of ICT in libraries has become inevitable in an era of information explosion and the emergence of wide range of new technologies. Effective application of ICT in libraries helps in performing their operations and services most efficiently. It requires imaginative, intelligent planning and huge investment of financial as well as human resources.

2. THE USE OF ICT BASED RESOURCES AND SERVICES IN SPECIAL LIBRARIES UNDER STUDY.

Following are the details of the statistical analysis and interpretations of the data collected from the library users through the structured questionnaire to assess:

General Information:

Status of the Library Users

Users were asked to indicate their designations or status. Table 2.4.70 indicates the designation wise distribution of library users in Special Libraries under study. The users' designations of some organisations are varies. But for comparison and uniformity it was recorded according to the status, scale of pay and nature of duties into the common pattern of designation in scientific research institutions like scientists, principle investigators, technical officer, technical assistant, research fellow, research associate, supporting staff, etc.

Table 2.4.70 Status Wise Distribution of Library Users

Designation	*Central Government*	*Central Government Autonomous*	*State Government*	*State Government Autonomous*	*Grand Total*
Principle Investigator	17(7.2 %)	34(7.6 %)	4(13.8 %)	14(8 %)	69(7.8 %)
Scientist	61 (25.7 %)	166 (37.1 %)	7(24.1 %)	44(25 %)	278 (31.3 %)
Technical Officer	44 (18.6 %)	61 (13.6 %)	7 (24.1 %)	32 (18.2 %)	144 (16.2 %)
Technical Assistant	49 (20.7 %)	44 (9.8 %)	2 (6.9 %)	22 (12.5 %)	117 (13.2 %)
Research Fellow	34 (14.3 %)	59 (13.2 %)	-	33 (18.8 %)	126 (14.2 %)
Research Associate	6(2.5 %)	14(3.1 %)	-	3(1.7 %)	23(2.6 %)
Supporting Staff	1(0.4 %)	17(3.8 %)	-	9(5.1 %)	27(3 %)
Others	25 (10.5 %)	52 (11.6 %)	9 (31 %)	19 (10.8 %)	105 (11.8 %)
Grand Total	**237** (100 %)	**447** (100 %)	**29** (100 %)	**176** (100 %)	**889** (100 %)

The different designations of users are scientists (31.3

per cent), technical officer (16.2 per cent), research fellow (14.2 per cent), technical assistant (13.2 per cent), principle investigator (7.8 per cent), research associate (2.6 per cent), supporting staff (3 per cent) and others (11.8 per cent).

It is found that from all the categories of organisations a good number of users are either scientists or persons having similar designation. The other major categories of users are technical officers, technical assistants and research fellows.

Age Range of the Library Users

Users were asked to indicate their age by selecting one of the four age ranges provided. Table 2.4.71 shows the distribution of users according to their age.

Table 2.4.71 Age Wise Distribution of Library Users in Special Libraries under study

Age Range	*Central Government*	*Central Government Autonomous*	*State Government*	*State Government Autonomous*	*Grand Total*
20-30	107(45.1 %)	208(46.5 %)	11(37.9 %)	101(57.4 %)	427(48 %)
31-40	79(33.3 %)	120(26.8 %)	3(10.3 %)	36(20.5 %)	238(26.8 %)
41-50	38(16 %)	79(17.7 %)	3(10.3 %)	22(12.5 %)	142(16 %)
51-60	13(5.5 %)	40(8.9 %)	12(41.4 %)	17(9.7 %)	82(9.2 %)
Grand Total	237 (100 %)	447 (100 %)	29 (100 %)	176 (100 %)	889 (100 %)

The analysis shows that a good number (48 per cent) of the library users are between 20-30 years of age. About 238 (26.8 per cent) users have 31-40 years of age. A few (16 per cent) users have 41-50 years of age and a very few (9.2 per cent) users have 51-60 years of age.

The majority (57.4 per cent) of the library users of State Government autonomous institutions and a good number of Central Government institutions (45.1 per cent) and Central Government autonomous institutions (46.5 per cent) are between 20-30 years of age. A good number (41.4 per cent) of the users of State Government institutions are between 51-60 years of age.

It is found that a good number of users of special libraries in Kerela are between 20-30 years of age. A few users are between 31-40 and 41-50 years of age and only a very few users are above 50 years of age.

Gender wise Distribution of Library Users

Table 2.4.72 gives the gender wise distribution of library users in Special Libraries under study. The analysis shows that majority (58.3 per cent) of them are male and 41.7 per cent of them are female.

Table 2.4.72 Gender wise Distribution of Library Users in Special Libraries under study

Gender	*Central Government*	*Central Government Autonomous*	*State Government*	*State Government Autonomous*	*Grand Total*
Male	151(63.7 %)	257(57.5 %)	16(55.2 %)	94(53.4 %)	518(58.3 %)
Female	86(36.3 %)	190(42.5 %)	13(44.8 %)	82(46.6 %)	371(41.7 %)
Grand Total	**237 (100 %)**	**447 (100 %)**	**29 (100 %)**	**176 (100 %)**	**889 (100 %)**

The majority of the library users of Central Government institutions (63.7 per cent), Central Government autonomous institutions (57.5 per cent), State Government institutions (55.2 per cent), and State Government autonomous institutions (53.4 per cent) are male.

It is found that majority of library users are male. It is also found that majority of the library users of all the categories of institutions are male.

USE OF ICT BASED LIBRARY SERVICES / RESOURCES / UTILITIES/TOOLS / DEVICES

Users were asked whether they use any of the ICT based library services / resources / utilities / tools / devices and the responses are summerised in Table 2.4.73.

Table 2.4.73 Use of ICT Based Services / Resources / Utilities / Tools / Devices

Information Handling Tools/ Utilities/ Devices	*Central Government*	*Central Government Autonomous*	*State Government*	*State Government Autonomous*	*Grand Total*
Floppy	47 (19.8 %)	308 (68.9 %)	11 (37.9 %)	101 (57.4 %)	467 (52.5 %)
Magnatic tape	2 (0.8 %)	20 (4.5 %)	-	-	22 (2.5 %)
CD-ROM	41 (17.3 %)	276 (61.7 %)	17 (58.6 %)	89 (50.6 %)	423 (47.6 %)
DVD	8 (3.4 %)	47 (10.5 %)	6 (20.7 %)	4 (2.3 %)	65 (7.3 %)
VCD	6 (2.5 %)	44 (9.8 %)	-	7 (4 %)	57 (6.4 %)
Printer	44 (18.6 %)	246 (55 %)	17 (58.6 %)	86 (48.9 %)	393 (44.2 %)
Scanner	10 (4.2 %)	122 (27.3 %)	-	15 (8.5 %)	147 (16.5 %)
Smart Card	-	-	-	-	-
Laptop Computer	-	8 (1.8 %)	-	1 (0.6 %)	9 (1 %)
CD-Net Server	26 (11 %)	125 (28 %)	-	39 (22.2 %)	190 (21.4 %)
CD-Tower	-	53 (11.9 %)	-	-	53 (6 %)
Bibliographic databases	66 (27.8 %)	314 (70.2 %)	12 (41.4 %)	95 (54 %)	487 (54.8 %)
Full text databases	8 (3.4 %)	200 (44.7 %)	-	57 (32.4 %)	265 (29.8 %)
E-Book	-	2 (0.4 %)	-	-	2 (0.2 %)
Telephone	2 (0.8 %)	109 (24.4 %)	-	36 (20.5 %)	147 (16.5 %)
Fax	-	25 (5.6 %)	-	-	25 (2.8 %)

Information Handling Tools/ Utilities/ Devices	*Central Government*	*Central Government Autonomous*	*State Government*	*State Government Autonomous*	*Grand Total*
E-mail	93 (39.2 %)	366 (81.6 %)	9 (31 %)	115 (65.3 %)	583 (65.6 %)
WWW	114 (48.1 %)	290 (64.9 %)	17 (58.6 %)	107 (60.8 %)	528 (59.4 %)
Ftp	8 (3.4 %)	35 (7.8 %)	-	-	43 (4.8 %)
Telnet	-	49 (11 %)	-	2 (1.1 %)	51 (5.7 %)
Listserve	-	18 (4 %)	-	-	18 (2 %)
Usenet/ Newsgroup	-	23 (5.1 %)	-	-	23 (2.6 %)
E_Journals	52 (21.9 %)	260 (58.2 %)	11 (37.9 %)	81 (46 %)	404 (45.4 %)
Library's Website	-	127 (28.4 %)	5 (17.2 %)	43 (24.4 %)	175 (19.7 %)
OPAC	21 (8.9 %)	263 (58.8 %)	12 (41.4 %)	74 (42 %)	370 (41.6 %)
Web OPAC	-	2 (0.4 %)	-	-	2 (0.2 %)

The electronic resource/tools used by the largest percentage of users is the e-mail. Majority (65.6 per cent) of them indicated that they are accessing e-mail from the library. The next most widely used resource is WWW, which is using by nearly 60 per cent of the users. It is also found that majority of them are using floppy (52.2 per cent), and bibliographical databases (54.8 per cent). A good number of the users are using CD-ROM (47.6 per cent), printer (44.2 per cent), e-journals (45.4 per cent) and OPAC (41.6 per cent).

All other resources and services received quite low use. A few users are using scanner (16.5 per cent), CD-Net server (21.4 per cent), full text databases (29.8 per cent), telephone

(16.5 per cent) and library's website (19.7 per cent). A very few users are using magnetic tape (2.5 per cent), DVD (7.3 per cent), VCD (6.4 per cent), laptop computer (1 per cent), CD tower (6 per cent), e-books (0.2 per cent), fax (2.8 per cent), ftp (4.8 per cent), telnet (5.7 per cent), listserve (2 per cent), usenet/ newsgroup (2.6 per cent) and WebOPAC (0.2 per cent). Nobody is using smart card technology in the library. It is also found that users of Central Government autonomous institutions are better in the use of various ICT based library services / resources / utilities / tools / devices.

It is revealed that the electronic resource used by the largest percentage of users is the e-mail. Majority of them indicated that they are accessing e-mail from the library. The next most widely used resource is WWW, which is being used by nearly 60 per cent of the library users. It is also found that majority of them are using floppy, and bibliographical databases. A good number of users are using CD-ROM, printer, e-journals and OPAC. It is also found that users of Central Government autonomous institutions are better in the use of various ICT based library resources and services.

Frequency of Use of the different ICT based Library Resources and Services

The users were asked to indicate the frequency with which they used various ICT based library services/ resources/utilities/tools/devices. The responses are summarised in the Tables 2.4.74 to 2.4.78

Frequency of Use of the different ICT based Library Resources and Services in the Central Government Institutions

Table 2.4.74 shows the frequency of use of various ICT based library resources and services by library users of Central Government institutions.

The analysis shows that a large majority of them are not using various ICT based library services and resources at all. Nearly half of them are browsing Internet and a good number

Table 2.4.74 Frequency of Use of the different ICT based Library Resources and Services in the Central Government Institutions

Tools/Resources	*Nearly once in a month*	*Two or three times in a month*	*About once in a week*	*Two or three times in a week*	*Almost every day*	*No use*
OPAC	12(5.1 %)	-	3(1.3 %)	2(0.8 %)	-	220(92.8 %)
Bibliographic database	34(14.3 %)	18(7.6 %)	19(8 %)	7(3 %)	-	159(67.1 %)
Full text database	9(3.8 %)	5(2.1 %)	2(0.8 %)	4(1.7 %)	1(0.4 %)	214(90.3 %)
E-Journal	16(6.8 %)	6(2.5 %)	6(2.5 %)	2(0.8 %)	4(1.7 %)	203(85.7 %)
Web Browsing	48(20.3 %)	24(10.1 %)	15(6.3 %)	9(3.8 %)	22(9.3 %)	119(50.2 %)
E-mail	28(11.8 %)	15(6.3 %)	27(11.4 %)	6(2.5 %)	25(10.5 %)	136(57.4 %)
Ftp	9(3.8 %)	1(0.4 %)	-	4(1.7 %)	-	223(94.1 %)
Telnet	-	-	-	2(0.8 %)	1(0.4 %)	234(98.7 %)
Mailing list(List serve)	-	-	-	1(0.4 %)	-	236(99.6 %)
Usenet/ News group	2(0.8 %)	-	-	-	1(0.4 %)	234(98.7 %)
Scanner	4(1.7 %)	1(0.4 %)	4(1.7 %)	4(1.7 %)	-	224(94.5 %)
Printer	?(0.8 %)	-	4(1.7 %)	4(1.7 %)	5(2.1 %)	222(93.7 %)

of them are using E-mail. E-mail is the most frequently used tool. About 10.5 of them used e-mail almost everyday. Web browsing is the second most frequently used service/tool. About 9.3 per cent of them used web browsing almost every day. 5.1 per cent of them using OPAC nearly once in a month. Nearly 15 per cent of them are using bibliographic databases once in a month. 6.8 per cent users are using e-journals nearly once in a month. A very few of them are using ftp and about 3.8 per cent of them are using it nearly once in a month. A very few of them are using printer and nearly 2.1 per cent are using it almost every day.

It is found that a large majority of library users of Central Government institutions are not using various ICT based library resources and services at all. Nearly half of the users are browsing Internet and a good number of them are using E-mail. E-mail is the most frequently used tool. Web browsing is the second most frequently used service/tool. However, a very few of them are indicated that they used e-mail, www, and OPAC almost every day. A few users are using bibliographic databases and e-journals nearly once in a month.

Frequency of Use of the different ICT based Library Resources and Services in the Central Government Autonomous institutions

Table 2.4.75 shows the frequency of use of different ICT based library resources and services in the Central Government autonomous institutions. The analysis shows that majority of the users are using OPAC, bibliographic databases, full text databases, e-journals, web browsing, and e-mail. A good number of them are using printer and scanner and a few of them are using ftp, telnet, mailinglist (list serve) and usenet/newgroups.

In the case of Central Government autonomous institutions also e-mail is the most frequently used tool. Nearly 82 per cent of the users are using E-mail and about 47.4 per cent of them are using it almost every day, while 14.3 per cent

Table 2.4.75 Frequency of Use of the different ICT based Library Resources and Services in the Central Government Autonomous Institutions

Tools/Resources	*Nearly once in a month*	*Two or three times in a month*	*About once in a week*	*Two or three times in a week*	*Almost every day*	*No use*
OPAC	105(23.5 %)	61(13.6 %)	15(3.4 %)	15(3.4 %)	30(6.7 %)	160(35.8 %)
Bibliographic database	133(29.8 %)	68(15.2 %)	64(14.3 %)	18(4 %)	21(4.7 %)	97(21.7 %)
Full text database	71(15.9 %)	49(11 %)	40(8.9 %)	16(3.6 %)	35(7.8 %)	195(43.6 %)
E-Journal	59(13.2 %)	52(11.6 %)	24(5.4 %)	85(19 %)	63(14.1 %)	142(31.8 %)
Web Browsing	40(8.9 %)	13(2.9 %)	48(10.7 %)	92(20.6 %)	134(30 %)	103(23 %)
E-mail	28(6.3 %)	7(1.6 %)	51(11.4 %)	64(14.3 %)	212(47.4 %)	81(18.1 %)
Ftp	17(3.8 %)	8(1.8 %)	5(1.1 %)	7(1.6 %)	3(0.7 %)	345(77.2 %)
Telnet	5(1.1 %)	3(0.7 %)	9(2 %)	3(0.7 %)	16(3.6 %)	342(76.5 %)
Mailing list (List serve)	3(0.7 %)	1(0.2 %)	10(2.2 %)	13(2.9 %)	17(3.8 %)	328(73.4 %)
Usenet/ News group	-	-	16(3.6 %)	7(1.6 %)	6(1.3 %)	341(76.3 %)
Scanner	54(12.1 %)	52(11.6 %)	11(2.5 %)	16(3.6 %)	18(4 %)	279(62.4 %)
Printer	38(8.5 %)	15(3.4 %)	21(4.7 %)	39(8.7 %)	86(19.2 %)	242(54.1 %)

of them are using it two or three times in a week. Bibliographic databases are the second most frequently used resources and nearly 79 per cent of them are using bibliographic databases. About 29.8 per cent of them are using it nearly once in a month. 77 per cent of users are using web browsing and 30 per cent of them are using it almost every day. Nearly 65 per cent users are using OPAC and 6.7 per cent users are using it almost everyday. Majority (56.4 per cent) of the users are using full text databases and about 15.9 per cent of them are using it nearly once in a month. Nearly 70 per cent users are using e-journals and about 14.1 per cent using it almost everyday. 3.8 per cent users are using ftp nearly once in a month and 3.6 per cent users are using telnet almost everyday. A good number of the users are using printer and about 19.2 per cent of them using it almost every day.

It is found that in the case of Central Government autonomous institutions also e-mail is the most frequently used tool. Nearly 82 per cent of the users are using E-mail and a good number of them use it almost every day. Bibliographic databases are the second most frequently used resources and nearly 79 per cent of them are using bibliographic databases. Majority of them are using web browsing and OPAC and a few of them use it almost every day. Majority of users are using full text databases and a few of them use it nearly once in a month. Nearly 70 per cent of the users are using e-journals and a few of them are using it almost everyday. A good number of users are using printer and a few of them use it almost every day.

Frequency of Use of the different ICT based Library Resources and Services in the State Government Institutions

Table 2.4.76 shows the frequency of use of different ICT based library resources and services in the State Government institutions. The analysis shows that majority of the users are using OPAC, bibliographic databases, full text databases, e-journals, web browsing, and printer. Nobody is using ftp,

Table 2.4.76 Frequency of Use of the different ICT based Library Resources and Services in the State Government Institutions

Tools/Resources	Nearly once in a month	Two or three times in a month	About once in a week	Two or three times in a week	Almost every day	No use
OPAC	-	-	6(20.7 %)	6(20.7 %)	-	5(17.2 %)
Bibliographic databases	-	4(13.8 %)	6(20.7 %)	6(20.7 %)	-	13(44.8 %)
Full text Database	-	-	-	20(69 %)	-	9(31 %)
E-Journal	5(17.2 %)	-	12(41.4 %)	-	-	12(41.4 %)
Web Browsing	-	-	6(20.7 %)	-	11(37.9 %)	12(41.4 %)
Email	-	-	-	-	11(37.9 %)	18(62.1 %)
Ftp	-	-	-	-	-	29(100 %)
Telnet	-	-	-	-	-	29(100 %)
Mailing list(List serve)	-	-	-	-	-	29(100 %)
Usenet/ News group	-	-	-	-	-	29(100 %)
Scanner	-	-	-	-	-	29(100 %)
Printer	12(41.4 %)	-	5(17.2 %)	-	-	12(41.4 %)

telnet, mailing list, usenet/newsgroup and scanner. E-mail and web browsing are the most frequently used tool. A few (37.9 per cent) users indicated that they use e-mail and web browsing almost every day. Majority (69 per cent) of the users indicated that they use full text databases two or three times in a week. Nearly 20.7 per cent of them indicated that they use OPAC and bibliographic databases two or three times in a week. Still another 20.7 per cent of them indicated that they use OPAC and bibliographic databases about once in a week. A good number (41.4 per cent) of them indicated that they use e-journals about once in a week. Majority of users are using printer but a good number (41.4 per cent) of them use it nearly once in a month.

In the case of State Government institutions also e-mail and web browsing are the most frequently used tools. A few users indicated that they use e-mail and web browsing almost every day. Majority of users indicated that they use full text databases two or three times in a week. A few users indicated that they use OPAC and bibliographic databases two or three times in a week. A good number of them use e-journals about once in a week. Majority of the users are using printer but a good number of them use it nearly once in a month.

Frequency of Use of the different ICT based Library Resources and Services in the State Government Autonomous Institutions

Table 2.4.77 shows the frequency of use of different ICT based library resources and services in State Government autonomous institutions.

The analysis shows that most of the users are preferred the 'no use' option. Majority of them are using bibliographic databases, e-journals, web browsing, and e-mail. Here also e-mail is the most frequently used tool and 31.8 per cent of them use it almost every day. Nearly 60 per cent of the users are using web browsing and a few (29 per cent) users indicated they use it almost every day. Majority of users are using e-

Table 2.4.77 Frequency of Use of the different ICT based Library Services and Resources in the State Government Autonomous Institutions

Tools/Resources	*Nearly once in a month*	*Two or three times in a month*	*About once in a week*	*Two or three times in a week*	*Almost every day*	*No use*
OPAC	49(27.8 %)	2(1.1 %)	8(4.5 %)	6(3.4 %)	7(4 %)	102(58 %)
Bibliographic database	38(21.6 %)	11(6.3 %)	10(5.7 %)	2(1.1 %)	1(0.6 %)	84(47.7 %)
Full text database	20(11.4 %)	16(9.1 %)	30(17 %)	8(4.5 %)	-	100(56.8 %)
E-Journal	19(10.8 %)	11(6.3 %)	16(9.1 %)	16(9.1 %)	32(18.2 %)	80(45.5 %)
Web Browsing	11(6.3 %)	13(7.4 %)	12(6.8 %)	9(5.1 %)	51(29 %)	72(40.9 %)
E-mail	9(5.1 %)	6(3.4 %)	24(13.6 %)	21(11.9 %)	56(31.8 %)	58(33 %)
Ftp	-	2(1.1 %)	-	-	-	168(95.5 %)
Telnet	-	-	-	1(0.6 %)	2(1.1 %)	169(96 %)
Mailing list(List serve)	4(2.3 %)	-	-	2(1.1 %)	-	164(93.2 %)
Usenet/ News group	-	-	-	-	-	170(96.6 %)
Scanner	4(2.3 %)	3(1.7 %)	7(4 %)	-	4(2.3 %)	154(87.5 %)
Printer	23(13.1 %)	11(6.3 %)	23(13.1 %)	5(2.8 %)	6(3.4 %)	106(60.2 %)

journals and a few (18.2 per cent) of them use it almost every day. 27.8 per cent of the users are using OPAC nearly once in a month. Nearly 53 per cent of the users are using bibliographic databases, but a good number of them use it nearly once in a moth.

Majority of library users of State Government institutions indicated that they are using bibliographic databases, e-journals, web browsing, and e-mail. Here also e-mail is the most frequently used tool and a few of them use it almost every day. Nearly 60 per cent of them are using web browsing but only a few of them use it almost every day. Majority of the users are using e-journals and a few of them use it almost every day. A few users are using OPAC nearly once in a month. Majority of users are using bibliographic databases, but good number of them uses it nearly once in a moth.

Chi-Square Values for Comparing Frequency of Using each Resource/Tool Between Different Organisations

Chi-Square tests were conducted to compare the frequencies of using each resource/tool between different organisations. Table 2.4.78 shows the values obtained through Chi-Square testing.

Table 2.4.78 Chi-Square Values for Comparing Frequency of Using each Resource/Tool Between Different Libraries

Tools/Resources	***Chi Square Values***
OPAC	356.778
Bibliographic databases	217.277
Full text Database	426.905
E-Journal	281.336
Web Browsing	180.611
Email	196.110
Ftp	77.2
Telnet	95.615
Mailing list(List serve)	115.803
Usenet/ News group	105.331
Scanner	133.518
Printer	222.979

Here all the Chi-Square values are found to be significant indicating that the frequencies of using all the tools are different among different organisations.

Users Rating for different ICT based Library Services and Resources/Tools

Users were asked to indicate their ratings for different ICT based library services and resources / tools. The responses are summarized in the tables 2.4.79 – 2.4.84.

Users Rating for different ICT based Library Services and Resources / Tools in Central Government Institutions

Table 2.4.79 gives the users rating for different ICT based library services and resources/tools in Central Government institutions.

Table 2.4.79 Users Rating for different ICT based Library Services and Resources / Tools in Central Government Institutions

Tools/Resources	*Excellent*	*Very Good*	*Good*	*Poor*
OPAC	-	2(0.8 %)	9(3.8 %)	18(7.6 %)
Bibliographic database	2(0.8 %)	8(3.4 %)	42(17.7 %)	51(21.5 %)
Full text database	-	5(2.1 %)	32(13.5 %)	58(24.5 %)
CD- ROM database	-	4(1.7 %)	62(26.2 %)	33(13.9 %)
CD-Networking	-	-	46(19.4 %)	14(5.9 %)
Internet service	-	12(5.1 %)	91(38.4 %)	47(19.8 %)
E-Journal	6(2.5 %)	7(3 %)	20(8.4 %)	112(47.3 %)
Speed of Internet	-	8(3.4 %)	36(15.2 %)	174(73.4 %)
Computer Infrastructure	4(1.7 %)	5(2.1 %)	20(8.4 %)	189(79.7 %)
ICT skill and expertise of library staff	6(2.5 %)	8(3.4 %)	22(9.3 %)	191(80.6 %)
ICT skill and expertise of library users	6(2.5 %)	12(5.1 %)	15(6.3 %)	192(81 %)
Printing service	-	6(2.5 %)	29(12.2 %)	193(81.4 %)
Training on ICT	-	2(0.8 %)	6(2.5 %)	220(92.8 %)

It is found that a few (17.7 per cent) users rated

bibliographic databases as good whereas 21.5 per cent of them rated it as poor. 24.5 per cent of the users rated full text databases as poor whereas 13.5 per cent users rated it as good. CD-ROM databases are good for 26.2 per cent of users whereas a few (13.9 per cent) of them rated it as poor. CD Networking is good for 19.4 per cent of the users and a few (5.9 per cent) of them rated it as poor. Internet service is good for 38.4 per cent of the users and a few (19.8 per cent) of them rated it as poor. A good number (47.3 per cent) of the users rated e-journals as poor, whereas a very few (8.4 per cent) users rated it as good. Majority (73.4 per cent) of the users rated speed of the Internet as poor but a few (15.2 per cent) of them rated it as good. Majority (79.7 per cent) of users indicated computer infrastructure as poor but a few (8.4 per cent) of them rated it as good. A large majority of users rated ICT skill and expertise of library staff (80. per cent), ICT skill and expertise of users (81 per cent) and printing service (81.4 per cent) as poor. Most (92.8 per cent) of the users rated training in ICT as poor and only 2.5 per cent of them rated it as good.

It is found that majority of the library users of Central Government institutions have rated the various ICT based library services/ resources/ tool/ devices as poor and only a few users rated them as good. A good number (47.3 per cent) of the users rated e-journals as poor, whereas a very few (8.4 per cent) users rated it as good. Majority (73.4 per cent) of the users rated speed of the Internet as poor but a few (15.2 per cent) of them rated it as good. Majority (79.7 per cent) of users indicated computer infrastructure as poor but a few (8.4 per cent) of them rated it as good. A large majority of users rated ICT skill and expertise of library staff (80.6 per cent), ICT skill and expertise of users (81 per cent) and printing service (81.4 per cent) as poor. Most (92.8 per cent) of the users rated training in ICT as poor and only 2.5 per cent of them rated it as good.

Users Rating for different ICT based Library Services and Resources / Tools in Central Government Autonomous Institutions

Table 2.4.80 gives the ratings of different ICT based library services and resources/tool by library users of Central Government autonomous institutions. A few (27.3 per cent) users rated OPAC as good and 10.5 per cent rated it as poor. 36.7 per cent of the users rated bibliographic database as good and it is very good for 23 per cent of the users and excellent for 12.1 per cent of the users. A few (26.4 per cent) users rated the full text databases as good but 8.3 per cent of them rated it as poor. Full text database is very good for 17.4 per cent of

Table 2.4.80 Users rating for different ICT based Library Services and Resources / Tools in Central Government Autonomous Institutions

Tools/Resources	*Excellent*	*Very Good*	*Good*	*Poor*
OPAC	44(9.8 %)	34(7.6 %)	122(27.3 %)	47(10.5 %)
Bibliographic database	54(12.1 %)	103(23 %)	164(36.7 %)	44(9.8 %)
Full text database	48(10.7 %)	78(17.4 %)	118(26.4 %)	37(8.3 %)
CD- ROM database	61(13.6 %)	90(20.1 %)	77(17.2 %)	88(19.7 %)
CD-Networking	24(5.4 %)	44(9.8 %)	45(10.1 %)	69(15.4 %)
Internet service	71(15.9 %)	104(23.3 %)	156(34.9 %)	72(16.1 %)
E-Journal	42(9.4 %)	91(20.4 %)	130(29.1 %)	113(25.3 %)
Speed of Internet	36(8.1 %)	96(21.5 %)	175(39.1 %)	109(24.4 %)
Computer Infrastructure	56(12.5 %)	93(20.8 %)	175(39.1 %)	83(18.6 %)
ICT skill and expertise of library staff	40(8.9 %)	68(15.2 %)	207(46.3 %)	110(24.6 %)
ICT skill and expertise of library users	20(4.5 %)	74(16.6 %)	217(48.5 %)	114(25.5 %)
Printing service	25(5.6 %)	45(10.1 %)	161(36 %)	184(41.2 %)
Training on ICT	-	10(2.2 %)	61(13.6 %)	311(69.6 %)

the users and 10.7 per cent of them rated it as excellent. A few (20.1 per cent) users rated CD-ROM databases as very good but 19.7 per cent of them rated it as poor. It is good for 17.2 per cent of the users and excellent for 13.6 per cent of the users.

A few (15.4 per cent) users rated CD Networking as poor and 10.1 per cent rated it as good. A good number (34.9 per cent) of the users rated Internet services as good and 23.3 per cent of them rated it as very good. Nearly 30 per cent of the users rated e-journals as good but a few (25.3 per cent) of them rated it as poor. A good number (39.1 per cent) of the users rated speed of the Internet as good but few (24.4 per cent) of them rated it as poor. Nearly 40 per cent users rated computer infrastructure as good and a few (20.8 per cent) of them rated it as very good. A good number (46.3 per cent) of users rated ICT skill and expertise of library staff as good but a few (24.6 per cent) of them rated it as poor. About half (48.5 per cent) of the users rated the ICT skill and expertise of library users as good but a few (25.5 per cent) of them rated it as poor. A good number (41.2 per cent) of the users rated printing service as poor but 36 per cent rated it as good. Majority (69.6 per cent) of the users rated training in ICT as poor and only 13.6 per cent of them rated it as good.

It is observed that more library users of Central Government autonomous institutions are rated OPAC, bibliographic databases, and full text databases as good and a few users rated them as very good or excellent. A few users indicated CD-ROM databases as very good, but some other users rated CD Networking as poor. A good number of users rated Internet services, e-journals, speed of the Internet, computer infrastructure, ICT skill and expertise of library staff and users as good. A few users rated them as poor. A good number of the users rated printing service as poor and majority of the users rated training in ICT as poor.

Users Rating for different ICT based Library Services and Resources / Tools in State Government Institutions

Table 2.4.81 gives the ratings of different ICT based library services and resources/ tool by library users of State Government institutions. A good number (41.4 per cent) of the users rated OPAC, bibliographic databases, CD-ROM databases, and Internet service as 'good'. A few (20.7 per cent) users rated full text databases, speed of Internet, and computer infrastructure as 'very good.' A good number (41.4 per cent) of the users rated computer infrastructure, ICT skill and expertise of library staff and users, printing service and training in ICT as 'poor', but majority (58.6 per cent) of them rated printing service and training in ICT as 'good'. A good

Table 2.4.81 Users Rating for different ICT based Library Services and Resources / Tools in State Government Institutions

Tools/Resources	*Excellent*	*Very Good*	*Good*	*Poor*
OPAC	-	-	12(41.4 %)	-
Bibliographic database	-	-	12(41.4 %)	-
Full text database	-	6(20.7 %)	6(20.7 %)	-
CD- ROM database	5(17.2 %)	-	12(41.4 %)	-
CD-Networking	-	-	-	-
Internet service	5(17.2 %)	-	12(41.4 %)	-
E-Journal	12(41.4 %)	5(17.2 %)	-	-
Speed of Internet	11(37.9 %)	6(20.7 %)	-	-
Computer Infrastructure	11(37.9 %)	6(20.7 %)	-	12(41.4 %)
ICT skill and expertise of library staff	-	12(41.4 %)	5(17.2 %)	12(41.4 %)
ICT skill and expertise of library users	-	12(41.4 %)	5(17.2 %)	12(41.4 %)
Printing service	-	-	17(58.6 %)	12(41.4 %)
Training on ICT	-	-	17(58.6 %)	12(41.4 %)

number (41.4 per cent) of users rated ICT skill and expertise of library users and staff as very good. A good number (41.4 per cent) of the users rated e-journals as excellent and it is 'very good' for 17.2 per cent of the users. 37.9 per cent of the users rated speed of Internet and computer infrastructure as 'excellent' and a few (17.2 per cent) of them rated CD-ROM database and Internet service as 'excellent'. It is also found that nobody is responded to CD-Networking.

It is revealed that a good number of library users of State Government institutions rated OPAC, bibliographic databases, CD-ROM databases, and Internet service as good. A few users rated full text databases, speed of Internet, and computer infrastructure as very good. A good number of them rated computer infrastructure, ICT skill and expertise of library staff and users, printing service and training in ICT as poor. Majority of users rated printing service and training in ICT as good and a good number of them rated ICT skill and expertise of library users and staff as very good. A good number of users rated e-journals, speed of Internet and computer infrastructure as excellent and a few of them rated CD-ROM database and Internet service as excellent.

Users Rating for different ICT based Library Services and Resources/Tools in State Government Autonomous Institutions

Table 2.4.82 gives the ratings of different ICT based library services and resources/tool by the library users of State Government autonomous institutions. Majority (63 per cent) of the users rated OPAC as 'poor' but a few (29 per cent) of them rated it as 'good'. A few (26.1 per cent) users rated bibliographic databases as 'good' and it is 'very good' for 14.2 per cent of the users. A few (22.7 per cent) users rated full text databases as 'good', and it is 'excellent' for 9.1 per cent of the users. CD ROM database is 'xcellent' for 17 per cent of the users, and it is 'very good' for 10.8 per cent users. Internet service is 'good' for 26.1 per cent of the users but a few (22.2 per cent) of them rated it as 'poor'.

A few (23.3 per cent) users rated e-journals as 'good' and 21 per cent of the users rated it as 'poor'. A good number (46 per cent) of the users rated speed of the Internet as 'poor', however, it is 'good' for 28.4 per cent of the users. 35.8 per cent users rated computer infrastructure as 'poor' but it is rated 'good' by 34.7 per cent users. A good number (42.6 per cent) of users rated ICT skill and expertise of library staff as 'poor' and it is 'good' for 34.7 per cent of the users. Majority (51.1 per cent) of the users rated ICT skill and expertise of users as 'poor' and a few (27.3 per cent) of them rated it as 'very good'. Majority (52.3 per cent) of the users rated printing service as 'good', but it is 'poor' for 32.4 per cent of the users. A large majority (81.8 per cent) of the user rated training in ICT as 'good'.

Table 2.4.82 Users Rating for different ICT based Library Services and Resources/Tools in State Government Autonomous Institutions

Tools/Resources	*Excellent*	*Very Good*	*Good*	*Poor*
OPAC	2(1.1 %)	13(7.4 %)	51(29 %)	11(6.3 %)
Bibliographic database	9(5.1 %)	25(14.2 %)	46(26.1 %)	19(10.8 %)
Full text database	16(9.1 %)	12(6.8 %)	40(22.7 %)	8(4.5 %)
CD- ROM database	30(17 %)	19(10.8 %)	18(10.2 %)	9(5.1 %)
CD-Networking	-	8(4.5 %)	5(2.8 %)	2(1.1 %)
Internet service	17(9.7 %)	33(18.8 %)	46(26.1 %)	39(22.2 %)
E-Journal	23(13.1 %)	25(14.2 %)	41(23.3 %)	37(21 %)
Speed of Internet	15(8.5 %)	5(2.8 %)	50(28.4 %)	81(46 %)
Computer Infrastructure	16(9.1 %)	14(8 %)	61(34.7 %)	63(35.8 %)
ICT skill and expertise of library staff	14(8 %)	11(6.3 %)	61(34.7 %)	75(42.6 %)
ICT skill and expertise of library users	-	23(13.1 %)	48(27.3 %)	90(51.1 %)
Printing service	4(2.3 %)	2(1.1 %)	92(52.3 %)	57(32.4 %)
Training on ICT	-	10(5.7 %)	144(81.8 %)	-

It is found that majority of the library users of State Government autonomous institutions rated ICT skill and expertise of users as poor. A few users rated bibliographic databases, full text databases, e-journals, computer infrastructure, Internet service, speed of the Internet, ICT skill and expertise of library staff, and ICT skill and expertise of users as good, but a few users rated them as poor. A good number of the users rated speed of the Internet, computer infrastructure, and ICT skill and expertise of library staff as poor. Majority of the users rated printing service as good. A large majority of the user rated training in ICT as good.

Chi-Square Values for Comparing Users Rating for different ICT based Library Services and Resources/Tools in different Organisations

Table 2.4.83 shows the Chi-Square values for comparing users rating for different ICT based library services and resources/tools in different organisations.

Table 2.4.83 Chi-square Values for Comparing Users Rating for different ICT based Library Services and Resources/Tools in different Organisations

Tools/Resources	*Chi Square Values*
OPAC	159.165
Bibliographic database	192.703
Full text database	148.105
CD- ROM database	167.829
CD-Networking	140.118
Internet service	149.388
E-Journal	193.633
Speed of Internet	295.782
Computer Infrastructure	304.695
ICT skill and expertise of library staff	242.234
ICT skill and expertise of library users	242.142
Printing service	175.770
Training on ICT	127.922

Here all the chi square values are highly significant at 1 per cent level of significance. This indicates that there is significant difference between the ratings of library users of different organisations.

Users' Opinion About Library Professionals' Help in Using ICT Based Library Resources and Services

Table 2.4.84 shows the distribution of users according to their opinion about library professionals' help in using ICT based library resources and services in Special Libraries under study. Majority (53.5 per cent) of them opined that library professionals help is inadequate and a good number (41.7 per cent) of them opined it is adequate and a very few (4.7 per cent) opined it is more than adequate.

Table 2.4.84 Users' Opinion about Library Professionals' Help in Using ICT Based Library Resources and Services

Organisation type	*Adequate*	*More than Adequate*	*Inadequate*	*Total*
Central Government	38(16 %)	5(2.1 %)	194(81.9 %)	237(100 %)
Central Government Autonomous	251(56.2 %)	17(3.8 %)	179(40 %)	447(100 %)
State Government	9(31 %)	12(41.4 %)	8(27.6 %)	29(100 %)
State Government Autonomous	73(41.5 %)	8(4.5 %)	95(54 %)	176(100 %)
Total	371(41.7 %)	42(4.7 %)	476(53.5 %)	889(100 %)

Chi-square value = 201.644**

Chi-Square value is significant at 1 per cent level indicating that there is significant difference between the help given by the library professionals in using ICT based resources and services between different types of organisations.

The large majority (81.9 per cent) of the library users of Central Government institutions and majority (54 per cent) of State Government autonomous institutions indicated that library professionals' help in using ICT based library resources and services is inadequate. However, majority (56.2 per cent) of the library users of Central Government autonomous institutions and a good number (41.5 per cent) of the users of State Government autonomous institutions indicated it is adequate. A good number (41.4 per cent) of the library users of State Government institutions opined that it is more than adequate.

It is found that majority of the users opined that library professionals' help is inadequate but a good number of users opined it is adequate. According to a large majority of the library users of Central Government institutions and majority of State Government autonomous institutions, library professionals' help is inadequate. However, majority of the library users of Central Government autonomous institutions and a good number of the users of State Government autonomous institutions opined it is adequate. A good number of library users of State Government institutions opinioned that it is more than adequate.

Users' Opinion about the Existing ICT Facilities in Special Libraries under study

Users were asked whether the existing ICT facilities in their libraries are underutilized or not. Table 2.4.85 shows the distribution of users according to their views about the existing ICT facilities in libraries of different organisations. The analysis shows that majority (56.8 per cent) of the users prefer the 'no' option indicating that the ICT facilities are not underutilized, but a good number (43.2 per cent) of them opined that it is underutilized. Majority of library users of Central Government institutions (55.7 per cent), Central Government autonomous institutions (59.1 per cent) and State Government autonomous institutions (54 per cent) opined the existing ICT facilities are not underutilized. But users of majority (51.7 per cent) of State Government institutions indicated that ICT facilities are underutilized.

Table 2.4.85 Users' Opinion About the Existing ICT Facilities

Organisation type	*ICT Facilities Are Underutilized?*		
	Yes	*No*	*Total*
Central Government	105(44.3 %)	132(55.7 %)	237(100 %)
Central Government Autonomous	183(40.9 %)	264(59.1 %)	447(100 %)
State Government	15(51.7 %)	14(48.3 %)	29(100 %)
State Government Autonomous	81(46 %)	95(54 %)	176(100 %)
Total	384(43.2 %)	505(56.8 %)	889(100 %)

Chi-square value = 2.479ns

Whether there is any dependency in the opinion of users on the organisation about the existing ICT facilities in libraries is tested using Chi-Square. The calculated value of chi-square was found to be significant at 5 per cent level indicating that there is no dependency. It implies that the percentage of users opinion about the existing ICT facilities in libraries in different type of organisation is almost same.

It is revealed that majority of the library users indicated that the ICT facilities are not underutilized, but a good number of them stated that it is underutilized. Majority of the library users of Central Government institutions, Central Government autonomous institutions and State Government autonomous institutions have expressed that the existing ICT facilities are not underutilized. However, library users of majority of State Government institutions indicated that ICT facilities are underutilized. Chi-square shows that the percentage of users opinion about the existing ICT facilities in libraries in different organisations is almost same.

Users' Opinion about the Adequacy of Existing ICT Facilities in Special Libraries under study

Table 2.4.86 shows the distribution of users according to their opinion about the adequacy of existing ICT facilities in their libraries. The analysis shows that majority (51.3 per cent) of them indicated that the existing ICT facilities in their libraries are inadequate.

Table 2.4. 86 Users' Opinion About the Adequacy of Existing ICT Facilities

Organisation type	*ICT Facilities Are Inadequate?*		
	Yes	*No*	*Total*
Central Government	182(76.8 %)	55(23.2 %)	237(100 %)
Central Government Autonomous	178(39.8 %)	269(60.2 %)	447(100 %)
State Government	6(20.7 %)	23(79.3 %)	29(100 %)
State Government Autonomous	90(51.1 %)	86(48.9 %)	176(100 %)
Total	456(51.3 %)	433(48.7 %)	889(100 %)

Chi-square value = 96.106**

Users' opinion about the adequacy of existing ICT facilities in libraries was tested using Chi square. The computed value of Chi-Square at 1 per cent level was significant. It means that adequacy of existing ICT facilities in libraries depends on the type of organisation. The 76.8 per cent of the library users of Central Government organisations have the opinion that the existing ICT facilities in their libraries are inadequate. 79.3 per cent of the library users of State Government institutions and 60.2 per cent of the users from the Central Government autonomous institutions have the opinion that the existing ICT facilities are not inadequate.

The majority of the library users of Central Government institutions (76.8 per cent) and State Government autonomous institutions (51.1 per cent) indicated that the existing ICT facilities are inadequate, however majority of the library users of Central Government autonomous institutions (·60.2 per cent) and State Government institutions (79.3 per cent) indicated that existing ICT facilities in their libraries are adequate.

It is revealed that majority of the library users indicated that the existing ICT facilities in their libraries are inadequate. Majority of the library users of Central Government institutions and State Government autonomous institutions indicated the existing ICT facilities are inadequate, however majority of the library users of Central Government autonomous institutions and State Government institutions indicated that existing ICT facilities in their libraries are adequate. The Chi-Square test shows that adequacy of existing ICT facilities in libraries depends on the type of organisation.

Users' Opinion about the Significant Change in Speed in Academic/Research Work by Using ICT

Table 2.4.87 shows the distribution of users according to their opinion about the significant change in speed in academic/research work by using the ICT in Special Libraries under study. The analysis shows that majority (54.3 per cent) of the users indicated that ICT is highly significant and a good number (43.4 per cent) of users indicated it is significant. A very few (2.2 per cent) users indicated it is not significant.

Table 2.4.87 Users' Opinion about the Significant Change in Speed in Academic / Research Work by Using ICT

Organisation type	*Highly Significant*	*Significant*	*Not Significant*	*Total*
Central Government	86(36.3 %)	147(62 %)	4(1.7 %)	237(100 %)
Central Government Autonomous	265(59.3 %)	180(40.3 %)	2(0.4 %)	447(100 %)
State Government	17(58.6 %)	8(27.6 %)	4(13.8 %)	29(100 %)
State Government Autonomous	115(65.3 %)	51(29 %)	10(5.7 %)	176(100 %)
Total	483(54.3 %)	386(43.4 %)	20(2.2 %)	889(100 %)

Chi-Square value = 83.471**

The calculated value of Chi Square was significant at 5 per cent level. This points to the result that opinion about the significant change in speed in academic/research work by using ICT in libraries depends on the type of organisation. 65.3 per cent of the library users of the State Government autonomous institutions indicated that ICT is highly significant in their academic/research work. A few (13.8 per cent) library users of the State government institutions indicated that ICT is not significant in their academic/research work.

The majority of the library users of Central Government autonomous institutions (59.3 per cent), State Government institutions (58.6 per cent) and State Government autonomous institutions (65.3 per cent) are indicated that ICT is highly significant in their academic/research work. Majority (62 per cent) of the library users of Central Government institutions, and a good number (40.3 per cent) of the users of Central Government autonomous institutions indicated that ICT is significant.

It is found that majority of the users indicated that ICT is highly significant in their academic/research work and a good number of users indicated it is significant. It is found that majority of the library users of Central Government autonomous institutions, State Government institutions and State Government autonomous institutions have indicated that ICT is highly significant in their academic/research work. Majority of the library users of Central Government institutions, and a good number of the users of Central Government autonomous institutions indicated that ICT is significant. The Chi Square test shows that opinion about the significant change in speed in academic/research work by using ICT in libraries depends on the type of organisation.

Users' Satisfaction with the Application of Information and Communication Technologies in Special Libraries under study

Users were asked to indicate what extent they were satisfied with the application of Information and Communication Technologies in their libraries. They were provided four options to indicate their responses. Table 2.4.88 shows the distribution of users according to their satisfaction with the application of ICT in their libraries.

Table 2.4.88 Users' Satisfaction with the Application of I C T

Type of Organisation	*Very Satisfied*	*Satisfied*	*Slightly Satisfied*	*Not Satisfied*
Central Government	5(2.1 %)	23(9.7 %)	32(13.5 %)	177(74.7 %)
Central Government Autonomous	76(17 %)	152(34 %)	72(16.1 %)	147(32.9 %)
State Government	5(17.2 %)	12(41.4 %)	-	12(41.4 %)
State Government Autonomous	25(14.2 %)	28(15.9 %)	35(19.9 %)	88(50 %)
Total	111(12.5 %)	215(24.2 %)	139(15.6 %)	424(47.7 %)

Chi-square value = 140.089**

The analysis shows that a good number (47.7 per cent) of the users are not satisfied with the present application of ICT in their libraries. About 24.2 per cent of them are satisfied and a few (15.6 per cent) are slightly satisfied.

Here the hypothesis tested was that the user's satisfaction with the application of ICT is independent on the type of organisation. The Chi Square value computed (140.089) was found to be highly significant. Hence, reject the hypothesis and conclude that Users' satisfaction with the application of ICT depends on the type of organisation.

The large majority (74.7 per cent) of the library users of Central Government institutions and 50 per cent users of State Government autonomous institutions are not satisfied with the application of ICT in their libraries. A good number (41.4 per cent) of the library users of State Government institutions indicated that they are satisfied with the application of ICT in their libraries, but the same percentage of users indicated they are not satisfied.

It is found that a good number of the users are not satisfied with the present application of ICT in their libraries. A few users are just satisfied and a very few are slightly satisfied. Majority of the library users of Central Government institutions and 50 per cent of the users of State Government autonomous institutions are not satisfied with the application of ICT in their libraries. A good number of the users of State Government institutions indicated that they are satisfied with the application of ICT in their libraries, but the same percentage of users indicated they are not satisfied. The Chi Square test shows that users' satisfaction with the application of ICT depends on the type of organization.

Reasons for Users' Dissatisfaction with the Application of ICT in Special Libraries under study

The questionnaire survey listed seven possible reasons to users to indicate their dissatisfaction and also provided an "other" category with the opportunity for users to write additional reasons, if they are indicated that they are not satisfied with the application of ICT in their libraries. Table 2.4.89 lists the various reasons and the percentage of library users in each type of organisation. Users were asked to indicate all the reasons they considered relevant. A good number (42.4 per cent) of them indicated 'inadequate ICT infrastructure' as their reason for dissatisfaction. Other reasons are 'users are not trained for ICT based information services' (35.1 per cent), 'Inadequately trained library professionals in ICT application' (20.2 per cent), 'Limited computer literacy among library users' (17.5 per cent), 'Inadequate publicity for the ICT based resources and services' (15.6 per cent), 'Rigid ICT use policies implemented by the library' (6.3 per cent) and 'Discouraging attitude of library' (4.9 per cent). Majority of the library users of Central Government institutions indicated 'inadequate ICT infrastructure' (67.9 per cent) and 'Users are not trained for ICT based information services' (66.7 per cent) as their reasons for dissatisfaction. A good number (41.4 per cent) of the library users of State Government institutions indicated 'Inadequate ICT infrastructure' and 'inadequately trained library professionals in ICT application' as their reasons for dissatisfaction. Library users of the State Government autonomous institutions indicated 'Inadequate ICT infrastructure '(42.6 per cent) and 'Users are not trained for ICT based information services' (30.1 per cent) and 'Inadequately trained library professionals in ICT application' (26.7 per cent) as their main reasons for dissatisfaction. A few library users of the Central Government autonomous institutions indicated 'Inadequate ICT infrastructure' (28.9 per cent) and 'Users are not trained for ICT based information services '(20.8 per cent) as their reasons for dissatisfaction.

Table 2.4.89 Reasons for Users' Dissatisfaction with the Application of Information and Communication Technologies

Reason for Dissatisfaction	*Central Government*	*Central Government Autonomous*	*State Government*	*State Government Autonomous*	*Grand Total*
Inadequate ICT infrastructure	161 (67. 9 %)	129 (28.9 %)	12 (41.4 %)	75 (42.6 %)	377 (42.4 %)
Limited computer literacy among library users	101 (42.6 %)	20 (4.5 %)	8 (27.6 %)	27 (15.4 %)	156 (17.5 %)
Users are not trained for ICT based information services	158 (66.7 %)	93 (20.8 %)	8 (27.6 %)	53 (30.1 %)	312 (35.1 %)
Inadequately trained library professionals in ICT application	89 (37.6 %)	32 (7.2 %)	12 (41.4 %)	47 (26.7 %)	180 (20.2 %)
Inadequate publicity for the	60 (25.3 %)	52 (11.6 %)	-	27 (15.3 %)	139 (15.6 %)

Reason for Dissatisfaction	*Central Government*	*Central Government Autonomous*	*State Government*	*State Government Autonomous*	*Grand Total*
ICT based resources and services					
Rigid ICT use policies implemented by the library	6 (2.5 %)	20 (4.5 %)	-	30 (17 %)	56 (6.3 %)
Discouraging attitude of library professionals towards their users	4 (1.7 %)	19 (4.3 %)	-	21 (11.9 %)	44 (4.9 %)

It is found that a good number of the users indicated 'inadequate ICT infrastructure' as their reason for dissatisfaction. Other reasons are 'Users are not trained for ICT based information services', 'Inadequately trained library professionals in ICT application', 'Limited computer literacy among library user's, 'Inadequate publicity for the ICT based resources and services', 'Rigid ICT use policies implemented by the library' and 'Discouraging attitude of library professionals towards their users'. Majority of the library users of Central Government institutions indicated 'inadequate ICT infrastructure' and 'Users are not trained for ICT based information services' as their reasons for dissatisfaction. A good number of the library users of State Government institutions indicated 'Inadequate ICT infrastructure' and 'inadequately trained library professionals in ICT application' as their reasons for dissatisfaction. Library users of State Government autonomous institutions indicated 'Inadequate

ICT infrastructure' and 'Users are not trained for ICT based information service's and 'Inadequately trained library professionals in ICT application' as their main reasons for dissatisfaction. A few library users of the Central Government autonomous institutions indicated 'Inadequate ICT infrastructure' and 'Users are not trained for ICT based information services' as their reasons for dissatisfaction.

User Education in ICT Based Library Resources and Services

Few questions were asked to find out whether user education in ICT is available in Special Libraries under study, if present how much users are satisfied, any need for a workshop or orientation program, etc.

Users Opinion about their Skill and Expertise to Use ICT based Library Resources and Services

Users were asked to indicate whether their skill and expertise are inadequate to use ICT based resources and services in their libraries. Table 2.4.90 shows the distribution of users according to opinion about their skill and expertise to use ICT based library resources and services.

Table 2.4.90 Users Opinion about their Skill and Expertise to Use ICT based Library Resources and Services

Type of Organisation	*Skill and Expertise are Inadequate to Use ICT based Resources and Services?*		
	Yes	*No*	*Total*
Central Government	177(74.7 %)	60(25.3 %)	237(100 %)
Central Government Autonomous	175(39.1 %)	272(60.9 %)	447(100 %)
State Government	12(41.4 %)	17(58.6 %)	29(100 %)
State Government Autonomous	48(27.3 %)	128(72.7 %)	176(100 %)
Total	412(46.3 %)	477(53.7 %)	889(100 %)

The analysis shows that majority (53.7 per cent) of the users indicated that their skill and expertise are not inadequate to use ICT based library resources and services. Majority of the library users of Central Government autonomous institutions (60.9 per cent), State Government institutions (58.6 per cent) and State Government autonomous institutions (72.7 per cent) indicated that their skill and expertise are not inadequate to use ICT based resources and services. However, majority (74.7 per cent) of the library users of Central Government institutions indicated that their skill and expertise are inadequate to use ICT based resources and services.

It is found that majority of the users indicated that their skill and expertise are not inadequate to use ICT based library resources and services. Majority of the library users of Central Government autonomous institutions, State Government institutions and State Government autonomous institutions indicated that their skill and expertise are not inadequate to use ICT based resources and services. However, majority of the library users of Central Government institutions indicated that their skill and expertise are inadequate to use ICT based resources and services.

USERS SUGGESTIONS FOR TRAINING

A total of 95 suggestions were given by the users in response to the open-ended question seeking suggestions about the areas in which they want training. For the purpose of data analysis, the suggestions and comments were grouped into five categories: database searching, Internet based information resources and services, information retrieval and dissemination, advanced searching and search query formulation and digital library. Table 2.4.91 gives the categories of suggestions. Of the 95 suggestions, 37 (39 per cent) were related to database searching. Users wanted training in database searching and data mining including CD-ROM, full text, online and multimedia databases. 24 suggestions (25 per cent) were related to Internet based information resources and services. Users wanted training in

Internet based information resources and services including Internet tools/resources/utilities, etc. 17 users pointed out the need for training in information retrieval and dissemination in general. Nine users wanted training in advanced searching and search query formulation. Eight users expressed the need for training in data mining from digital libraries.

Table 2.4.91 Users Suggestions with regard to Areas of Training

	Key Category of Suggestions	*No.*
1	Database searching (CD-ROM and Full text databases)	37
2	Internet based information resources and services	24
3	Information Retrieval and dissemination	17
4	Advanced searching and search query formulation	9
5	Data mining from digital library	8
	Total	95

It is found that a very few users responded to this open-ended question. They wanted training in database searching, Internet based information resources and services, information retrieval and dissemination, advanced searching and search query formulation and data mining from digital library.

User Education in Internet Services / Tools / Utilities in Special Libraries under study

Users were asked whether they get training / orientation in Internet services / tools / utilities. Table 2.4.92 shows the distribution of users according to training they get in Internet services/tools/utilities. The analysis shows that majority (79.1 per cent) of the users indicated that they are not getting any training/orientation in Internet services/tool/ utilities. A large majority (91.6 per cent) of the library users of Central Government institutions and majority of Central Government autonomous institutions (77.6 per cent), State Government institutions (55.2 per cent) and State Government autonomous institutions (69.9 per cent) indicated that they are not getting any training/orientation in Internet services/tools/utilities.

Table 2.4.92 User Education in Internet Services / Tools / Utilities

Type of Organisation	*User Education in Internet Services / Tools / Utilities*		
	Yes	*No*	*Total*
Central Government	20(8.4 %)	217(91.6 %)	237(100 %)
Central Government Autonomous	100(22.4 %)	347(77.6 %)	447(100 %)
State Government	13(44.8 %)	16(55.2 %)	29(100 %)
State Government Autonomous	53(30.1 %)	123(69.9 %)	176(100 %)
Total	186(20.9 %)	703(79.1 %)	889(100 %)

It is found that majority of the users indicated that they are not getting any training/orientation in Internet services/tool/utilities. A large majority of the library users of Central Government institutions and majority of the Central Government autonomous institutions, State Government institutions and State Government autonomous institutions indicated that they are not getting any training/orientation in Internet services/tools/utilities.

Users Opinion about the User Education in ICT :

To ascertain the level of user education/orientation, users were asked as to whether they felt "adequate", "more than adequate", or "inadequate". Table 2.4.93 shows the distribution of users according to their opinion about the user education/orientation in ICT. The analysis shows that majority (77.3 per cent) of the users indicated that the user education/orientation in ICT is inadequate and a few (17.7 per cent) users are indicated that the user education/orientation in ICT is adequate. Only 14 (1.6 per cent) users indicated that the user education/orientation in ICT is more than adequate.

Table 2.4.93 Users Opinion about User Education in ICT

Type of Organisation	*User Education in ICT*		
	Adequate	*More than Adequate*	*Inadequate*
Central Government	21(8.9 %)	1(0.4 %)	215(90.7 %)
Central Government Autonomous	104(23.3 %)	5(1.1 %)	309(69.1 %)
State Government	5(17.2 %)	6(20.7 %)	18(62.1 %)
State Government Autonomous	27(15.3 %)	2(1.1 %)	145(82.4 %)
Total	157(17.7 %)	14(1.6 %)	687(77.3 %)

Chi-square value = 123.425**

Whether the opinion about the user education is independent on the type of organisation is tested using Chi-Square test. The computed value was found to be significant indicating that opinion about user education depends on the type of organisation.

The large majority (90.7 per cent) of the library users of Central Government institutions and majority of the Central Government autonomous institutions (69.1 per cent), State Government institutions (62.1 per cent) and State Government autonomous institutions (82.4 per cent) indicated that the user education/orientation in ICT is inadequate. A few (23.3 per cent) users of the Central Government autonomous institutions indicated that the user education/orientation in ICT is adequate.

It is observed that majority of the users indicated that the user education/orientation in ICT is inadequate and a few are indicated user education/orientation is adequate. Only 14 users indicated that the user education/orientation is more than adequate. Large majority of the library users of

Central Government institutions and majority of Central Government autonomous institutions, State Government institutions and State Government autonomous institutions indicated that the user education/orientation in ICT is inadequate. The Chi Square test indicates that opinion about user education/orientation depends on the type of organisation.

Users Opinion About the Need for a Workshop / Orientation Program in ICT Based Library Resources and Services in Special Libraries under study:

In order to ascertain users' perception on the need for a workshop/orientation program, the users were asked whether they 'agree' or 'disagree' or were 'not sure' that there was a need for a workshop/orientation program on ICT based library resources and services. Table 2.4.94 shows the distribution of users according to their opinion about the need for a workshop/orientation program in ICT based library resources and services. The analysis shows that large majority (88.1 per cent) of the users agree that there is a need for a workshop/orientation program and a few (10.3 per cent) users are not sure.

Table 2.4.94 Users Opinion About the Need for a Workshop / Orientation Program in ICT Based Library Resources and Services

Type of Organisation	*Workshop/Orientation Program in ICT Based Library Resources and Services is required?*		
	Agree	*Disagree*	*Not Sure*
Central Government	216(91.1 %)	-	21(8.9 %)
Central Government Autonomous	380(85 %)	14(3.1 %)	53(11.9 %)
State Government	18(62.1 %)	-	11(37.9 %)
State Government Autonomous	169(96 %)	-	7(4 %)
Total	783(88.1 %)	14(1.6 %)	92(10.3 %)

Users' responses indicate that they are not getting proper education/orientation in ICT based information resources and services. It is very essential to provide user education / orientation / awareness to users in ICT based information resources and services. Lack of user education / orientation will lead to the underutilization of resources and services.

The most of the library users of State Government autonomous institutions (96 per cent), and Central Government institutions (91.1 per cent) and majority of the Central Government autonomous institutions (85 per cent) and State Government institutions (62.1 per cent) agree that there is a need for a workshop/orientation program in ICT based library resources and services. About 37.9 per cent of the library users of State Government institutions are preferred the option 'not sure'.

It is found that large majority of the users agree that there is a need for a workshop/orientation program in ICT based library resources and services. Most of the library users of State Government autonomous institutions, and Central Government institutions and majority of the Central Government autonomous institutions and State Government institutions agree that there is a need for a workshop/ orientation program in ICT based library resources and services.

USERS' ATTITUDE TOWARDS ICT APPLICATION

Attitude of users towards ICT based information resources and services are an important factor in the application of ICT in libraries. Usually libraries are introducing and implementing new services and resources according to the needs and demands of their clientele. Users with more demanding information needs and positive attitude towards ICT based information resources will help the libraries to introduce ICT based information resources and services. It is very relevant to assess the attitude of library users towards the ICT application in their libraries. Users were asked to indicate their attitude and responses were obtained and the same was analysed according to institutions wise.

Users' Attitude Towards ICT Application in Libraries of Central Government Institutions

In this section the attitude of the library users of Central Government institutions are analysed. The attitudes were formed into 9 variables and are stated in Table 2.4.95.

Table 2.4.95 Attitude Towards ICT Application by the Library Users of Central Government Institutions

Sl.No.	*Variable Description*	*Variable Code*	*Agree*	*Disagree*
1	ICT applications are to improve the quality of the library services	ATQUAL	237	0
2	ICT application improve the efficiency of the library	ATEFFI	237	0
3	ICT application enhance the knowledge and expertise	ATKNOW	232	5
4	ICT application makes an integration within the Organisation	ATINTE	211	26
5	ICT application are essential to improve the communication facilities	ATCOMM	220	17
6	ICT application improves the status of the library	ATSTAT	225	12
7	ICT use often disturb the routine work of the library	ATROUT	14	223
8	ICT takes over the traditional way of information handling in the library	ATTRAD	133	104
9	ICT application will spoil the image of the library	ATSPOIL	11	226

HIERARCHICALCLUSTERANALYSIS

Dendrogram using Average Linkage (Between Groups)

```
CASE       0      5     10     15     20     25
Label  Num +------+------+------+------+------+

ATQUAL     1 □□
ATEFFI   2 □□□□
ATKNOW     3 □□ □□□□□
ATSTATUS  6 □□□□ □□□
ATINTE    4 □□□□□□□□ □□□□□□□□□□□□□□□□□□□□
ATCOMM     5 □□□□□□□□□□        □□□□□□□□□□□□□□□□□□□□□□□□
ATTRAD    8 □□□□□□□□□□□□□□□□□□□□□□□□□□□□□         □
ATDISTUR  7 □□□□□□□□□□□□□□□□□□□□□□□□□□□□□□□□□□□□□□□□□□□□□□□□□□□□□□□
ATSPOIL   9 □□□□
```

Figure 2.4.3. Dendrogram- Users' Attitude Towards ICT Application in Libraries of Central Government Institutions

As seen in Figure 2.4.3the dendrogram shows that at 20 per cent distance level, three interpretable clusters have been formed. The first cluster consists of six variables, the second cluster consists of two variables and third cluster consists of one variable. The clusters formed are given in the Table 2.4.96.

Table 2.4.96 Clusters Formed

Cluster 1	*Cluster 2*	*Cluster 3*
1	7	8
2	9	
3		
4		
5		
6		

The first cluster is named as 'ICT Application Improves the Quality, Efficiency, Facilities and Status of the Library Resources and Services'. It is presented in Table 2.4.97.

Table 2.4.97 Cluster 1: ICT Application Improves the Quality, Efficiency, Facilities and Status of the Library Resources and Services

Sl.No.	*Variable Description*	*Variable Code*	*Agree*	*Disagree*
1	ICT applications are to improve the quality of the library services	ATQUAL	237	0
2	ICT application improve the efficiency of the library	ATEFFI	237	0
3	ICT application enhance the knowledge and expertise	ATKNOW	232	5
4	ICT application makes an integration within the Organisation	ATINTE	211	26
5	ICT application are essential to improve the communication facilities	ATCOMM	220	17
6	ICT application improves the status of the library	ATSTAT	225	12
	Total		**1362**	**60**

Agreement Ratio = $\overline{A}$ = 1362/237 = 5.75

Disagreement Ratio = 60/237 = 0.25

Cluster Centre : (5.75 : 0.25)

Agreement and Disagreement Ratio (23:1)

About six variables have been grouped for this cluster. The agreement and disagreement ratio is 23:1. This shows that library users have overwhelming positive attitude towards the application of ICT in their libraries. Most of them have the attitude that ICT application would improve the quality, efficiency, and status of the library services and resources. It would improve the facilities of the library and enhance the knowledge and expertise of library professionals and make integration with the organisation.

The second cluster is named as 'ICT Application Creates Problems to the Resources and Services of the Library' and it is given in the Table 2.4.98.

Table 2.4.98 Cluster 2: ICT Application Creates Problems to the Resources and Services of the Library

Sl.No.	Variable Description	Variable Code	Agree	Disagree
7	ICT use often disturb the routine work of the library	ATROUT	14	223
9	ICT application will spoil the image of the library	ATSPOIL	11	226
	Total		**25**	**449**

Agreement Ratio = $\overline{A}$ = 25/237 = 0.11
Disagreement = 449/237 = 1.89
Cluster Centre : (0.11 : 1.89)
Agreement and Disagreement Ratio (1:17)

Two variables have been grouped for this cluster. The agreement and disagreement ratio is 1:17. The analysis shows that library users have the attitude that ICT applications never create any problems to the resources and services of the library.

The third cluster is named as 'ICT Takes Away the Traditional Way of Information Handling in the Library' and is given in Table 2.4.99.

Table 2.4.99 Cluster 3: ICT Takes Away the Traditional Way of Information Handling in the Library

Sl.No.	Variable Description	Variable Code	Agree	Disagree
8	ICT takes over the traditional way of information handling in the library	ATTRAD	133	104

Agreement Ratio = $\overline{A}$ = 133/237 = 0.56
Disagreement Ratio = 104/237 = 0.44
Cluster Centre : (0.56 : 0.44)
Agreement and Disagreement Ratio (13:10)

This cluster is formed by only one variable. The

agreement and disagreement ratio is 13:10. The analysis gives a mixed response, but a slight majority of users agree that ICT takes away the traditional way of information handling in the library.

The library users have overwhelming positive attitude towards the application of ICT in their libraries. Most of them have the attitude that ICT application would improve the quality, efficiency, and status of the library resources and services. They indicated that ICT would improve the facilities of the library and enhance the knowledge and expertise of library professionals and make integration with the organisation. It is also observed that they have the attitude that ICT application never creates any problems to the resources and services of the library. A slight majority of them agree that ICT takes away the traditional way of information handling in the library.

Users' Attitude Towards ICT Application in Libraries of Central Government Autonomous Institutions

In this section the attitude of the library users of Central Government autonomous institutions are analysed. The attitudes were formed into 9 variables and are stated in Table 2.4.100.

Table 2.4.100 Attitude Towards ICT Application by the Library Users of Central Government Autonomous Institutions

Sl.No.	*Variable Description*	*Variable Code*	*Agree*	*Disagree*
1	ICT applications are to improve the quality of the library services	ATQUAL	444	3
2	ICT application improve the efficiency of the library	ATEFFI	428	19
3	ICT application enhance the knowledge and expertise	ATKNOW	415	32
4	ICT application makes an integration within the Organisation	ATINTE	358	89
5	ICT application are essential to improve the communication facilities	ATCOMM	393	54

Sl.No.	*Variable Description*	*Variable Code*	*Agree*	*Disagree*
6	ICT application improves the status of the library	ATSTAT	402	45
7	ICT use often disturb the routine work of the library	ATROUT	42	405
8	ICT takes over the traditional way of information handling in the library	ATTRAD	219	228
9	ICT application will spoil the image of the library	ATSPOIL	33	414

HIERARCHICALCLUSTERANALYSIS

Dendrogram using Average Linkage (Between Groups)

Rescaled Distance Cluster Combine

```
CASE        0    5    10   15   20   25
Label    Num +----+----+----+----+----+

ATQUAL     1 □□□□□□
ATEFFI     2 □□ □□□
ATKNOW     3 □□□□□□ □□□
ATSTATUS   6 □□□□□□□□ □□□□□
ATCOMM     5 □□□□□□□□□□ □□□□□□□□□□□□□□□□□□□□□□□□□□□□□□□□□□□
ATINTE     4 □□□□□□□□□□□□□□                      □
ATDISTUR   7 □□□□□□□□□□□□□□□□□□□□□□□□□□□□□□□           □
ATSPOIL    9 □□□□            □□□□□□□□□□□□□□□□□□□□□
ATTRAD     8 □□□□□□□□□□□□□□□□□□□□□□□□□□□□□□
```

Figure 2.4.4 Dendrogram- Users' Attitude Towards ICT Application in Libraries of Central Government Autonomous Institutions

As seen in Figure 2.4.4 the dendrogram shows that at 25 per cent distance level, three interpretable clusters have been formed. The first cluster consists of six variables, the second cluster consists of two variables and third cluster consists of one variable. The clusters formed are given in Table 2.4.101

Table 2.4.101 Clusters Formed

Cluster 1	*Cluster 2*	*Cluster 3*
1	7	8
2	9	
3		
4		
5		
6		

Table 2.4.102 gives the first cluster and it is named as 'ICT Application Improves the Quality, Efficiency, Facilities and Status of the Library Resources and Services'.

Table 2.4.102 Cluster 1: ICT Application Improves the Quality, Efficiency, Facilities and Status of the Library Resources and Services

Sl.No.	*Variable description*	*Variable Code*	*Agree*	*Disagree*
1	ICT applications are to improve the quality of the library services	ATQUAL	444	3
2	ICT application improve the efficiency of the library	ATEFFI	428	19
3	ICT application enhance the knowledge and expertise	ATKNOW	415	32
4	ICT application makes an integration within the Organisation	ATINTE	358	89
5	ICT application are essential to improve the communication facilities	ATCOMM	393	54
6	ICT application improves the status of the library	ATSTAT	402	45
	Total		**2440**	**242**

Agreement Ratio = $\overline{A}$ = 2440/447 = 5.5

Disagreement Ratio = 242/447 = 0.5

Cluster Centre : (5.5 : 0.5)

Agreement and Disagreement Ratio (11:1)

About six variables have been grouped for this cluster. The agreement and disagreement ratio is 11:1. This shows that library users have overwhelming positive attitude towards the application of ICT in their libraries. Most of them have the attitude that ICT application will improve the quality, efficiency, and status of the library resources and services. It will improve the facilities of the library and enhance the knowledge and expertise of library professionals and make integration with the organisation.

The second cluster is named as 'ICT Application Creates Problems to the Resources and Services of the Library' and is given in Table 2.4.103.

Table 2.4.103 Cluster 2: ICT Application Creates Problems to the Resources and Services of the Library

Sl.No.	Variable Description	Variable Code	Agree	Disagree
7	ICT use often disturb the routine work of the library	ATROUT	42	405
9	ICT application will spoil the image of the library	ATSPOIL	33	414
	Total		75	819

Agreement Ratio = $\overline{A}$ = 75/447 = 0.2

Disagreement ratio = 819/447 = 1.8

Cluster Centre : (0.2 : 1.8)

Agreement and Disagreement Ratio (1:9)

Two variables have been grouped for this cluster. The agreement and disagreement ratio is 1:9. The analysis shows that the library users have the attitude that ICT application never creates any problems to the services and resources of the library.

The third cluster is given in Table 2.4.104. It is named as 'ICT Takes Away the Traditional Way of Information Handling in the Library'.

Table 2.4.104 Cluster 3: ICT Takes away the Traditional Way of Information Handling in the Library

Sl.No.	Variable Description	Variable Code	Agree	Disagree
1	ICT takes over the traditional way of information handling in the library	ATTRAD	219	228

Agreement Ratio = $\overline{A}$ = 219/447 = 0.48

Disagreement : 228/447 = 0.51

Cluster Centre : (0.48 : 0.51)

Agreement and Disagreement Ratio (1:1)

This cluster is formed by only one variable. The agreement and disagreement ratio is 1:1. The analysis gives a mixed response, about half of the library users agree that ICT takes away the traditional way of information handling in the library.

It is found that the attitude of the library users of Central Government Autonomous institutions are almost same as the attitude of the users of Central Government institutions. They have overwhelming positive attitude towards the application of ICT in their libraries. Most of them have the attitude that ICT application would improve the quality, efficiency, and status of the library services and resources. They indicated that ICT would improve the facilities of the library and enhance the knowledge and expertise of library professionals and make integration with the organisation. It is also observed that they have the attitude that ICT application never creates any problems to the services and resources of the library. About half of them agree that ICT takes away the traditional way of information handling in the library.

Table 2.4.105 Attitude Towards ICT Application by the Library Users of State Government Institutions

Sl.No.	Variable Description	Variable Code	Agree	Disagree
1	ICT applications are to improve the quality of the library services	ATQUAL	29	0
2	ICT application improve the efficiency of the library	ATEFFI	29	0
3	ICT application enhance the knowledge and expertise	ATKNOW	23	6
4	ICT application makes an integration within the Organisation	ATINTE	15	14
5	ICT application are essential to improve the communication facilities	ATCOMM	23	6
6	ICT application improves the status of the library	ATSTAT	29	0
7	ICT use often disturb the routine work of the library	ATROUT	0	29
8	ICT takes over the traditional way of information handling in the library	ATTRAD	8	21
9	ICT application will spoil the image of the library	ATSPOIL	0	29

Users' Attitude Towards ICT Application in Libraries of State Government Institutions

In this section the attitude of the library users of State Government institutions are analysed. The attitudes were formed into 9 variables and are stated in Table 2.4.105.

HIERARCHICALCLUSTERANALYSIS

Dendrogram using Average Linkage (Between Groups)

Rescaled Distance Cluster Combine

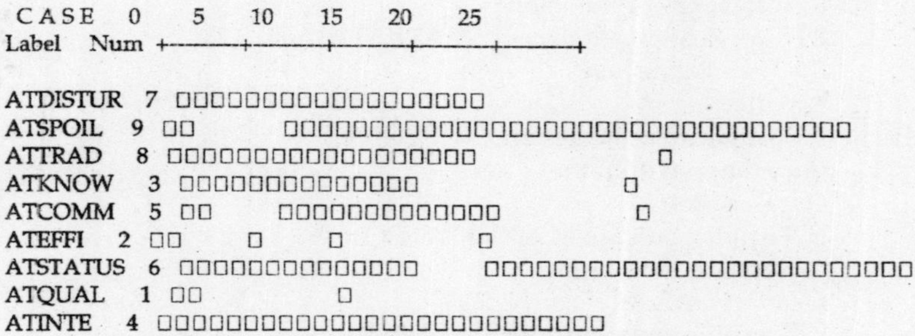

Figure 2.4.5 Dendrogram- Users' Attitude Towards ICT Application in Libraries of State Government Institutions

As in Figure 2.4.5 the dendrogram shows that at 55 per cent distance level, two interpretable clusters have been formed. The first cluster consists of six variables and the second cluster consists of three variables. The clusters formed are given in Table 2.4.106.

Table 2.4.106 Clusters Formed

Cluster 1	*Cluster 2*
1	7
2	8
3	9
4	
5	
6	

Table 2.4.107 shows the first cluster and it is named as 'ICT Application Improves the Quality, Efficiency, Facilities and Status of the Library Resources and Services'.

Table 2.4.107 Cluster 1: ICT Application Improves the Quality, Efficiency, Facilities and Status of the Library Resources and Services

Sl.No.	*Variable Description*	*Variable Code*	*Agree*	*Disagree*
1	ICT applications are to improve the quality of the library services	ATQUAL	29	0
2	ICT application improve the efficiency of the library	ATEFFI	29	0
3	ICT application enhance the knowledge and expertise	ATKNOW	23	6
4	ICT application makes an integration within the Organisation	ATINTE	15	14
5	ICT application are essential to improve the communication facilities	ATCOMM	23	6
6	ICT application improves the status of the library	ATSTAT	29	0
	Total		**148**	**26**

Agreement Ratio = $\overline{A}$ = 148/29 = 5.1
Disagreement Ratio = 26/29 = 0.9
Cluster Centre : (5.1 : 0.9)
Agreement and Disagreement (5.6:1)

About six variables have been grouped for this cluster. The agreement and disagreement ratio is 5.6:1. This shows that library users have overwhelming positive attitude towards the application of ICT in their libraries. Most of them have the attitude that ICT application would improve the quality, efficiency, and status of the library services and resources. It would improve the facilities of the library and enhance the knowledge and expertise of library professionals and make integration with the organisation.

The second cluster is named as 'ICT Application Creates Problems to the Resources and Services of the Library' and is given in Table 2.4.108.

Three variables have been grouped for this cluster. The agreement and disagreement ratio is 1:9. The analysis shows

Table 4.108 Cluster 2: ICT Application Creates Problems to the Resources and Services of the Library

Sl.No.	Variable Description	Variable Code	Agree	Disagree
7	ICT use often disturb the routine work of the library	ATROUT	0	29
8	ICT takes over the traditional way of information handling in the library	ATTRAD	8	21
9	ICT application will spoil the image of the library	ATSPOIL	0	29
	Total		8	79

Agreement Ratio = $\overline{A}$ = 8/29 = 0.3
Disagreement Ratio = 79/29 = 2.7
Cluster Centre : (0.3 : 2.7)
Agreement and Disagreement Ratio (1:9)

that the negative aspects hold in the variables are not agreed by the library users of State Government institutions in Kerala. Most of them have the attitude that ICT application never creates any problems to the resources and services of the library.

The cluster analysis revealed that the library users of State Government institutions have overwhelming positive attitude towards the application of ICT in their libraries. Most of them have the attitude that ICT application would improve the quality, efficiency, and status of the library resources and services. They indicated that ICT would improve the facilities of the library and enhance the knowledge and expertise of library professionals and make integration with the organisation. It is also observed that the negative aspects holds in the variables are not agreed by the library users of State Government institutions in Kerala. Most of them have the attitude that ICT application never creates any problems to the resources and services of the library.

Users' Attitude Towards ICT Application in Libraries of State Government Autonomous Institutions

In this section the attitude of the library users of State

Government autonomous institutions are analysed. The details are stated in Table 2.4.109.

Table 2.4.109 Attitude towards ICT Application by the Library Users of State Government Autonomous Institutions

Sl.No.	Variable Description	Variable Code	Agree	Disagree
1	ICT applications are to improve the quality of the library services	ATQUAL	174	2
2	ICT application improve the efficiency of the library	ATEFFI	176	0
3	ICT application enhance the knowledge and expertise	ATKNOW	166	10
4	ICT application makes an integration within the Organisation	ATINTE	138	38
5	ICT application are essential to improve the communication facilities	ATCOMM	161	15
6	ICT application improves the status of the library	ATSTAT	169	7
7	ICT use often disturb the routine work of the library	ATROUT	6	170
8	ICT takes over the traditional way of information handling in the library	ATTRAD	70	106
9	ICT application will spoil the image of the library	ATSPOIL	1	175

HIERARCHICALCLUSTERANALYSIS

Dendrogram using Average Linkage (Between Groups)

Rescaled Distance Cluster Combine

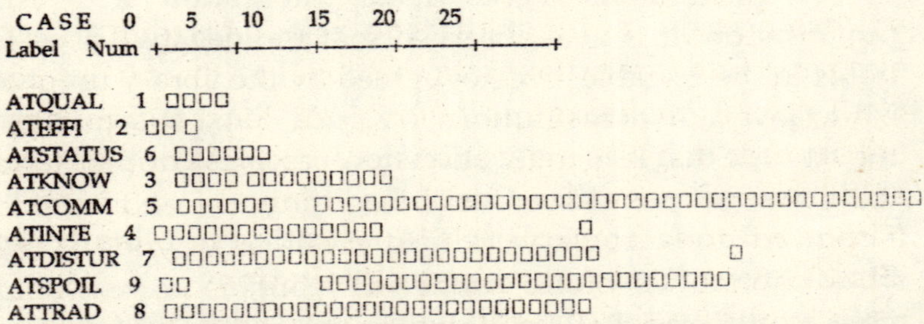

Figure 2.4.6 Dendrogram- Users' Attitude Towards ICT Application in Libraries of State Government Autonomous Institutions

As seen in Figure 2.4.6 the dendrogram shows that at 55 per cent distance level, two interpretable clusters have been formed. The first cluster consists of six variables; and the second cluster consists of three variables. The clusters formed are given in the Table 2.4.110.

Table 2.4.110 Clusters Formed

Cluster 1	*Cluster 2*
1	7
2	8
3	9
4	
5	
6	

The First Cluster is named as 'ICT Application Improves the Quality, Efficiency, Facilities and Status of the Library Resources and Services' and is given in Table 2.4.111.

Table 2.4.111 Cluster 1: ICT Application Improves the Quality, Efficiency, Facilities and Status of the Library Resources and Services

Sl.No.	*Variable Description*	*Variable Code*	*Agree*	*Disagree*
1	ICT applications are to improve the quality of the library services	ATQUAL	174	2
2	ICT application improve the efficiency of the library	ATEFFI	176	0
3	ICT application enhance the knowledge and expertise	ATKNOW	166	10
4	ICT application makes an integration within the Organisation	ATINTE	138	38
5	ICT application are essential to improve the communication facilities	ATCOMM	161	15
6	ICT application improves the status of the library	ATSTAT	169	7
	Total		984	72

Agreement Ratio = $\overline{A}$ = 984/176 = 5.6
Disagree ment Ratio = 72/176 = 0.4
Cluster Centre : (5.6 : 0.4)
Agree ment and Disagreement Ratio (14:1)

About six variables have been grouped for this cluster. The agreement and disagreement ratio is 14: 1. This shows that library users have overwhelming positive attitude towards the application of ICT in their libraries. Most of them have the attitude that ICT application would improve the quality, efficiency, and status of the library resources and services. It would improve the facilities of the library and enhance the knowledge and expertise of library professionals and make integration with the organisation.

The second cluster is presented in Table 2.4.112 and it is named as 'ICT Application Creates Problems to the Resources and Services of the Library'.

Table 2.4.112 Cluster 2: ICT Application Creates Problems to the Resources and Services of the Library

Sl.No.	*Variable Description*	*Variable Code*	*Agree*	*Disagree*
7	ICT use often disturb the routine work of the library	ATROUT	6	170
8	ICT takes over the traditional way of information handling in the library	ATTRAD	70	106
9	ICT application will spoil the image of the library	ATSPOIL	1	175
	Total		77	451

Agreement Ratio = $\overline{A}$ = 77/176 = 0.4
Disagreement Ratio = 451/29 = 2.6
Cluster Centre : (0.4 : 2.6)
Agree ment and Disagree ment Ratio (1: 6.5)

Three variables have been grouped for this cluster. The agreement and disagreement ratio is 1: 6.5. The analysis shows that the negative aspects hold in the variables are not agreed by the library users of State Government autonomous institutions in Kerala. Most of them have the attitude that ICT application never creates any problems to the services and resources of the library.

The library users have overwhelming positive attitude towards the application of ICT in their libraries. Most of them have the attitude that ICT application would improve the quality, efficiency, and status of the library resources and services. They indicated that ICT would improve the facilities of the library and enhance the knowledge and expertise of library professionals and make integration with the organisation. It is also observed that the negative aspects holds in the variables are not agreed by the library users of State Government autonomous institutions in Kerala. Most of them have the attitude that ICT application never creates any problems to the services and resources of the library.

Users' Comments and Suggestions about the Current State-of-the-Art Application of ICT in their Libraries

The numerous comments and suggestions given by the users in response to the open-ended question about the state-of-the-art application of ICT are categorised and analysed. A total of 555 suggestions and comments were received from the users. For the purpose of data analysis, these suggestions and comments were grouped into seven key categories: ICT based resources; ICT infrastructure; Internet; ICT based services; User training; Staff related comments and suggestions and miscellaneous. Table 2.4.113 gives the key categories of comments and suggestions. Of the 555 suggestions and comments, 33.3 per cent were related to ICT based resources. Of these, 40 per cent of the suggestions were to provide electronic/ online journals. 74 users were suggested acquisition of more e-journals. 35 users suggested acquisition of more full text databases. 22 users wanted more bibliographic databases, 13 users expressed the need for digital library and 14 users requested more frequent updating of databases.

Sixty-nine suggestions (14 per cent) were related to ICT infrastructure. 24 users wanted more computer terminals in the library, and 14 users pointed out that the ICT infrastructure is very poor. 8.8 per cent of the suggestions were related to Internet. 28 users wanted high bandwidth. 17 suggestions (3 per cent) were related to ICT based services. Of these, 9 users wanted digitization of documents. Of the 555 suggestions and comments, 25.6 per cent were related to user education/ training. 79 users wanted user education in ICT based library resources and services, 32 users wanted awareness in ICT and 29 users expressed the need for workshop/orientation programme in ICT based resources and services. 76 comments (13.7 per cent) were related to staff and 37 users suggested training for library staff in ICT based resources and services. 32 users commented that ICT knowledge of staff is very poor. Apart from these, seven users stated that the system is not user friendly and one user wanted WebOPAC facility.

It is found that users wanted more electronic resources like e-journals, full text databases, bibliographic databases, more terminals, and high Internet bandwidth. They also expressed the need for training in ICT based resources and services for both library staff and users.

CONCLUSION

The use of ICT based information resources and services in Special Libraries under study are not up to the expected level. Majority of the libraries do not have adequate ICT infrastructure and ICT based information resources. Generally users are not satisfied with the current condition and they want more electronic resources and services. As far as the use of electronic resources is concerned, e-mail is the most widely used resource/tool followed by World Wide Web. Majority of the library users are rated various ICT based library services and resources as poor and opinioned that library professionals' help is inadequate. Majority of them indicated that the ICT facilities in the libraries of different organisations are not underutilised, but the existing ICT facilities are inadequate. They indicated that ICT is highly significant in their academic/research work and Internet is more resourceful than library resources. A good number of the users are not satisfied with the present application of ICT in

Table 4.113 Users' main Comments and Suggestions

	Category	*No*
1	ICT Based Resources	185
	Provide electronic/online journals	74
	Provide more full text databases	35
	Provide more bibliographic databases	22
	Provide more electronic databases	14
	More frequent updating	14
	Digital library facility required	13
	Provide multimedia databases	9
	Provide e-books	4
2	ICT Infrastructure	78
	More terminals to be provided	24
	ICT infrastructure is poor	14
	ICT infrastructure is good	8
	CD-Writer is required	8
	Scanner is required	7
	Improved network facility required	5
	CD-Net Server facility required	4
	Access through intranet	4
	Provide more printers	4
3	Internet	49
	Provide high bandwidth	28
	More online resources to be provided	11
	Internet connection is very slow	8
	24 hour internet facility required	2
4	ICT Based Services	17
	Digitisation of documents	9
	Current contents through web	4
	Remote access to resources	4
5	User Education/Training in ICT	142
	Provide training in ICT based library resources and services	79
	Provide awareness in ICT	32
	Provide workshops/orientation programs	29
	Provide online training	2
6	Staff Related Comments	76
	Provide training in ICT based library resources and services	37
	Poor in ICT	32
	Cooperative and helpful	7
7	Miscellaneous	8
	System is not user friendly	7
	Provide WebOPAC facility	1

their libraries and inadequate ICT infrastructure is the reason for dissatisfaction. Majority of them indicated that their skill and expertise are adequate to use ICT based library resources and services and they are not getting any training in Internet services/tools/utilities. They admitted that the user education/orientation in ICT is inadequate and large majority of the users agreed that there is a need for a workshop/orientation program in ICT based library resources and services. They have overwhelming positive attitude towards the application of ICT in their libraries.

2.5
Summary of the Findings and Suggestions

This chapter provides a summary of the major findings of the research study and suggestions for improving the application of ICT in special libraries in Kerala.

SUMMARY OF THE MAJOR FINDINGS

The application of Information and Communication Technologies in libraries is of continuing interest to the information profession. The present investigation has achieved its aim, in that it has provided a useful summary of the state-of-the-art application of ICT in special libraries in Kerala. The major findings of the study are the following:

GENERAL INFORMATION

1. Libraries of Central Government Autonomous Institutions have gone far ahead in computerization and automation compared to the libraries of other categories of institutions. The total membership of the majority of the libraries is below 200. A few (33.3 per cent) libraries have between 200 and 500 members. There are three libraries with more than 500 members.

2. A good number (31.3 per cent) of the library users are either scientists or persons having similar designation. The other major categories of users are technical officers, technical assistants and research fellows. A good number (48 per cent) of the users are between 20-30 years of age. A few users are between 31-40 and 41-50

years of age and only a very few (9.2 per cent) users are above 50 years of age. Majority (58.3 per cent) of the library users of all the categories of institutions are male.

LIBRARY BUDGET

3. A good number (33.3 per cent) of the special libraries in Kerala have below 10 lakhs of average annual budget. Libraries of Central Government Autonomous institutions have substantial annual budget compared to the libraries of other categories of institutions. Majority of them have above 10 lakhs of average annual budget and three of them have above 50 lakhs of average annual budget. Libraries of RRL and SCTIMST have around 50 lakhs of average annual budget. VSSC library has 2.5 crores of average annual budget.

4. About half of the special libraries in Kerala do not have enough financial resources for their needs. They are struggling to introduce ICT based resource and services. Due to limited budgets, they are not able to provide electronic journals and electronic databases. Only three libraries are participating in consortia based subscription, therefore they are better in providing more full text electronic journals. About 40 per cent of the libraries get financial assistance from their parent institution according to their needs. But most of them are not able to provide more advanced ICT based services and resources like full text electronic journals and databases.

LIBRARY COLLECTIONS

5. Most of the libraries have different types of collections like books, journals, bound volumes of journals, etc. A few (26.7 per cent) of them have subscribed to online journals and full text databases. Majority of them have bibliographic databases and CD-ROM databases.

6. Majority (70 per cent) of the special libraries in Kerala

have below 10000 volumes of books. A few libraries have greater than 10000 volumes of books. Two of them have more than 50000 volumes of books and they are attached to the Central Government autonomous and State Government autonomous institutions.

7. Majority (86 per cent) of the libraries subscribe to less than 100 foreign journals. A few libraries are subscribing to 50-100 foreign journals. Only 3 libraries are subscribing more than 100 foreign journals and they are attached to the Central Government autonomous and State Government autonomous institutions. Majority (80 per cent) of libraries are subscribing below 100 Indian journals. A few of them are subscribing less than 25 Indian journals and four libraries are subscribing more than 100 Indian journals. Majority of libraries are receiving less than 50 gratis journals and a very few libraries are receiving more than 50 gratis journals. Three of them are receiving more than 100 gratis journals.

8. A few (26.7 per cent) libraries are subscribing or receiving online/electronic journals and about half of them are attached to the Central Government autonomous institutions. Only libraries of IIITMK, NIO and RRL are subscribing or getting more than 1000 electronic/online journals.

9. Majority (63.3 per cent) of the institutions have back volumes of journals in their libraries. Libraries of majority of Central Government institutions and Central Government autonomous institutions have back volumes of journals. Four of them have more than 20000 back volumes of journals.

10. About half of the libraries have theses collection and majority of them have less than 100 theses. Majority of Central Government autonomous institutions have thesis collection. A few (26.7 per cent) libraries have dissertations/project reports. Three of them have more

than 100 dissertations/project reports. A good number (43.3 per cent) of special libraries in Kerala have standards. A few of them have less than 1000 standards. Only 2 libraries have more than 5000 standards. About half (53.3 per cent) of the libraries have technical reports in their collection and majority of them have less than 1000 technical reports. Only one library has more than 5000 technical reports.

11. Most (90 per cent) of the special libraries in Kerala have CD-ROM collection and majority of them have less than 100 CD-ROMs. A few of them have 100-500 CD-ROMs and 2 of them have more than 500 CD-ROMs. Majority (66.7 per cent) of libraries have CD-ROM databases, and most of them are attached to the Central Government autonomous institutions. About half of them have less than 5 CD-ROM databases and three libraries have 5-10 CD-ROM databases. Only two libraries have more than 10 CD-ROM databases.

12. About half of the special libraries in Kerala are poor in electronic resources. However, libraries of Central Government autonomous institutions are better in electronic resources. In most of the cases the libraries have their bibliographic databases in electronic form and one or two CD-ROM databases.

LIBRARY PROFESSIONALS

13. Majority (57.1 per cent) of libraries in all the category of institutions the number of library professionals vary from 1-4. Six libraries have more than 9 numbers of professionals and out of which five are attached to the Central Government autonomous institutions.

14. A slight majority (53 per cent) of library professionals in different categories of institutions are Postgraduates and there are three who hold a PhD degree in Library and Information Science. Majority (51 per cent) of them

are above 45 years of age. Libraries of autonomous institutions have comparatively younger workforce.

15. ICT based resources and services of majority of libraries are managed by a single library professional. In most of the cases the library professionals are not trained in ICT based resources and services. The skill and expertise of library professionals of a good number of libraries are inadequate. The main problem of the special libraries in Kerala is lack of qualified library professionals in Information and Communication Technologies. Most of the libraries are getting support from the computer professionals of the institute or libraries depend on them for rectifying any problems in the hardware, software or network.

INFORMATION AND COMMUNICATION TECHNOLOGY INFRASTRUCTURE

16. Majority of the special libraries in Kerala have basic hardware facilities like servers, computers, printers, etc. The libraries of Central Government autonomous institutions have better hardware facilities including scanner, barcode printer, barcode scanner, Net Server, CD-ROM Tower, CD-Writer, etc.
17. The hardware facilities of majority of the libraries are either not properly utilised or are underutilised. Most of the library professionals are not properly aware of the operations of the hardware, so they are underutilised. A good number of them need more computer terminals and devices like printers to provide ICT based resources and services. Seven libraries have very poor hardware.
18. All the libraries have library management software, and majority of them are commercially prepared. CDS/ISIS is the most used library management software and Libsys is the second. Central Government autonomous

institutions are better in the use of library management software as most of them are using good library management software. Seven libraries (23.3 per cent) reported to have developed the library management software in-house. Majority of libraries have Network Operating System, DTP Software and Anti Virus Software, a few of them have digital library software, CD Net Management Software and DBMS/RDBMS. Windows NT is the most (46.7 per cent) used Network Operating System, followed by Linux. The use of DBMS/RDBMS is very less and CDS/ISIS and ORACLE are the two successfully used software. Very few of them are using digital library software and majority of them are using MS Office and Norton Antivirus software.

19. Majority of the libraries are either not successful in using the library management software or the software is not sufficient for complete automation and ICT application in their libraries. About 40 per cent of them have somewhat good software collection, including library management software and other software like MS Office, AntiVirus, etc., but in this case also except a few libraries most of them are not using their software properly, some modules are not at all utilised or library professionals do not know how to use them properly.

COMPUTER APPLICATIONS

20. Library automation in special libraries in Kerala largely commenced during the period 1990-2000. All the libraries of Central government institutions were automated before the year 2000. A good number (46.1 per cent) of libraries of Central Government Autonomous institutions were automated before 1990. All the State Government institutions surveyed were automated after 1990. Majority (57.1 per cent) of State Government autonomous institutions were automated

between 1990 and 2000. Chi-square test also indicates that there is no association between year of automation and type of organisation.

21. Library management software of majority (71.4 per cent) of the libraries are network version and have online help and OPAC facilities.

22. Only a few libraries are using barcode technology for circulation and stock verification of documents. Four libraries (30.8 per cent) of Central Government autonomous institutions are using it for both circulation and stock verification. No library has introduced smart card technology but one Central Government autonomous institution is going to introduce this technology in recent future in the library.

PRESENT STATUS OF LIBRARY AUTOMATION

23. The library catalogue proved to be the most popular area for automation; followed by circulation system. All the libraries of Central Government institutions, Central Government autonomous institutions, State Government institutions and majority of State Government autonomous institutions have computerised their cataloguing work. Majority (60 per cent) of them have computerised circulation systems. Few libraries of Central Government institutions and majority of the libraries of Central Government autonomous institutions, State Government institutions and State Government autonomous institutions have OPAC facility. Only two libraries of Central Government autonomous institutions are doing budget control using library management software. Central Government autonomous institutions are better in library automation compared to the libraries of other categories of institutions.

24. Majority (60 per cent) of libraries' acquisition process is

purely manual. Even though majority of them have library management software and computers, they are doing acquisition work manually. This is due to the lack of well-accepted library management software, and the library professionals are not aware of the complete process of acquisition work using the computer and library management software. The acquisition process of about 40 per cent of them is semi-automated. They are using library management software, computer, Internet, etc for the acquisition work, but are not fully automated. They are doing some aspects manually, for example budget control, preparation of letters, etc.

25. The special libraries in Kerala are in different stages of automation of their cataloguing work. A good number (33 per cent) of them have automated cataloguing system and most of them are attached to the Central Government autonomous institutions. Few libraries have automated in their cataloging work in part and the retrospective conversion process is in progress. A sizeable number (40 per cent) have only manual catalogues. The classification work is purely manual in all special libraries in Kerala.

26. A few (16.7 per cent) special libraries in Kerala have fully automated circulation system. They are attached to Central Government autonomous institutions and all are using barcode technology in the circulation process. About 40 per cent of the libraries have not completed the automation of their circulation work, though they are using computer and library management software. A good number (43.3 per cent) of libraries under study are doing their circulation work manually. There are several reasons for this situation like, lack of sufficient infrastructure, lack of well-accepted library management software, lack of qualified library professionals, etc.

27. Majority (56.7 per cent) of special libraries in Kerala are purely manual in their serial control and a good number of libraries are in the process of automating their serials control. There are several reasons for this like lack of well accepted library management software, lack of computer infrastructure, lack of qualified library professionals, or library professionals are not trained in computerised serial control.
28. About half of the special libraries in Kerala have no OPAC. A few (33.3 per cent) libraries have good OPACs, some are excellent in their performance. Most of them are attached to Central Government autonomous institutions.
29. Majority (56.7 per cent) of the libraries are getting help and support from the computer professionals of the parent institute. Most of them are attached to the Central Government autonomous institutions. The system administration of a good number libraries are by their library professionals alone. The skill and expertise of library professionals are inadequate to manage and administer ICT based resources and services.

USE OF DATABASE FOR INFORMATION RETRIEVAL AND THE NATURE OF INFORMATION RETRIEVED

30. Only a few (20 per cent) libraries are using commercial online databases, which are accessible through terminals situated both inside and outside the library. Majority of libraries are using CD-ROM databases, but few of them are using full text databases. It is accessed through terminals situated inside the library and through remote terminals situated outside the library. Majority of them are attached to the Central Government autonomous institutions. A few libraries are using databases for storing internal records and two of them are using it for storing full text information.

DIGITAL LIBRARY

31. Majority (56.7 per cent) of the special libraries in Kerala have no digital library or digital library initiatives. A few libraries have started to develop a digital library or started digitization of some of their collection or have digital library initiatives. Two libraries have separate digital libraries, but these are not organised in a proper manner and they are in the beginning stage. The main components of these digital libraries are electronic databases, full text e-journals through Science Direct, Emerald, etc., publications of the institute research community, e-books, discussion groups, online news, and in house databases. A few libraries have Greenstone Digital Library Software and IIITMK library has Acado software, and VSSC library has very good hardware for digital library development, but this library is not systematic in the digitisation process. It lacks proper guidance, and qualified library professionals in the collection development and management.

TELECOMMUNICATION AND NETWORKING

32. Majority (80 per cent) of the special libraries in Kerala have telephone facility and a few of them have both telephone and fax facility. Most (90 per cent) of them are connected to the institute network or Intranet. About half (46.7 per cent) of the libraries have separate library network. Majority of them are attached to the Central Government autonomous institutions. A few libraries are connected to the institute LAN or intranet with one terminal for accessing the Internet. A few libraries have no separate network and are not connected to the institute LAN or Intranet and they are working with standalone machines.
33. A good number (46.7 per cent) of libraries have CD-Net Server/CD Tower and majority (76.9 per cent) of them

are attached to the Central Government autonomous institutions.

LIBRARY CONSORTIA

34. Only three special libraries in Kerala are participating in library consortia and this is for accessing electronic journals. IIITMK library is participating in INDEST consortium for accessing e-journals. NIO library is also participating in consortium for e-journal subscription. RRL library is participating in CSIR Consortium on e-journals. By participating in this consortium this library has launched the e-journal access facility by subscribing to the Science Direct.

INTERNET

35. There are five Internet Service Providers in special libraries in Kerala, namely VSNL, NICNET, ASIANET, Sathyam and BSNL and majority (73.3 per cent) of them are accessing Internet through the VSNL. Majority (56.7 per cent) of them have leased line connections and a few have ordinary dial up and VSAT connections. Most of them have access to Internet through institute's or library network. A good number (43.3 per cent) of the libraries have only one computer node with Internet access and the Central Government autonomous institutions have more terminals with Internet access. Majority (56.7 per cent) of libraries are using Internet Explorer as their Internet browser software and a few libraries are using Netscape Navigator for browsing Internet. Majority (86.7 per cent) of libraries have a website or at least a link in the home page of the parent institute. About half of them are providing their profile through these websites or links. A few of them are providing online catalogue and databases.

36. The use of Internet for library and information services is found to be very less. Majority of Central Government

autonomous institutions are using Internet for acquisition work and SDI services. All the State Government institutions and majority of State Government autonomous institutions are using Internet for CAS and SDI services.

ICT BASED LIBRARY SERVICES

37. All the special libraries in Kerala are providing Current Awareness Services using different methods and majority of them are providing access to bibliographical databases, OPAC, and SDI Services. The other services provided are access to e-journals, WebOPAC, multimedia service, automated indexing service, scanning and forwarding of documents, and e-books. Libraries of Central Government autonomous institutions are better in providing ICT based library services.

38. ICT based resources and services of majority (63.3 per cent) of special libraries in Kerala are very poor and not adequate. They are providing a few services like bibliographic searching, Internet browsing, etc and this too not in a successful manner. Most of them lack proper infrastructure and qualified library professionals. Only a few (36.7 per cent) of them are providing different services like electronic database service, online databases service, online journals services, SDI, CAS, content service, internet services, etc. Libraries of Central Government autonomous institutions are better in this regard. Some of them have separate sections for services like Internet and some have CD-Net based information services.

39. All the special libraries in Kerala are providing E-mail and World Wide Web facilities. Majority of the libraries of Central Government autonomous institutions are providing ftp, Telnet, ListServe and Usenet/

Newsgroups services. They are better in Internet based services or facilities than the libraries of other categories of institutions.

TRAINING IN ICT BASED SERVICES AND OPERATIONS

40. Majority (60 per cent) of the special libraries in Kerala are providing training to their staff in ICT based operations and services. Majority (61.5 per cent) of them are attached to the autonomous institutions. Although a variety of training methods are used, the most frequently used methods are self-learning and in house workshops. A good number them have responded 'outside workshops', 'through trial and error' and 'through attending short training courses' as the training methods.
41. Majority (80 per cent) of special libraries in Kerala are providing various facilities for career advancement and knowledge improvement to their staff like facilities for attending workshops, seminars, short-term courses and in some of them are encouraging higher studies like Ph.D. But most of the library staffs are not using these facilities properly. A few institutions are not providing any such facilities for their staff.
42. Majority (73.3 per cent) of the special libraries in Kerala are providing user education in library management software, CD-ROM searching and Internet services/tools/utilities. Majority of them are attached to the Central Government autonomous institutions. But the user education and orientation programmes are not systematic and not in a useful manner.

OBJECTIVES OF INFORMATION AND COMMUNICATION TECHNOLOGY APPLICATION

43. Major objectives of ICT application in special libraries in Kerala are to render effective services to the user community, to keep the users up to date in their fields,

to modernise the library activities, to improve access to library collection, to improve the quality of existing services and to reduce routine and time consuming clerical works.

FACTORS INFLUENCING THE PROVISION OF ICT BASED LIBRARY RESOURCES AND SERVICES

44. The budget allocations to majority of the libraries are not adequate. There is no association in the allocation of budget among different type of organisation. The ICT skill and expertise of library staffs of majority (53.3 per cent) of libraries are stated as just satisfactory. Majority of State Government autonomous institutions and about half of Central Government autonomous institutions stated that skill and expertise of library staffs are good. The ICT skill and expertise of library staff depends on the type of organisation.

45. Majority (53.3 per cent) of the libraries have stated that the ICT awareness of library users are good and majority of these libraries are attached to the Central Government autonomous institutions. There is no association between the ICT awareness of library users and type of organisation, i.e., it is independent of type of organisation. Most (90 per cent) of libraries have stated that training in ICT is only satisfactory or it is inadequate. Training in ICT depends on the type of organisation. Majority (70 per cent) of libraries have stated that ICT infrastructure is only satisfactory or it is inadequate. A few (38.5 per cent) libraries of Central Government autonomous institutions have good ICT infrastructure. The ICT infrastructure is independent of the type of organisation.

BARRIERS TO ICT APPLICATION

46. About three fourth of the librarians feels that the main barriers to ICT application in special libraries in Kerala

are inadequately trained library professionals, inadequate ICT infrastructure and insufficient fund. Majority of them also feel that lack of ICT knowledge on the part of users is a barrier towards the successful application of ICT and a good number of them also feels that lack of well accepted and standard library management software package is a barrier towards the ICT application in special libraries in Kerala.

47. Majority of the librarians did not agree that lack of awareness, interest and initiation of library professionals towards ICT application in the library are the barriers of ICT application. A large majority of librarians have negatively responded to the barriers like ICT operational cost is exceeding year by year, inability to absorb recurring costs, increasing costs of procuring hardware and software, political and administrative changes, lack of official/policy guidelines, and non availability of less expensive library management software. Librarian of ICRI has reported that power failure is the main problem, as this institute is located in a remote hilly region and another librarian of Technopark has reported that the availability of web based resources is the main barrier of ICT application in the library.

LIBRARIANS' ATTITUDE TOWARDS THE APPLICATION OF ICT

48. The librarians have overwhelming positive attitude towards the application of Information and Communication Technologies in the special libraries in Kerala. Most of them have the attitude that ICT application will improve the status of the library by improving the quality and efficiency of the resources and services. Most of them are of the view that ICT application will in no way affect the resources and services of the library.

FUTURE PLANS

49. Majority (70 per cent) of librarians stated digital library as their future plan. A few librarians stated subscription of CD-ROM databases, establishment of CD-Networking, web based administration & management, introduction of multimedia systems, smart cards and bar coding, and setting up of intranet as their future plans.

USE OF ICT BASED LIBRARY SERVICES/RESOURCES/ UTILITIES/TOOLS/DEVICES

50. The electronic resource/tool used by the largest percentage of users is the e-mail. Majority (65.6 per cent) of them are accessing e-mail from the library. The next most widely used resource is WWW, which is being used by nearly 60 per cent of the library users. Majority of users are using floppy, and bibliographic databases. A good number of them are using CD-ROM, printer, e-journals and OPAC. Library users of Central Government autonomous institutions make more use of various ICT based library services and resources.

FREQUENCY OF USE OF THE DIFFERENT ICT BASED LIBRARY RESOURCES AND SERVICES

51. A large majority of library users of Central Government institutions are not using various ICT based library resources and services at all. Nearly half (49.8 per cent) of the users are browsing Internet and a good number (42.6 per cent) of them are using E-mail. E-mail is the most frequently used tool. Web browsing is the second most frequently used service/tool. However, a few users are using e-mail, www, and OPAC almost every day. A few users are using bibliographic databases and e-journals nearly once in a month.

52. In the case of Central Government autonomous institutions also e-mail is the most frequently used tool.

Nearly 82 per cent of users are using E-mail and majority of them use it almost every day. Bibliographic databases are the second most frequently used resource. Majority of users are using web browsing (77 per cent) and OPAC (64.2 per cent) and a few of them use it almost every day. Majority of users are using full text databases and a few of them use it nearly once in a month. Nearly 70 per cent users are using e-journals and a few of them are using it almost everyday. A good number of users are using printer and a few of them use it almost every day.

53. In the case of State Government institutions also e-mail and web browsing are the most frequently used resource or tool. A few (37.9 per cent) of them are using e-mail and web browsing almost every day. Majority (69 per cent) of users access full text databases two or three times in a week. A few (20.7 per cent) users access OPAC and bibliographic databases two or three times in a week. A good number (41.4 per cent) of users access e-journals about once in a week. Majority of users are using printer but a good number of them use it nearly once in a month.

54. Majority of the library users of State Government autonomous institutions are using bibliographic databases, e-journals, web browsing, and e-mail. Here also, e-mail is the most frequently used tool and a good number of them are using it almost every day. Nearly 60 per cent of the users are browsing the web but only a few of them do it almost every day. Majority of users are accessing e-journals and a few of them are using it almost every day. Some users are using OPAC and bibliographic databases nearly once in a month.

55. The Chi-Square values are found to be significant indicating that the frequencies of using all the services,

resources/tools are different among different organisations.

USERS' RATING FOR DIFFERENT ICT BASED LIBRARY SERVICES AND RESOURCES/TOOLS

56. Majority of the library users of Central Government institutions have rated the various ICT based library services/resources/tool/devices as poor and only a few users rated them as good. A good number (47.3 per cent) of the users rated e-journals as poor, whereas a very few (8.4 per cent) users rated it as good. Majority (73.4 per cent) of the users rated speed of the Internet as poor but a few (15.2 per cent) of them rated it as good. Majority (79.7 per cent) of users indicated computer infrastructure as poor but a few (8.4 per cent) of them rated it as good. A large majority of users rated ICT skill and expertise of library staff (80.6 per cent), ICT skill and expertise of users (81 per cent) and printing service (81.4 per cent) as poor. Most (92.8 per cent) of the users rated training in ICT as poor and only 2.5 per cent of them rated it as good.
57. More library users of Central Government autonomous institutions have rated OPAC, bibliographic databases, and full text databases as good and a very few users rated them as very good or excellent. A few (20.1 per cent) users indicated CD-ROM databases as very good, and some other (15.4 per cent) users rated CD Networking as poor. A good number of users rated Internet services, e-journals, speed of the Internet, computer infrastructure, ICT skill and expertise of library staff and users as good. A good number (41.2 per cent) of users rated printing service as poor and majority (69.6 per cent) of users rated training in ICT as poor.
58. A good number (41.4 per cent) of the library users of State Government institutions rated OPAC,

bibliographic databases, CD-ROM databases, and Internet services as good. A few (20.7 per cent) users rated full text databases, speed of Internet, and computer infrastructure as very good. A good number (41.4 per cent) of the users rated computer infrastructure, ICT skill and expertise of library staff and users as poor. Majority (58.6 per cent) of users rated printing service and training in ICT as good and a good number of users rated ICT skill and expertise of library users and staff as very good. A good number of users rated e-journals, speed of Internet and computer infrastructure as excellent and a few users rated CD-ROM database and Internet service as excellent. It is also found that nobody has responded to CD-Networking.

59. Majority (51.1 per cent) of the library users of State Government autonomous institutions rated ICT skill and expertise of users as poor. A few users rated bibliographic databases, full text databases, e-journals, computer infrastructure, Internet service, speed of the Internet, ICT skill and expertise of library staff and users as good, but a few users rated them as poor. A good number of users rated speed of the Internet, computer infrastructure, and ICT skill and expertise of library staff as poor. Majority (52.3 per cent) of users rated printing service as good. A large majority (81.8 per cent) of them rated training in ICT as good.

60. The chi square values are highly significant at 1 per cent level of significance. There are significant differences between the ratings for different ICT based services, and resources/tools by library users of different organisations.

USERS' VIEWS ABOUT ICT APPLICATION IN SPECIAL LIBRARIES IN KERALA

61. Majority (53.5 per cent) of the users opined that library

professionals' help in using ICT based library resources and services is inadequate but a good number (41.7 per cent) of them considered it as adequate. According to a majority (81.9 per cent) of the library users of Central Government institutions and majority of State Government autonomous institutions, library professionals' help is inadequate. However, the opinion of majority (56.2 per cent) of the library users of Central Government autonomous institutions and a good number (41.5 per cent) of the users of State Government autonomous institutions are adequate. A good number (41.4 per cent) of the library users of State Government institutions opined that it is more than adequate.

62. Majority (56.8 per cent) of the library users indicated that the existing ICT facilities in their libraries are not underutilized, but a good number (43.2 per cent) of users stated that it is underutilized. Majority of the library users of Central Government institutions, Central Government autonomous institutions and State Government autonomous institutions have expressed that the existing ICT facilities are properly used. But library users of majority (51.7 per cent) of the State Government institutions indicated that ICT facilities are underutilized. Chi-square test shows that the percentage of users opinion about the existing ICT facilities in libraries in different organisations is almost same.

63. Majority (51.3 per cent) of the library users indicated that the existing ICT facilities in their libraries are inadequate. Majority of the library users of Central Government institutions and State Government autonomous institutions indicated that the existing ICT facilities are inadequate, but majority of the library users of Central Government autonomous institutions and State Government institutions indicated that the

existing ICT facilities in their libraries are adequate. The chi-square test shows that adequacy of existing ICT facilities in libraries depends on the type of organisation.

64. Majority (54.3 per cent) of the users indicated that ICT is highly significant in their academic/research work and a good number of users indicated it is significant. Majority of the library users of Central Government autonomous institutions, State Government institutions and State Government autonomous institutions have indicated that ICT is highly significant in their academic/research work. Majority of the library users of Central Government institutions, and a good number of users of Central Government autonomous institutions indicated that ICT is significant. The Chi Square test shows that the opinion about the significant change in speed in academic/research work by using ICT in libraries depends on the type of organisation.

65. A good number (47.7 per cent) of the users are not satisfied with the present application of ICT in their libraries. A few (24.2 per cent) users are just satisfied and very few users are slightly satisfied. Majority of the library users of Central Government institutions and 50 per cent users of State Government autonomous institutions are not satisfied with the application of ICT in their libraries. A good number of the users of State Government institutions are satisfied with the application of ICT in their libraries, but the same percentage of them are not satisfied. The Chi Square test shows that users' satisfaction with the application of ICT in their libraries depends on the type of organisation.

66. A good number (42.4 per cent) of the users indicated 'inadequate ICT infrastructure' as their reason for dissatisfaction with the present application of ICT in

their libraries. Majority of the library users of Central Government institutions indicated 'inadequate ICT infrastructure' and 'users are not trained for ICT based information services' as their reasons for dissatisfaction. A good number of the library users of State Government institutions indicated 'inadequate ICT infrastructure' and 'inadequately trained library professionals in ICT application' as their reasons for dissatisfaction. Library users of State Government autonomous institutions indicated 'inadequate ICT infrastructure', 'users are not trained for ICT based information services' and 'inadequately trained library professionals in ICT application' as their main reasons for dissatisfaction. A few library users of Central Government autonomous institutions indicated 'inadequate ICT infrastructure' and 'users are not trained for ICT based information services' as their reasons for dissatisfaction.

USER EDUCATION IN ICT BASED LIBRARY RESOURCES AND SERVICES

67. Majority (53.7 per cent) of the users indicated that their skill and expertise are adequate to use ICT based library resources and services. Majority library users of Central Government autonomous institutions, State Government institutions and State Government autonomous institutions indicated that their skill and expertise are adequate to use ICT based resources and services. But majority (74.7 per cent) of the library users of Central Government institutions indicated that their skill and expertise are inadequate to use ICT based resources and services.

68. Majority (79.1 per cent) of the users indicated that they are not getting any training/orientation in Internet services/tools/utilities. A large majority of the library users of Central Government institutions and majority of the Central Government autonomous institutions,

State Government institutions and State Government autonomous institutions indicated that they are not getting any training/orientation in Internet services/tools/utilities.

69. Majority (77.3 per cent) of the users indicated that the user education in ICT based resources and services are inadequate and a few (17.7 per cent) users indicated it is adequate. Only 14 users indicated that the user education in ICT is more than adequate. Large majority of the library users of Central Government institutions and majority of the Central Government autonomous institutions, State Government institutions and State Government autonomous institutions indicated that the user education in ICT is inadequate. The Chi Square test indicates that the opinion about user education in ICT based resources and services depend on the type of organisation.

70. Large majority (88.1 per cent) of the users agree that there is a need for workshop/orientation program in ICT based library resources and services. Most of the library users of State Government autonomous institutions, and Central Government institutions and majority of Central Government autonomous institutions and State Government institutions agree that there is a need for workshop/orientation program in ICT based library resources and services.

USERS ATTITUDE TOWARDS INFORMATION AND COMMUNICATION TECHNOLOGY APPLICATION IN LIBRARIES OF DIFFERENT ORGANISATIONS

71. The users of special libraries in Kerala have overwhelming positive attitude towards the application of ICT in their libraries. Most of them have the attitude that ICT application would improve the quality, efficiency, and status of the library resources and services. They indicated that ICT would improve the

facilities of the library and enhance the knowledge and expertise of library professionals and make integration with the organisation. They have the attitude that ICT application never creates any problems to the services and resources of the library. About half of the library users of Central Government institutions and Central Government autonomous institutions agree that ICT takes away the traditional way of information handling in the libraries.

SUGGESTIONS FOR IMPROVING ICT APPLICATION IN SPECIAL LIBRARIES

It is true that no library or information centre, whether it is in developed or in developing countries afford to lag behind in reaping the benefits of advances in ICT, but in practice, libraries and information centres particularly in the developing countries like India are finding it hard to keep pace with this transformational environment. Firstly, financial crunch, secondly non-availability of skilled/trained manpower, thirdly inherited administrative and organizational problems are some of the bottlenecks in utilising the ICT in libraries. It is in this context the investigator felt it necessary to understand the state-of-the-art application of ICT in special libraries in Kerala and the issues therein. The neumerous views and comments offered by the librarians and users have enabled the investigator to offer some feasible suggessions for achieving optimal utilization of ICT based library resources and services in libraries. The investigator found that serious efforts are required to raise the librarians' level of knowledge in Information and Communication Technologies. The following suggestions can be offered in developing countries like India to strengthen the application of Information and Communication Technologies in libraries and information centres.

LIBRARY BUDGET / FINANCE

Special libraries need better funding/finance, if they are to give more productive and effective information resources and services. Automation and ICT applications are very essential in the libraries. In order to access electronic journals and databases, substantial amount of money is needed. Systematic utilisation of this budget is also very important. It will be very useful to categorise budget according to the needs of library like library automation, collection development, etc. It is the responsibility of librarian to acquire necessary budget from the authorities. Special libraries can also raise funds through marketing of their resources and services. It is very essential to increase the budget/financial assistance according to current needs, especially in the escalating costs of electronic resources.

ICT INFRASTRUCTURE

Libraries should have sufficient hardware like servers, computer terminals, printers, scanners, barcode scanners, data caputure unit, CD-Tower, CD-writers, DVD drives, VCD players, UPS, etc. It should be maintained properly. Software is the lifeblood of hardware. It is very essential to have good software to apply ICT for library operations and services. Libraries should have very good library management software to operate all the functions of the library. It will be very nice if the software is an integrated version and it should have online help and OPAC/WebOPAC facilities. Libraries should use DBMS/RDBMS for managing the different databases of the library. Libraries should have very good antivirus software and it should be updated frequently. Software should have adequate security measures and it should be protected from computer viruses. Library should be able to get local support from the software company and should be able to access a secure master copy in case the copy in use is corrupted or lost. It can be avoided by taking backup copies of major software. All software and new files should be regularly checked by reputable anti-virus software. The system administrator should keep a software toolkit for troubleshooting.

COLLECTION DEVELOPMENT

In view of the increasing importance of digital information resources and the widespread use of information and communication technology for information handling, it is suggested that special libraries in Kerala, strive a right choice between printed and electronic resources. It is appreciable that most of the special libraries in Kerala have a good resource in hardcopy; however, the same cannot be said about electronic resources. These libraries must go a step ahead and provide electronic resources like online/electronic journals, bibliographic databases, fulltext databases, CD-ROM databases, multimedia databases, and access to web based resources, etc. Libraries should invest in developing library web pages/portals and provide web-based services like WebOPAC, and access to digital resources. However, they are lacking ICT based resources and services. Usually special libraries will concentrate on a particular subject. Journals related to this subject will be the major collection of these libraries, because journal articles have more primary research information. Today most of the subjects have very good electronic journals and databases. Online journals have lot of advantages than their hardcopy counterparts, for example, multimedia and hypertext facility. Special libraries should access online journals to satisfy the information needs of their clientele. Libraries can form consortia to acquire online journals by shared subscription of these journals. It will reduce the cost of online journals and libraries can get more electronic journals. Online journals have the facility to access back volumes of journals and libraries can preserve these back volumes by copying them into CDs and can save lot of space compared to their harcopy counterparts. In order to access databases through online CD-ROM Server, CD-Tower, etc will be very useful. It is essential to update databases frequently. It will be safe to take a copy of CD-ROM databases for preservation and for security. Internet has lot of web accessible information resources. Use of these electronic resources is very essential in special libraries to meet the information requirements of its users. Individual libraries can access several types of electronic resources and services through library consortia and library networks.

MANPOWER DEVELOPMENT

This investigation has seriously considered the lack of manpower and skill and expertise of library staff as the major factors that hindered the ICT application in special libraries in Kerala. Hence, it urges the authorities to appoint qualified library professionals in special libraries in Kerala. Libraries can provide quality information resources and services with the use of information and communication technologies in their operations. Library staff should have good knowledge in library automation, ICT application, and resources, and Internet based resources and services. They should have good qualification and acquire new skills and expertise in information handling. Realising the importance of manpower in the process of ICT based information storage, retrieval and dissemination, the following programmes are suggested to achieve the goals of manpower development in the ICT era. (i) recruitment of expertise in Information and Communication Technology, (ii) establishment of Information and Communication Technology laboratories in the libraries, (iii) provision of online and digital information facilities, and (iv) research and Development programmes in ICT based information handling.

ATTITUDE OF LIBRARY PROFESSIONALS TOWARDS ICT

More emphasis should be placed on improving librarians' attitude toward technology. Librarians' knowledge in ICT, experience in computer use, level of awareness of technology, recency in ICT training are key factors impacting their attitudes toward information and communication technology. The attitude of librarians towards ICT application is an important factor. Usually library staffs have positive attitude towards ICT application, but there is no strong initiation from their part for computerization and ICT application in their libraries. No authority will give a library a bag full of money and it is the duty of librarian to get finance from the authroties or from other sources and it is very essential to implement ICT in their libraries.

SKILL AND EXPERTISE OF LIBRARY STAFF

Library professionals have undergone a drastic change, which had not been seen ever before. The library professionals responsible for the implementation of ICT in libraries should combine ICT and library and information science qualifications, skills, competencies and expertise. There are lot of skills related to ICT based resources and services required for library professionals. Firstly, library professionals should have skills to handle ICT products, particularly, operating system, software, telecommunication products, DBMS, data and file management, DTP, word processing, generation of reports, etc. The next level of skills includes skills required to apply ICT for service management in general and information processing, search and retrieval in particular. This involves collection and organisation of data in electronic form, indexing techniques, selection and evaluation of sources, searching techniques, updation techniques, etc. The library professionals should also have Internet skills and skills required for accessing networked resources as well as marketing of electronic information. They should have skills to manage documents and data archives. Library professionals should have skills in programming, system administration, hardware maintenance and troubleshooting, networking, system migration skills, etc. They need to have managerial skills required for information management in teams and marketing of services, particularly marketing themselves and their skills.

They should have system analysis, self-development, negotiation and communication skills. Internet technology provides an avenue for information professionals to show they are professionals who have adapted to the new technology. There have been so many opportunities for the library professionals for involvement in an information-based society including electronic and multimedia pubishing, internet based-information services, global networking, web based digital resources, etc.

RESOURCE SHARING AND NETWORKING

In view of the increased pressure on the libraries and information centres for the provision of variety of information resources and services, they are forced to depend on other library resources. Therefore, it is suggested that the special libraries in Kerala shall share both hardcopy and digital resources. Therefore it is argued for the total rejuvenation of the existing attempts in the direction of networking and resource sharing among the special libraries in Kerala. Libraries should have telephone, fax, and e-mail facilities and it will help them to provide lot of services. The library networks should be protected from unauthorized access by various techniques such as encryption, remote access regulations, etc. Libraries should ensure security by setting devices like routers, firewalls, proxy servers, etc

INTERNET BASED RESOUCES AND SERVICES

In view of the explosive growth of the Internet and widespread use of web based information resources, it is suggested that the Internet based resources and services such online journals and online databases shall be made available to the clientele of the libraries. Internet connection is an important requirement of special libraries in Kerala. It will help them to access different types of web based information resources and services. Library users can access digital resources like e-journals through Internet. Internet connection should be provided through a good Internet service provider. Leased line connection is good for special libraries in Kerala and connection should have high bandwidth. It will be helpful to provide Internet connection through library network and library staff can access Internet from different sections of the library and it will increase their use of Internet. Libraries should have sufficient terminals and good Internet browsers for accessing Internet. Libraries can provide lot of web based resources and services like WebOPAC, Current Contents, e-journals, electronic databases by creating a good website or portal for the library. Internet alone can be used for providing different services like e-mail, ftp, telnet, newsgroups, etc. Library staff should have a commanding power in Internet based resources and services.

USER AWARENESS AND TRAINING IN ICT

This investigation explicitly states that special libraries in Kerala are lacking in the programmes of users awareness and training in ICT. This is more important than any other in the overall use of ICT based resources and services by users. In order to meet the same, each library has to have compulsory user awareness and training programmes in ICT. A significant effort is required to increase awareness of new technologies among the library professionals in special libraries in Kerala. Majority of library professionals have inadequate knowledge about ICT and their potential in library and information services. Libraries should promote ICT awareness and knowledge by providing short courses, organizing workshops, seminars, conferences, and public lectures and organizing hands on training programmes.

Training is very important for providing quality information services in an electronic environment. Libraries should provide training in hardware, software, communication facilities, digital library, library management software, etc. In-house training programmes are more effective in training the staff about the operations of ICT based resources and services. A separate budget should be allocated for training whenever a new technology is acquired even if it is highly expensive. Librarians should initiate orientation programs for staff and users for newly implemented systems and technologies.

Library users should get adequate training in using different ICT based information resources and services. Users should be given training in data mining, information searching, database searching and Internet use. Libraries should provide career advancement facilities for their staff enabling them to attend workshops, seminars, short-term courses, and to undergo higher studies. More and more staff may also be encouraged to participate in seminars/workshops and to engage in research work.

DIGITAL LIBRARY

Digital library initiatives are the main features of present day global information society including library and information centres. Realising its importance and potential use of digital information resources, it is suggested that the library and information centres in Kerala shall make attempts to go in for creating digital libraries so as to keep pace with the modern trends. While problems and challenges still exist in Indian context, there is an urgent need to establish digital libraries.

LIBRARY CONSORTIA

Library consortium is a collective activity of any group of libraries towards a common goal. The term is now used perhaps too broadly encompassing each and every routine as well as special activities of library. The main reason for forming a library consortium is to improve information resources and services to the library users and to gain financial benefits. The standardised policy in collection development and bargaining power of a consortium can help to reduce costs of documents. Shared subscription to electronic resources is the main activity of a library consortium and it can be a viable solution in order to increase the access to electronic resources across institutions at a lower cost. The consortia-based subscription can be successfully deployed to meet the pressures such as diminishing budget, increased user's demand and rising cost of electronic resouces. The collective strength of consortia members facilitates the libraries to get the benefit of wider access to electronic resources at affordable cost and at the best terms and conditions. Special libraries in Kerala can form different levels of consortia like consortium of ICAR institutes, consortium of CSIR institutes, consortium of State Government autonomous institutes, consortium of Government departmental libraries, etc.

INFORMATION MARKETING

The marketing of library and information services is a recent development in India. The escalating costs of library infrastructure, documents especially electronic resources and shrinking budgets are forcing the library and information centres to market their products and services. Realising the significance and benefits of information marketing, it is suggested that there is every need for the library and information centres in India in general and Kerala in particular, to develop strategies for the promotion of marketing their information products and services.

LIBRARY AND INFORMATION SCIENCE CURRICULUM

The influence of Information and Communication Technology on every discourse of human knowledge is undisputed and is also considered all pervasive. The contemporary scenario predominated by information and knowledge perspectives indicate the pressing need to educate and train the library and information manpower. In this context a new model curriculum integrating the traditional and, modern knowledge and thought has to be devised and implemented. Information and Communication Technology should be a core component of formal Library and Information Science education in India. Library schools need to upgrade their syllabi regularly according to the job market and future requirements. LIS schools should promote research and development in ICT

CONCLUSION

Application of ICT in special libraries has become inevitable in an era of information explosion and widespread use of digital information resources. Effective application of ICT in libraries helps in performing their operations and services most efficiently. In Kerala many special libraries have been applying ICT for providing efficient services and resources. This investigation has provided a useful summary of current state-of-the-art application of ICT in special libraries in Kerala. Though the special libraries in Kerala have hardware and software facilities to some extent, ICT based resources and services are not reaching the users to the expected extent. The application of ICT in special libraries in Kerala is not systematic and it is very slow. This was severely affected the provision of ICT based resources and services. This state of affairs has been largely due to inadequate finance, inadequate infrastructure and inadequately trained library professionals. Most of the libraries are struggling to introduce ICT based library resources and services. About half of them have very poor hardware and electronic resources. The skill and expertise of library staff in ICT based resources and services are not adequate. Majority of libraries have commercially prepared library management software and CD-ROM databases, but very few of them are using commercial online databases. Majority of libraries have no digital library or digital library initiatives. Only three libraries are participating in library consortia and this too is for accessing electronic journals. The use of Internet for library and information services is found to be very less. ICT based resources and services of majority of libraries are very poor and not adequate. Majority of the libraries are providing training to their staff and users. Majority of library users rated various ICT based library resources and services as poor. They opined that library professionals' help in using ICT based library resources and services is inadequate. They have indicated that the existing ICT facilities in their libraries are not underutilised, but they are inadequate and ICT is highly significant in their academic/ research work. A good number of the users are not satisfied with the present application of ICT in their libraries and they have indicated inadequate ICT infrastructue as their reason for dissatisfaction. Majority of users indicated that their skill and expertise are adequate to use ICT based library resources and services and they are not getting any training in Internet services/tools/utilities. They pointed out that the training in ICT based resources and services are inadequate and large majority of users agreed that there is a need for a workshops/ orientation programs in ICT based resoucers and services. The librarians and users have overwhelming positive attitude towards the application of ICT in their libraries.

It is in this context, the suggessions and recommendations of the study would be relavant and useful. In an era when a large number of useful information products are available only in digital format, the gap between so-called 'information rich' and 'information poor' countries is widening further. Rather, information poor countries are now under the threat of 'information starvation'. To overcome this unfortunate situation, library management in developing countries need to review their policies and, instead of heavily depending on traditional information resources, should set aside adequate resources for collecting digital information. They also need to give priority to staff training, and user education in regard to ICT based resources and services. The study concludes that most of the special libraries in Kerala need proper ICT infrastructure including hardware, software and humanware and library staff have to be trained properly to make use of the resources optimally both conventional and digital resources.

Bibliography

Abdoulaye, Kaba & Majid, Shaheen. (2000) **Use of the Internet for reference services in Malaysian academic libraries.** *Online Information Review*, 24 (5), pp.381-289.

Adam, L. & Wood, F. (1999) **An investigation of the impact of information technology in Sub-Saharan Africa.** *Journal of Information Science*, 25 (4), pp.307-318.

Adeniran, O. R. & Adigun, T.A. (1993) **The use of microcomputers in Nigerian libraries and information centers.** *Journal of Information Science*, 19, pp.239-246.

Agnew, Grace.B. (1996) **The Internet initiative at the Atlanta-Fulton public library.** *DESIDOC Bulletin of Information Technology*, 16 (1) January, pp. 25-29.

Alemie, L. (1998) **How is information technology shaping the economy and society?** *Information Development*, 14 (4), pp. 181-183.

Ali, Amjad. (2004) **Application of information technology in the educational media libraries in Delhi.** IN: Proceedings of the XX *IATLIS National Conference on Globalization of Library and Information Science Education*, 21-23 November 2003, DLISc., University of Madras, Chennai. Hyderabad, IASLIC. pp. 89-96.

Allen, Mathew & Retzlaff, Lothar. (1998) **Libraries and information technology: towards the twenty-first century.** *The Australian Library Journal*, February, pp. 91-99.

Amekuedee, J.O. (1995) **Barriers to successful university library automation in Ghana with particular reference to the Balme Library.** *International Information and*

Library Review, 27, pp. 171-181.

Amritpal Kaur & Naresh Nandan. (2000) **Impact of IT on university libraries: a case study of Bhai Gurdas library, GNDU, Amritsar.** *Library Herald*, 38 (1), pp. 43-51.

Amritpal Kaur. (1999) **Use of computer and CD-ROM in the libraries of agricultural universities and research institutes in the states of Punjab, Haryana and Himachal Pradesh: a study.** *ILA Bulletin*, 32 (3-4), pp. 5-10.

Arbour, D. (1994) **Information technology in the US library market: what the numbers tell us.** *The Electronic Library*, 12 (6), pp. 367-369.

Awogbami, Popoola A. (1992) **The diffusion of CD-ROM into Nigerian libraries.** *CD-ROM Librarian*, 7 (5) May, pp. 30-33.

Baby, M.D. (2000) **Library of future-today: CUSAT-a case study.** IN: *Proceedings of the Seventh National Convention for Automation of Libraries in Education and Research on Information Services in a Networked Environment in India.* Ahmedabad, INFLIBNET Centre. pp. 3.113-3.119.

Barlow, Lisa J. & Graham, Margaret E. (1999) **The use of information and communication technologies in commercial libraries in the UK.** *Program*, 33 (2) April, pp. 109-128.

Bertot, John Carlo & McClure, Charles R. (1997) **Impacts of public access to the Internet through Pennsylvania public libraries.** *Information Technology and Libraries*, December, pp. 151-164.

Bharat Kumar. (2003) **Automation in university libraries of Haryana.** *ILA Bulletin*, 39(3) July-September, pp. 15-21.

Biddiscombe, Richard. (2001) **The development of information professionals' needs for Internet and IT skills: experiences at the university of Birmingham.**

Program, 35 (2), April, pp. 157-166.

Blecic, Deborah D. et al (1998) **Using transaction log analysis to improve OPAC retrieval results.** *College and Research Libraries,* 59 (1) January, pp. 39-50.

Blunden-Ellis, J.A. (1992) **UK market survey of library automation system vendors (1990-91).** *Program,* 26 (3), pp. 291-305.

Borgman, C.L. (1996) **Automation is the answer, but what is the question? progress and prospects for central and eastern European libraries.** *Journal of Documentation,* 52 (3) September, pp. 252-295.

Borgman, C.L. (1996) **Why are online catalogs hard to use?: lessons learned from information retrieval studies.** *Journal of the American Society for Information Science,* 47, pp. 493-503.

Borgman, C.L., Hirsh, S.G. & Hiller, J. (1996) **Rethinking online monitoring methods for information retrieval systems: from search product to search process.** *Journal of the American Society for Information Science,* 47, pp. 568-583.

Breeding, Marshall. (1997) **Designing secure library networks.** *Library Hi Tech,* 57-58 (15:1-2), pp. 11-20.

Budd, J.M. & Connaway, L.S. (1997) **University faculty and networked information: results of a survey.** *Journal of the American Society for Information Science,* 48 (9), pp. 843-852.

Bukhari, A. A. & Meadows, A. J. (1992) **The use of information technology by scientists in British and Saudi Arabian universities: a comparative study.** *Journal of Information Science,* 18, pp. 409-415.

Burton, P.F. (1999) **Information professionals and the world wide web.** *Online and CD-ROM Review,* 23 (2), pp. 103-104.

Carrasco, Laura Ortega & Vanderkast, Egbert Sanchez. (1998) **The information professional in a networked society**. *Aslib Proceedings,* 50 (5), May, pp. 95-99.

Chandra, S. (1999) **Libraries by the year 2020 AD**. *University News,* 37 (51), pp. 17-20.

Chaya Devi. (1997) **Attitude of the end-users towards online information retrieval-a case study**. *Annals of Library Science and Documentation,* 44 (1), pp. 18-31.

Chen, Ching-Chin. (1997) **Multimedia technologies.** *World Information Report 1997/98* Paris, UNESCO. pp. 206-255.

Cherry, Joan M. (1998) **Bibliographic displays in OPACs and web catalogs: how well do they comply with display guidelines?** *Information Technology and Libraries,* 17 (3), September, pp 124-137.

Cherry, Joan M. et al. (19ç 1) **OPACs in twelve Canadian academic libraries: an evaluation of functional capabilities and interface features.** *Information Technology and Libraries,* September, pp. 174-191.

Chopra, Y.L. & Mukherjee, Bhaskar. (2000) **Use of IT in library services at R.D.University, Jabalpur: users' reaction**. IN: Proceedings of the Seventh National Convention for Automation of Libraries in Education and Research on Information Services in a Networked Environment in India. Ahmedabad, INFLIBNET Centre. pp. 253-1.260.

Choukhande, Vaishali & Dongre, Sandesh M. (2004) **An analytical study of electronic sources and services provided to users with special reference to research scholars of Visvesvaraya National Institute of Technology Library, Nagpure**. IN: Proceedings of the Second International CALIBER on Road Map to New Generation of Libraries Using Emerging Technologies, Febrary 11-13, New Delhi. Ahmedabad, INFLIBNET Centre. pp. 100-106.

Commings, K. (1997) **Libraries of the future.** *Computers in Libraries*, 17 (1), January, pp. 20-21.

Connaway, Lynn Silipigni., Johnson, Debra Wilcox. & Searing, Susan E. (1997) **Online catalogs from the users' perspective: the use of focus group interviews.** *College and Research Libraries*, 58 (5) September, pp. 403-420.

Crawford, J.C. (1999) **A qualitative study of the use of networked software and electronic software and electronic information services at Glasgow Caledonian university library**. *Education for Information*, 17, pp. 101-111.

Cronin, B. (1998) **Information professionals in the digital age**. *International Information and Library Review*, 30, pp. 37-50

Cronin, B. & Overfelt, K. (1995) **E-journals and tenure.** *Journal of the American Society for Information Science*, 46 (9), pp. 700-703

D'Elia, George. et al. (2002) **The impact of the internet on public library use: an analysis of the current consumer market for library and internet services**. *Journal of the American Society for Information Science and Technology*, 53 (1) August, pp. 802-820.

Davarpanah, Mohammad Reza. (2001) **Level of information technology application in Iranian university libraries.** *Library Review*, 50 (9), pp. 444-450.

De Stricker, Ulla. (1998) **New information technologies: possible implications for libraries.** *Computers in Libraries*, February, pp. 61-65.

Demilew, Petros. (2001) **The potential of electronic document delivery services for academic libraries in Ethiopia**. *Bulletin of the American Society for Information Science and Technology*, August/September, pp. 14-19.

Dhiman, A.K. (1998) **Modern technology in resource sharing**

for information handling. *Library Progress,* 18 (1-2), pp. 19-21.

Dickstein, Ruth., Greenfield, Louise. & Rosen, Jeff. (1997) **Using the world wide web at the reference desk.** *Computers in Libraries,* September, pp. 61-66.

East, Harry & Leach, Kathryn. (1998) **The continuing prominence of CD-ROMs in academic libraries: the findings and evaluation of a survey.** *Aslib Proceedings,* 50 (8) September, pp. 208-214.

Evald, Pierre. (1996) **Information technology in Danish public libraries.** *Program,* 30 (2) April, pp. 121-131.

Farajpahlou, A Hossein. (1994) **Status of library automation in Iranian academic libraries.** *International Information and Library Review,* 26, pp. 107-137.

Fitzgerald, Brendan & Savage, Frances. (2004) **Public libraries in Victoria, Australia: an overview of current ICT developments, challenges, and issues.** *OCLC Systems & Services,* 20 (1), pp. 14-30.

Furner-Hines, Jonathan & Willett, Peter. (1995) **The use of the world-wide web in UK academic libraries.** *Aslib Proceedings,* 47 (1) January, pp. 23-32.

Furness, Karen L. & Graham, Margaret E. (1996) **The use of information technology in special libraries in the UK.** *Program,* 30 (1) January, pp. 23-37.

Gardner, Mike & Pinfield, Stephen. (2001) **Database-backed library web sites: a case study of the use of PHP and MySQL at the university of Nottingham.** *Program,* **35 (1), pp. 33-42.**

Giordano, Tommaso. (2002) **Library co-operation on ICT in Italy: an overview.** *Program,* 36 (3), pp. 144-151.

Griffiths, Jose-Marie. (1999) **Why the web is not a library.** *FID Review,* 1(1), pp. 13-20.

Gustitus, Cheryl. (1998) **The push is on: what push technology**

means to the special librarian. *Information Outlook,* January, pp. 21-25.

Haider, Syed Jalaluddin. (1998) **Library automation in Pakistan.** *International Information and Library Review,* 30 , pp. 51-69.

Hallmark, Julie & Garcia, C. Rebecca. (1996) **Training for automated systems in libraries.** *Information Technology and Libraries,* 15 (3) September, pp. 157-168.

Hamade, S.N. (1995) **Computer services in libraries and information centers of Saudi Arabia.** *Libri,* 45 (1), pp. 31-35.

Hauptman, R. & Anderson, C.L. (1994) **The people speak: the dispersion and impact of technology in American libraries.** *Information Technology and Libraries,* 13 (4), pp. 249-256.

Hewitson, Andrew. (2002) **Use and awareness of electronic information services by academic staff at Leeds Metropolitan university-a qualitative study.** *Journal of Librarianship and Information Science,* 34 (1) March, pp. 43-52.

Hsieh-Yee, Ingrid. (1996) **Student use of online catalogs and other information channels.** *College and Research Libraries,* 57 (2), March, pp. 161-175.

Jeevan, V.K.J. (1999) **Information technology for library services at IIT Kharagpur.** *Annals of Library Science and Documentation,* 46 (1), March, pp. 9-17.

Johnston, Colin. (1998) **Electronic technology and its impact on libraries.** *Journal of Librarianship and Information Science,* 30 (1) March, pp. 7-21.

Kamalavijayan, D. (1999) **Retrospective conversion: the Reserve Bank of India's experience.** *IASLIC Bulletin,* 44 (2), pp. 75-78.

Kaminer, N. (1999) **Scholars and the use of the internet.**

Library and Information Science Research, 19 (4), pp. 329-345.

Kannappanavar, B.U. & Vijayakumar, M. (2001) **Use of IT in university of agricultural science libraries of Karnataka: a comparative study.** *DESIDOC Bulletin of Information Technology*, 21 (1) January, pp. 21-26.

Kasirao, V. (2000) **Application of information technology (IT) in special libraries, information and documentation centres (LIBIDOCS) in Chennai: a study of its impact on LIS**. IN: Proceedings of the Seventh National Convention for Automation of Libraries in Education and Research on Information Services in a Networked Environment in India. Ahmedabad, INFLIBNET Centre. pp. 1.245-1.252.

Kelly, Sarah & Nicholas, David. (1996) **Is the business cybrarian a reality? internet use in business libraries**. *Aslib Proceedings*, 48 (5) May, pp. 136-144.

Kirkpatrick, Teresa E. (1998) **The training of academic library staff on information technology within the libraries of the Minnesota state colleges and universities system**. *College and Research Libraries*, 59 (1) January, pp. 51-59.

Kogannurmath, M.M. & Jange, Suresh. (1999) **Use of internet by Social Science research scholars: a study.** IN: Proceedings of the Sixth National Convention for the Automation of Libraries in Education and Research on Academic libraries in Internet Era, 18-20 Febrary, Nagpur. Ahmedabad, INFLIBNET Centre. pp. 239-245.

Konomos, Philip & Herrington, Scott. (2000) **Evaluating the use of public PC workstations at the Arizona state university libraries.** *The Electronic Library*, 18 (6), pp. 403-408.

Lazonder, Ard W., Biemans, Harm J.A. & Wopereis, G.J.H. (2000) **Differences between novice and experienced**

users in searching information on the world wide web. *Journal of the American Society for Information Science,* 51 (6), pp. 576-581.

Majid, Shaheen. (2001) **Trends in using CD-ROM in academic libraries of three South Asian Countries-Pakistan, Bangladesh and Sri Lanka**. *Aslib Proceedings,* 53 (2), February, pp. 68-76.

Malaisamy, T.K. (1998) **Information technology in library management and education.** *IASLIC Bulletin,* 43 (1), pp. 27-31.

Mambo, Henry L. (2001) **Tanzania: an overview of information communications technology (ICT) development in libraries and information services.** *The International Information & Library Review,* 33 (1) March, pp. 89-96.

Matheson, Nina W. (1996) **The idea of the library in the twenty-first century."** *Bulletin of Medical Librarians' Association,* 83 (1), pp. 38-43.

Mathews, Paula L. (1997) **An investigation into internet training for academic library staff.** *New Library World,* 98 (3), pp. 84-97.

Matoria, Ram Kumar & Upadhayay, P.K. (2002) **Design and development of web-enabled databases in libraries with special reference to RDBMS: Selection of tools and technologies**. *DESIDOC Bulletin of Information Technology,* 22 (4-5) July-September, pp. 9-15.

McCarthy, Cheryl A., Krausse, Sylvia C. & Little, Arthur A. (1997) **Expectations and effectiveness using CD-ROMs: what do patrons want and how satisfied are they?** *College and Research Libraries,* 58 (2) March, pp. 128-143.

Mendelsohn, Henry N. (1997) **Services in automated libraries: challenges and opportunities**. *IASLIC Bulletin,* 42 (1), pp. 27-34.

Mittal, Abha & Agarwal, Deepti. (2001) **Computerization of CBRI library: a practical approach.** *Annals of Library and Information Studies,* 48 (3) September, pp. 111-116.

Mohamed Haneefa, K. & Bavakutty, M. (2001) **Wireless networking in libraries: a conceptual introduction.** IN: Proceedings of the National Seminar on Library Co-operation in a Networked World, 25-26 May, University of Calicut. New Delhi, Ess Ess Publications. pp. 132-145.

Mohamed Haneefa, K. (2003) **Security for libraries in the digital networked environment.** *Library Progress (International),* 23 (2), pp. 143-149.

Mohamed Haneefa. K. (2004) **Application of wireless technologies in libraries.** IN: Proceedings of the Second International CALIBER on Road Map to New Generation of Libraries Using Emerging Technologies, Febrary 11-13, New Delhi. Ahmedabad, INFLIBNET Centre. pp. 366-373.

Moorthy, A.L. & Karisiddappa, C.R. (2001) **Information infrastructure and use of electronic media in Indian libraries**. IN: Proceedings of the First South Indian Library Conference on Role of University and College Libraries in the Changing Information Scenario, 18-19 October. Hyderabad, Potti Sreeramulu Telugu University Library and ILA-South Zone. pp. 148-162.

Moorthy, A.L. & Karisiddappa, C.R. (2000) **Mass storage technologies for libraries and information centres**. *DESIDOC Bulletin of Information Technology,* 20 (5) September, pp. 3-20.

Moorthy, A.L. & Murthy, S.S. (1998) **Information technology and Indian libraries**. IN: 50 Years Library and Information Services in India. Jain, M K ed. Delhi, Shipra Publications, pp. 249-260.

Moscoso, Purificacion & Molina, Teresa Malo De. (1999) **And after automation, what? Spanish libraries and the challenge of modernization.** *Journal of Librarianship and Information Science,* 31 (2) June, pp. 111-117.

Moscoso, Purificacion., Nogales, J. Tomas. & Caridad, Mercedes. (1995) **The use of online and CD-ROM databases in Spanish university centralised bibliographic services.** *Online and CD-ROM Review,* 19 (1), pp. 3-12.

Muhammad Ramzan. (2004) **Does level of knowledge impact librarians' attitude toward information technology (IT) applications?** IN: Proceedings of the Second International CALIBER on Road Map to New Generation of Libraries Using Emerging Technologies, Febrary 11-13, New Delhi. Ahmedabad, INFLIBNET Centre. pp. 21-31.

Mujoo-Munshi, Usha. (1997) **Information technology training for library and information science professionals: some perspectives.** *Journal of Library and Information Science,* 22 (1-2) June-December, pp. 36-46.

Mulimila, R.T. (2000) **Information technology applications in East Africa government-owned university libraries.** *Library Review,* 49 (4), pp. 186-192.

Murthy, S.S. (1996) **Library networks in India-an overview.** *DESIDOC Bulletin of Information Technology,* 16 (1), pp. 3-9.

Murthy, S.S. (1999) **Role of librarians in the new millennium of information technology.** *DESIDOC Bulletin of Information Technology,* 19(4-5), pp. 3-10.

Mutula, Stephen M. (2001) **The IT environment in Kenya: Implications for libraries in public universities.** *Library Hi Tech,* 19 (2), pp. 155-166.

Neena Singh. (2001) **Internet: importance and usage for library and information professionals.** *DESIDOC*

Bulletin of Information Technology, 21 (3) May, pp. 17-28.

Nithyanandam, K & Manorama Srinath. (1996) **Impact of automation on the employees of engineering college libraries.** IN: Proceedings of the XLI All India Library Conference on Human Relations in Librarianship, Vijayawada. Delhi, Indian Library Association. pp. 371-378.

O, Neill, E T. (1998) **Characteristics of web accessible information.** *IFLA Journal,* 24 (2), pp. 114-116.

Oduwole, A.A. (2001) **Use of CD-ROM databases in Nigerian academic libraries.** *Information Technology and Libraries,* 20(1) March, pp. 43-46.

Ojha, D.C. et. al. (2000) **Impact of information technology on libraries: a futuristic approach.** *ILA Bulletin* , 36 (3), pp. 87-92.

Ormes, Sarah. (1998) **Internet services in Danish public libraries.** *Journal of Librarianship and Information Science,* 30 (2) June, pp. 123-132.

Ortiz-Repiso, Virginia & Rios, Yolanda. (1994) **Automated cataloguing and retrospective conversion in the university libraries of Spain.** *Online and CD-ROM Review,* 18 (3), pp. 157-166.

Palmini, Cathleen C. (1994) **The impact of computerization of library support staff: a study of support staff in academic libraries in Wisconsin.** *College and Research Libraries* 55(2) March, pp. 119-127.

Pandian, M.Paul., Jambhekar, Ashok. & Karisiddappa, C.R. (2002) **IIM digital library system: consortia-based approach.** *The Electronic Library,* 20(3), pp. 211-214.

Park, Iljon. (1997) **A comparative study of major OPACs in selected academic libraries for developing countries-user study and subjective user evaluation.** *International Information and Library Review,* 29, pp. 67-83.

Patil, S.K. (2000) **Infrastructure requirement for networking and network based services in university libraries: a case study of university of Pune**. IN: Proceedings of the Seventh National Convention for Automation of Libraries in Education and Research on Information Services in a Networked Environment in India. Ahmedabad, INFLIBNET Centre. pp. 3.135-3.139.

Patkar, Vivek N. (2000) **Information technology adoption by libraries: opportunities and barriers.** *Information Studies,* 6 (2) April, pp.125-140.

Payette, S.D & Rieger, O.Y. (1998) **Supporting scholarly inquiry: incorporating users in the design of the digital library.** *Journal of Academic Librarianship,* 24 (2), pp. 121-129.

Poole, Carolyn E. & Denny, Emmett. (2001) **Technological change in the workplace: a statewide survey of community college library and learning resources personnel.** *College and Research Libraries,* November, pp. 503-515.

Prasad, A.R.D. (1997) **Application of OCR in building bibliographic databases**. *DESIDOC Bulletin of Information Technology,* 17 (4) July, pp. 17-19.

Qari, Abdulghafoor A. (1999) **Training for information technology at king Abdulaziz university library.** *Journal of Librarianship and Information Science,* 31 (1) March, pp. 39-44.

Ramesh Babu, B. (2000) **The emergence of web OPACs in the 21st century: Challenge for Indian libraries.** IN: Proceedings of the Seventh National Convention for Automation of Libraries in Education and Research on Information Services in a Networked Environment in India. Ahmedabad, INFLIBNET Centre. pp. 1.185-1.192.

Ramesh Babu, B. & Gopalakrishnan, S. (1998) **Internet: a survey of its use in Chennai**. IN: Proceedings of the

49th FID Conference and Congress on Towards the New Information Society of Tomorrow: Innovations, Challenges and Impact, 11-17 October, New Delhi. New Delhi, INSDOC. pp. I.9-I.13.

Ramesh Babu, B. & Tamizhchelvan, M. (2003) **An investigation into the features of OPACs in Tamil Nadu (India)**. *Library Review,* 52 (6), pp. 257-267.

Ravichandra Rao, I.K. (1997) **Impact of recent advances in information technology on collection development**. *DESIDOC Bulletin of Information Technology,* 17 (1) January, pp. 3-6.

Remesh, B.D. Kumbar & Satish Kanamadi. (2004) **Evaluation of IT based services on the basis of user requirements and satisfaction: a case study of university libraries of Karnataka state.** IN: Proceedings of the Second International CALIBER on Road Map to New Generation of Libraries Using Emerging Technologies, Febrary 11-13, New Delhi. Ahmedabad, INFLIBNET Centre. pp. 61-72.

Sada, Ellis. (1999) **Training users in the electronic era.** *Information Outlook,* December, pp. 22-29.

Sajjad Ur Rehman., Abu Baker, Ahmad Bakeri. & Majid, Sheheen. (1998) **Needed capabilities and development strategies for future information professionals: a Malaysian perspective**. *International Information and Library Review,* 30, pp. 123-141.

Sajjad Ur Rehman., Abu Baker, Ahmad Bakeri. & Majid, Sheheen. (1997) **Defining competencies for special library professionals: Malaysian experience.** *Aslib Proceedings,* 49 (6) June, pp. 162-169.

Sambasivan, K. (1998) **Impact of internet in information technology in India.** *Herald of Library Science,* 37 (2-3), pp. 210-213.

Sashikala Subbarao, V. (1997) **Identifying and informing potential end-users: a case study of information services by network at IIT-Bombay central library.** IN: Proceedings of the Fourth National Convention for Automation of Libraries in Education and Research on Information Technology Application in Academic Libraries. Ahmedabad, INFLIBNET Centre. pp. 94-96.

Satyanarayana, Pattnaik and Saravanan, A. (1999) **Internet in India: an overview.** *Yojna,* April, pp. 44-45.

Schofield, Frances., McMenemy, David. & Henderson, Kay. (2004) **People's network libraries: comparative case studies of old and new ICT learning centers.** *Library Review,* 53 (3), pp. 157-166.

Sherwell, John. (1997) **Building virtual library: the case of Smithkine Beachem.** *Aslib Managing Information,* 4 (5), pp. 35-36.

Siddiqui, Moid A, (1997) **The use of information technology in academic libraries in Saudi Arabia.** *Journal of Librarianship and Information Science,* 29 (4), December, pp. 195-203

Singh, S.P. (2001) **Computer applications in Indian institutes of technology libraries.** *The Electronic Library,* 19 (2), pp. 92-101.

Sinha, Manoj Kumar. (2004) **Scenario of automation and networking of library and information centres (LICs) of north eastern region of India: an evaluative study.** In Proceedings of the Second International CALIBER on Road Map to New Generation of Libraries Using Emerging Technologies, Febrary 11-13, New Delhi. Ahmedabad, INFLIBNET Centre. pp. 61-72.

Siriwongworawat, Suwakhon. (2003) **Use of ICT in Thai libraries: an overview.** *Program: Electronic Library and Information Systems,* 37 (1), pp. 38-43.

Siwatch, Ajit Singh. (2000) **Computer application in National Library on Dairying-a case study.** IN: Proceedings of the Seventh National Convention for Automation of Libraries in Education and Research on Information Services in a Networked Environment in India. Ahmedabad, INFLIBNET Centre. pp. 1.166-1.170.

Slone, Debra J. (2000) **Encounters with the OPAC: on-line searching in public libraries.** *Journal of the American Society for Information Science,* 51 (8) June, pp. 757-773.

Smith, Judith M. & Templeton, Emma-Jane. (1999) **A comparison of the range and value of use of the internet with traditional reference sources in Scottish public libraries.** *Journal of Information Science,* 25 (1), pp. 27-33.

Sowards, Steven W. (2000) **Libraries and imagination at the dawn of the world wide web.** *Libri,* 50, pp. 137-156.

Sridhar, M.S. (1999) **Skill requirements of LIS professionals in the New E-World.** *Library Science with a Slant to Documentation and Information Studies,* 36 (3), pp. 141-149.

Sridhar, M.S. (2000) **Modernisation of library service using IT potential and trends.** *Herald of Library Science,* 39 (1-2) January-April, pp. 28-41.

Sridhar, M.S. (2004) **OPAC vs card catalogue: a comparative study of user behaviour.** *The Electronic Library,* 22 (2), pp. 175-183.

Starkweather, W.M & Wallin, C. Clark. (1999) **Faculty responses to library technology: insights on attitudes.** *Library Trends,* 47, pp. 640-668.

Storey, Colin. (1995) **The impact of information technology on management and organization: the case of Hong Kong polytechnic university library.** *Library Management,* 16 (2), pp. 22-33.

Stricher, Ulla de. (1998) **New information technology:**

possible implications for libraries. *Computers in Libraries,* 18 (2) February, pp. 61-65.

Subba Rao, S. (1996) **CD-ROM technology: world scenario and Indian experience.** *Information Today and Tomorrow,* 15 (2), pp. 3-16.

Subba Rao, S. (2001) **Networking of libraries and information centres: challenges in India.** *Library Hi Tech,* 19 (2), pp. 167-178.

Sumati Sharma. (1999) **Information technology in special library environment.** *DESIDOC Bulletin of Information Technology,* 19 (6) November, pp. 17-30.

Tadasad, P.G., Maheswarappa, B.S. & Alur, Seema A. (2003) **Use of internet by undergraduate students of P D A college of engineering, Gulbarga.** *Annals of Library and Information Studies,* 50 (1), pp. 31-42.

Taylor, Mary K. (2000) **Library webmasters: satisfactions, dissatisfactions, and expectations.** *Information Technology and Libraries,* 19 (3), pp. 116-124.

Tilloston, J. (1995) **Internet use through the university of Toronto library: demographics, destinations, and users' reactions. Information Technology and Libraries,** 14 (3) September, pp. 190-198.

Tonta, Y. (1996) **Scholarly communication and the use of networked information sources.** *IFLA Journal,* 22 (3), pp. 240-245.

Tran, Lan Anh & Gorman, G.E. (1999) **The implementation of information technology in Vietnamese libraries: results of a survey.** *Asian Libraries,* 8 (10), pp. 380-395.

Veena Sharma. (1997) **Automation of library procedures in Nagpur university**. IN: Proceedings of the Fourth National Convention for Automation of Libraries in Education and Research on Information Technology Application in Academic Libraries. Ahmedabad, INFLIBNET Centre. pp. 19-21.

Venkata Ramana, P. & Chandrasekhar Rao, V. (2003) **Use of information technology in central university libraries of India.** *DESIDOC Bulletin of Information Technology,* 23 (2), pp. 25-42.

Vijayakumar, J.K. & Manju Das. (2000) **CD-ROM to DVD-ROM: a new era in electronic publishing of databases and multimedia reference sources.** *IASLIC Bulletin,* 45 (2), pp. 49-54.

Vijayaraghavan, M.S. (2000) **Information technology-a force multiplier extraordinary.** *DESIDOC Bulletin of Information Technology,* 20 (1-2) January & March, pp. 21-28.

Vishwanathan, T. (1998) **Application of information technology in libraries**. *Annals of Library Science and Documentation,* 38 (1), pp. 1-7.

Vohra, R. & Davarpanah, M.R. (2000) **Application of information technology (IT) in A.C.Joshi library.** IN: Proceedings of the Seventh National Convention for Automation of Libraries in Education and Research on Information Services in a Networked Environment in India. Ahmedabad, INFLIBNET Centre. pp. 1.160-1.165.

Watson, J.S. (1998) **'If you don't have it, you can't find it': a close look at students' perceptions using technology**. *Journal of the American Society for Information Science,* 49 (11), pp. 1024-1036.

Yadagiri, A. (1999) **Application of information technology in library services in the central library, REC Warangal : a case study.** *IASLIC Bulletin,* 44 (3) September, pp. 111-115.

Yan, Wong Chi & Gorman, G.E. (1998) **The use of CD-ROM in Australian academic library acquisitions procedures**. *Asian Libraries,* 7 (6), pp. 123-130.

Yan, Wong Chi & Gorman, G.E. (1998) **The use of CD-ROM**

in Hong Kong academic library acquisitions procedures. *Asian Libraries*, 7 (12), pp. 367-374.

Younis, Abdul Raseq. (1990) **Library automation in Jordan.** *International Library Review*, 22, pp. 19-29.

Zhang, Y. (1998) **The impact of internet-based electronic resources on formal scholarly communication in the area of library and information science: a citation analysis**. *Journal of Information Science*, 24 (4), pp. 241-254.

Zhang, Y. (2001) **Scholarly use of internet-based electronic resources.** *Journal of the American Society for Information Science and Technology*, 52 (8) June, pp. 628-654.

Web References

A working definition of digital library. (2001) [Internet] Digital Library Federation. Available from: <*http://www.diolib.org/pubs/ar9899p1.html*> [Accessed June 3rd 2004].

Benjes-Small, Candice, M. & Just, Melissa L. (2004) The library and information professional's guide to plug-ins and other web browser tools: selection, installation, troubleshooting. **Program: Electronic Library & Information Systems** [Internet] 37(2), pp. 135-136. Available from: <*http://haly.emeraldinsight.com/vl=859682/cl=18/nw=1/rpsv/~5999/v37n2/s1009/p135*> [Accessed August 11th 2004].

Biddiscombe, Richard. (2001) The development of information professionals' needs for internet and IT skills: experiences at the university of Birmingham **Program: Electronic Library & Information Systems** [Internet] 35 (2), pp. 157-166. Available from: *http://haly.emeraldinsight.com/vl=859682/cl=18/nw=1/rpsv/~5999/v35n2/s4/p157*>[Accessed August 11th 2004].

Chowdhury, Gobinda G. (2004) Digital libraries and reference services: present and future. **Journal of Documentation** [Internet] 58(3), pp. 258-283. Available from: <*http://haly.emeraldinsight.com/vl=859682/cl=18/nw=1/rpsv/~5997/v58n3/s1/p258*> [Accessed August 11th 2004].

Cullen, Rowena. (2003) The digital divide: a global and national call to action. **The Electronic Library** [Internet] 21 (3), pp. 247-257.Available from: <*http://ariel.emeraldinsight.com/vl=7697037/cl=54/nw=1/*

fm=html/rpsv/cw/mcb/02640473/v21n3/s7/p247> [Accessed June 7th 2004]

Darch, Colin & Underwood, Peter G. (1999) Dirt road or yellow brick superhighway? information and communication technology in academic libraries of South Africa. **Library Hi Tech** [Internet] 17 (3), pp. 285 – 298. Available from: *<http://ariel.emeraldinsight.com/vl=6997816/cl=101/nw=1/rpsv/~1137/v17n3/s8/p285>* [Accessed June 4th 2004].

Debowski, Shelda. (2000) The hidden user: providing an effective service to users of electronic information sources. **OCLC Systems & Services** [Internet] 16 (4), pp. 175-180. Available from: *<http://haly.emeraldinsight.com/vl=859682/cl=18/nw=1/rpsv/~1183/v16n4/s3/p175>*[Accessed August 11th 2004].

Dutton, William H. (2004) Information and communication technologies: visions and realities. **Information Technology & People** [Internet] 12 (1), pp. 113 – 115. Available from: *<http://ariel.emeraldinsight.com/vl=6997816/cl=101/nw=1/rpsv/~1188/v12n1/s2001/p113>* [Accessed June 30th 2004].

Fifarek, Aimee. (2002) Technology and privacy in the academic library **Online Information Review** [Internet] 26 (6), pp. 366-374. Available from: *<http://haly.emeraldinsight.com/vl=859682/cl=18/nw=1/rpsv/~1184/v26n6/s1/p366>*[Accessed August 11th 2004].

Garrod, Penny. (2004) Skills for new information professionals (SKIP): an evaluation of the key findings **Program: Electronic Library & Information Systems** [Internet] 32 (3), pp. 241-263. Available from: *<http://haly.emeraldinsight.com/vl=859682/cl=18/nw=1/rpsv/~5999/v32n3/s3/p241>*[Accessed August 1st 2004].

Gladney, Henry M. (1997) Safeguarding digital library contents and users. **D-Lib Magazine** [Internet] June.

Available from: <*http://www.dlib.org/dlib/june97/ibm/06gladney.html.*> [Accessed May 3rd 2004].

Glossary of flexibility working and ICT terms. (2004) [Internet] Cambridge, HOP Associates. Available from: <*http://www.flexibility.co.uk/helpful/glossary.html*> [Accessed June 3rd 2004].

Heeks, R. (1999) **Information and Communication Technologies, Poverty and Development.** Manchester, Institute for Development Policy and Management. Available from: <*http://www.man.ac.uk/idpm/idpm_dp.htm#devinf_wp*> [Accessed June 3rd 2004].

Hiller, Steve. (2002) The impact of information technology and online library resources on research, teaching and library use at the university of Washington. **Performance Measurement and Metrics: The International Journal for Library and Information Services** [Internet] 3 (3), pp. 134-139. Available from: <*http://ariel.emeraldinsight.com/vl=7697037/cl=54/nw=1/fm=html/rpsv/cw/mcb/14678047/v3n3/s3/p134*> [Accessed June 7th 2004].

Hofmann, Ulrich. (1995) Developing a strategic planning framework for information technologies for libraries. **OCLC Systems & Services** [Internet] 11 (4), pp. 22-32. Available from: <*http://haly.emeraldinsight.com/vl=859682/cl=18/nw=1/rpsv/~1183/v11n4/s4/p22*> [Accessed August 11th 2004]

Hwang, Gyu-hee. (2003) Information and communication technologies and changes in skills. **International Journal of Manpower** [Internet] 24 (1), pp. 60 – 82. Available from: <*http://ariel.emeraldinsight.com/vl=6997816/cl=101/nw=1/rpsv/~1197/v24n1/s4/p60*>[Accessed June 4th 2004].

Jimba, Samuel W. & Oladele, Benedict A. (1997) The constraints of providing a CD-ROM-based information service in a developing environment: a case study of the national veterinary research institute library, Vom. **OCLC Systems & Services** [Internet] 13 (2), pp. 67-71. Available from: <*http://haly.emeraldinsight.com/vl=859682/cl=18/nw=1/rpsv/~1183/v13n2/s4/p67*> [Accessed August 11th 2004].

Koehler, Wallace. (1999) **Digital libraries and world wide web sites and page persistence**.[Internet]. Available from: <*http://www.shef.ac.uk/~is/publications/infres/paper60.html*> [Accessed May 3rd 2004].

Lancaster, F.W. & Warner, Amy. (2004) Intelligent technologies in library and information service applications. **Program: Electronic Library & Information Systems** [Internet] 37 (1), pp. 63-64. Available from: <*http://haly.emeraldinsight.com/vl=859682/cl=18/nw=1/rpsv/~5999/v37n1/s1005/p63*> [Accessed August 11th 2004].

Manjunath, G.K. (2004) **Library automation: why and how**? [Internet]. Available from: <*http://www.igidr.ac.in/lib/paper1.htm*> [Accessed June 4th 2004].

McCaskill, Sandra., Goettler, Elaine. & Hawthorn, Margaret. (1990) How a medium-sized library became a leader in CD-ROM technology. **OCLC Systems & Services** [Internet] 6 (1). Available from: <*http://haly.emeraldinsight.com/vl=859682/cl=18/nw=1/rpsv/~1183/v6n1/s8/p0*> [Accessed June 4th 2004].

Ojedokun, Ayoku A. (2003) Transforming the library into a "teaching-learning laboratory": the case of university of Botswana library. **Campus-Wide Information Systems** [Internet] 20 (1), pp. 25-31. Available from: <*http://haly.emeraldinsight.com/vl=859682/cl=18/nw=1/rpsv/~1141/v20n1/s3/p25*> [Accessed August 11th 2004].

Ornager, Susanne. (2003) Development of ICT for library and information professionals: a training package for developing countries in Asia and Pacific from UNESCO. **Program: Electronic Library & Information Systems** [Internet] 37 (2), pp. 109-112. Available from: <*http://ariel.emeraldinsight.com/vl=7697037/cl=54/nw=1/rpsv/~5999/v37n2/s5/p109*> [Accessed June 7th 2004].

Pickard, Alison. (1998) **The impact of access to electronic and digital information resources on learning opportunities for young people : a grounded theory approach**. [Internet]. Available from: <*http://www.shef.ac.uk/~is/publications/infres/isic/pickard.html*> [Accessed June 7th 2004].

Roberts, D Hywel E & Everitt, Jean. (1999) A study of information and communications technologies in museums with particular reference to Wales. **Program: Electronic Library & Information Systems** [Internet] 33 (4), pp. 291-301. Available from: <*http://ariel.emeraldinsight.com/vl=7697037/cl=54/nw=1/rpsv/~5999/v33n4/s1/p291*> [Accessed June 7th 2004].

Saeed, Hamid. et al. (2000) Internet use in university libraries of Pakistan. **Online Information Review** [Internet] 24 (2), pp. 154-160. Available from: <*http://haly.emeraldinsight.com/vl=859682/cl=18/nw=1/rpsv/~1184/v24n2/s7/p154*> [Accessed August 11th 2004].

Schofield, Frances., McMenemy, David. & Henderson, Kay. (2004) People's network libraries: comparative case studies of old and new ICT learning centres. **Library Review** [Internet] 53 (3), pp. 157-166. Available from: <*http://ariel.emeraldinsight.com/vl=7697037/cl=54/nw=1/rpsv/~1150/v53n3/s4/p157*> [Accessed June 7th 2004].

Searching and Researching on the Internet and the Web Glossary. [Internet]. Available from: <*http://www.webliminal.com/search/glossary.html*> [Accessed June 7th 2004].

Shakkarwar, Rajesh. (1998) Host-based DVD: arriving on PC

platforms today. **Intelinsight** [Internet] 2 (1), pp. 8-19. Available from: (*http://developer.intel.com/solutions.tech/dvd/dvdpr10.pdf*) [Accessed June 3rd 2004].

Sharmila Ghosh. (2003) Service evaluation in a special library: supporting development research at the institute of social sciences library, New Delhi. **Library Review** [Internet] 52 (2), pp. 76-83. Available from: <*http://ariel.emeraldinsight.com/vl=6997816/cl=101/nw=1/fm=html/rpsv/cw/mcb/00242535/v52n2/s4/p76*> [Accessed June 4th 2004].

Shaw, Wendy. (2001) The use of the internet by academics in the discipline of English literature: a quantitative and qualitative approach.[Internet]. Available from: <*http://www.shef.ac.uk/~is/publications/infres/ws8.html.*> [Accessed March 3rd 2004].

Storey, Colin. (1995) The impact of information technology on management and organization: the case of Hong Kong polytechnic university library. **Library Management** [Internet] 16 (2), pp. 22-33. Available from: <*http://ariel.emeraldinsight.com/vl=7697037/cl=54/nw=1/fm=html/rpsv/cw/mcb/01435124/v16n2/s3/p22*> [Accessed June 7th 2004].

Swanepoel, Marinus., Toit, Adeline Du. & Brakel, Pieter A Van. (2001) Management of information technology in academic information services. **Aslib Proceedings: New Information Perspectives** [Internet] 53 (6), pp. 224-237. Available from: <*http://haly.emeraldinsight.com/vl=859682/cl=18/nw=1/rpsv/~5996/v53n6/s3/p224*> [Accessed August 7th 2004].

Tanner, Simon. (2001) Librarians into the digital age: planning digitization projects. **Program: Electronic Library & Information Systems** [Internet] 35 (4), pp. 327-337. Available from: <*http://haly.emeraldinsight.com/vl=859682/cl=18/nw=1/rpsv/~5999/v35n4/s1/p327*>

[Accessed August 11th 2004].

Tebbetts, Diane R. (2000) The costs of information technology and the electronic library. **The Electronic Library** [Internet] 18 (2), pp. 127-136. Available from: <*http://ariel.emeraldinsight.com/vl=7697037/cl=54/nw=1/rpsv/~1091/v18n2/s5/p127*> [Accessed June 3rd 2004].

Tellis, Winston. (1997) Information technology in a university: a case study. **Campus-Wide Information Systems** [Internet] 14 (3), pp. 78-91. Available from: <*http://haly.emeraldinsight.com/vl=859682/cl=18/nw=1/rpsv/~1141/v14n3/s2/p78*> [Accessed August 11th 2004].

Warner, Julian. (2000) What should we understand by information technology (and some hints at other issues)?" **Aslib Proceedings: New Information Perspectives** [Internet] 52 (9), pp. 350-370. Available from:*http://haly.emeraldinsight.com/vl=859682/cl=18/nw=1/rpsv/~5996/v52n9/s4/p350*> [Accessed August 11th 2004].

Webb, Sylvia P. (1995) Pursuing quality in special libraries. **Library Review** [Internet] 44 (7), pp. 5-7. Available from: <*http://ariel.emeraldinsight.com/vl=6997816/cl=101/nw=1/fm=html/rpsv/cw/mcb/00242535/v44n7/s1/p5*> [Accessed June 4th 2004].

Wisner, William H. (2001) Whither the postmodern library? libraries, technology and education in the information age. **Library Review** [Internet] 50 (3), pp. 146-159. Available from: <*http://ariel.emeraldinsight.com/vl=7697037/cl=54/nw=1/rpsv/~1150/v50n3/s1011/p146*> [Accessed June 7th 2004].

APPENDIX A

QUESTIONNAIRE

(To the Librarian)

Dear Sir / Madam,

This questionnaire is intended to collect data for the study *"Application of Information and Communication Technologies in Special Libraries in Kerala"* under the guidance of Prof. M. Bavakutty. I seek your valuable cooperation and help in obtaining the necessary information. I assure that all information supplied by you will be treated with the utmost confidence. The questionnaire has been designed in such a way as to minimize the time and effort required to complete. Thank you very much for answering all the questions and for your comments. Please return your completed questionnaire to the researcher.

Mohamed Haneefa K
Senior Research Fellow
Department of Library
and Information Science
University of Calicut.

A. General Information

Please indicate your responses with a '✓' (tick mark) or write in the spaces provided.

1. Name of the Institution:
2. **Please indicate the type of your Institution/ Organisation**:

   State Government ☐ / Central Govt ☐ Semi Govt ☐ / Autonomous (Central Govt.) ☐ / Autonomous (State Govt.) ☐ / Public Sector ☐ Private Sector ☐ / Others (Please specify):
3. Name of the Library/Information Centre:
4. Address:

   Telephone: E-mail :

   Fax: URL :
5. Name of the Librarian/ Person-in-charge of the Library:
6. Total Membership of the Library/Information Centre:

8. Annual Budget (Please specify the annual budget of the Institution and Library)

Years	*Annual Budget of the Institution*	*Annual Budget of the Library/Information Centre*
2001-2002		
2002-2003		
2003-2004		

B. Collection of the Library / Information Centre

(Please specify the collection as 0n 31st December 2004)

Sl. No	*Document*	*Collection*
1	Books	
2	Foreign Journals	
3	Indian Journals	
4	Gratis Journals	
5	Online/Electronic Journals	

6	Back Volumes of Journals
7	Theses
8	Dissertations/Project Reports
9	Standards
10	Patents
11	Technical Reports
12	Reprints
13	Audio Cassettes
14	Video Cassettes
15	Microforms
16	Bibliographic Databases
17	Full Text Databases
18	CD-ROM Databases
19	CD-ROMs
20	DVDs
21	VCDs
22	Others (Please specify)

C. Library Staff

1. Strength of the staff in the Library / Information Centre:

   Professional staff: Technical staff:

   Semi-professional staff: Others:

   If other, please specify:

2. Please give the following details of your library staff?

Sl.No	*Designation*	*Scale of Pay*	*Age*	*Qualifications Educational/ Professional/ Technical*
1				
2				
3				
4				
5				
6				
7				
8				

D. Information and Communication Technology Infrastructure

D.1. Hardware (Please give the following details of the hardware)

Sl.No	*Nomenclature*	*Make*	*Quantity*
1	Server		
2	Clients/ Computer Workstations		
3	Dot Matrix Printer		
4	Ink Jet Printer		
5	Laser Printer		
6	Barcode Printer		
7	Scanner		
8	Barcode Scanner		
9	CD-Net Server		
10	CD-ROM Tower		
11	Systems with DVDs		
12	Back up Device		
13	LCD Projector		
14	CD-Writer		
15	UPS		
16	Others (Please specify)		

D.2. Software (Please give the following details of the software)

Sl.No	*Nomenclature*	*Product Name*	*Quantity*
1	Network Operating System		
2	Library Management Software		
3	Digital Library Software		
4	CD-Net Management Software		
5	DTP Software		
6	Database/Relational Database Management System		
7	Antivirus Software		
8	Others (Please specify)		

E. Computer Applications

1. Year of starting of the computer automation:
2. Whether the library management software is a Network version? Yes/No
3. Whether the library management software has online help for users? Yes/No
4. Whether the library management software has OPAC facility? Yes /No
5. Whether the library management software has Web OPAC facility? Yes/No
6. What is the level of Library Automation? (Please give the following details)

Sl. No	*Library Functions*	*Computerized (Please tick)*
1	Acquisition	
2	Cataloguing	
3	Circulation	
4	Serial Control	
5	OPAC	
6	Annual Stock Verification	
7	Budget Control	
8	Others (Please specify)	

7. Whether your library has introduced Barcode Technology? Yes\No

   If yes, mention the functions activated using Barcode Technology?

   a. Annual Stock Verification ☐

   b. Circulation ☐

8. Whether your library has introduced Smart Card Technology? Yes\No
9. Please indicate the type of databases you use for information retrieval, and the nature of information

retrieved: (Please tick the appropriate)

Database Type	*Search Software Products Use*	*Used To Retrieve Bibliographical Information?*	*Full Text?*
Commercial Online Database			
CD-ROM Database			
Internal Records			
Others (Please specify)			

10. Please indicate the extent of end-user access to available electronic databases (Please tick the appropriate)

Database Type	*Is end-user access permitted Via terminals situated in the library?*	*Via terminals situated outside of the library?*
Commercial Online Database		
CD-ROM Database		
Internal Records		
Others (Please specify)		

11. Do you have a Digital Library? Yes/No

F. Telecommunication and Networking

1. Do you have the following telecommunication facilities? Telephone / Fax
2. Whether your library has an independent Library Network? Yes/No
3. Whether your library is part of Institute Network? Yes/No
4. What is the type of network?

   LAN ☐ / MAN ☐ / Intranet ☐/ Extranet ☐ / WAN ☐ /Wireless ☐
5. Does your library network include a CD-Net/CD-ROM Server/CDTower? Yes/No

6. Does your library is participating in any library consortium? Yes/No

   If yes, what is the name of the consortium? Please specify the main activities of the consortium: ....

F.1. Internet

1. Do you have Internet connectivity in the library or information centre? Yes/No

   If yes, Name of the Internet Service Provider(s) (ISP)

   a. ERNET ☐
   b. VSNL ☐
   c. NICNET ☐
   d. ASIANET ☐
   e. Satyam ☐
   f. BSNL ☐
   g. Others (please specify) :

2. Type of Internet connection? Leased line ☐ /Ordinary Dial up ☐/ ISDN Dial up ☐/ VSAT ☐/Others (Please specify):

3. Is this Internet facility available over the network of your library? Yes/ No

   If yes, how many nodes are configured with Internet access facility: ______Nos.

4. Internet browsers available in the library

   a. Netscape ☐
   b. Internet Explorer ☐
   c. Mosaic ☐
   d. Lynx ☐
   e. Opera ☐
   f. Neo Planet ☐
   g. Others (Please specify) :

5. Do you have a separate web site or a link in the web site of your Institute? Yes/No

   If yes, what constitutes the web site?

   a. Library profile ☐
   b. Web OPAC ☐
   c. Online databases ☐
   d. Audio/Video ☐
   e. Others (Please specify)

6. Do you use Internet for following library operations and services? (Please tick)

   a. Acquisition ☐
   b. Cataloguing ☐
   c. Classification ☐
   d. Bibliographic databases ☐
   e. SDI ☐
   f. CAS ☐
   g. Others (Please specify)

G. Services

1. What are the services provided by your library using information and communication technologies? (Please tick as appropriate)

Sl. No.	*Types of Services*	*Please Tick*
1	Access to full text databases	
2	Access to bibliographical databases	
3	OPAC	
4	Web OPAC	
5	Multimedia Service	
6	Automated indexing service	
7	Current Awareness Service	
8	Selective Dissemination of Information	
9	Scanning of documents and forwarding	

10	E-journals
11	e-books
12	Others (Please specify)

2. Internet services provided: (Please tick marks the appropriate box (es)):

   a. E-mail ☐
   b. Ftp ☐
   c. Telnet ☐
   d. List Serv ☐
   e. Usenet/Newsgroups ☐
   f. WWW ☐
   g. Others (Please speecify):

H. Training

H.1. Training the Staff

1. Do you conduct any training for the library professionals? Yes/ No
2. Training Method (Please tick as appropriate)

Sl. No.	*Training Method*	*Please tick*
1	Self-learning through reading manuals/ documentation	
2	Through trial and error	
3	Through attending short training courses	
4	Staff attachment with institutions already using ICT	
5	Individualized training by coworker	
6	In-house workshops	
7	Individualized training by supervisor	
8	Outside workshops	
9	Vendor workshops	
10	Others (Please specify)	

H.2. User Education in ICT Based Resources and Services

1. Do you conduct user education in ICT based resources and services? Yes / No
2. Which of the following modules have been included in the user education in ICT?
   a. Computer and network fundamentalso ☐
   b. Library management software ☐
   c. Internet services/tools/utilities ☐
   d. CDROM searching ☐
   e. Others (Please specify)

I. Objectives of Information and Communication Technology Application

1. Please indicate the cbjectives of information and communication techno ogy applications in your library or information centre.

Sl. No.	*Objectives*	*Please tick*
1	To modernise the library activities	
2	To render effective services to the user community	
3	To keep the users up to date in their fields	
4	To improve access to library collection	
5	To improve the quality of existing services	
6	To reduce routine and time consuming clerical works	
7	To improve cooperation and resource sharing among libraries	
8	To easily participate and utilise national and international computer networks	
9	To reduce the number of library staff required	
10	To improve prestige and visibility of library	
11	To provide competitive and strategic information needed for research and development	
12	Others (Please specify)	

J. Factors Influencing the Provision of Information and Communication Technology (ICT) Based Services

1. Please indicate the factors influencing the provision of ICT based services in your library

Sl.No.	*Factors*	*Excellent*	*Very Good*	*Good*	*Satisfactory*
1	Allocation of budget				
2	ICT Skills and expertise of library staff				
3	ICT awareness of library users				
4	ICT Training				
5	ICT Infrastructure				
6	Others (Please specify)				

K. Barriers of ICT Application

(Please indicate the barriers you face in applying ICT in your Library or Information Centre)

Sl. No.	*Barriers of ICT Applications*	*Please tick*
1	Insufficient funds	
2	Inadequate ICT infrastructure	
3	Library professionals are not interested in ICT adoption in the library	
4	Inadequately trained library professionals	
5	Lack of initiative on the part of the library professionals	
6	Lack of awareness among library professionals about the potential of IT	
7	Lack of ICT knowledge on the part of users	
8	ICT operational cost is exceeding year by year	
9	Inability to absorb recurring costs	

Sl. No.	*Barriers of ICT Applications*	*Please tick*
10	Increasing costs of procuring hardware and software	
11	Political and administrative changes	
12	Lack of well accepted & standard library management software package	
13	Lack of official/policy guidelines	
14	Non availability of less expensive library management software	
15	Non availability of consultancy services	
16	Others (Please specify)	

L. Attitude Towards the Application of ICT

Please indicate your attitude towards the application of ICT in your library or information centre

Sl.No	*Attitude*	*Agree*	*Disagree*
1	ICT applications are to improve the quality of the library services		
2	ICT application improve the efficiency of the library		
3	ICT application enhance the knowledge and expertise		
4	ICT application makes an integration within the organization		
5	ICT application are essential to improve the communication facilities		
6	ICT application improves the status of the library		
7	ICT use often disturb the routine work of the library		
8	ICT reduces the work load of the library professionals		
9	ICT takes over the traditional way of information handling in the library		
10	ICT application will spoil the image of the library		

Sl.No	*Attitude*	*Agree*	*Disagree*
11	ICT applications will increase the number of supporting staff		
12	ICT affects regular budgeting provision		
13	ICT takes major share from the library		

M. Future Plans

1. Please indicate the future plans of your library towards Information and Communication Technology application

Sl. No.	*Future plans*	*Please tick*
1	Intranet	
2	CDROM database	
3	Multimedia system	
4	CD-Networking	
5	Barcoding	
6	Smart Cards	
7	Web based administration & management	
8	Digital Library	
9	Others (Please specify)	

N. Do you have any comments or suggestions you wish to make about the state-of-the-art application of Information and Communication Technologies in your library or information centre?

Signature

APPENDIX B

QUESTIONNAIRE

(To the Users of the Library / Information Centre)

Dear Sir / Madam,

This questionnaire is intended to collect data for the study *"Application of Information and Communication Technologies in Special Libraries in Kerala"* under the guidance of Prof. M. Bavakutty. I seek your valuable cooperation and help in obtaining the necessary information. I assure that all information supplied by you will be treated with the utmost confidence. The questionnaire has been designed in such a way as to minimize the time and effort required to complete. Thank you very much for answering all the questions and for your comments. Please return your completed questionnaire to the researcher.

Mohamed Haneefa K
Senior Research Fellow
Department of Library
& Information Science
University of Calicut. 673 635

A. General Information

1. Name of the Institution:
2. Please tick the box which best describes your designation:

   Director ☐ Principle Investigator ☐ Scientist ☐ Technical Officer ☐

   Technical Assistanto Research Fellow ☐ Research Associate ☐

Supporting Staff ☐

Other (please specify) .... ☐

3. Please tick the box which best describes your age group:

under 20 ☐ 20 - 30 ☐ 31 - 40 ☐ 41 - 50 ☐ 51 - 60 ☐

61 and over ☐

4. Sex (Please tick the appropriate box): Male/ Female
5. Educational Qualifications:
6. Area (s) of study/research:

B. Use of ICT Based Services/Resources/Utilities/Tools/ Devices

1. Do you use any of the following information handling tools/utilities/devices/ services/ resources in your library? (Please tick all that you use)

No	*Tools/utilities/devices/ services/ resources*	*Please Tick*
1	Floppy	
2	Magnetic Tape	
3	CD-ROM	
4	DVD	
5	VCD	
6	Printer	
7	Scanner	
8	Smart Card	
9	Laptop Computer	
10	CD-Net Server	
11	CD-Tower	
12	Bibliographic Database	
13	Full Text Database	
14	E-Books	
15	Telephone	
16	Fax	
17	E-mail	

No	Tools/utilities/devices/ services/ resources	Please Tick
18	WWW	
19	Ftp	
20	Telnet	
21	ListServe	
22	Usenet/Newsgroup	
23	E-Journals	
24	OPAC	
25	WebOPAC	
26	Others (Please specify)	

2. How frequently do you use the following tools and resources in your library? (Please tick the appropriate boxes)

No	Tools/ Resources	Nearly once in a month	Two or three times in a month	About once in a week	Two or three times in a week	Almost every day	No use
1	OPAC						
2	Bibliographic Database						
3	Full Text Database						
4	E-Journal						
5	Web Browsing						
6	E-mail						
7	Ftp						
8	Telnet						
9	Mailing list (ListServe)						
10	Usenet/ Newsgroup						
11	Scanner						
12	Printer						
13	Others (Please specify)						

3. How do you rate the following in your library or information centre? (Please tick appropriate boxes)

No	*Services/Resources/ Tools/Utilities/ Devices*	*Very Good*	*Good*	*Poor*	*Excellent*
1	OPAC				
2	Bibliographic Database				
3	Full text Database				
4	CD-ROM Database				
5	CD-Networking				
6	Internet Service				
7	E-Journals				
8	Speed of the Internet				
9	Computer Infrastructure				
10	ICT Skill and Expertise of Library Staff				
11	ICT Skill and Expertise of Library Users				
12	Printing Service				
13	Training in ICT				
14	Others (Please specify)				

4. How do you find the library professionals' help in using ICT based resources and services?

   Adequate ☐

   More than adequate ☐

   Inadequate ☐

5. Do you feel that the existing ICT facilities in your library are under utilized? Yes/ No

6. Do you feel that the existing ICT facilities in your library are inadequate? Yes/ No

7. Do you find any significant change in speed in your academic/research work by using the Information and Communication Technologies?

Highly significant ☐
Significant ☐
Not significant ☐

8. To what extent are you satisfied with the application of Information and Communication Technologies in your library or information centre?

Very satisfied ☐
Satisfied ☐
Slightly satisfied ☐
Not satisfied ☐

If you are not satisfied, please specify the reason(s) (Please tick appropriate boxes)

a. Inadequate ICT infrastructure ☐
b. Limited computer literacy among library users ☐
c. Users are not trained for ICT based information services ☐
d. Inadequately trained library professionals in ICT application ☐
e. Inadequate publicity for the ICT based resources and services ☐
f. Rigid ICT use policies implemented by the library ☐
g. Discouraging attitude of library professionals towards their users ☐

C. User Education in ICT based Library Resources and Services

1. Do you think that your skill and expertise are inadequate to use ICT based resources and services? Yes/ No

If yes, in which area(s) do you want training? ....

2. Do you get education/training on Internet services/ tools/utilities? Yes/ No
3. How do you find the user education in ICT based resources and services?

   Adequateo More than adequate ☐

   Inadequate ☐
4. Do you think that there is a need for a workshop/ orientation program in ICT based resources and services?

   Agree ☐ / Disagree ☐ / Not sure ☐

D. Attitude towards Information and Communication Technology Application (Please tick appropriate boxes)

Sl.No	*Attitude*	*Agree*	*Disagree*
1	ICT application improve the quality of the library services		
2	ICT application improve the efficiency of the library		
3	ICT application enhance the knowledge and expertise		
4	ICT application makes an integration within the organization		
5	ICT application is essential to improve the communication facilities		
6	ICT application improves the status of the library		
7	ICT application often disturb the routine work of the library		
8	ICT takes over the traditional way of information handling in the library		
9	ICT application will spoil the image of the library		

E. Please give your suggestions and comments in a paragraph or two, to improve the ICT based information resources and services in your library or information centre?

....

....

....

....

....

Signature

APPENDIX C

INTERVIEW SCHEDULE

(With Chief Librarians)

A. General Information

1. Name :
2. Name of the Institute :

B. Application of Information and Communication Technologies (ICT)

1. Please discuss the adequacy / success / problems in the following resources / services / facilities in your library
   a. Library Budget
   b. Library's Electronic Resources
   c. Skill and Expertise of Library Staff
   d. Hardware
   e. Software
   f. Internet Facilities and Services
   g. ICT based Services
2. Please describe your success and problems in the following house keeping operations
   a. Acquisition
   b. Cataloguing
   c. Classification
   d. Circulation
   e. Serial control
   f. OPAC
   g. System Administration

3. What are the major barriers to the ICT application in your library?
4. Do you provide carrier advancement facilities to your library professionals? Please explain?
5. Do you provide training in ICT based operations and services to your library professionals? Please explain?
6. Do you provide user education in ICT based library resources and services? Please explain?

APPENDIX D
OBSERVATION SCHEDULE

Application of Information and Communication Technologies

1. Electronic Resources of the Library
2. Skill and Expertise of Library Staff
3. ICT Infrastructure of the Library
    - i. Hardware
    - ii. Software
    - iii. Communication Facilities
4. Library Automation
    - 4.1 Acquisition
    - 4.2 Cataloguing
    - 4.3 Classification
    - 4.4 Circulation
    - 4.5 Serial control
    - 4.6 OPAC
    - 4.7 System Administration
5. Library Network
6. Internet Facilities in the Library
7. ICT based Library Services
8. Barriers to the ICT Application in the Library
9. Digital Library

APPENDIX E

LIST OF SPECIAL LIBRARIES STUDIED

1. Central Institute of Fisheries Technology (CITF), Cochin
2. Central Marine Fisheries Research Institute (CMFRI), Cochin
3. Cntral Pantation Crops Research Institute (CPCRI), Kasaragod
4. Central Tuber Crops Research Institute (CTCRI), Trivandrum
5. Centre for Development Studies (CDS), Trivandrum
6. Coconut Development Board (CDB), Cochin
7. DOECC Center (CRDT), Calicut
8. Electronic Research and Development Centre (ER & DC), Trivandrum
9. Fact Engineering and Design Organisation (FEDO), Cochin
10. Fluid Control Research Institute (FCRI), Palakkad
11. Indian Cardamom Research Institute (OCRI), Myladumpara
12. Indian Institute of Information Technology and Management Kerala (IIITMK), Trivandum
13. Indian Institute of Spices Research (IISR), Calicut
14. Kerala Forest Research Institute (KFRI), Trichur
15. Kerala Industrial Training and Consultany Organisation (KITCO), Cochin
16. Kerala Institute of Local Administration (KILA), Thrissur

17. Kerala State Planning Board (KSPB), Trivandrum
18. Kochin Refinaries, Cochin
19. Liquid Propulsion Systems Center (LPSC) Valiamala, Trivandrum
20. Marine Products Exports Development Authority (MPEDA), Cochin
21. National Institute of Oceanography (NIO), Cochin
22. Regional Cancer Centre (RCC), Trivandrum
23. Regional Research Laboratory (RRL), Trivandrum
24. Rubber Research Institute of India (RRII), Kottayam
25. Spices Board, Cochin
26. Sree Chithira Tirunal Institute for Medical Sciences and Technology, (BMT Wing), Trivandrum
27. Sree Chithira Tirunal Institute for Medical Sciences and Technology, (Hospital wing), Trivandrum
28. Technopark Library, Trivandrum
29. Tropical Botanical Garden and Research Institute (TBGRI), Trivandrum
30. Vikram Sarabhai Space Centre (VSSC), Trivandrum

Index